GENDER, SEX, AND TECH!

GENDER, SEX, AND TECH!

AN INTERSECTIONAL FEMINIST GUIDE

Edited by Jennifer Jill Fellows and Lisa Smith

WOMEN'S
PRESS

Toronto | Vancouver

Gender, Sex, and Tech! An Intersectional Feminist Guide
Jennifer Jill Fellows and Lisa Smith

First published in 2022 by
Women's Press, an imprint of CSP Books Inc.
425 Adelaide Street West, Suite 200
Toronto, Ontario
M5V 3C1

www.womenspress.ca

Library and Archives Canada Cataloguing in Publication

Title: Gender, sex, and tech! : an intersectional feminist guide / edited by
    Jennifer Jill Fellows and Lisa Smith.
Names: Fellows, Jennifer Jill, editor. | Smith, Lisa (Lecturer), editor.
Description: Includes bibliographical references.
Identifiers: Canadiana (print) 20220223335 | Canadiana (ebook) 20220223408 |
    ISBN 9780889616356 (softcover) | ISBN 9780889616363 (PDF) |
    ISBN 9780889616370 (EPUB)
Subjects: LCSH: Technology—Social aspects. | LCSH: Sex. | LCSH: Feminism.
Classification: LCC T14.5 .G46 2022 | DDC 303.48/3—dc23

Cover design by Rafael Chimicatti
Page layout by S4Carlisle Publishing Services

22 23 24 25 26 5 4 3 2 1

Printed and bound in Ontario, Canada

Canadä

J. J. F.: For my daughter, Audrey. May she know a digital landscape that is more equitable than the one I see now.

L. A. S.: For my parents—Stan and Donna. Thank you for encouraging curiosity, cherishing collaboration, and holding space for multiple truths. My world, digital and otherwise, is better for having you in my life.

Contents

PART I: DISRUPT

PART II: CONNECT

PART III: SURVEILLANCE

PART IV: BODIES

PART V: RECLAIM

Acknowledgements

This book has many beginnings, and there are so very many people to thank and acknowledge. However, we would like to begin in a somewhat unconventional way—by thanking *space*. The physical spaces we occupy and the digital spaces we reached for in the time of the COVID-19 pandemic. The reason this book exists at all is not due to any individual person or group but is, in part, due to space. A hallway, to be exact. We (Jill and Lisa) both work at an institution where the humanities and social science instructors have offices altogether in one long hallway. The conversations in this space are almost always guaranteed to be lively, interesting, and interdisciplinary. Our institution, Douglas College, is located on the unceded traditional territories of the Coast Salish peoples of the Qiqéyt (Qayqayt) and kʷikʷəƛ̓əm (Kwikwetlem) Nations. It is on this land that we have the privilege to think, learn, and share knowledge as scholars. And it was on this land, in a hallway surrounded by anthropologists, historians, political scientists, administrators, and psychologists, that we first crafted the rough outline of what would become this book.

Pulling a book of this nature together while working full time and parenting children was no small feat, and many people were involved in helping this book become a reality. We would like to thank our acquisitions editor at CS/WP, Sarah Powell, who believed in this project and helped shepherd us through the initial stages of drafting a proposal. We would also like to thank Natalie Garriga, our editor at CS/WP, who happily addressed all our questions, which, as this was the first time either of us had taken on a project like this, was a lot of questions! We would also like to thank our copy editor, Kristy Lynn Hankewitz, for her diligence and attention to detail. Thanks are also due to each one of the authors who submitted their work to this volume, helping to shape it into an engaging and diverse representation of scholarly work in the field of gender, sex, and technology. We would also like to thank Deyvika Srinivasa and Ana Brito, who offered their careful and thoughtful comments on initial chapter drafts through the eyes of an undergraduate student. We would like to thank the six anonymous reviewers who read the book carefully and critically offered helpful suggestions and uplifting praise in equal measure. Neither of us has ever experienced such a supportive and helpful peer review process, and to whoever you all are, we are grateful for your insights and suggestions. The comments from reviewers made the volume as a whole stronger, sharper, and more refined.

I (Jill) would also personally like to thank my daughter for her tolerance of how much mummy was working, and even for her willingness to work alongside me, making beautiful drawings at the side of my desk during the early days of the COVID-19 pandemic. And I'd like to thank my husband, Evan Sklarski, for taking on more than his share of childcare and household duties so that I had time to devote to this book, as well as for many late-night discussions about the tech industry and feminism. He is still my knight in orange Gore-Tex! Finally, I would like to thank my wonderful co-editor, Lisa Smith. Her energy, attention to detail, and ability to plan and organize helped keep me on track when I lost sight of where we were and what we needed to do next. Thank you, Lisa, for keeping me enthused all the way to the end!

I (Lisa) wish to thank my partner, Mathieu Beaudoin, who supports all that I do and every hare-brained scheme I cook up. More than anything, he also reminds me of the importance of taking a break, stepping back, and not taking everything so seriously. Je t'aime. I am equally grateful to my children, Amédée and Loïc. My work takes up a lot of space in my life, but nothing is more important to me than you. Finally, I would like to extend a special thanks to my collaborator, Jill Fellows. I feel we walked this journey together and I greatly value your sense of curiosity, joy, and wonder. You are a true philosopher and friend.

A Brief Introduction to Sex and Tech: From Everyday to Extraordinary

Jennifer Jill Fellows and Lisa Smith

START, PAUSE, REPEAT

As you *start* this book, we invite you to *pause* and take stock of all the technological devices that are close at hand. If you are a typical North American, you likely have access to a phone (probably even a smartphone), a computer, and much more. We would also suspect that you do not tend to think of these everyday things as having much to do with gender or sex. However, just a glimpse below the surface can give you a hint that they do. From the way in which dating sites are set up, to the portrayal of gender-coded bodies in video games, to the use of technology to track fertility and manage or mitigate pregnancies, the tech lying around you is already saturated in cultural processes that reify and define gender and sex. The relationship between gender, sex, and tech becomes even more apparent when we consider the designers of the tech we regularly use and *who* that tech has been designed *for*. Marginalized groups often find themselves frustrated by tech, whether it be because of a lack of representation online, a lack of tools to meet their needs, or oppressive and discriminatory practices offline being reproduced online. For example, it is often difficult for trans or nonbinary people to use dating apps because many of these apps have been designed with cis people in mind. This is just one of the ways in which an intersectional approach is necessary when considering technology.

In this collection, we will not be covering everything that could be said about sex and tech. The topic is massive; we are scratching the surface. What we offer here are glimpses into all the ways that technology affects, and is affected by, cultural perceptions of gender and sex. We hope the topics covered in this text are thought-provoking for you (we certainly found them to be so as we were putting this collection together). But we hope, even more important than the topics, that the tools, concepts, approaches, and arguments laid out in this volume will leave you with a valuable takeaway, so that you can continue to explore the relationship between gender, sex, and tech well beyond the last page of this book. As such, what we offer here is a guide to help you explore this fascinating and challenging topic on your own. Each chapter in this collection models and illustrates how to use an intersectional feminist lens to critically reflect on the technologies we use every day, and at the end of each chapter, there are questions, suggested materials, and activities designed to help you further your explorations on your own.

So: Start—read this text carefully, and note any places where you are confused, interested, or both! Pause—take a moment to revisit those places that caught your interest and consider what is being said. And finally: Repeat. Read more, learn more, reflect more!

THREE EXAMPLES OF GENDER, SEX, AND TECH

If you are still wondering why a volume examining gender, sex, and tech is needed, these three examples should help illustrate some of the themes we will explore in this volume.

Example 1: Janet Vertesi, Secret Pregnancies, and Big Data

Janet Vertesi is a sociologist who examines the relationship between society, science, and technology. In 2014, she conducted a "personal experiment" to see if she could keep her pregnancy a "secret." But who was Vertesi trying to keep her pregnancy "secret" from? The answer might surprise you. Vertesi did not mean her employers or family and friends; she was trying to keep her pregnancy secret from big data (Vertesi, 2014).

Many pregnant people (Lisa and Jill included) have had Enfamil (a brand of infant formula) and other pregnancy- and baby-related promotional items mysteriously arrive in the mail, without ever requesting samples. For a lot of people, this is surprising. For some it might be amusing or even welcome. You may say, "One less thing to think about when getting ready for a new baby." For others, it is frightening or even devastating. It only takes a moment of scanning the internet to find stories of people who were planning to get an abortion, who had undergone unsuccessful in vitro fertilization treatment, or who miscarried only to have formula samples arrive at their door (Marchitelli, 2019). You might pause and wonder: how did these companies know about the most intimate details of one's reproductive body? But of course, we know how they know. "They" are digitally watching us, all the time, and the reach of big data continues to grow. As Lupton (2015) observes, our reproductive bodies have become digitized in a number of ways, from pregnancy apps to data tracking.

Vertesi asked, "Could I go the entire nine months of my pregnancy without letting these companies know I was expecting?" (Vertesi, 2014). This was harder than it might at first seem. Pregnancy and babies are big business, and a lot of companies have invested a lot of energy into identifying pregnant people online. Obviously, this meant that Vertesi could not announce her pregnancy on social media and that she could not browse for maternity or baby-related items online. But that wasn't the end of it. When she did need to buy maternity clothes or a crib or any of the other many items one needs when pregnant and preparing for a baby, she had to use cash or gift cards.

This experiment cost Vertesi in ways both expected and unexpected. When an uncle congratulated her on social media about her pregnancy, she had to quickly delete the comment and unfriend him. She hastily contacted him offline to explain why she had taken these actions, which on the surface came across as quite rude and combative (Vertesi, 2014). This was only one of several social strains she had with her friends and family members. But these social strains, while important, were not the end of the story.

Sometimes, there were products that could only be purchased online. In addition, as many pregnant people know, the internet can be a valuable resource for soothing anxieties and answering questions about gestation. Vertesi downloaded Tor, a private browser that routes internet traffic through foreign servers, obscuring the user's location, in order to access the net when she needed to. And when purchases needed to be made online, they were made through temporary email accounts, and the address Vertesi gave was a post office box that she acquired for the purpose. Finally, all online purchases were made using gift cards.

The heavy reliance on Tor, and on gift cards, is often flagged as evidence of criminal behaviour. In the end, Vertesi was able to successfully keep her pregnancy secret from data mining's all-seeing eye. The cost of this secret was that her husband was flagged as suspect when he went to the grocery store to buy enough gift cards to purchase the stroller they wanted online. In effect, her privacy was flagged as a criminal act. Vertesi (2014) declared, "No one should have to act like a criminal just to have some privacy from marketers and tech giants."

Example 2: Joy Buolamwini, Robotics, and the White Mask

Joy Buolamwini is a computer scientist and digital activist at Massachusetts Institute of Technology (MIT). During her undergraduate studies, Buolamwini was working on social robotics (a field that works on developing robots that can interact autonomously with humans); she found that the robots she was working with did not recognize her. These social robots were programmed to use facial recognition software to identify humans for the process of interacting with them, but they did not consistently or easily identify Buolamwini when compared with her lighter-skinned classmates. In fact, she found that the technology worked best only when she literally put a white mask over her face (Benjamin, 2019). At the time, she dismissed this as a weird glitch that could be sorted out later (Tucker, 2017).

Several years later, she was surprised to confront the same issue in the labs where she was working at MIT. She discovered that both MIT and her undergraduate program (as well as many other programs around the world) were using the same open-source facial recognition software. The same bias extended across a whole host of programs, robots, and other tools that rely on facial recognition.

Buolamwini discovered that the problem was that the software had been trained on the faces of mostly white researchers. The data set that was used to test the software was an unrepresentative one. But once the software was working well on that data set, the developers launched it, and no one had ever noticed a problem, much less went back to correct it, in the intervening years (Tucker, 2017). This was mildly annoying for many darker-skinned people who were not easily recognized by facial recognition software. But Buolamwini points out that the problem can go well beyond minor annoyance. These software programs are currently being used in self-driving cars to help them identify pedestrians in order to avoid them (O'Brian, 2019). This results in self-driving cars being unable to identify Black pedestrians unless they literally wear white masks.

Why had no one noticed a problem? Because most software engineers are light skinned. The software worked well on identifying their faces (no surprise there: it was trained on their faces). Further, it is often difficult to know when an algorithm is biased. Many of us (especially those of us who are not software engineers) "don't even know it's an option" and so aren't even looking for bias (Tucker, 2017). Sociologist Ruha Benjamin takes this analysis further, arguing that many algorithms have recreated the Jim Crow era of the past in what she calls the "new Jim Code" (Benjamin, 2019). Algorithms are offered as a quick, objective, and unbiased fix to many of the discriminatory problems of the past and of today. But, too often, these algorithms end up reinforcing and reifying the discrimination already present in the societies that created them (Benjamin, 2019). As Buolamwini and Gebru (2018, p. 1) observe, machines are not objective as they are made by people, meaning racism and sexism are built in.

Example 3: Riley Constantine, Trans Identities, and Online Avatars

In 2018, Riley Constantine wrote a piece for the *Escapist* magazine (an online video game magazine) with the title "I'm a Transgender Woman Because of Video Games." In this powerful and deeply personal piece, Constantine details how her experiences with massively multiplayer online games shaped her understanding of herself and allowed her the freedom to explore her own gender identity.

Constantine notes that growing up in the United States in the late 1990s and early 2000s, she felt abandoned by her society. Gender identity was not discussed at school or in any of her other social circles, and trans identities were viewed as taboo and sinful. So as she went through puberty and became increasingly anxious and uncomfortable with her body, Constantine turned to video games as an escape. But it was when she discovered online role-playing games that she began to identify the root causes of her distress.

Instead of playing with a stock character designed by game developers, role-playing games allow the player to customize a character. Players can often choose hairstyle, facial features, skin colour, and gender, to name a few of the options available in most role-playing games. Constantine reports that she would spend hours making a female avatar to play these games, only to delete the avatar in shame at the idea that she wanted to play as a woman and what that might signify.

The turning point for Constantine came while playing *Fable 2*. Constantine played *Fable 2* with a male avatar, but there was a quest that granted a potion capable of changing one's avatar's gender upon completion. The catch: the player had to use the potion immediately upon receiving it. Constantine reports agonizing over whether to use the potion or not and feeling confronted with her own secret desire to change her own gender. Finally, she decided not to use the potion. She reports that "the sense of regret was instant" (Constantine, 2018), leading her to frantically search the web to watch videos of those who had chosen to use the potion. What she found instead surprised her. She found a vibrant trans community. She found that the potion that had been offered to her avatar in the game was something that could be replicated in real life. She discovered trans women and learned about hormone therapy. In short, she gained knowledge, support, and a sense of belonging.

Though feminists have rightly criticized video games for their (typically overly sexualized) representation of female bodies, Constantine's story serves as a reminder that most technology, including video games, are more complicated than is usually portrayed in the media. These tools can be, and are being, utilized for good. And the creators of technology often cannot predict or even imagine all the uses that technology will be put to in the hands of the public. Constantine used video game technology as a safe way to explore her own gender identity, and through this exploration, she discovered another often-celebrated facet of modern technology: its ability to make information widely available, create communities, and give people a sense of belonging. Constantine's story is not unique. There are other such stories of transgender youth discovering and exploring their identities online, often through role-playing games (Dale, 2014).

Read together, these three examples illustrate some of the complex issues that are at play when we seek to delve deeper into understanding gender, sex, and tech. First and foremost, we are trying to study something that is part of everyday life, even if we experience it as "new" or "novel." Innovation—meaning new things or ways of doing something—is a significant part of the development of and social reception of technology. Big data, social robotics, and online gaming personas all speak to our present reality and hint at things to come. At the same time, these seemingly new technologies are shaped by existing systems of power and oppression. Racism, sexism, gender discrimination, and classism do not disappear with new technologies, even though technology has in some cases been a force for transformation. Said another way, technology is not value neutral; feminists of science would say science and, by extension, technology are socially constructed— meaning they are shaped by human societies and culture (see Martin, 1991).

WHO YOU ARE MATTERS

Maybe it seems obvious to say, but who you are matters; it matters in how your personal and social identity shape you as an individual. But it also matters in terms of shaping how you study and the questions you ask. As this volume is an opportunity to adopt a bird's eye view of what is going on while keeping two feet firmly on the ground, being transparent about perspective is important. Currently, too many of us are using tech all the time without really looking at it. In fact, we bet that most readers do not reflect upon or notice the tech they are using unless it breaks down. Instead of unreflectively using tech, we seek to examine tech itself. To use a sociological concept, we seek to "make the strange familiar" or take a second look at taken-for-granted objects and social processes. Doing so involves adopting a critical stance by asking thoughtful and thought-provoking questions. We have provided questions for discussion at the end of each chapter to get you going.

Part of this work also involves being aware of how our own experience shapes and informs all academic work. *Reflexivity* means acknowledging that what we know is connected to who we are, where we live, and the culture we are familiar with (Mauthner & Doucet, 2003). When we engage in reflexivity, we are being mindful of our positionality and privilege, or the ways our opportunities have been shaped by where we are situated in relation to others. Some groups have more, some have less, and this is not just coincidental. To make this work transparent, we have invited all authors to identify their positionality in their respective chapters. However, it is important to note that reflexive positioning is not the same as self-disclosure. Though a mindful reflexive positioning can give you, the reader, a sense of who we are and how our lived experiences have shaped our perspectives, a reflexive positioning is not, and cannot be, the full picture of a person. The authors in this volume have generously shared aspects of themselves with you, but only aspects they feel comfortable sharing. In addition, while people may reach for categories like "gay" or "cis" to describe themselves, some of these categories fit better or worse for some people. This, too, is part of the challenge and opportunity of reflexive positioning. We reflect on our positionality relative to a set of categories, classifications, and social norms. As such, our reflections are always already situated in context, and our expressions of ourselves may be limited by such context. But recognizing this context and its potential opportunities and limitations is vital, especially in a volume examining technology. All too often, technological tools have been sold (either figuratively or literally) with a promise of achieving objectivity. No technology has ever fulfilled this promise. Objectivity, in terms of a "view from nowhere," is not possible, and many feminists also argue that it is not desirable (Haraway, 1988; Harding, 1998, 2015). A commitment to a plurality of voices and perspectives is a much richer place from which to gain knowledge.

In this introductory chapter, we will begin this work of reflexive positioning by sharing our own.

My name is Jennifer Jill Fellows. I grew up just outside of Calgary, Alberta, on the traditional lands of the Tsuut'ina Nation. I am a white, cisgender, heterosexual, nondisabled woman. I have one daughter and am in a long-term monogamous relationship. I have a PhD in philosophy, a discipline that is still dominated by white men. Currently, only 25 percent of philosophy professors are women, and the number of racialized philosophers and disabled philosophers working professionally in the field is troublingly small. As a woman working in philosophy, I have faced sexism on several occasions and have been made to feel uncomfortable because of my gender. Though I was a child of the 1980s, my family had a computer in the home, and I had access to technology and was encouraged to use it long before many of my peers. Overall, I have a position of privilege. I have benefited from my whiteness, from my conventional performance of womanhood, from my family's settler status on traditional Indigenous lands, and from my higher education.

My name is Lisa Smith and I was born in North Vancouver, British Columbia, on the unceded territory of the Coast Salish Peoples, including the territories of xʷməθkʷəyə̓m (Musqueam), Sḵwx̱wú7mesh (Squamish), and səlilwətaɬ (Tsleil-Waututh) Nations. I am white, cisgender, heterosexual, middle class, nondisabled, a mother of two, a scholar, and a college professor. My ancestors immigrated to Canada in several waves, in some cases fleeing poverty and persecution, seeking life and security on land that was not theirs to occupy. As a white woman who conforms in many ways to social expectations of gender and sexual expression, I navigate my surrounding social world with ease. I have not experienced systemic forms of racial and colonial violence, nor have I had to justify or explain my gendered or sexed body to others. I benefit from the status that higher education affords. I have lived experience with abortion, childbirth, and sexual abuse and violence. I often see myself reflected in statistics that document gendered patterns of inequity; however, I am well aware that I am capable of pulling the levers of society to my advantage in ways that many other groups and individuals are not. I take for granted that I have access to phones and computers and am employed in a relatively stable sector. My passion for sociology grew out of many things, including a period of dispossession and drug use during my teens, as well as growing up in an unconventional and incredibly diverse family.

Who we are is not inconsequential. Further, the consequences of technology, and what is at stake, vary dramatically depending on who you are and where you are. At the end of each chapter, we have included questions to prompt such reflection, and "Invitations to Go Deeper" to encourage readers to reflect on and engage with these themes.

SOME WORKING DEFINITIONS

We suspect *gender*, *sex*, and *tech* are not new terms to you. At the same time, it is worthwhile to establish some common ground in terms of what these words mean when we are aiming to think more deeply about them. In this section, we provide working definitions of key terms and concepts that are central to this volume—technology, social construction of science and technology, gender and sex, intersectionality, sexualities and heteronormativity, gender identity and cis-normativity, (in)equality and (in)equity, colonialism and neocolonialism—and reflect on them from a Canadian context. We will address each in turn.

Technology

Technology is central to the scholarly work discussed herein. But technology means different things to different people. No doubt, when we say *technology*, you probably think of the internet, smartphones, retinol scanners, and maybe big data surveillance. But what about glasses, bikes, and sticks, or the actions you take to shape who you are? You may also think of science, as people often view science and technology as closely related. And while they are, there is an important distinction to make. The word *technology* comes from the ancient Greek word *technê*, which is typically translated as "craft" or "art." The root word can also be seen in words like *technique.* So while we often think of technology as material or digital tools, it's useful to keep in mind that technologies can also refer to new skills, crafts, or arts: in short, technology refers to ways of remaking the world and ourselves. As philosopher Henryk Skolimowski (1966) said, science studies what is the case, whereas technology focuses on what could be. Science documents. Technology transforms. And of course, this means that technology has the power to transform science too, which it has done, multiple times.

In this text, we will work with a broad definition of technology as things and practices that are used to augment or transform human capacity or experience. Notice that with this definition, we can be referring to tools that we use to manipulate the environment, but we can also be referring to things we do to work on or develop who we are as people. Thinking about technology in this way draws us away from the nuts and bolts of a given technology and towards the social dimension. These are of course connected, but we are more interested in the latter in this text. Think about your immediate family. Do you notice differences in the ease with which people use a particular technology? It is highly likely that you are very comfortable using a smartphone and all the associated apps. You would likely be less adept at morse code and the telegraph. You may have seen VHS tapes and a VCR, but have you ever used one in your lifetime? Elkind (2003) refers to this as the technology generation gap. Similarly, Prensky (2001) refers to the divide between tech-savvy young people and their parents; the former he refers to as *digital natives* and the latter as *digital immigrants.* In the contemporary context, Clark and Roberts (2010) speak of surveillance technology as being disproportionately unfair towards younger generations, who are much more likely to have the follies of their youth immortalized online than older generations are.

Social Construction of Science and Technology

Overall, this volume contributes to the broader body of feminist scholarship around the social construction of science and technology. As we discussed in Joy Buolamwini's story above, technological development and, by extension, science are often framed as objective and value neutral. The role of the people creating a given technological tool are rarely understood as influencing the shape of how technology functions (or doesn't). However, as we have already shown, technologies are not value neutral but come with lots of extras, including racism, sexism, and classism. These observations reflect the insights of feminist scholars of science and technology. As Thomas S. Mullaney says,

> Inequality, marginalization, and biases are transposed from the social and political world, where they can (at least in theory) be struggled over in the light of day, and rendered more durable, invisible, unavailable to human audit, and thus largely unassailable within the realm of computation. (Mullaney et al., 2021, p. 6)

Dominant mainstream narratives of technology often see tech as objective, as progressive, and as an unqualified good or a mark of progress towards something better. It is through the growing body of scholarship in the social construction of science and tech that we can see how technologies rarely deliver on these promises. Further, the more troubling side of tech often remains hidden from view. Many authors in this collection bring to light the ways that technologies all too often reproduce and reinforce the social structures that exist in the societies that create them.

Gender and Sex

Gender and sex may appear to be simple enough on the surface; however, in this text, we want to go beyond the basics. For many people, these terms are interchangeable, and often the term *gender* is viewed as a polite way to refer to sex. However, in gender studies programs, a distinction is typically made. *Sex* is biological, and *gender* is a socially created category. But when we investigate further, these two classifications are not as straightforward as they might seem.

Most people trace the origin of the sex/gender distinction to Simone de Beauvoir's famous statement: "One is not born, but rather becomes, a woman"

(1953, p. 267). The sex/gender distinction was largely a product of second-wave feminism and grew out of a desire to fight against essentialism. Many second-wave feminists accepted that sex was binary and that there were biological differences between men and women. However, they disputed that these differences had any social salience in terms of the roles or occupations to which women were suited. They argued, for example, that women were overrepresented in the caring professions not because of any biological drive to care and nurture but because women were socialized to be caring. Gender, then, was a social category. And if it was social, it could be socially transformed.

However, third-wave feminism challenged this distinction. Judith Butler (1990) argues that the distinction between sex and gender was a false one, because biology was always already viewed through a binary lens. In effect, scientists found two sexes because they were looking for two sexes. But this implied that sex itself was social. As Talia Mae Bettcher (2012) points out, there is nothing necessarily masculine about a penis, and we could just as easily view the penis as feminine (and many trans subcultures do, though they often prefer to refer to this biological organ by a different name).

Many third- and fourth-wave feminists, trans activists, and members of the 2SLGBTQ+ (Two-Spirit, lesbian, gay, bisexual, trans gender, queer, and others) community have argued that gender and sex are both best viewed as a spectrum, and several follow Butler's argument to not draw a distinction between sex and gender. The advantages of not distinguishing between the two is that one can examine the gendered assumptions that are attached to the sexed body itself. Some feminists fear that the loss of the sex/gender distinction will lead to an erosion of the category of "woman" entirely. And they worry that without that category, there will be no common core for feminists to rally around. Feminists are supposed to represent and advocate for women. But if sex itself is a social category and open to change, some worry this leaves it unclear *who* feminists are advocating *for*. In response, third-wave feminists such as Amia Srinivasan (2017) have argued that it might be helpful to move from a descriptive claim of what a woman *is* to a prescriptive claim of what a woman *should be*. She posits we should think of *woman* as a term of political solidarity rather than a metaphysical identity. Srinivasan argues that this move can allow us to reconceptualize the definition of woman to include all individuals who self-identify as women. This is only one of many various ways feminist theorists have offered for how to rethink the category of woman under a third-wave feminist paradigm.

One last thing to note about the sex/gender distinction is that it is one that has a specific North American origin and significance. While the divide does trace its lineage back to de Beauvoir, it is not a distinction that all languages make. Thus, not all feminist movements globally divide sex and gender or even do so in the way outlined above. The point here is that the sex/gender distinction has a history and an origin. And it, too, might be said to be socially constructed.

But wait. We've said that gender is socially constructed and open to revision, that sex too might be socially constructed and open to revision, and that the sex/gender distinction is also socially constructed! Does that mean none of this is real?

Not at all. Money is socially constructed. It only has value because we all believe it does. But as anyone carrying any debt at all will tell you, it is all too real and has real impacts on our lives. To say that gender, sex, and the sex/gender distinction are all social constructions is not to say they are not real or that they don't really matter. Instead, it is to say we should be very careful in how we think about them, employ them, and collectively construct and reconstruct these terms. For just like money and debt, these terms can have real positive and negative consequences on people's lives.

Intersectionality, Colonialism, and the Canadian Context

Intersectionality is a key concept for this text. The term originates in the work of two key Black American feminist scholars: Patricia Hill Collins (1994, 2000, 2015) and Kimberlé Williams Crenshaw (1989, 1991). Collins (1994) states, "Black feminist thought … fosters an enhanced theoretical understanding of how race, gender, and class oppression are part of a single, historically created system" (p. 618). It is not enough to look at power and oppression in relation to gender alone; we must understand the relationship to race and class. Further, gender cannot be separated from one's experience of race and class, and doing so can be considered a form of violent dismissal and silencing of the experiences of marginalized groups.

Similarly, in her work, Crenshaw (1989) seeks to articulate the inseparability of race, class, and gender, as tied to the operation of power and oppression. As we write this introduction, it is early summer 2020. The violent and open murder of George Floyd by police has incited mass gatherings of outrage in the United States and around the world. George Floyd's death is tragic on so many levels, including for members of his family and loved ones. His murder by police is also very real evidence that the United States continues to carry out and reproduce brutal and systemic forms of violence and oppression against Black folks.

Crenshaw delivered a Ted Talk in 2017 entitled "The Urgency of Intersectionality" where she calls on us to "bear witness to race and gender bias and speak up for victims of prejudice." She also speaks to police violence and the fact that police violence against Black men receives more coverage than police violence against Black women. An intersectional lens helps us to understand how certain stories come to the surface, while others, like the murder of Breonna Taylor, are sidelined. Crenshaw and Collins first started writing about this concept in the 1980s, and we have not come very far since then. To be clear: it is not that we should not focus on George Floyd. It is that we should focus on Breonna Taylor *as well*. Crenshaw's insight was that the sexism Black women face is different from the sexism white women face because of racism. Black women don't just face racism and sexism (though they do) but also racialized sexism and racial fetishization. When a Black woman's murder is less focused on than a Black man's, that is racialized sexism. When Black women's bodies are exoticized and objectified in music videos, it is a unique form of racial fetishization that white women don't typically experience. Intersectionality is not merely additive. It is not a matter of adding racism to sexism. It is transformative. Racism and sexism work together to create new forms of oppression for people who are at these intersecting identities. The work of understanding and using intersectional analysis began with two Black American women scholars (Crenshaw and Collins) but has since been expanded to focus on the experiences of 2SLGBTQ+ people, Indigenous people, disabled people, and many other marginalized groups, thus showing how fruitful intersectionality has become. It is, however, important, in using intersectionality, to remember that it is a tool that was first designed to explain and explore the experiences of Black American women specifically.

Canada, the "great white North," continues to willfully ignore police brutality and the systemic and institutionalized racism that has informed the colonial state. Canada, like the United States and many other parts of the world, is a settler colonial state. *Colonialism* refers to the violent occupation of land and subjugation of people who inhabit that land. The founding of the Canadian state has been shaped by colonial processes and systems that have involved extensive and varied forms of economic exploitation and destruction of Indigenous lands, dispossession of Indigenous Peoples from those lands, and multiple and ongoing attempts to extinguish Indigenous identities, cultures, and relations. In the contemporary context, Indigenous Peoples continue to experience violence at the hands of the Canadian settler state—in direct and indirect ways. Consider the huge outpouring of support from protests related to the murder of George Floyd in Canada from Toronto to Vancouver, with the comparatively little attention to the killing of Colten Boushie. Of course, people interested in social justice should support the protests against the murder of George Floyd; however, the lack of attention given to the killing of Colten Boushie—where police brutality and gender and systemic racism intersected—highlights the invisibility and erasure of the ongoing violence of settler colonialism across Canadian settler society. In part, this is a result of the globalization of media. The United States remains a powerful and influential neighbour. But in part, it is also an active ignorance that far too many Canadians practice with regard to the oppression and violence faced by Indigenous Peoples. An intersectional lens can help support critical reflection in this regard. Intersectionality is a call for understanding experiences of oppression as inextricably tied together; but it is not just about adding things together. To this end, it is important to situate power and oppression within the unique historical and social context being examined. There may be similarities between Canada and the United States, as both are the products of colonialism, but there are also differences.

The scholarly work in this collection focuses mostly on the Canadian context, but the issues are not neatly confined by geography. Technology is part of broader globalizing forces as it increases our capacity to extend beyond the limitations of our own borders and to equally control our engagement with the outside world. Trans and multinational tech giants play a significant and defining role in moderating our capacity to access the latest communication technologies, pharmaceuticals, personal mobility devices, and much more.

Heteronormativity and Cisnormativity

The gender binary is the assumption that there are only two genders (male and female). This binary is often justified by turning to the sexed body. However, the relation of sex to gender is far from clear, as discussed above. Furthermore, scientific investigations into sex strongly support the view of sex as a spectrum rather than a strict binary. Five key markers or traits are used by biologists and medical researchers to determine sex: chromosomes, sex hormones, secondary sex characteristics (such as breasts), external genitalia (such as a penis or vulva), and internal genitalia (such as ovaries). An individual may well have some characteristics out of the five that would mark them as male while having others that would mark them as female:

> For example, a person could count as male on the basis of some markers (i.e., testosterone levels; or testicles, perhaps undescended), yet female on the basis of others (i.e., could have a vagina). Determining someone's sex has never been straightforward, in spite of current assumptions, and has required negotiation and attention to context. (Freeman & López, 2018, p. 248)

Thus, there are many people who do not have bodies that align with the strict sex binary many of us were taught in high school biology. These people are collectively known as *intersex*. But though the science of sex suggests a spectrum approach is best, the assumption of a strict sex binary, and gender binary resting unproblematically upon this sex binary, has long prevailed. This assumption of a binary is important to keep in mind as we examine some other key concepts.

Heteronormativity is the view that it is normal or natural for humans to be heterosexual. Typically, this view is not just that heterosexuality is normal but that heterosexual pair bonding is normal. In other words, gay and queer relationships, as well as polyamorous relationships, are viewed as abnormal, deviant, or in some way unnatural. The assumption that gender is best understood as a binary helps to support and reinforce heteronormativity. We often hear heterosexual people described as (or describe themselves as) being attracted to the "opposite" gender or sex. This idea of opposites is used to justify the naturalness of heterosexuality. Men and women are opposite, with different (and opposing) strengths and weaknesses. For example, where men are rational, women are emotional. So men are able to make the hard decisions, and women are able to do the work of empathy and comfort. This lends itself readily to a picture wherein men and women belong together, each having skills that the other lacks. It begins to look as though men and women were two puzzle pieces that fit together. So the gender binary, by its very nature, makes heterosexuality seem almost inevitable and, by contrast, makes queer relationships seem unnatural. This mistaken view that heterosexuality is logical, natural, and normal is known as heteronormativity.

Cisnormativity is supported by the assumption that sex and gender are binary as well. To be *cis* is to have a gender identity that matches the gender one was assigned at birth (or, increasingly with the advent of technology, in the womb). To be *trans* is to have a gender identity that is different from the one assigned at birth. But notice that to someone who accepts the gender binary, and who further accepts the unscientific view that the gender binary is supported by a sex binary, to be trans seems unnatural. This is because cisnormativity assumes that the gender assigned at birth unproblematically follows from a clear and unambiguous sexed body, and cisnormativity further supposes that there is no meaningful difference between gender and sex. The first assumption erases intersex people. The second assumption erases trans people. Cisnormativity holds that it is normal and natural to be cis and that the sexed body connects unproblematically to one's gender identity. Ultimately, cisnormativity leads to essentializing people, both cis and trans, by reducing their gender identities to their genitalia. This leads to the harmful view that the most important thing about a woman is the possession of a uterus, an essentialist view that feminist of all genders should strongly oppose.

(In)equity and (In)equality

Throughout this text, various chapters will explore (in)equity as opposed to (in)equality. You may ask, well what is the difference? *Equality* implies that everyone gets the same thing; but because everyone is different, treating everyone the same in all situations is not necessarily fair and can lead to inequitable results. *Social equity* is trying to achieve equitable outcomes for all people by ensuring everyone gets what is *right for them* (Anzovino et al., 2019, p. 13).

A lot of technological "fixes" claim to address inequality by treating everyone the same. But many of these fixes increase inequity. For example, as discussed by Smith in Chapter 1, in the early days of the birth control pill, it was assumed by many people that having access to reproductive control meant freedom for *all* women (Tone, 2002). Yet, in Canadian society, Indigenous women, racialized women, disabled women, and other groups at the margins have been the target of state-mandated violence via forced sterilization for many years. For this reason, women who have been excluded from, left out of, or pushed to the margins of the broader reproductive rights movements have articulated a distinct notion of autonomy in relation to reproductive rights through the reproductive justice movement. Organizations and individuals that advocate for reproductive justice centre the experiences of racially marginalized women and girls provide a far broader and varied definition of choice in relation to childbearing, situate the importance of access to services (e.g., contraception, abortion, etc.), and highlight the right to healthy and clean environments as central to reproductive rights. Within the reproductive justice movement, we find that equity, not equality, is at the centre; freedom is not directly tied to one specific technology—such as the birth control pill—that all women need access to.

In Canada, if we were to adopt an intersectional lens, we would consider intersecting patterns of (in)equity including, but not limited to, the following: Indigeneity, age, ability, gender/sex, race, sexual orientation, socio-economic status, religion, immigration status, education, and geographic location. This list points us in the direction of understanding that oppression is not experienced on one "axis" alone and, further, that they cannot be easily separated out.

BOOK OVERVIEW

This book has humble beginnings. We (Jill and Lisa) met to discuss designing a new course on sex and tech (our first working title). After completing the course syllabus to submit to our department for review, we realized that there was no existing text for such a course. Of course, given that we had nothing but time on our hands (!!!), we thought, "Let's write a book!" and further, "Let's write a book with a whole bunch of other amazing scholars!" As such, at its core, this book is meant to build a foundation for further study by gathering scholars interested in investigating gender, sex, and tech. Feminist work on collective biography and other forms of group investigation highlight that there is a richness in more than one voice, a recurrent theme throughout the book.

In working with contributors to this collection, we have sought to ensure the volume is accessible, without shying away from academic rigour. Overall, themes that unite the different contributions in this volume include a critical stance towards technology, and we have encouraged authors to engage with intersectional feminist scholarship in ways fitting for their object(s) of study. Authors took up the challenge and worked with care and diligence to explore the complex ways that an intersectional lens can help deepen our understanding of a range of technologies, both expected and unexpected.

The scholarship collected in this volume reminds us that technology is made and used by people, and as such, it is never neutral or value free. Technology is connected to agendas, values, and beliefs, but it also speaks to power, oppression, violence, and of course resistance. Across the collection, authors have sought to avoid fearmongering—tech avoidance—or equally, lauding technology as saviour—the answer to all our woes. Instead, authors have sought to highlight the importance of perspective and the value in cultivating space for understanding and reflection. A recurrent theme, however, is that in these explorations, there are things at stake; the consequences are real and are not experienced equitably.

The collection is organized into five sections. The authors in Part I: Disrupt push us to identify and trouble common narratives about gender, sex, and technology. Smith's chapter explores the strong tendency to associate technologies with progress for women—and, in particular, relative increases in autonomy and freedom to men—through a rapid-fire exploration of three everyday technologies: birth control pills, baby bottles, and bikes. In particular, Smith considers the stories we tell about technology and invites us to consider who is left out, why, and what we can do about it. Friesen and Brito take a closer look at what gets defined as technology and to what end through pushing us to see menstruation supplies as technologies. By shifting our perspective, they highlight the need to consider what gets labelled as technology and what it means to bring gendered tech into broader discussions of tech equity. McHardy introduces the reader to technology-facilitated sexual violence (TFSV) generally and homes in on the implications for post-secondary institutions. McHardy's chapter provides a key intervention into the ways that new tech often eclipses existing regulations and extends gender-based violence in new and disturbing ways. Across this section, authors push us to consider assumptions we may hold regarding technology and how it connects to intersecting social identities and experiences.

The authors in Part II: Connect offer insight into the promise of technology as a facilitator of intimacy and relationship. Through an in-depth autoethnography, Orchard focuses on dating apps to explore life transitions, female sexuality, and the use of tech to make and navigate intimate relationships online. In contrast, Dietzel shares research findings that highlight the ways that dating apps reproduce and reify deep patterns of systemic racism among men who have sex with men. Finally, Manji takes a closer look at the omnipresence of smartphones within our lives and, more specifically, the role they play within heterosexual committed relationships.

In Part III, we turn to the theme of Surveillance, where authors dig deep into what it means to live in the era of the surveillance society. Drawing on the philosophy of Hegel, Fellows helps us to situate computers within gendered social relations of work. Her account situates the gendering of virtual assistants within the broader historical trajectory of which they are a part. Polzer et al. highlight the changing nature of tech produced to manage and make sense of the reproductive body. As they show, understanding menstrual, fertility, and self-tracking apps through the lens of postfeminist biopedagogies can help us understand the power relations at play within this form of surveillance. Finally, Raza provides a comprehensive account that illuminates the deep roots of bias and systemic discrimination within technologies that support the surveillance society.

In Part IV: Bodies, authors take a closer look the intersection of technology and the body. Hites-Thomas draws on her recent research to consider the role played by a range of experts in defining and delimiting "authentic" gender, with a focus on transition surgery and "male enhancement." Banbury and Fritsch draw on critical disability scholarship to examine gamification and the ways mainstream transhumanist narratives continue to frame the disabled body as a problem to overcome.

The authors in Part V: Reclaim explore the ways we use, hold, and make space within and through technology, placing a particular focus on the digital realm. Brown and Knowles build on the work of decolonial scholars to illustrate the ways Indigenous groups are taking up social media as a tool for holding space for resistance and movement building. Tomsons invites students to consider their classrooms from their own perspectives, as well as "from the other side of the desk" in terms of the decisions instructors are making. She considers the ways feminist ethics of care can help inform the work of post-secondary instructors and transforms our view of digital classrooms as places where caring can manifest or where people can fail to care. Since many of our readers are likely students, this chapter may well resonate with you as one of the few shared lived experiences you likely have with your fellow readers. Finally, Yard examines feminist use of zines as do-it-yourself (DIY) technology and how this technology can be brought into the digital realm, as well as into the classroom. The authors in this final section offer critiques of the digital realm, but they also remind us that within social constraints, we can find and make spaces for creativity, play, strength, and perhaps most importantly, resistance.

At the end of each chapter, should anything catch your interest or leave you wanting to know more, you will find links and citations for additional resources, as well as questions for discussion and reflection. We very much hope that this book brings you into a deeper understanding of just some of the profound ways that tech shape our lives, from the everyday to the extraordinary, and that the concepts, ideas, and theories developed here help you mindfully navigate your own use of technology.

Voices That Are Missing

As you are reading, pay attention not only to what has been said but also to the silences, the gaps, and the voices that are missing. For example, there is no chapter in this volume addressing lesbians and technology, nor is there any chapter discussing the role of technology in the Black Lives Matter movement. We have tried to solicit manuscripts from a wide variety of perspectives, but we were not always successful. We suspect that this might, in part, be because of the pressures of the COVID-19 pandemic and the added stressors that this pandemic has placed on marginalized and vulnerable populations. Further, we don't claim to have identified all the missing voices in this manuscript. So keep your eyes open and take up the invitations from authors to add to the conversation outside the boundaries of this text (e.g., hold a Wikipedia edit-a-thon, make your own zine with a community of folks who share your passions for social justice and equity, and tell your neighbours and friends about the real history behind computers)!

We hope this introductory chapter has piqued your interest and given you some tools to work with as you go forwards. So, without further ado, let's start.

QUESTIONS FOR DISCUSSION

1. According to you, what is technology? How does your definition compare with the definition discussed in this chapter? If it is the same, have you always thought that way? If it's different, what are the differences you notice?
2. Within fourth-wave feminism, many scholars argue that intersectional analysis is increasingly centred across scholarship, activism, and politics. Can you think of a recent example where intersectionality is discussed in relation to technology? What intersecting social locations or experiences does your example consider or reflect? In your example, does technology aid in resistance, further oppression, or fall somewhere in between?
3. When you think about Canadian society, what kinds of debates do you notice circulating in society about gender, sex, and technology? Do these debates relate to the themes we outlined in this chapter? Do these debates acknowledge or reflect an intersectional perspective? Which of these debates interests you the most? Why?

INVITATIONS TO GO DEEPER

For the Invitations to Go Deeper at the end of each chapter, we encourage you to engage in personal introspection by taking the time to write just for you. If writing does not work for you, try recording or drawing your reflections. Either way, take some considered time to reflect on who you are and how this shapes the ways you know and respond to the topics we are exploring. If you have someone you trust, we suggest speaking about these questions with them. Often, dialogue is a good way of exploring and clarifying ideas.

1. Who are you? How does who you are shape your relationship to technology?
2. What is a story that relates to gender, sex, and technology that you have come across in recent months that stands out in your memory? This could be something you saw in the news or that came across your social media feed, or it could be something that you experienced. Recount the story in simple terms and from memory only. Why does this story stand out for you? What themes stand out to you in this story? Can you relate on a personal level to what the story is about? If yes, how so? If not, what are the gaps in your own experience that might make it difficult for you to fully relate to the experience in the story? How does your own relationship to the experience change the way you understand the issues?

3. Take a good look at your home. Make a comprehensive list of every single technology that you can think of in your home. If you had never encountered any of these technologies before, and all of them were new, what kinds of conclusions might you draw?

READ MORE

Duportail, J. (2017, September 26). I asked Tinder for my data. It sent me 800 pages of my deepest, darkest secrets. *The Guardian.* https://www.theguardian.com/technology/2017/sep/26/tinder-personal-data-dating-app-messages-hacked-sold

Horowit-Hendler, S., & Hendler, J. (2020, January 14). Conversational AI can propel social stereotypes. *Wired.* https://www.wired.com/story/opinion-conversational-ai-can-propel-social-stereotypes/

Martin, E. (1991). The egg and the sperm: How science has constructed a romance based on stereotypical male–female roles. *Signs, 16*(3), 485–501.

Noble, S. U. (2018). *Algorithms of oppression: How search engines reinforce racism.* NYU Press.

LISTEN MORE, WATCH MORE

"How I'm fighting bias in algorithms," Joy Buolamwini, TED Talk, November 2016: https://www.ted.com/talks/joy_buolamwini_how_i_m_fighting_bias_in_algorithms?language=en

"How systemic racism works during a pandemic: COVID-19," Tricia Rose, Brown University: https://www.youtube.com/watch?v=mpfCkawO2RY&list=PLTiEffrOcz_5PzYIeQWH3I-MMgkkIsetx&index=4&t=0s

"The urgency of intersectionality," Kimberlé Crenshaw, TED Talk, December 2016: https://www.youtube.com/watch?v=akOe5-UsQ2o

REFERENCES

Anzovino, T., Oresar, J., & Boutilier, D. (2019). *Walk a mile: A journey towards justice and equity in Canadian society.* Nelson.

Benjamin, R. (2019). *Race after technology.* Polity Press.

Bettcher, T. M. (2012). Trans women and the meaning of "woman." In N. Power, R. Halwani, & A. Sobe (Eds.), *The Philosophy of Sex: Contemporary Readings* (6th ed., pp. 233–250). Rowman and Littlefield.

Buolamwini, J., & Gebru, T. (2018). Gender shades: Intersectional accuracy disparities in commercial gender classification. In S. A. Friedler & C. Wilson (Eds.), *Proceedings of Machine Learning Research, volume 81: Conference on fairness, accountability and transparency, 23–24 February 2018, New York, NY, USA* (pp. 1–15). http://proceedings.mlr.press/v81/buolamwini18a/buolamwini18a.pdf

Butler, J. (1990). *Gender trouble: Feminism and the subversion of identity.* Routledge.

Clark L. A., & Roberts, S. J. (2010). Employers' use of social networking sites: A socially irresponsible practice. *Journal of Business Ethics, 95*(4), 507–525.

Collins, P. H. (1994). *Black feminist thought: Knowledge, consciousness, the politics of empowerment.* Routledge.

Collins, P. H. (2000). *Black feminist thought: Knowledge, consciousness, the politics of empowerment* (2nd ed.). Routledge.

Collins, P. H. (2015). Intersectionality's definitional dilemmas. *Annual Review of Sociology, 41,* 1–20.

Constantine, R. (2018, October 2). I'm a transgender woman because of video games. *The Escapist.* https://www.escapistmagazine.com/v2/im-a-transgender-woman-because-of-video-games/

Crenshaw, K. W. (1989). Demarginalizing the intersection of race and sex: A Black feminist critique of discrimination doctrine, feminist theory and antiracist practice. *University of Chicago Legal Forum, 89,* 139–167.

Crenshaw, K. W. (1991). Mapping the margins: Intersectionality, identity politics, and violence against women of color. *Stanford Law Review, 43,* 1241–1299.

Crenshaw, K. W. (2017, October 16). The urgency of intersectionality. *TED Talks.* https://www.ted.com/talks/kimberle_crenshaw_the_urgency_of_intersectionality?language=en

Dale, L. K. (2014, January 23). How World of Warcraft helped me come out as transgender. *The Guardian.* https://www.theguardian.com/technology/gamesblog/2014/jan/23/how-world-of-warcraft-game-helped-me-come-out-transgender

de Beauvoir, S. (1953). *The second sex* (H. M. Parshley, Trans. & Ed.). Everyman's Library.

Elkind, D. (2003). The reality of virtual stress. *CIO* (fall/winter), 44–45.

Freeman, L., & López, S. A. (2018). Sex categorization in medical contexts: A cautionary tale. *Kennedy Institute of Ethics Journal, 28*(3), 243–280.

Haraway, D. (1988). Situated knowledges: The scientific question in feminism and the privilege of partial perspective. *Feminist Studies, 14*(3), 575–599.

Harding, S. (1998). *Is science multicultural? Postcolonialisms, feminisms, and epistemologies.* Indiana University Press.

Harding, S. (2015). *Objectivity and diversity: Another logic of scientific research.* University of Chicago Press.

Lupton, D. (2015). "Mastering your fertility": The digitised reproductive citizen. In A. McCosker, S. Vivienne, & A. Johns (Eds.), *Negotiating digital citizenship: Control, contest and culture* (pp. 81–94). Rowman and Littlefield.

Marchitelli, R. (2019, January 27). "No right to make money off us that way": Woman targeted by baby product marketing after miscarriage. *CBC News.* https://www.cbc.ca/news/business/woman-targeted-by-baby-product-marketers-after-miscarriage-1.4989945

Martin, E. (1991). The egg and the sperm: How science has constructed a romance based on stereotypical male–female roles. *Signs, 16*(3), 485–501.

Mauthner, N. S., & Doucet, A. (2003). Reflexive accounts and accounts of reflexivity in qualitative data analysis. *Sociology, 37*(3), 413–431.

Mullaney, T. S., Peters, B., Hicks, M., & Philip, K. (2021). *Your computer is on fire.* MIT Press.

O'Brian, M. (2019, April 8). MIT researcher exposing bias in facial recognition tech triggers Amazon's wrath. *Insurance Journal.* https://www.insurancejournal.com/news/national/2019/04/08/523153.htm

Prensky, M. (2001). Digital natives, digital immigrants part 1. *On the Horizon, 9*(5), 1–6. https://doi.org/10.1108/10748120110424816

Skolimowski, H. (1966). The structure of thinking in technology. *Technology and Culture, 7*(3), 371–383.

Srinivasan, A. (2017, January 1). What is a woman? *Philosophy Bites Podcast.* https://philosophybites.com/2017/01/amia-srinivasan-on-what-is-a-woman.html

Tone, A. (2002). *Devices and desires: A history of contraceptives in America.* Hill and Wang.

Tucker, I. (2017, May 28). A white mask worked better: Why algorithms are not colourblind. *The Guardian.* https://www.theguardian.com/technology/2017/may/28/joy-buolamwini-when-algorithms-are-racist-facial-recognition-bias

Vertesi, J. (2014, May 1). My experiment opting out of big data made me look like a criminal. *Time.* https://time.com/83200/privacy-internet-big-data-opt-out/

PART I

DISRUPT

Birth Control Pills, Baby Bottles, and Bikes: Dancing on the Edge of Social Transformation

Lisa Smith

"My Washdays are Holidays Now!" (Inglis Automatic Washer advertisement)

"Roll dishpan drudgery out of her life!" (General Electric washer advertisement)

TECHNOLOGY, GENDER, AND "PROGRESS" IN REAR-VIEW

In the 1950s in North America, many advertisements for new household technologies such as electric and automatic washers heralded the arrival of a new era for women. Reading these advertisements in the present can inspire laughter to be sure. The overly enthusiastic proclamations depict outdated images of domestic labour, family life, and gender roles that are profoundly out of step with contemporary sensibilities. In the advertisement quotes above, the new technologies—automatic and electric washers—are sold to consumers as a marker of progress and innovation in the home, and it is implied these items will change the status of women for the better. Women are depicted as a homogenous and unified group, and men, in the second example, are characterized as possessing the power to purchase these technologies *for* women. New tech here is made for women by men to change their lives, who dole it out in world-changing and life-altering installments at their discretion within the safety of the nuclear family home. While the specific messages for these advertisements may be out of date, the tendency to associate technology as the answer to the problems facing women persists even today. Of course, tech—while significant—is rarely the solution or saviour; more often, tech glosses over or, even worse, augments deep and profoundly unfair social arrangements. For example, electric and automatic washers are now relatively commonplace fixtures in most North American households, and yet household labour remains inequitable on both individual and systemic levels. In Canada, women continue to bear the burden of the second shift, tackling housework on top of career pursuits. Further, racialized women are overrepresented in precarious domestic labour, including house cleaning and other care work that is essential to the public and private spheres. Race, class, and gender collide here to shape how domestic labour is carried out and by whom (Guppy & Luongo, 2015). This has little to do with the kind of tech that is in homes and more to do with power structures that legitimate and perpetuate inequity—patriarchy, racism, heteronormativity, and much more. So, in rear-view, it would be better to say that technological advancements—such as electric and automatic washers—do not equal freedom for anyone, and certainly not for all women. (I understand that the former statement is perhaps not the best advertising copy.)

The story of technology and the impact of technologies on women has not been shaped by men alone. Women have often been excluded from access to the benefits that flow from technological innovation. As a result, there are many cases where women have fought for and actively supported technological innovation to enhance bodily autonomy and freedom. Women have pushed, and continue to push, back against and transform systems that govern what technologies do and whom they are for. However, such a generalized view of the impact of technology on women's lives and experiences hides the privilege of white, middle-class, able-bodied, cisgender women to engage with technology as a choice independent from structural violence and oppression. We need to do more with our analysis, and intersectionality is key in this regard. This chapter takes a critical look at the ways the "myth of progress" continues to shape narratives about the impact of technology on women's lives and experiences through a cursory examination of three everyday technologies: the birth control pill, baby bottles, and bikes. Why these three technologies? Well, it is not just because they all start with the letter "B," though this is a nice coincidence. These items are useful introductory entry points into thinking broadly about technology as a site of social transformation within the context of intersecting identities and social locations.

These accounts are by no means exhaustive, and this chapter's intent is to provide a jumping-off point to delve deeper and even add to broader social and cultural representations of these technologies (e.g., see invitation in Questions for Discussion to hold your own edit-a-thon to add to the stories of Black American feminist cyclists in past and present on Wikipedia!). The subtitle for this chapter is "Dancing on the Edge of Social Transformation," drawing our attention towards the multiple, the varied, and the edge, whereby some people win, some people lose, and some people fall in between when tech is integrated into life. "Dishpan drudgery" and "washday holidays" cannot be solved by simple quick fixes, nor are the experiences they refer to limited to the individual. Change requires a closer look at the social arrangements that support inequity within the home and beyond. To this end, we may conclude that a given technology is part of the solution; however, it is absolutely not the whole story.

"MOM, YOU LIKE OLD PHONES AND YOU NEVER GET NEW PHONES"

I am curious to know if you consider yourself a modern individual. If so, are the technologies you use part of what allows you to define yourself as such? The other day, as I was watching YouTube with my two children (aged 9 and 12), the inevitable ad interrupted the latest video release from one of their favourite YouTubers (they are convinced they need the "merch"!). The advertisement was for yet another new iPhone, and as the remote was not close to hand, I let the ad run. Images of lives lived figured prominently, reflecting the extent to which smartphones have become an extension of not just who we are but how we are every day. The next morning on our way to the school bus, my 12-year-old son expressed how important it was for him that he have the new iPhone. While part of his logic related to his desire for the device, he also felt the need to point out the difference between us. He said, "Mom, you only like old phones and you never get new phones." To be clear, the implication was that this was a bad thing.

In some ways, my son was expressing what could be construed as a modernist view of technology. New is better. Obtaining the latest technology will make his life better. My son's desire for the latest and newest technologies, as well as the dilemma it presents for me, are expected. As a white, middle-class, cis women living in Canada, I inhabit and navigate a particular experience of parenting and decision-making as it relates to technology, and digital technologies specifically. While I would not consider myself updated on the latest and most up-to-date innovations, for the most part, digital technologies flow freely into our home. My son expects a certain level of access to tech that is commensurate with his peers and social world. His main dilemma is convincing his parents to buy it for him. As a parent, the dilemmas I face are varied to be sure; however, they mostly fall within making choices—in consultation with my partner—about what technologies my children will or will not use. The capacity to access and employ a given technology is a function of social status, including class, gender, race, geographic location, age, and much more. Yet, the social processes that bring technologies to us are hidden from view, such that the appearance of any technology in our lives seems incidental and inevitable—pure progress, delivered straight to our door. Further, the social meanings attached to technologies appear finite and concrete. Of course, nothing could be further from the truth.

MAKING SENSE OF GENDER, TECHNOLOGY, AND SOCIAL TRANSFORMATION

As discussed in the introduction to this text, technologies are connected to and part of changing patterns of gendered relations at both individual and societal levels. The birth control pill, baby bottles, and bikes reflect complex and varying dimensions of social change as connected to gender and technologies. As this chapter focuses mostly on these items within the North American and Western cultural tradition, I begin with a discussion of modernism as it relates to technology and views about social progress, placing a particular focus on the unique context of gender and technology. I then turn to a discussion of intersectional and critical feminist scholarship, as well as social constructionism, as potential starting points for moving beyond straightforward accounts of gender relations and technology.

Within late modern capitalist societies, modernist views of technology continue to permeate and inform culture and daily life: "Modernism holds that change equals progress, that what is modern or new will automatically be better than the older thing it replaces" (Steckley, 2017, p. 434). Most critical scholars would seek to disrupt such a view even if they may agree that technology can be a driving force for social change. For example, the development of factory machinery is commonly connected with many wider social transformations, such as where we work and live, how we work, and who works, as well as with reshaping the global economic system. New contraceptive technologies, from condoms to the oral contraceptive pill, are often associated with changing social relations from who we have sex with and when we have sex with them, to why we have sex with them (i.e., to reproduce or not), as well as the role played by manufacturing and pharmaceutical companies in shaping what we can get (McLaren, 1990; Tone, 2001). Most critical scholars quickly reject a modernist view of technology as too simplistic and, further and most importantly for this text, problematic for the erasure of broader systemic patterns of inequity as related to technology. As noted previously, women have often been excluded from the benefits of technological innovation; the push for reproductive technologies by feminist activists is one such example, and indeed, historically, the female reproductive body was left out of medical and social innovation. Nevertheless, the myth of progress as it relates to the status of women, whether speaking of reproductive or other technologies, necessitates a second look.

For example, narratives of technology as enhancing freedom and choice for women homogenize and leave unproblematized the category of woman. Within popular framings of gender and tech, women are often presented as a one-dimensional, single-layered social category. Intersectional feminist scholars (see Collins, 1992; Crenshaw, 1989) push us to go beyond this framing and beyond surface-level inclusion, at the level of theory and practice. Class, ability, gender, Indigeneity, sexuality, and nationality cannot be parsed out as separate things independent from the relations of domination and oppression they bring to bear on the individual. As people engage with things—whether the law, or institutions, or tech—power relations are always present, and intersecting positionalities shape experiences within and of those things. In late modern capitalist societies, colonialism, patriarchy and misogyny, systemic racism, and global capitalism underpin and shape how technologies circulate as part of daily life and experience. Sometimes the connection between these deep power structures is obvious, while in other cases, the links are hidden, silent, or difficult to perceive. Intersectionality is a key intervention within the context of Black American feminist scholarship, and it should be noted that there is continued discussion about and engagement in its use within contemporary feminist scholarship and related areas. For the purposes of this chapter, an intersectional lens is key for illuminating the ways tech intersects with who people are—inhabiting multiple overlapping and inseparable social identities—and where they are—situated within social relations of power and oppression.

Eileen Leonard's (2003) *Women, Technology, and the Myth of Progress* provides an in-depth critique of the modernist view of technology, particularly as it relates to gender. Leonard troubles the notion that technology moves society towards better things and increases autonomy and freedom for women as a unified group. Importantly, she argues that the myth of progress ignores the intersection of class, gender, and race that shapes the change flowing from new technologies. As Leonard highlights, the mainstream media plays a key role in perpetuating overly simplistic accounts of technology and its impact on gender relations. It is not hard to find examples of "the myth of progress," technology, and women within mainstream media. I encourage readers to seek out examples of their own across a range of media, whether print, social media, or other. Most importantly, Leonard posits that the myth of progress draws attention away from the difficult work of social change that must take place at the level of day-to-day life through grassroots community organizing, ongoing collective political work, and movement building. For Leonard, tech matters; but the things that people do, both with and related to tech, matter more.

Like many scholars who are critical of a modernist view of technology, Leonard employs a social constructionist lens whereby she understands that meaning about technologies is formed within social and cultural relations and systems. Processes of social construction are thus circulating and being formed all the time and often occur at the level of representation. For example, gendered meanings are layered onto cultural objects and artifacts, and are a key mechanism for communicating social expectations for gender performance; this happens in both subtle and not so subtle ways. Bikes sold to young boys are often dark blue, black, red, or orange. Bikes sold to young girls are often pink or purple. The use of these cultural markers of masculinity and femininity is arbitrary and is an everyday example of the social construction of gender. However, as I will discuss later, social construction also involves who is and who is not represented. For example, the history of Black female cyclists is not commonly known, nor is it included on the current (as of June 17, 2021) Wikipedia page entitled "Bicycle," even though there is a section exploring "Female Emancipation," where the history of the bicycle as part of feminist organizing is covered in great detail. It is not that this omission is intentional; rather, it is an instance where we see that certain stories come to light to the exclusion of others. To this end, power and power relations shape both what we see and what we know about technologies as social things that create change. Technologies, and the things we say about them, intersect with pre-existing social categories and experiences that are often part of sustaining systemic violence and oppression (see Harding, 1991, 1998; Martin, 1991). Thus, we want to pay attention to what is represented—but also to what is absent or omitted.

So, what *can* we *do*? Well, a lot. Maybe. It depends. People take up and use technologies within the context of constrained social relations that simultaneously limit and open possibilities in human experience and interaction. The accounts that follow provide a brief overview of three examples that help flesh out themes discussed in this section. I explore each tech item in turn, consider general representations, and offer at least one example of ways individuals or groups have sought to disrupt or reshape through action. The aim here is to put tech back in its place, reaffirm and draw attention to the social and cultural processes that give it a certain meaning, and understand the impacts of social situation and privilege.

THE BIRTH CONTROL PILL: TOWARDS THE HORRIFYING, REVOLUTIONARY, AND UNEXPECTED

"No woman can call herself free who does not own and control her body. No woman can call herself free until she can choose consciously whether she will or will not be a mother." (Margaret Sanger, 1919)

"Birth control was revolutionary because it was birth control that enabled women to seize control of their own reproductive abilities, to plan their pregnancies, to plan their children, to have sex without babies ... so birth control was massively liberating." (Interview with Debora Spar, Author of *Women and Machines: How Technology Has Shaped Gender Roles*, CBC Radio, 2021)

Within a text examining technology and gender, a discussion of the birth control pill—or *the pill* as it is commonly known—would be expected. Though separated by just over one hundred years, in the quotes above, Sanger and Spar articulate a similar notion—birth control means freedom for women. Indeed, since its origins in the mid-20th century, the pill has come to be a well-known popular culture icon for allowing women to realize choice and autonomy. At the same time, the pill has always been rife with controversy within society generally, among feminist scholars, and for grassroots and community organizers and activists. It has never not been controversial. The story of the pill is helpful for illuminating the ways that technologies are perceived as tied to transformations in our gendered lives, but also gender relations more generally. During the 20th century, reproductive control, which the pill is perceived to allow, has come to be strongly associated with freedom and autonomy for women (Granzow, 2007; Ruhl, 2002; Smith, 2014a, 2014b; Tone, 2001). However, as Cream (1995) points out, the desire to control reproduction reflects the experience of white middle-class cis women, where reproductive control remains a marker in the performance of appropriate and successful heterosexual femininity. As the long-reigning poster child for reproductive control, the pill is worth taking a closer look at, as well as the ways we might illuminate a not so straightforward path for thinking about this piece of tech.

To be clear, we might agree that reproductive control is important and see and feel the benefits of widespread access to contraceptive devices such as the pill. The point here is not to say people should not be able to get access to the pill or any other such contraceptive device. Instead, we seek to trouble the strong association of the pill with a straightforward account of progress for all women.

In North America, throughout the 20th century, calls to take up reproductive control as a symbol of women's freedom were criticized by Black and Indigenous feminists. Eugenics and population control have been, and continue to be, intimately intertwined with the broader development of technologies that facilitate reproductive control and, to this day, disproportionality impact racialized, disabled, and impoverished women. As such, associating technologies that facilitate reproductive control with freedom for all women is highly problematic and willfully ignorant of deep patterns of structural inequity and violence. Reproductive control and free choice-making in relation to contraception remain complex and highly contingent on one's social position within the broader web of power relations. In the North American context, the pill is not just about reproductive control; it is embedded within ongoing legacies of colonialism, racism, and classism that intersect to enact control on women's bodies.

A particularly important example of the deep interrelationship between reproductive technologies, and the pill specifically, with colonial systems of power and violence lies in the early trials of the pill in Puerto Rico. Drug developers sought a captive population outside of the mainland of the United States. As Lebron (2017) observes,

> Scholars and activists have long argued that Puerto Rico functions as a colonial laboratory for the United States. Instances of unethical medical and scientific experimentation in Puerto Rico—including testing of the birth control pill and use of Agent Orange—provide perhaps the clearest examples of the oppressive dimensions of U.S. colonial rule in Puerto Rico and its deleterious effects on the land and people. (p. 328)

Lebron's account is important for how it highlights the complex political and social relationships within Puerto Rico that facilitate ongoing forms of structural violence and inequity. In addition, Lebron highlights links between the pill and other forms of scientific experimentation, beyond reproductive technologies. Even though it can seem like a discrete thing, tech does not live in one place, nor does it serve just one end within webs of power.

The ways that the history of the pill is embedded within colonial violence are not regularly discussed within mainstream news media stories that celebrate the anniversary of the pill (see Allemang, 2010; CBC News, 2010; NPR, 2010). Instead, the news media tends to lean into controversy surrounding women, sex, and changing social values, as well as controversies relating to the use of pharmaceutical technologies. For example, in the *Globe and Mail* article "The Pill Turns 50," the author states,

> And yet after 50 years, it's hard to dispute the Pill's place in the annals of reproduction: It's outlasted and outdistanced its cumbersome rivals, made the leap from utopian and dangerous to everyday and normal, offered easy liberation in a convenient oral format and fended off all its critics, as if they were the exception and it had become the rule. (Allemang, 2010)

Across popular news media stories, the pill is presented as a form of tech that speaks to women's bodies and experiences in a unified fashion, while confining the controversy to the realm of sexual mores, ethics and informed consent, and reproductive control more generally.

Such a narrative situates the pill as being for one thing—reproductive control—and one kind of woman—straight, cis, most likely middle-class, and, up until recently, most likely white. Of course, since its inception, the pill has been used for many things. Further, in the contemporary context, pharmaceutical marketing reflects key changes in the place of the pill within the broader spectrum of contraceptive options and views about reproductive control. In advertisements for the pill, brands such as Alesse feature racial diversity and target, in particular, younger women (Smith, 2014a). Advertisements for Alesse also market the lifestyle benefits of the pill, such as menstrual flow management and reduced acne, even if reproductive control remains a prominent feature. Despite these shifts within pharmaceutical marketing, the pill's strong association with heterosexual sex and cis women persists and ignores the various ways gender intersects with pharmaceutical technologies and the different stakes at play in reproductive control and autonomy.

Like all pharmaceutical technologies, the pill can be and is used for other things beyond reproductive control. For example, the pill is often taken continuously by nonbinary folks and trans men to stop menstruation. Use of the pill by gender-diverse individuals is not discussed in mainstream news stories about the pill. This omission reflects broader social views about the technology and whom it serves, whether on a day-to-day basis or in regard to social change more generally. A recent article published in *Teen Vogue* entitled "7 Things to Know about Birth Control if You Are Transgender or Nonbinary" (Weiss, 2019) reflects one instance of the uptake of the pill within mainstream media as being for someone other than straight, cis folks. Beyond this one case, representation of gender-diverse people's use of the pill within the mainstream media is relegated to niche status. This omission within popular culture mirrors social supports and services available to trans and nonbinary folks seeking to navigate reproductive and sexual health care.

Supports and services are generally lacking, and practitioners are often not up to speed about the reproductive and health needs of trans and nonbinary patients.

For example, in my research on the use of the pill, a participant who identified as queer shared that when they turned 16, their doctor automatically prescribed them the pill, stating, "Well … you're 16 … you should probably be on the pill" (Smith, 2014b). The doctor cited a list of benefits, ranging from lighter periods to less acne, and tacked on reproductive control as a side benefit, assuming that their patient would be having heterosexual sex with cis men. This example highlights just one such case where the pill enters social relations and is framed as meeting the needs of a seemingly unified subject—young, cis, hetero, and in need of reproductive control, with a few side benefits—with little regard to the unique positionalities and needs of the individual. An assumption that the pill's impact can be confined to the sexual and reproductive body, or that it circulates freely within a homogenous group of women, is beyond problematic. Pharmaceutical technologies are always already complex and continue to be shaped by intersecting patterns of inequity and power relations in action.

GLASS + VULCANIZED RUBBER = FREEDOM FOR WOMEN?

"Breastfeeding vs. Formula: The Pros and Cons" (Healthline)

"The Benefits of Breastfeeding vs. Bottle Feeding Formula" (American Pregnancy Association)

If the pill is expected within a text on gender and tech, I hazard to guess that baby bottles would be somewhat unexpected. We don't think of these things as tech. But they are. What is commonly understood as a baby bottle today is a modified version of older models that came into existence in the 1800s, made of glass bottles and rubber nipples. Initial models grew out of technological innovation during the industrial revolution, which included the production of raw materials required (e.g., glass blowing and vulcanization of rubber). Today, in Canadian society, baby bottles can be purchased at most major children's supply stores, such as Babies"R"Us, as well as pharmacies and grocery stores, such as Shoppers Drug Mart and Save-on-Foods. Baby bottles are commonly used to feed infant children previously pumped breast milk, infant formula, and, in other cases, milk and milk alternatives, such as juice or water. Within North American society, baby bottles are commonly associated with impacting gender and the distribution of care work—specifically infant feeding; however, as Hausman (2008) notes, choice-making in relation to infant feeding is often reduced to and perceived as an individual choice. On the web, articles abound from blogs, websites, and more, framing a debate between breastfeeding and bottle feeding and offering to guide mothers (not parents) through this choice-making process.

When I was a new mother, I was overwhelmed with the amount of advice I received from well-meaning friends, family members, and even community members regarding how best to care for—and feed—my infant. While much of this advice related to sleep habits and clothing choices, a lot of advice also heralded the freedom I would find once I "got my baby on the bottle." "You will be able to go out again!" "Your partner can be part of the feeding process!" People even offered kindly to share the tech I would need—bottles and breast pumps—something I greatly appreciated as a parent on a tight budget. While I did use baby bottles filled with expressed milk on a few occasions, I mostly relied on breast feeding for reasons that don't really matter here. The same advice-givers readily offered their thoughts on my seemingly poor uptake of bottle feeding. I got the sense that some, not all, thought I had just not tried hard enough. The indirect message I received from some people was akin to the following: "Why are you not enjoying your freedom to the full extent that you could?" For these folks, baby bottles meant freedom, and I *should* be using what I have access to, to the fullest extent possible.

My choice to use baby bottles in a dispirited fashion was thus perceived by some as troubling and in need of correction and guidance. Indeed, when we examine and understand baby bottles as gendered tech, we can illuminate intersecting social structures and processes that define choice and autonomy across social space and within social relations. As Hausman (2008) argues, in the contemporary North American context, the use of baby bottles is situated within broader discussions about choice-making in relation to infant feeding. In North American society, debates about breast feeding versus bottle feeding intersect with the redefinition of women's place in public life and, in particular, the workplace. Yet, the privilege to pick and choose methods of nourishing one's child belies the extent to which infant care is shaped by a variety of considerations, including biological limitations of the body, as well as gender, race, relationship status, class, culture, family relationships, and many other factors. As always, bottles and the extent to which they lead to increased autonomy for parents remains highly contingent and situational. Engagement with, and use of, technologies that facilitate infant feeding is not a uniform experience.

At the level of representation in the media, Duckett's (2012) work highlights that baby bottle marketing is characterized by a seemingly generic appeal to all women. Continued class inequity between strata of women shapes views about breastfeeding versus bottle feeding, impacting, in particular, working- and lower-class women. Duckett (2012) finds that mainstream parenting magazines continue to reproduce existing patterns of gender-based class inequity in relation to bottle feeding with formula. She states that

> magazines targeting working- and lower-class women … repeatedly discuss the need for women to add supplements to their assumedly inadequate diets, while upper-class women need not worry because they can afford to purchase and prepare more expensive organic meals. (p. 243)

As Duckett points out, the framing of bottle feeding within mainstream media as a "better choice" for working- and lower-class women reflects the broader history of popular health messaging that continues to reify class-based inequities in relation to infant feeding choice-making by women.

Mainstream media representations of baby bottle use are thus perched between complex and often contradicting views about what and how mothers ought to carry out nourishing their infants. As Hausman (2008) observes, "choice" in this case should not be confused with "liberation" (p. 3) for women, even if it is presented as such. Infant feeding continues to intersect with the broader constraints facing mothers on a day-to-day basis that are rooted in structural inattention to caregiving as a form of essential and undervalued labour. As such, though they are seemingly banal and everyday items, baby bottles are part of the re-envisioning of gendered relations across late modern capitalist societies. The deep edge of social transformation remains out of reach as the choice of breast versus bottle is continually centred within popular narratives as an individual versus social issue.

For me, baby bottles were in large part the inspiration for this chapter and reflect my own internal reflexive process in reconsidering my preconceived notions about technology as they intersect with gender relations and social change. About a year ago, I heard a news story while heading home from work and listening to the radio. The story was about an archeologist's discovery of infant feeding vessels at a prehistoric dig site in eastern Europe. Something about this story grabbed me, and I immediately started to imagine all the things I thought the discovery of these "incredibly cute" ancient baby bottles implied (CBC News, 2019). The archeologists associated with the dig site do make some claims about what these vessels might mean for our understanding of gender relations at that time. However, after seeking more insight from a colleague, who is an anthropologically trained archeologist, she reminded me that "when studying ancient societies, we have to leave all of our preconceptions about gender behind." Further, "We can't know much as we have no capacity to know the full complexity of the social system and structure where these vessels were used." The takeaway here is that placing tech in place means taking a closer look at social relations within a given society, and this means recognizing that there are things we cannot know, especially things that happened in the past. Bringing this same sense of distance to the present, and identifying what we think we know, is a core element of bringing a critical and intersectional lens to the technologies we employ within daily life that are taken for granted or not seen as extraordinary tech—like baby bottles.

BIKES: ROLLING TOWARDS INTERSECTIONS

If the pill is an expected topic for discussion, and baby bottles are unexpected, I would say bikes will be expected for some. Depending on who you are and what you know about bikes, you may or may not associate them with having anything to do with gender. However, since the early days of cycling, bikes have been looped into existing patterns of exclusion and inequity. More recently, critical scholars and, in particular, feminist historians have sought to bring to light the ways cycling is connected to gender relations and the movement for suffrage and equality.

Hallenbeck's (2016) aptly titled work *Claiming the Bicycle* highlights the vast and varied ways that women have pushed for access to, engaged with, reshaped, and taken up the bicycle as a site of liberation and transformation. For example, Hallenbeck brings to light the hidden histories of female riders within the American cycling movement of the 1880s. As she notes, the increase in women cyclists was facilitated, in part, by technological innovation that made bikes that could adapt to women's dress and body sizes. Women's fashions (another kind of tech!) were being adapted to encourage increased movement and mobility. At the same time, women did indeed have to fight for the right to ride. One opponent to women cyclists claimed the bicycle was "the devil's advance agent" and asserted that it "would bring about women's moral and religious demise" (p. 31). To this end, simply taking up cycling could be seen as a form of critique, resistance, and pushing back. Bicycles facilitated movement, and thus it is not surprising that many women saw possibilities, personal and political, in using this technology, regardless of the perceived threat to morality. Indeed, the bicycle went on to become a key symbol of the Suffragette movement in England and America, and was a regular feature in political action and activism. Hallenbeck's work also highlights histories of African American women cyclists, such as Kittie Knox and Idella Johnson, and draws attention to the racism and sexism experienced by early Black American women cyclists. For example, many early Black American women cyclists were excluded from Black American men's cycling clubs—because of sexism—but also were "unable to race white women racers"—because of racism (p. 182).

Today (as of June 1, 2021), a quick search of the net yields many interesting and insightful videos, from documentaries to animated shorts, about the role of bikes in women's liberation and feminism more generally. Acknowledging that Google searches reflect personalization, there is an abundance of links, articles, and websites that conform to a modernist view of access to technology as progress for women. In many of these, we see highlighted the struggle to gain access to bikes as tied to broader political emancipation for white middle-class women. Historical or contemporary stories about racialized women and otherwise marginalized groups who have engaged in political mobilization through cycling do not appear quite as readily via web searches or within information-sharing sites. At the same time, it is worth acknowledging that the connection between cycling and feminism generally is often buried within other content. For example, the Wikipedia page entitled "Bicycle" (as of June 17, 2021) is one of the few bike-related articles that discusses social aspects of cycling. The page has a subsection entitled "Female Emancipation" and provides some detail about the history of cycling and suffrage. The Wikipedia page entitled "Cycling in the United States" has a one-line entry naming Ayesha McGowan "the first African American female professional road cyclist." Suffice it to say the presence of the rich history of Black American female ridership, in past and present, including its importance for marginalized and racialized groups in political and community organizing, is lacking on Wikipedia. I encourage readers to do something about this lack (see Questions for Discussion). However, for now, allow me to highlight that when seeking information on the internet, one would have to know that there was a history of Black American female ridership and be intentional in the search terms employed. I know because my sister is part of the bike industry and helped me understand more fully the complex and varied history of the bicycle. Silencing, invisibility, and erasure in this case are no accident and continue to shape bicycle ridership to this day.

In the contemporary context, despite being a multi-billion-dollar industry globally, in North America, the bike industry remains very much a white- and male-dominated milieu. This extends across production, mechanics, and sales, as well as leisure and competitive contexts. A key example is discussed by Buehler and Pucher (2012), who note that racialized women continue to be underrepresented as cyclists. Cultural expectations, financial barriers, and many other factors play a role (Lubitow et al., 2019). Despite this, many individuals and groups are pushing back against social and cultural barriers to reshape whom bicycles are for and to encourage diverse ridership.

One example of an organization that seeks to hold space for racialized women riders is Black Girls Do Bike. There are many more. The Black Girls Do Bike organization aims to grow and "support a community of women of color who share a passion for cycling." They champion "efforts to introduce the joy of cycling to all women, but especially, women and girls of color" (Black Girls Do Bike, 2021). In a recent interview for VeloNews, Monica Garrison, the founder and creator of Black Girls Do Bike, expresses the value of the organization for broader social justice work, as well as creating a safe space for Black women and other racialized women:

> I think if all things were equal you'd see yourself reflected in all aspects of cycling. As a person of color, I don't see that. We know things aren't equal because there's not a reflection in the quality of advertising and in other aspects of the industry. (Welch, 2021)

Garrison is naming a social issue—inequitable access to and representation in relation to a technology—and acting, in this case through taking up cycling and building a social organization. In doing so, Garrison is challenging and remaking the stories that are told about a given technology—the bike—and who this technology is for—not only white cis men.

I hope by now we can agree that new tech does not lead to a one-dimensional kind of progress; however, dare I say, people working together can make something with tech that is meaningful to their social world and experience. And sometimes, just sometimes, we see a glimmer of hope beyond power, violence, and oppression. It is fleeting, though, like a bike ride on the weekend. Better to ride together, with communities of activists and general feminist troublemakers, and do so often.

CONCLUDING THOUGHTS AND TOWARDS THE INTERNET OF THINGS

> There's an interesting kind of restraint that you find. There's not a lot of cursing or swearing. There's not a lot of personal cuts. There's not a lot of put downs that one would expect to find. There's not screens full of "go to hell," which is surprising. The kind of liberation is mixed. It's interesting because one would think if you're anonymous you'd do anything you want. But people in a group have their own sense of community and what we can do. The thing that I'm always left with, when I leave, is this sense of overwhelming

desire of people to feel rooted. And the only way they feel rooted is through another person. And if this is the only way, maybe the only way that they can talk to somebody, this is how they'll do it. (CBC Archives, 1993)

The above excerpt comes from an interview called "A Computer Network Called Internet," featured in the CBC Archives. A computer programmer speaks to the positive and controlled atmosphere of this new connective technological tool— the internet. I get where he is coming from; there is a comfort in proclaiming that things will be good, that things will be better. That comfort of "better times ahead" is part of the attraction of modernism. The myth of progress has reared its familiar head in a big way during the COVID-19 pandemic, in which the internet has emerged as the "solution" to massive social upheaval and shut-downs. I understand that saying "it's complicated" is not the best selling point, and certainly not the stuff of headlines. Through the gaze of the present, we all know this programmer was just as off-base as those automatic and electric washer advertisements. Disrupting the myth of progress, and particularly the ways that technology is situated as poised to transform the status of women, is a key aspect of this entire collection. Doing so, in part, involves challenging modernist views of technology that are deeply embedded within our social and cultural understandings of technology, my own included. Social constructionism helps us to see that technologies come into being within the context of human societies and that they reflect the cultures, values, ideas, and beliefs of those societies. We can get part of the way by starting to notice the constant stream of representations that shape how we see, understand, and in some cases use tech. However, an intersectional feminist lens necessitates moving beyond the surface to the ways technologies serve and feed into power relations, which reproduce inequity in often violent and oppressive ways. Unpacking power relations is no easy task and not one that should be taken lightly. The collective wisdom in this collection reflects that it takes many voices, experiences, and positionalities to do this important work.

To close, I will say that wash days are not holidays, and dishpan drudgery persists, even if advertisements continue to tell a very different story. Indeed, people can and do use technology to push back and create new things, in big and small ways, within social constraints that we may or may not be aware of. If we are dancing on the edge of social transformation, it means the end is not yet determined. It is just that complicated, but also that simple, and in that I find hope.

QUESTIONS FOR DISCUSSION

1. Pick one of the three technologies discussed in this chapter: bikes, baby bottles, or the birth control pill. Discuss as a group the following prompts:
   - What words come to mind when you think about this technology?
   - What did you know about this technology prior to reading this chapter?
   - Do you associate this technology with social change? If yes, how so? For whom?
2. Make a list of technologies (other than tech already discussed in this chapter) that are commonly associated with impacting gender relations. Select one or two and conduct a search of online news stories or social media posts about that technology. What themes do you notice about how that technology is represented across social space? What do these stories reflect about race, ability, gender, sexual orientation, and so on, as related to that technology? To what extent do the stories you found reflect an intersectional lens? If they do, in what way? If they do not, how might this be addressed?
3. As a group, explore pages on Wikipedia related to cycling. Consider the range of content available and focus in on content related to intersecting social identities. Who is missing? What could be added? Carry out further research and hold an edit-a-thon to add to existing content (see links below under Read More).

INVITATIONS TO GO DEEPER

1. Take some time to consider your relationship to technology. Do you associate technology with progress? If yes, how so? Explore your thoughts through reflecting on a technology that you have recently started using, that is, something that is "new" for you.
2. Make a list of the technologies that you regularly employ as part of your day-to-day life. For each item on the list, answer the following: How did this technology come to be a part of your life? Are you aware of a broader social story related to this technology? Does awareness of this story impact, inform, or change how you think about the technology? At the end of the day, what does the technology mean to you (this could be progress, also something else, maybe many things)?
3. Select a technology that you employ on a regular basis. What is it supposed to be or intended to be used for? Are there other uses that you might consider? Be creative and seek beyond the expected. Try to think of as many possibilities as you can.

READ MORE

Art + Feminism. (2020). *Quick guide for editing on Wikipedia.* https://artandfeminism. org/wp-content/uploads/2020/12/EN_Quick-Guide-for-Editors-2020.pdf

CBC News. (2019, September 26). "Incredibly cute" ancient baby bottles discovered by archeologists. https://www.cbc.ca/news/science/ baby-bottles-1.5296792

Devlin, H. (2019, September 25). Historic find suggests bottle-feeding not a modern phenomenon. *The Guardian.* https://www.theguardian.com/ science/2019/sep/25/prehistoric-babies-were-fed-animal-milk-from-pots-says-study

Edit-a-thon. (2021, December 8). *Wikipedia.* https://en.wikipedia.org/wiki/ Edit-a-thon

Eugenics Archives. (n.d.). Homepage. https://eugenicsarchive.ca/

Szczepanski, C. (2013, March 20). Women's (bike) history: 3 days, 5 women, 250 miles. *News from the League.* https://bikeleague.org/content/ womens-bike-history-3-days-5-women-250-miles

Tomanek, T. (2009). Baby bottles: A pictorial history. *Contemporary Pediatrics*, *26*(5), 36–39.

LISTEN MORE, WATCH MORE

Afghan cycles, Sarah Menzies, 2018: https://nwfilm.org/films/afghan-cycles/

The pill, PBS, 2003: https://www.pbs.org/wgbh/americanexperience/films/pill/

REFERENCES

Allemang, J. (2010, May 7). The pill turns 50. *The Globe and Mail.* https://www. theglobeandmail.com/life/health-and-fitness/health/conditions/the-pill-turns-50/ article572652/

Bicycle. (2021, June 7). In Wikipedia. https://en.wikipedia.org/wiki/Bicycle

Black Girls Do Bike. (2021). Purpose. https://www.blackgirlsdobike.com/home

Buehler, R., & Pucher, J. (2012). International overview: Cycling trends in Western Europe, North America, and Australia. In J. Pucher & R. Buehler (Eds.), *City cycling* (pp. 9–29). MIT Press.

CBC Archives. (1993, October 8). A computer network called Internet. *Prime Time News.* https://www.cbc.ca/archives/entry/a-computer-network-called-internet

CBC News. (2010, May 7). Birth-control pill turns 50. https://www.cbc.ca/news/birth-control-pill-turns-50-1.908892

CBC News. (2019, September 26). "Incredibly cute" ancient baby bottles discovered by archeologists. https://www.cbc.ca/news/science/baby-bottles-1.5296792

CBC Radio. (2021, March 2). Harvard professor explores how technology shaped the role of women in society. https://www.cbc.ca/radio/ideas/harvard-professor-explores-how-technology-shaped-the-role-of-women-in-society-1.5933577

Collins, P. H. (1992). *Black feminist thought: Knowledge, consciousness, and the politics of empowerment*. Routledge.

Cream, J. (1995). Women on trial: A private pillory. In S. Pile & N. Thrift (Eds.), *Mapping the subject: Geographies of cultural transformation* (pp. 158–169). Routledge.

Crenshaw, K. (1989). Demarginalizing the intersection of race and sex: A Black feminist critique of discrimination doctrine, feminist theory and antiracist practice. *University of Chicago Legal Forum*, *89*, 139–167.

Cycling in the United States. (2021, June 7). In Wikipedia. https://en.wikipedia.org/wiki/Cycling_in_the_United_States

Duckett, N. D. (2012). Rethinking the importance of social class: How mass market magazines portray infant feeding. In P. H. Smith, B. L. Hausman, & M. Labbok (Eds.), *Beyond health, beyond choice: Breastfeeding constraints and realities* (pp. 236–248). Rutgers University Press.

Granzow, K. (2007). De-constructing "choice": The social imperative and women's use of the birth control pill. *Culture, Health & Sexuality*, *9*(1), 43–54.

Guppy, N., & Luongo, N. (2015). The rise and stall of Canada's gender-equity revolution. *The Canadian Review of Sociology / Revue canadienne de sociologie*, *52*(3), 241–265.

Hallenbeck, S. (2016). *Claiming the bicycle: Women, rhetoric, and technology in nineteenth-century America*. Southern Illinois University Press.

Harding, S. (1991). *Whose science? Whose knowledge? Thinking from women's lives*. Cornell University Press.

Harding, S. (1998). *Is science multicultural? Postcolonialisms, feminisms, and epistemologies*. Indiana University Press.

Hausman, B. L. (2008). Women's liberation and the rhetoric of "choice" in infant feeding debates. *International Breastfeeding Journal*, *3*, Article 10.

Lebron, M. (2017). Puerto Rico and the colonial circuits of policing. *NACLA Report on the Americas*, *49*(3), 328–334.

Leonard, E. (2003). *Women, technology, and the myth of progress*. Pearson.

Lubitow, A., Tompkins, K., & Feldman, M. (2019). Sustainable cycling for all? Race and gender-based bicycling inequalities in Portland, Oregon. *City & Community*, *18*(4), 1181–1202.

Martin, E. (1991). The egg and the sperm: How science has constructed a romance based on stereotypical male–female roles. *Signs, 16*(3), 485–501.

McLaren, A. (1990). *A history of contraception*. Basil and Blackwell.

NPR. (2010, May 9). The pill turns 50. https://www.npr.org/templates/story/story.php?storyId=126646877

Ruhl, L. (2002). Dilemmas of the will: Uncertainty, reproduction and the rhetoric of control. *Signs, 27*(3), 641–663.

Smith, L. (2014a). Girl power and the pill: Unpacking web-based marketing for Alesse and Yasmin. In S. Paterson, F. Scala, & M. Sokolon (Eds.), *Fertile ground: Reproduction in Canada* (pp. 257–279). McGill-Queen's University Press.

Smith, L. (2014b). "You're 16 … you should probably be on the pill": Girls, the non-reproductive body, and the rhetoric of self-control. *Studies in the Maternal, 6*(1), 1–26.

Steckley, J. (2017). *Elements of sociology: A critical Canadian introduction*. Oxford University Press.

Tone, A. (2001). *Devices and desires: A history of contraceptives in America*. Hill and Wang.

Weiss, S. (2019). 7 Things to know about birth control if you are transgender or nonbinary. *Teen Vogue*. https://www.teenvogue.com/story/things-to-know-about-birth-control-trans-non-binary

Welch, B. (2021). Yes, Black girls do bike. https://www.velonews.com/culture/yes-black-girls-do-bike/

CHAPTER 2

Flowing with Tech: Bringing an Intersectional Lens to Menstruation Technologies

Lauren Friesen and Ana Brito

"Women's regular bleeding engenders phantoms." (Paracelsus)

"Contact with [menstrual blood] turns new wine sour, crops touched by it become barren, grafts die, seed in gardens are dried up, the fruit of trees fall off, the edge of steel and the gleam of ivory are dulled, hives of bees die, even bronze and iron are at once seized by rust, and a horrible smell fills the air; to taste it drives dogs mad and infects their bites with an incurable poison." (Pliny the Elder, *Natural History: A Selection*)

"Simplify the laundress problem." (Headline of a 1920s Kotex advertisement for Cellucotton pads)

INTRODUCTION

Menstruation is a normal biological function, and yet, there exists an uncomfortable silence that affects the daily life of women and girls, and trans and nonbinary menstruators. Taboo and shame shape all aspects of menstruation, including the things used to manage menstrual blood flow—menstruation technologies. In this chapter, we argue that period products—disposable pads, tampons, menstrual cups, and more—are technology and should be viewed as such. Further, drawing on an intersectional feminist framework, we observe that menstruation technologies are not accessed equitably by menstruators, creating an issue of tech equity. Once period technology is included in conversations regarding tech equity, we are able to analyze how it is designed and marketed to serve certain populations at the expense of others. Furthermore, the vast majority of period tech we use contributes to the duality of menstruation as a site of both shame and celebration.

Period technology has made strides forwards in efficiency and safety, but a cultural lag can be observed in the surrounding discourse. To speak candidly about menstruating is still a taboo in cultures globally (Kiefer & Fitzgerald, 2018). The way we think and talk about menstrual technology reflects this taboo. For example, ensuring control over when and how a period will occur is of utmost importance to hide any stains, smells, or indication that menstruation is happening.

Technology is defined as the tools or artifacts used to achieve goals and make life easier; it is often thought of as computers, handheld devices, or sophisticated digital devices and equipment used within daily tasks. However, many technologies are used to enhance or aid bodily functions. As an example, hearing aids are digital processors that help people cope with hearing deficiencies. In a similar fashion, menstrual technologies are used by menstruators to manage blood flow. Physical products for managing periods are not usually thought of as technology, in part because they are essentially designed to not be thought of at all.

Generally speaking, throughout history, most technologies built to manage menstruation have been designed to hide or mask the fact that people menstruate; this is reflected in advertisements for products that employ euphemism and feminine imagery. This marketing rarely displays realistic or even scientifically accurate portrayals of menstruation. For example, for most of their history, tampons and pad commercials replaced menstrual blood with blue liquids. In 2011, Always finally started using red liquid to show the efficacy of their products (Stamper, 2011). The fact that blue liquid is used as a visual euphemism illustrates that not all types of blood are considered equal: realistic menstrual blood is taboo in the media, while blood that comes from violent situations is shown as perfectly normal red blood. In the contemporary context, period tech, in its various forms, is being developed on a grander scale than ever before (Hughes, 2020), swiftly becoming normalized in its control of the menstruating body using high-tech gadgets and personalized apps.

Reflecting on my own[1] experience with period education serves to contextualize the changing landscape of period shame across generations. Growing up, my mother repeatedly told me about her first period, or "menarche." She was 12 years old, playing kickball at school in her white gym shorts in the early 1970s. Upon her realization that her shorts were no longer white, she sprinted all the way home, without stopping to ask a teacher or classmate for help. She believed there was something horribly wrong with her body and was too embarrassed to seek help because of where the blood was coming from. Her mother had never told her how a period would occur or what to do. When *my* first period occurred, I knew what was happening. I was prepared for how to manage it and who to ask for help. I was at the beach the day I got my first period—I remember my first thought being the irrational fear that I would attract a shark in the water. Despite my knowledge and preparedness for menarche, I distinctly recall being terrified to tell my mother that it had happened. It was like a dirty secret. Unfortunately, in many places, my mom's experience is still the norm, and my childhood sense of vague embarrassment is a seemingly universal sentiment.

When my[2] grandmother was young, women in Argentina were granted a "feminine day" once a month to use if they were experiencing menstrual cramps or discomfort. After the 1976 coup, the feminine day was abolished. Nowadays, some collective bargaining agreements allow employees to take a day off if they are experiencing menstrual pain. However, in most cases, employees are not aware of such rights and do not take advantage of them. I remember my first job. At 19 years old, I was hired as a call centre agent to work for a multinational technology company. During my 8-hour shift, I had three breaks of 10 minutes each and my 40-minute lunch hour. Those days that I had my period at work were brutal, as I did not find 10 minutes long enough to go to the washroom, change my pad, stretch my legs, and sometimes take a painkiller to manage my cramps. Menstrual pain can affect women's lives in many ways, interfering in daily activities (Weisberg et al., 2016). Recognizing cups, tampons, and pads as technology to manage menstruation is important because it extends into the daily lives of menstruators.

As two cisgender women who have relatively easy access to menstruation technologies, we recognize that our experience does not reflect all, or even most, menstruators' relationship with their periods. We both hold the privilege to pick and choose which technologies we use to manage menstruation. We usually have no need to miss work or school when we bleed. Throughout this chapter, if you menstruate or have menstruated, we invite you to think about your experience with, and perception of, menstruation. Do you categorize tampons as technology, with a long history and complex process of design evolution? Further, how does the way we gender technology affect the way we view menstrual products? Finally, consider the ways that access to menstruation technologies is limited and why.

A FEMINIST FRAMEWORK

Media, marketing, and education all serve to reinforce shame within the experience of menstruation. Feminist scholarship can help us understand how our perceptions of menstruation operate. Gender schema theory suggests that contemporary society seeks to dichotomize the biologies and experiences of male and female bodies, pushing us to place more importance on what makes us different rather than what makes us similar, stating, "The distinction between male and female serves as a basic organizing principle for every human culture" (Bem, 1981, p. 354). Further, gender schema theory says that from a young age, boys and girls learn to code behaviour, products, and facets of everyday life as "masculine" versus "feminine," adapting by aligning themselves with one option or the other. Employing this theory, within mainstream North American society, menstruation is coded as a distinctly female experience that *only* affects women and, by extension, should only be cared about by women. This trend not only alienates non-menstruators from understanding what menstruation is really like but erases male-identifying people from discussions about menstruation; but trans men and many nonbinary people menstruate and rely on menstruation technologies. To this end, socialization shapes who is permitted to care about periods and why. Furthermore, treating menstruation as a "women's problem" obscures the multiple positionalities that shape the experience of menstruation; for example, people in different socio-economic positions may have varying degrees of ease or difficulty accessing menstruation technologies. Relegating all information about periods to a distinctly feminine sphere serves to make issues like period poverty seem like an issue that only affects women and that should therefore be solved by them.

Coined by scholar Kimberlé Crenshaw (1989) in the late 1980s, *intersectionality* is an analytical framework used to consider how one's gender, race, class, and other socio-political identities overlap and converge to create a distinct experience. Such factors represent advantages and disadvantages in society. Intersectional feminism invites us to examine how our experiences as women are not universal but rather stratified by various intersecting and overlapping social identities and experiences. Sexism informs and is informed by racism, ableism, homophobia, and so on, to a point where these forces become inextricably linked and make a unique experience of marginalization. For a more in-depth discussion of intersectionality, refer to the introduction of this collection. As intersectional feminists, it is integral to take these distinctions into account, as they inform the way we move through the world and impact biological experiences, including menstruation.

MENSTRUATION AND THE ROOTS OF SHAME

Menstruation technologies such as pads, tampons, cups, and underwear are employed to manage menstrual flow. A wide range of options exist to obscure the fact that bleeding is happening. From intense flow pads to cups that last up to 12 hours, menstruation technologies hide the fact that menstruation is occurring. A 2005

Tampax Compak commercial features two high school girls sitting in class, getting caught passing a tampon between them. When the teacher forces the student to approach the front of the classroom to present the item, he cannot identify it as a tampon and mistakes it for a snack, remarking, "Well, I hope you brought enough for everyone." The commercial promises, "So discreet, only *you'll* know it's a tampon" (Tampax, 2016). This trend in marketing makes two promises: management of blood flow and discreet concealment. In this chapter, we ask you to rethink the implications of period technology being marketed as something to be hidden.

The exact origins of the menstrual taboo are unknowable. Periods have often been represented in opposing ways: simultaneously powerful, marking fertility and the power of the female reproductive system, and disgusting or dangerous, reflected in patterns of physical isolation and exclusion from society (Knight, 1991, as cited in Rajak, 2015). Kothari (2010) suggests that negative perceptions of menstruation stem, at least in part, from early human relationships with blood: "Menstrual blood [was] considered dirty and black and the hunters' sacrificial blood as good and bright red" (p. 45). Blood, as a life-giving force, is afforded a great sense of cultural power. It comes as no surprise that many humans would associate fear and a sense of sacred ability with women's habitual bleeding. Some cultural practices, such as in Orthodox Judaism's *mikveh* (Freidenfelds, 2009), require women to conduct ritual cleansing after menstruation to restore their purity. Historically, the menstruating woman has been viewed as a threat to the workings of everyday life: for example, her skin will tarnish silver (Whelan, 1975, p. 106) and bronze; Pliny the Elder theorized that "crops touched by [menstrual blood] become barren" (Lister, 2020, p. 258). Menstruation has virtually never been wholly perceived as a positive process to embrace as normal and natural but rather as something inherently *wrong* or threatening.

Periods are perceived as many things at once in various cultural spaces. A plethora of societies view "Aunt Flow" as powerful in some way while simultaneously toxic, dangerous, or unclean. The most frequently held beliefs, according to a 1974 American Anthropological Association study, are as follows:

1. Generalized belief that menstrual fluid is unpleasant, contaminating, or dangerous.
2. Menstruants may not have sexual intercourse.
3. Personal restrictions are imposed upon the menstruants, such as food taboos, restriction of movement, talking, etc.
4. Restrictions are imposed upon contact made by menstruants with men's things, i.e., personal articles, weapons, implements used in agriculture

and fishing, craft tools, "men's crops," and religious emblems and shrines, where men are the guardians.

5. Menstruants may not cook for men.
6. Menstruants are confined to menstrual huts for the duration of their periods. (Montgomery, 1974, p. 155)

Most, if not all, of these patterns are still in place in some form and can be analyzed in centuries of preceding social history.

While it would be convenient to believe that we have advanced past euphemism to describe menstruation as a natural, necessary process, the language and culture surrounding menstruation remains grounded in shame. This shame bleeds into the technology and language we use, the apps we download, and the branding we pay for.

To this end, language is one of the most important instruments in upholding menstrual taboo. Euphemism lets us skirt around medical terms to directly address periods and anatomy. The influential 12th-century midwifery text the *Trotula* suggests using alternative names for female anatomy to avoid the shame of using medical terms (Freidenfelds, 2009, p. 20). While one is "on the rag," being unable to speak about their "monthlies" can extend to a general sense of shame and secrecy about the female body and sexuality—especially that of young girls—as a whole (Schooler et al., 2005). While girls are educated on menstruation, they are taught stigma and social perception alongside it (Freidenfelds, 2009). If we cannot speak about menstruation in plain language, it will remain shrouded in shame.

Secrecy and shame surrounding menstruation go hand in hand with what Laws (1990) identifies as "Menstrual Etiquette": a collection of socially constructed, discreet procedures to conceal menstruation from public perception, particularly from men. This is furthered by the act of physical separation that may be enacted during menstruation. Menstrual huts epitomize this; women are confined to a separate physical space while they are considered "impure" or "untouchable" for the duration of their period (Lister, 2020, p. 258). In a modern context, this manifests in many ways—consider period products with "silent" packaging. Tampax Pocket Pearl tampons boast a patented "QuietTouch™ Wrapper" to keep period management a secret (London Drugs, n.d.). The need for secrecy stems from the wide-ranging belief that menstruation or menstrual blood is unclean, impure, and dangerous. Further, we can examine the term *feminine hygiene*: this term frames menstruation as something that is dirty and emphasizes the need to clean up. Ultimately, the association with hygiene reinforces periods as a source of shame.

Have you ever wondered how women in the Middle Ages managed *les malades secrettes* (Freidenfelds, 2009, p. 20)? While we can infer based on materials available at the time, much of the information informally and intergenerationally passed between women would have been done in a clandestine manner, rarely, if ever, being recorded for us to analyze today. There is a severe knowledge gap in menstrual history due to taboo; the majority of texts regarding menstruation have been written by and for men and, as such, do not contain the lived experience of menstruators.

We can infer that in ancient times, people who menstruated used natural materials to deal with blood flow. Among other materials, sphagnum moss, papyrus, and sea sponges could be wadded to resemble what we would recognize as pads and tampons today (Stein & Kim, 2009). More advanced tech began to develop in the 19th century, with 185 patent grants for "catamenial" devices from 1854 to 1921 (Goldberg, 2016). In the United States, Lister's Towels became the first disposable pads in 1896. For those who could afford them, period belts would be worn to hold cloth in place with pins and a belt. Outer clothes could be protected from bloodstains using "sanitary aprons" made of rubber. For lower- and middle-class women, cloth was used to absorb blood and painstakingly cleaned as covertly as possible (Friedenfelds, 2009, pp. 30–31).

The 20th century witnessed a medicalization of the female body, with the "tendency to define normal events in women's lives (such as menstruation, pregnancy, and menopause) and natural states (such as small breast size) as pathological and requiring medical attention" (Purdy, 2001, p. 249). Simultaneously, the association of personal hygiene with morality became widespread. As a consequence, disposability became a key trend in menstrual products. After its original purpose of bandaging soldiers in World War I, Cellucotton found widespread use as the first commercial menstrual pad made by Kotex in 1920. In the 1930s, Earle Cleaveland Haas patented the first tampon featuring an applicator, and Leona Chalmers developed the first usable commercial menstrual cup in 1937 (MUM.org, n.d.). The disposability of these products meant that they could be used more discreetly, though stigma attached to publicly purchasing them was still a great deterrent for women. As for Chalmers' menstrual cup, widespread use was partially deterred by the need to physically touch one's vagina (North & Oldham, 2011). The cup and other insertable technologies were slow to gain popularity due to concerns about virginity and sexual promiscuity (Renault, 2019). Many continued to use reusable cloth and bricolage[3] into the latter half of the 20th century and into the modern day; cloth pads and period underwear have seen a resurgence in recent years in response to environmental concerns about the disposability of period products.

Methods of dealing with periods were and continue to be heavily stratified across class lines. Durkin (2017) explains that the financial cost of menstrual supplies can be a burden for people in lower socio-economic positions and that menstrual equity is one tool to help women cope with this economic obstacle.

WHAT'S NEW IN PERIOD TECH?

While much about our world has changed, particularly in terms of technological advancement, various taboos still rear their heads in popular discourse. From public officials' capabilities being questioned because they menstruate (Rutherford-Morrison, 2016) to the long-held myth of tampons "taking" one's virginity, menstrual myths continue to spread across society. In contrast, the technologies we use to manage menstruation have undergone a substantial overhaul. Today, within the Global North, a plethora of technology exists that can be used to track and manage periods. Digital technologies designed to track and manage menstruation are simultaneously innovative and invasive, forcing us to renegotiate our relationship with menstruation as well as our willingness to share the most private details of our cycles with large tech corporations. By 2025, the "Femtech" industry is estimated to be worth US$50 billion (Rosas, 2019, as cited in Shipp & Blasco, 2020).

While menstrual tracking has been around for as long as periods, the digital aggregation of data regarding reproductive health has never been performed on such a large scale, with popular apps garnering upwards of 100 million downloads (Shipp & Blasco, 2020). Apps such as Clue, Flo, Ovia, and Eve collect data such as the following: period symptoms, sexual activity, frequency of orgasm, ovulation tracking, and basal body temperature. These apps have unprecedented access to personal information about reproductive health and are virtually always coded as highly feminine: clipart of flowers and bright pink thumbnails are commonplace.[4] Later in this text, Polzer et al. take an in-depth look at these apps and consider how we can understand them more fully through the lens of feminist biopedagogies (Chapter 8).

In addition to new kinds of tracking apps, a shift in physical period technology has occurred. A Kickstarter for LOONCUP, "the world's first smart menstrual cup" (LOONCUP, 2021), is an example of how our societal relationship with periods is evolving. While the menstrual cup was patented in the 1930s, aversion to physical insertion and removal of the cup played a key role in its delayed popularity. In contrast, the LOONCUP provides an unprecedented amount of information and intimacy with one's reproductive system; the cup "predicts women's health and disease through quantifying menstrual blood" (LOONCUP, 2021). It provides a gentle vibrating alert when almost full and syncs with a smartphone to record one's menstrual cycle, blood colour, and basal body temperature. The LOONCUP's aggregation of intimate data is reflected in other "wellness tracker" technologies such as the Bellabeat, a menstrual and hormonal cycle tracker that can be worn in the form of jewellery. Bellabeat aims to allow women to "look deeper into [their] hormonal shifts and learn how to use them to [their] advantage" (Bellabeat.com, n.d.). The opportunity to understand the intricacies of one's own hormonal cycle with the click of a button represents an immeasurable progression in the way we deal with menstruation. However, both products are very subtle in appearance when compared with other body technologies such as glasses or glucose trackers. Bellabeat, as described in its packaging and website, claims to be designed for the "female body" (Bellabeat.com, n.d.). This product offers no design clue to its real function, as it can pass for an ordinary water bottle and a leaf-style pendant. The construction of menstruation as a problematic female function begets its medicalization. Such medicalization defines which processes are considered normal and which require intervention. If periods are seen as problematic, new products arise to prevent women from showing any signs that indicate that they are, in fact, menstruating. For example, the LOONCUP proactively helps people who menstruate avoid spillovers or odours that might arise if the cup becomes full. The period product industry has developed a pattern of capitalizing on the idea of "saving" women from the perceived shame of menstruating, commodifying the ability to prevent any signs of a period. In addition, menstruation technologies are evolving to address pain in new ways. Daye (2021) is one example—a cannabidiol (CBD)-infused tampon that eases menstrual cramps. Livia (2021) is a clip-on transcutaneous electrical nerve stimulation (TENS) machine marketed as "undetectable" and "discreet" to be used for managing cramps. It is worth noting that women's pain is more likely to be treated inadequately and taken less seriously than men's (Hoffman & Tarzian, 2001). Methods of treating dysmenorrhea[5] that are designed by and for women are a step in the right direction, though the emphasis on discretion persists.

The continued commodification of menstruation capitalizes on the notion of the female body as shameful and in need of apps, products, and services in order to be adequately managed. The companies that sell such products benefit from this portrayal, ensuring that if women feel that menstruation is unhygienic and dirty, products are available for purchase to "fix" the ways their bodies naturally exist.

WHO DOES PERIOD TECH SERVE?

Menstrual technology such as tampons, pads, and cups are gendered products. Their marketing strategies utilize highly feminized packaging and design, with colours and imagery that solidify menstruation as a distinctly female issue. Most pad brands market solely to feminine-looking bodies that menstruate. By gendering packages and marketing, physical menstrual tech anchors menstruation within the feminine sphere. The understanding of "women" without a sex/gender distinction can be problematic as it disregards trans and nonbinary folks' experiences. Frank (2020) explains that menstruation is seen as a bodily function that differentiates women from men. Normative sex assumptions that identify menstruation as an exclusive feminine bodily function generate stigma for nonbinary, gender non-conforming, and transgender folks who menstruate. Nonbinary menstruators are obligated to navigate geographies tailored specifically to heterosexual, cisgender women, forcing public management of menstrual flow in spaces where they might not feel safe. Trans and nonbinary people are compelled to hide their actions under the risk of being outed, or they experience gender dysphoria due to an unnecessarily gendered market.

Gendered menstrual geographies dictate who belongs in certain places and who is considered an outsider. Frank (2020) explains that men's bathrooms are specially tailored for heterosexual, cisgender men's bodies. Because of this, they are usually not equipped with sanitary disposal bins for pads or tampons. As a result, trans and nonbinary folks who menstruate can feel out of place when managing their menstrual flow within the restroom that they use. As Frank (2020) states, "menstruation as a stigmatized marker of difference from men is partly responsible for the division of sex assigned restrooms in Western culture" (p. 375). Period products are often only available for purchase in women's restrooms. The message is clear: there is no space for menstruation in men's spaces.

The menstrual supplies aisle is another example of gendered menstrual geographies.[6] Usually, disposable pads and tampons are placed alongside hairdryers and feminine shampoos. Menstrual supplies are grouped with other feminine products. Because periods are seen as impure and dirty (Frank, 2020, p. 374), women are made to feel embarrassed or ashamed when purchasing menstrual supplies. The menstrual supplies aisle is designed to welcome women and drive away men. Such gendered places are designed specifically to serve the gender binary, aligning one's explicit appearance with gender. Folks that exist outside the gender and sex binary are likely to experience dysphoria when confronted with rows of flowery boxes in the "feminine" hygiene aisle. The heavy gendering of menstruation acts as an unwelcome reminder that mainstream discourse believes some menstruators have "the wrong parts" (Frank, 2020, p. 382).

While hyperfeminization of menstrual resources remains a huge issue, there have been many strides in the right direction in recent years. Brands such as Aisle, a Vancouver-based, gender-neutral period technology provider, are looking for ways to make the market more accessible. The advent of trans-friendly products such as Aisle's boxer brief—designed to replace up to four tampons—are paving the way for a new kind of menstrual experience that transcends gender (Aisle, 2021). Other companies like Thinx and Saalt also opt for branding in neutral colours and avoiding hyperfeminine language (Saalt, n.d.; Thinx, 2021). Considering these trends, the future of menstrual tech seems to be expanding its inclusivity of nonbinary and trans menstruators.

However, though menstruation technologies are becoming more inclusive in some ways, many equity issues persist. This can be most clearly seen when examining period poverty. Period poverty is defined as the lack of economic resources to access sufficient menstrual supplies. Many women and gender non-conforming folks might also encounter socio-economic difficulties in accessing facilities and washrooms with clean water to manage their menstrual flow. This extends to the digital technology used for tracking periods and managing menstrual pain, which are not fully accessible options for marginalized groups. Because menstruation is still considered a taboo subject, period poverty is relegated under a shroud of silence, making the problem invisible. Period poverty is a pervasive social issue in Canada and throughout the world (Smith et al., in press). Although most menstruators bleed for two to seven days a month, every month, for at least 40 years, menstruation is considered a personal issue, and as such, it is expected to be dealt with in private (Smith et al., in press). This makes reaching out for help in order to access products a difficult feat for many due to embarrassment or financial strain.

The consequences of period poverty are serious: studies show that many girls and young women miss or skip school because of a lack of menstrual supplies or access to water and sanitary spaces to manage menstrual flow (Cousins, 2020; Smith et al., in press). The lack of access to menstrual supplies can lead to the use of makeshift pads and menstrual supplies made with unsterile rags that can cause serious reproductive health problems (Cousins, 2020). Certain social groups can experience period poverty more severely, such as the homeless population. Vora (2020) explains that for many years the experiences of women living in the streets or precarious conditions have been overlooked. The author explains the difficulties that homeless women face while seeking to manage their blood flow, noting that the inability to access menstrual products makes women and people who menstruate feel shame as they rely on shelters or food banks for such products. The author highlights how the invisibility of menstruation as an issue for the homeless populations leads to a lack of legislation and successful policy making in this regard.

This is a particularly pervasive issue for many Indigenous communities in Canada, where "having your period is just not affordable" (Malone, 2017). A pack of tampons in rural northern communities can sell for double the price one would find in the city,[7] forcing menstruators to treat them as luxury items that are out of reach. Not only does this put people who have periods under financial stress, but it sends the message that because period products are not accessible, they—and, by extension, menstrual health—are unimportant.

Some suggest the solution of reusable period products, then—if disposable products are unaffordable. Why not use an option that can be used repeatedly each month, such as a menstrual cup or cloth pads? This ignores a pervasive issue in Canada: the lack of clean water on Indigenous reserves. Drinking water advisories on reserves are an ongoing issue in Canada that cannot be fully discussed in this chapter, but for now we will put it bluntly: how can you sanitize a menstrual cup if you do not have access to clean water? How does one wash a cloth pad multiple times throughout their period if laundry is a luxury (Human Rights Watch, 2016)? It is clear, through means of advertising and access, who menstrual technology is serving—and who it is not. While having reusable and technologically sophisticated choices for managing menstruation may be a step in the right direction, menstruation technologies continue to serve cisgender and middle- to higher-income women.

Canada has made some steps in an attempt to tackle period poverty. Smith et al. (in press) note that some Canadian provinces and cities such as "British Columbia, Nova Scotia, Toronto, [and] Whitehorse" have implemented policies that require public schools to provide free menstrual supplies in their restrooms. Such policies would help students manage their menstrual flow in bathrooms rather than having to ask a friend or a teacher for menstrual supplies. In Canada, the fight to provide free menstrual supplies in all public restrooms persists. Despite many changes, period supplies remain treated as luxuries, rather than necessities.

Period poverty is about poverty; but we can also understand it as a tech equity issue. As we mentioned at the outset of this chapter, normally, when discussing inequitable access to technology, we think of computers or cellphones. Menstruation technologies are specifically used to address the needs of menstruators and are therefore not afforded the status as a tool for living a good life. Technologies used to manage menstruation are delegitimized because they are gendered. These are not technologies that menstruators can use to make cis men's lives easier or provide care for other people. It is understood only as a means for managing "women's problems." As long as this trend of assigning technologies created for menstruator's bodies as unimportant persists, period poverty will exist alongside it.

CONCLUSION

Menstruation exists in a paradoxical state: hidden and taboo, and yet necessary for the fulfillment of prescribed ideals of femininity. While menstruation technologies have evolved over thousands of years, societal perception and access to these essential tech items lag behind. For example, requests for a spare tampon are whispered privately, almost with embarrassment; Indigenous, homeless, transgender, or otherwise marginalized people with periods must make impossible decisions between buying tampons or buying food; when a female-presenting person displays certain emotions, she is asked if she's "on the rag." The technology we use to manage menstruation connects to and is part of deeply ingrained processes of gendering; menstrual supplies have been relegated to the status of "luxury products" or something non-instrumental to daily health and well-being. We suggest it is not considered a legitimate form of technology because it is designed to accommodate the female body. Periods remain particularly unmentionable in patriarchal systems where discussion of sexual health is uncommon, exacerbating the effects of period poverty among marginalized women and girls, trans, and gender non-conforming people. If we cannot openly discuss an inequity so systemic, there is no chance of meaningful change. This problem is part of a bigger picture of women and girls' bodies being placed under immeasurable, systematic control. Our bodies continue to be regularly policed by patriarchy, even in the age of self-regulating menstrual cups and CBD-infused tampons. As much as things have changed, there is still so much that remains the same. We hope one day we can say that periods are normal, period, and that the tech we use will reflect that as well. That would be truly revolutionary.

QUESTIONS FOR DISCUSSION

1. Can you think of an example of how menstruation technologies are gendered (e.g., advertisements, packaging, etc.)? How is gender communicated in the example you chose?
2. Prior to reading this chapter, did you consider tampons, pads, menstrual cups, or other period supplies as technology? Why or why not?
3. In the society you live in, where do people get information about menstruation? Do you believe people have adequate information to deal with menarche?

INVITATIONS TO GO DEEPER

1. If you were responsible for explaining menstruation to someone who has yet to have their first period, what kind of information would you share with them? What aspects of menstruation would you focus on?
2. How does media impact the way we think about menstruation and menstruation supplies? Find a commercial or other piece of marketing material (website, social media account, etc.) and examine how it represents the menstrual tech it is advertising. Is it gendered? How does it present menstruation? What messages are and are not being sent?
3. Referencing the product that you discussed in prompt 2 above, explore whether this product is a piece of tech that could serve every menstruator's needs. Why or why not?

READ MORE

Frank, S. E. (2020). Queering menstruation: Trans and non-binary identity and body politics. *Sociological Inquiry*, *90*(2), 371–404. https://doi.org/10.1111/soin.12355

Mahdawi, A. (2021, April 21). Pinky Gloves are just the latest ludicrous attempt to monetise the vagina. *The Guardian*. https://www.theguardian.com/commentisfree/2021/apr/21/pinky-gloves-are-just-the-latest-ludicrous-attempt-to-monetise-the-vagina

Malone, G. (2017, February 18). The women trying to make periods more affordable in northern Indigenous communities. *Vice News*. https://www.vice.com/en/article/ez8g87/the-women-trying-to-make-periods-more-affordable-in-northern-indigenous-communities

Vora, S. (2020). The realities of period poverty: How homelessness shapes women's lived experiences of menstruation. In C. Bobel, I. T. Winkler, B. Fahs, K. A. Hasson, E. A. Kissling, & T. A. Roberts (Eds.), *The Palgrave handbook of critical menstruation studies* (pp. 31–47). Palgrave Macmillan, Singapore. https://doi.org/10.1007/978-981-15-0614-7_4

LISTEN MORE, WATCH MORE

"How Thinx got its provocative ads on the New York City subway," Miki Agrawal, founder of period underwear company Thinx, speaks on her experience with putting "provocative" ads in the New York subway system: https://www.youtube.com/watch?v=sjvxTBsXxrs&t=96s&ab_channel=Inc

"The story of menstruation (1946)," a Walt Disney production through
the courtesy of Kotex products: https://www.youtube.com/
watch?v=vG9o9m0LsbI&t=486s&ab_channel=OldTVTime

NOTES

1.   Speaking as Lauren Friesen.

2.   Speaking as Ana Brito.

3.   *Bricolage* is a term for taking household or common items and turning them into something
     new. In this case, women could use materials such as outgrown clothing, pillowcases and
     linens, and other fabrics to create period products for themselves.

4.   Namely: Flo, Period Tracker by GP apps, My Calendar—Period Tracker, Femometer Period
     Tracker, and countless others.

5.   *Dysmenorrhea* is a medical term for menstruation-related pain.

6.   *Gendered geography* is defined as spaces and places (physical or metaphorical) that relate
     more to one gender than to another. For example, when thinking about a nail salon, one would
     assume it is more a woman's place than a man's place.

7.   Malone (2017) notes that in the First Nation community of Attawapiskat in northern Ontario,
     a 40-pack of tampons costs $17.89. This price becomes $7.97 at Walmart locations "down
     south."

REFERENCES

Aisle. (2021). https://periodaisle.ca/

Bellabeat.com. (n.d.). https://www.bellabeat.com/

Bem, S. L. (1981). Gender schema theory: A cognitive account of sex typing.
  Psychological Review, 88(4), 354–364.

Cousins, S. (2020). Rethinking period poverty. *The Lancet (British Edition), 395*(10227),
  857–858. https://doi.org/10.1016/S0140–6736(20)30605-X

Crenshaw, K. (1989). Demarginalizing the intersection of race and sex: A Black feminist
  critique of antidiscrimination doctrine, feminist theory and antiracist politics.
  University of Chicago Legal Forum, 1989(8), 139–167.

Daye. (2021). http://www.yourdaye.com/

Durkin, A. (2017). Profitable menstruation: How the cost of feminine hygiene products
  is a battle against reproductive justice. *The Georgetown Journal of Gender and the Law,
  18*(1), 131–172.

Frank, S. E. (2020). Queering menstruation: Trans and non-binary identity and body
  politics. *Sociological Inquiry, 90*(2), 371–404. https://doi.org/10.1111/soin.12355

Freidenfelds, L. (2009). *The modern period: Menstruation in twentieth-century America*. Johns-Hopkins University Press.

Goldberg, J. (2016, March 4). *"Solving woman's oldest hygienic problem in a new way": A history of period products*. New York Academy of Medicine.

Hoffmann, D. E., & Tarzian, A. J. (2001). The girl who cried pain: a bias against women in the treatment of pain. *The Journal of Law, Medicine & Ethics, 28*, 13–27. https://doi.org/10.1111/j.1748-720X.2001.tb00037.x

Hughes, M. (2020, July 21). The rise of femtech and period-management technology. *Top Business Tech*. http://www.tbtech.co/the-rise-of-femtech-and-period-management-technology/

Human Rights Watch. (2016, June 7). *Make it safe: Canada's obligation to end the First Nations water crisis*. http://www.hrw.org/report/2016/06/07/make-it-safe/canadas-obligation-end-first-nations-water-crisis

Kiefer, T., & Fitzgerald, G. (2018, May 28). Let's talk about menstrual hygiene. *UN Dispatch*. https://www.undispatch.com/lets-talk-about-menstrual-hygiene/

Kothari, B. (2010). Perception about menstruation: A study of rural Jaipur, Rajasthan. *Indian Anthropologist, 40*(1), 43–54.

Laws, S. (1990). *Issues of blood: The politics of menstruation*. Macmillan.

Lister, K. (2020). *A curious history of sex*. Unbound Press.

Livia. (2021). http://www.mylivia.com/

London Drugs. (n.d.). Tampax Pearl Pocket compact tampons—regular/super/super plus—34s. https://www.londondrugs.com/tampax-pearl-pocket-compact-tampons---regular%2Fsuper%2Fsuper-plus—-34s/L0966809.html

LOONCUP. (2021). https://www.looncup.com/

Malone, G. (2017, February 18). The women trying to make periods more affordable in northern Indigenous communities. *Vice News*. https://www.vice.com/en/article/ez8g87/the-women-trying-to-make-periods-more-affordable-in-northern-indigenous-communities

Montgomery, R. E. (1974). A cross-cultural study of menstruation, menstrual taboos, and related social variables. *Ethos, 2*(2), 137–170. https://doi.org/10.1525/eth.1974.2.2.02a00030

MUM.org. (n.d.). Museum of menstruation and women's health. https://www.mum.org/

North, B. B., & Oldham, M. J. (2011). Preclinical, clinical, and over-the-counter postmarketing experience with a new vaginal cup: Menstrual collection. *Journal of Women's Health, 20*(2), 303–311. https://doi.org/10.1089/jwh.2009.1929

Purdy, L. (2001). Medicalization, medical necessity, and feminist medicine. *Bioethics, 15*(3), 248–261.

Rajak, I. (2015). *She got her period: Men's knowledge and perspectives on menstruation* (Publication No. 429) [Master's thesis]. Cornerstone Minnesota State University. https://cornerstone.lib.mnsu.edu/cgi/viewcontent.cgi?article=1428&context=etds

Renault, M. (2019, August 23). Menstrual cups were invented in 1867. What took them so long to gain popularity? *Popular Science.* https://www.popsci.com/menstrual-cups-history-period-care/

Rosas, C. (2019). The future is femtech: Privacy and data security issues surrounding femtech applications. *Hastings Business Law Journal, 15*(2). 319–341.

Rutherford-Morrison, L. (2016, October 17). Why this letter about Hillary Clinton is wrong. *Bustle.* https://www.bustle.com/articles/189974-hillary-clinton-cant-be-president-because-of-menstruation-claims-this-letter-to-the-editor-but-thats

Saalt. (n.d.). https://saalt.com/

Schooler, D., Ward, M., Merriwether, A., & Caruthers, A. (2005). Cycles of shame: Menstrual shame, body shame, and sexual decision-making. *The Journal of Sex Research, 42*(4), 324–334. https://doi.org/10.1080/00224490509552288

Shipp, L., & Blasco, J. (2020). How private is your period? A systematic analysis of menstrual app privacy policies. *Proceedings on Privacy Enhancing Technologies, 2020*(4), 491–510. https://doi.org/10.2478/popets-2020-0083

Smith, L., Gacimi, R., Adolph, N., Hope, J., & Tribe, S. (in press). Flow of inequity: Period poverty and the COVID-19 pandemic. In S. Shariff (Ed.), *Navigating mental health, wellness, and social challenges during COVID-19.* Peter Lang.

Stamper, L. (2011, July 6). Always runs first feminine hygiene ad to show blood. *Huffpost.* https://www.huffpost.com/entry/always-runs-first-feminin_n_891546

Stein, E., & Kim, S. (2009). *Flow: The cultural story of menstruation.* St. Martin's Griffin Press.

Tampax [jj vowers]. (2016, April 30). *Tampax Compak commercial sun, 6/12/2005* [Video]. YouTube. https://www.youtube.com/watch?v=AbCvzYOUonU&t=30s&ab_channel=jjvowers

Thinx. (2021). https://www.shethinx.com/

Vora, S. (2020). The realities of period poverty: How homelessness shapes women's lived experiences of menstruation. In C. Bobel, I. T. Winkler, B. Fahs, K. A. Hasson, E. A. Kissling, & T. A. Roberts (Eds.), *The Palgrave handbook of critical menstruation studies* (pp. 31–47). Palgrave Macmillan, Singapore. https://doi.org/10.1007/978-981-15-0614-7_4

Weisberg, E., McGeehan, K., & Fraser, I. S. (2016). Effect of perceptions of menstrual blood loss and menstrual pain on women's quality of life. *The European Journal of Contraception & Reproductive Health Care, 21*(6), 431–435. doi.org/10.1080/1362518 7.2016.1225034

Whelan, E. (1975). Attitudes toward menstruation. *Studies in Family Planning, 6*(4), 106–108. https://doi.org/10.2307/1964817

Technology-Facilitated Sexual Violence, Student Sexuality, and Post-Secondary Institutions

Shaina McHardy

INTRODUCTION

Since its inception, social media use has become a normalized element in the lives of many Canadians, particularly young adults. Social media platforms have many social benefits, such as providing an inexpensive mode of communication and allowing for long-distance communication. Nevertheless, it is becoming increasingly apparent that such platforms have also been used for harmful purposes, such as cyberstalking and cyberbullying. As more industries are taking greater advantage of available technologies, even post-secondary institutions have begun embracing technological advancements, utilizing online forums for information management, communication, and marketing. As a result, what is considered "campus" is becoming increasingly blurred (Quinlan et al., 2017). It has been argued that university campuses "simultaneously [occupy] virtual and physical worlds," requiring institutional administrators to reconceptualize how they address transgressions that occur among students (Quinlan et al., 2017, p. 119). This blurring of campus borders makes it difficult to determine what is considered "on campus" or "off campus," further complicating an institution's ability to address student behaviour.

In 2017, several provincial governments mandated that all publicly funded post-secondary institutions implement sexual violence policies. While these post-secondary institutions complied, there has been continued criticism regarding the effectiveness of these policies (Schwartz, 2018). Very few institutions have policies explicitly addressing students' online behaviours, including their use of technology to victimize other students. Despite this, some of the policies use language that is vague enough to potentially include online forms of sexual violence, such as revenge porn. For example, some policies define sexual violence as any form of sexual violation, which would conceptually include technology-facilitated sexual violence (TFSV), as punishable behaviours. As part of an ongoing project (hereafter referred to as the "current research"), 30 interviews were conducted with campus community members (i.e., students, faculty, and staff) at a mid-sized southern Ontario university, and a variety of unobtrusive sources were analyzed to explore the phenomenon of TFSV and the role Canadian post-secondary institutions can and should take in responding to incidents that occur among students.[1] As a Canadian student and victim of sexual violence myself, with an expertise in interpersonal violence and victimization, investigating the emerging problem of TFSV among Canadian students has become an important project of mine. It should be noted that due to my personal background, my acceptance of TFSV as an act of violence does not definitively determine that this is the position of all academics. The goal of this research is to better inform policy makers and future policy development on how to best serve community members, investigate the perceptions of campus community members regarding TFSV and its associated harms, and build upon the growing body of literature focusing on the unique Canadian context.

This chapter will explore the phenomenon of TFSV among Canadian students. Research on TFSV is relatively new, and little of the current literature examines the Canadian context, despite it being addressed in Canada's *Criminal Code* under section 162.1. The following will discuss the significance of this context and examine the phenomenon from both a theoretical and lived-experience perspective, drawing upon both the limited existing literature and the current project. As research on this phenomenon is both new and limited, this chapter concludes with suggestions for improving institutional engagement and responses to incidents of TFSV among their students.

TFSV AND COLLOQUIALISMS: DEFINITIONS AND EXAMPLES

Since the 1990s, online crime has been thoroughly researched; however, the majority of research has focused on those sexual crimes that involve child victims. Henry and Powell (2016) have sought to address this oversight in the Australian context. Their research focuses on adult female victims of TFSV while acknowledging that male adults are also victimized by similar behaviours. In recent years, research into such behaviours as "revenge porn" are more prevalent. This research tends to be fragmented, focusing on specific behaviours, and tends to use colloquialisms that frequently get reduced to cyberbullying, which is often equated with schoolyard harassment. Furthermore, most (if not all) of the available literature on TFSV assumes a gender binary and often does not include information regarding sexual orientation, race/ethnicity, or socio-economic status. To address the fragmented nature of the current state of the literature, Henry and Powell (2016) define TFSV, which encompasses any behaviours "where mobile and online technologies are used as tools to blackmail, control, coerce, harass, humiliate, objectify or violate another person" (p. 398). These include image-based behaviours that sexually exploit, harass, enable a sexual assault, or otherwise abuse an individual based on gender or sexuality (Powell & Henry, 2018). This definition allows for a more accessible discussion of the phenomenon as it amalgamates the behaviours without conflating or diminishing the severity of them. There are many terms given to various behaviours and categories of behaviours that fall under the TFSV umbrella—some of which have been more extensively discussed in academia, popular media, and news media than others. The following will briefly outline some of these behaviours and the colloquialisms used.

The first term commonly used among scholars and criminal justice system personnel is *intimate images*. Section 162.1(1) of the Canadian *Criminal Code* defines the behaviour associated with intimate images as follows:

> Everyone who knowingly publishes, distributes, transmits, sells, makes available or advertises an intimate image of a person knowing that the person depicted in the image did not give their consent to that conduct, or being reckless as to whether or not that person gave their consent to that conduct.

Intimate images themselves are any images or video recording involving nudity or the exposure of genitals or anal or breast regions. The intimate images statute covers such behaviours as revenge porn. Revenge porn typically occurs when a former romantic partner shares intimate images without the other former partner's consent. This type of behaviour is so common that numerous websites that are dedicated to such images exist (Fonrouge, 2017). A major concern about this specific behaviour is that due to the seemingly permanent nature of the internet, published images may resurface years after they were taken, further victimizing the subjects of the images.

Another form of TFSV that has become all too common is referred to as *sexploitation*. As a colloquialism, this term is often used in different ways depending on the context. One use refers to instances in which individuals coerce victims into sending them explicit images. Another use refers to coercing victims to perform physical sexual acts or otherwise extorting victims with the threat of disseminating intimate images that they may or may not actually have. One such case, *R. v. S.S.* (2018), resulted in the accused being convicted of both exploitation under section 346(1) of the Canadian *Criminal Code* and distribution of intimate images under section 162.1(1) when he published intimate images of the victim after attempting to extort money. Regardless of the context, these types of behaviours also fall under the term *cyberharassment*. Like cyberbullying, cyberharassment is a term that was created to encompass all harassing behaviours that occur online or through telecommunication technologies. While it does not have to be of a sexual nature, the term cyberharassment is most often used in discussing various forms of TFSV.

One final behaviour that can be included under the umbrella of TFSV is often referred to as sharing a *dick pic*, which is an image of an individual's penis. This type of image becomes harmful when it is sent without the subject's knowledge and/or when it is unsolicited and sent to an unsuspecting recipient. According to a poll conducted in the United Kingdom, 41% of women aged 18 to 36 years had received an unsolicited dick pic, suggesting that this behaviour is quite common (Mandau, 2019). Research suggests this behaviour has become normalized, and most recipients shrug it off as rude but expected. Sending dick pics is particularly common within social media apps such as Snapchat and dating applications such as Tinder. Due to the widespread nature of the internet and related communication technologies, the harm of TFSV cannot be judged based solely on the experiences of the average student, as this does not account for those who might be more likely to be traumatized by the behaviours, such as those with experiences of sexual violence and children. All of the aforementioned behaviours, as well as others, fall under the definition of TFSV, further emphasizing the need for this broader term to allow for efficient discussion of such behaviours among academics and policy makers alike.

PREVALENCE OF TFSV

Determining the prevalence of the various behaviours considered to be forms of TFSV is difficult. As with physical sexual violence, unless incidents are reported, official records will not be accurate reflections of the prevalence of the issue. According to a news article, since the introduction of section 162.1 of the *Criminal Code* in 2014, "[police] forces in Canada are on track to handle more than 5,000 complaints of allegedly sharing intimate images or videos without consent" (Allen, 2019, para. 1). Of those five thousand complaints, approximately

20 percent of cases (851 as of 2018) resulted in criminal charges (Allen, 2019). Official accounts suggest that more than one thousand incidents of the distribution of intimate images are reported each year (Statistics Canada, 2017, 2018). Statistics Canada (2020) has found that 13 percent of female respondents and 6 percent of male respondents had received sexually suggestive messages or images; 7 percent of female respondents and 2 percent of male respondents were pressured to share intimate images of themselves; and, finally, 2 percent of both male and female participants were victims of either the distribution or threat of distribution of intimate images. What these results demonstrate is that women are more likely to be victims of TFSV except in the case of the dissemination of intimate images. Given the relatively new nature of these types of offences, these findings are significant. While the dissemination of intimate images does not appear to be a gendered crime, other forms of TFSV that are illegal have a definite gendered nature.

THE CANADIAN CONTEXT: THE PCOCA AND CANADIAN POST-SECONDARY INSTITUTIONS

Canada presents a unique context for investigating TFSV, as the Canadian government passed the *Protecting Canadians from Online Crime Act* (PCOCA) in 2014. This act had three main effects on Canadian legislature. The first applies to juveniles, as it provides an alternative legal route for dealing with youths under the age of 18 engaging in the act of disseminating intimate images. Prior to the passing of this act, the only legal option was to pursue charges of the creation and dissemination of child pornography. The second is establishing section 62.1 of the *Criminal Code*, which makes the dissemination of intimate images among adults explicitly illegal. This makes acts such as revenge porn illegal. Finally, it extends existing statutes to include analogous behaviours that occur through the use of technology, such as cyberstalking and identity fraud. These progressive legal reforms not only make Canada a unique jurisdiction but also demonstrate the nation's unwillingness to accept these behaviours.

TFSV was coined to encompass the range of behaviours as well as the severity of the repercussions. When one engages in illegal behaviours through technology, the PCOCA redirects criminal justice system personnel to alternative statutes and vice versa. Voyeurism, the act of watching others engaged in sexualized activities, is now covered under section 162—looking at an individual through a window is now viewed as no different than looking at an individual through a screen. On the other hand, harassing an individual in person is now equivalent to harassing that individual via the internet. For example, what has been known as cyberbullying was difficult to address prior to 2014. Now, these behaviours are covered under the criminal harassment statute. While this may seem like an innocuous legal manoeuvre, this theoretically accomplishes what Henry and Powell (2016) were attempting to achieve by defining TFSV and demonstrating the severity of acts that would otherwise be brushed off as schoolyard bullying.

Because of the aforementioned provincial mandates, many Canadian post-secondary institutions now have sexual violence policies. Some post-secondary institutions have also implemented additional prevention and response strategies. In some cases, this has also led to the creation of sexual violence response coordinator positions to better inform university policy, response, and educational programs regarding sexual violence on campus. Unlike in the United States, where Title IX provisions provide some level of guidance and an avenue for victims to address their experiences, Canadian post-secondary institutions have no equivalent legislation, meaning university administrations are left to determine their own policies and procedures. Of those post-secondary institutions that have implemented sexual violence policies, few include any explicit mention of TFSV. It is hoped that the current and similar research will help better inform Canadian institutions on how to address TFSV and other forms of non-physical sexual violence.

THE CONSEQUENCES OF TFSV

There is a common sentiment that what happens in cyberspace does not have consequences "in the real world." Despite this belief, research suggests that people can cultivate extremely real and intimate relationships of many kinds through technology (Harris, 2016; Tsai & Pai, 2012). As those who have experienced TFSV have attested, even when no physical interaction occurs, there can be serious effects (CBC News, 2014). While some incidents of TFSV begin with a physical assault that is either recorded or photographed, the effects of the subsequent TFSV not only compound the trauma of the initial assault but also have their own consequences. As will be discussed shortly, regardless of whether a physical assault occurred prior to the TFSV, some victims ultimately resort to suicide to end their ongoing suffering. The following will discuss the concept of violence, as well as some well-publicized examples of incidents of TFSV in both Canada and abroad.

TFSV as Violence

One of the most common questions that arises when investigating TFSV is whether it is appropriate to refer to non-physical forms of sexual victimization as violence. During the conception of the current research, several academics questioned the validity using the term *violence*. This also came up during the interviews. It was not until discussing the consequences and harms associated with TFSV that many participants decided that violence is an accurate description of the behaviours, while others immediately acknowledged examples of TFSV as violent incidents. As stated by Henry and Powell (2015), violence "can be defined as physical, emotional, symbolic, and structural" (p. 759). This coincides with the majority of research on intimate partner violence, whereby behaviours are referred to as violence, regardless of the lack of physicality, such as economic violence (depriving the victim of financial independence). It is arguable that the harms associated with TFSV and other non-physical forms of sexual violation should be considered violence.

To some extent, the concept of violence is one that is taken for granted—it is assumed that there is an implicit understanding of the term, and therefore, it is rarely explicitly defined. Hamby (2017) argues that the scientific standards that are applied to defining and categorizing biological entities should also be applied to more abstract concepts, such as violence. Both the Centers for Disease Control and Prevention and the World Health Organization have included non-physical acts such as threats in their definitions of violence (Hamby, 2017; Herrenkohl et al., 2011). Hamby (2017) argues that a typology should be applied to defining violence, which includes behaviours that are "(a) intentional, (b) unwanted, (c) nonessential, and (d) harmful" (p. 168). This typology would include non-physical forms of behaviours that are harmful, such as psychological abuse, but would exclude either unintentional or essential behaviours, such as accidents or doctors rebreaking a bone to set it correctly. This typology can be useful for both policy makers and legislators to better allow them to determine how to respond to behaviours such as TFSV more decisively.

Canadian Examples

It is one thing to discuss the concepts of harm and violence in the abstract, but it is another to view them in the context of concrete examples. Two Canadian examples of the consequences of TFSV have been highly publicized: the deaths of Amanda Todd and Rehtaeh Parsons. In 2012, Amanda Todd, a 15-year-old secondary school student in British Columbia, took her own life after being relentlessly harassed both online and at school. Prior to her suicide, Todd met a man online and developed a relationship with him. At some point during a video call, the man asked her to expose her breasts and she complied. Unbeknownst to her, the man took an image of this encounter. When he later asked her to repeat the act and she refused, he proceeded to share that image with her schoolmates, resulting in her being harassed by not only that man but her classmates as well. This harassment ultimately culminated in her posting a video to YouTube in which she describes her torment and suicidal ideation. While most accounts of the Todd case refer to her experiences as cyberbullying, she was a victim of TFSV, and the harms she experienced extended far beyond cyberspace. In this case, she fell victim to not only an adult stranger but was also victimized by her peers, some of whom she considered friends. This further emphasizes the potential dangers of technological advancements, as individuals can be victimized regardless of where the perpetrator physically resides.

One year after Todd's suicide, a Nova Scotia teenager, also 15 years old at the beginning of her torment, followed suit. Rehtaeh Parsons went to a party, got intoxicated, and was raped. At some point, another partygoer took a photograph of the assault and subsequently shared that image with Parsons's peers. Like the Todd case, the sharing of that image resulted in her being harassed at school and online, by both her peers and strangers. After years of such abuse, Parsons attempted suicide and was placed on life support, ultimately resulting in her death. This case became highly publicized and resulted in new provincial legislation that was short-lived, but it was also one of the catalysts for the creation of the PCOCA. In this case, the TFSV occurred after a physical assault. Following the immense publicity Parsons's experiences and suicide garnered, her situation became known as "Canada's Steubenville" in reference to a similar case in Steubenville, Ohio (Dodge, 2016). As this and similar cases demonstrate, new technologies and media can be and have been used as tools to exacerbate the trauma of sexual violence and, in turn, become tools of violence themselves. Increasingly, secondary and post-secondary school institutions are becoming the arena in which young Canadians begin exploring and understanding their sexuality. Particularly due to the disparity among conceptions of sexuality, how it is expressed, and how it can be explored (safely), young Canadians, especially young women, are at a greatly disproportionate risk of experiencing some form of TFSV, making it both a gendered and intersectional problem.

International Examples

While it is argued that Canada is a unique jurisdiction due to its legislation, it is not unique in the occurrences of incidents of TFSV. In a disturbingly similar situation to Parsons, another 15-year-old girl in Saratoga, California, Audrie Pott, also took her life after images of her sexual assault were circulated among her peers. Similar to Parsons, Pott went to a party, became intoxicated to the point of inebriation, and was sexually assaulted. Partygoers also took turns writing defamatory and derogatory words and phrases on her body with permanent marker. Several pictures were taken both during and after the assault, which were then distributed over the internet and via text message. The harassment and taunting that Pott experienced following the incident was so severe that she took her own life just over a week after the party. Pott's story became widely publicized and was eventually part of the documentary *Audrie and Daisy* (Cohen & Shenk, 2016). According to friends of Pott, as recounted in the documentary, they were surprised and outraged by the very public humiliation Pott experienced from her peers and strangers, and they were additionally disturbed by how cruel other girls were. When another young girl experienced similar trauma and attempted her own suicide, she stated that it was hearing about Pott and her family's grief that helped her deal with her own struggles. This documentary not only brought a great deal of national and international attention to the issue of TFSV but also demonstrated how widespread and terrifyingly common such behaviours are, as well as how devastating the impact is on the victims and their loved ones.

It is not unusual for American news media to be consumed in Canada, allowing Canadians to learn about such tragedies as Audrie Pott's suicide. However, TFSV and TFSV resulting in suicide is not a North American phenomenon; it is just less likely for Canadians to know about international incidents of it. While all of the cases discussed thus far have involved young secondary school students, older women are also similarly affected. A 28-year-old K-pop singer took her own life after a former partner threatened to release a video of them having sex (Kwon, 2019). While it has been speculated that her fame and the pressures of being a K-pop star contributed to her previous suicide attempts and eventual successful attempt, it appears that it was the threat from her former partner that ultimately made the decision. In Spain, a 32-year-old factory worker died by suicide after more than two hundred of her co-workers accessed intimate images of her and began harassing her at work (Valdez, 2019). In this case, investigators have still not discovered where the images originated or who instigated the sharing. Similarly, a 26-year-old Argentinian policewoman, Belen San Roma, shot herself after an ex-boyfriend uploaded a revenge porn video to the internet (Rogers, 2020). In her suicide note, she included her social media and device passwords, seemingly in hopes of leading the police to the man who leaked the video (Rogers, 2020).

For each of these victims, the TFSV they experienced was seemingly, at least initially, committed by a specific person, and their victim status has gone unquestioned. In other cases, victims of TFSV are not seen as victims at all and in some situations are actually blamed for their own victimization. In 2014, the internet was flooded with nude images of more than one hundred celebrities by individuals who hacked their iCloud accounts (Chittley, 2014). During the interviews conducted for the current research, few participants initially thought of this incident when asked if they had heard of any cases of TFSV; however, when it was mentioned at a later point in the interview, all of the participants acknowledged the behaviour as no different than revenge porn. For whatever reason, because these victims are celebrities, they are not afforded the same empathy and understanding as others. These individuals were targeted because of both their gender and their celebrity status; thus, age and gender are not the only risk factors in becoming a victim of TFSV. The media attention surrounding this incident has sparked significant debate among the general population regarding the culpability of victims in their violation. For example, many have shared the opinion that "if you don't take nude photos, they can't be stolen" (Gibson, 2014). While this chapter is not intended to discuss the issue of victim blaming, it is noteworthy that opinions regarding the status of victimhood can depend not only on one's notion of whether TFSV is truly violence but also on who the victim is. As technologies continue to develop and expand their capabilities, from increased communication capabilities to remote storage of information and images, the risk of being electronically victimized has also increased.

SOCIAL MEDIA USE

A common question that arose during the interviews for the current research was what is considered to be social media. As technologies and platforms continue to evolve, this question becomes even more pertinent. For example, YouTube is primarily a video-sharing platform but has also become a social media platform due to the ability to comment on shared content and respond to the comments of others. Millions of Canadians use various social media platforms, the most popular platform being Facebook, with the majority of users aged 15 to 24 years (Gruzd & Mai, 2020). Among those who use social media, most report using them in some capacity daily. With approximately 16 percent of Ontario students using social media for at least five hours a day, there is growing concern among mental health professionals (Canadian Mental Health Association, 2021). Research has suggested that social media users enjoy social media for a variety of reasons, ranging from communication to its use as a creative outlet (Statistics Canada, 2021). The use of different social media platforms also depends on their purposes.

For example, Instagram is predominantly an image-sharing platform, while Twitter is more commonly used for text communication. All social media platforms can be used in problematic ways. Regardless of the intended use of the platform, the rate at which young people are habitually using social media puts youths, along with other subsets of the population (e.g., celebrities and public figures), at increased risk over the rest of the population. Especially during the COVID-19 pandemic, many are using social media as a means of maintaining social contact, creating the need for post-secondary institutions to ensure the safety of their students—both physically and emotionally.

Why Do Students Use Social Media?

Depending on the platform, students use social media for a variety of reasons, reflected in both previous research and the current research. While some students have actively decided to "quit" social media (Little, 2020), social media use is still very popular among post-secondary students (Gruzd & Mai, 2020). One of the most common reasons for using social media, particularly Facebook and Twitter, is to "keep up to date" (Bridgestock, 2021). In an interview for the current research, one student referred to her Twitter feed as her "daily newspaper," stating that she used Twitter not only as her main method of communication but also as her news source. In another interview, a mature student who is a grandmother stated that she uses Facebook to keep tabs on her family and communicate with family members that do not live locally. During this interview, she laughed and admitted that she first created her Facebook account because her daughter wanted to play online games with her. The ability to communicate and interact with others regardless of their physical location is one of the major benefits of social media. As one interviewee noted, however, this ease of (mass) communication can also be detrimental. While she stated that she uses social media as her main method of communication with peers and loved ones, she has also experienced and witnessed TFSV on those same platforms. The ability to instantly communicate with several people simultaneously is both potentially wonderful and dangerous.

Another common reason for using social media platforms is as a creative outlet. Platforms such as Facebook, Instagram, and Pinterest all have strong creative elements. Many participants in the current research stated that one of their favourite aspects of social media is getting ideas for their various creative pursuits. From artwork to cooking recipes, several social media platforms allow individuals to share their creative works with ease and in a public forum. Similarly, many social media users utilize such functions as Facebook groups to communicate and interact with others for the purpose of video games or other activities. Such functions enable individuals to connect with others regardless of geographical location or other connections to one another. It has been noted, however, that while these groups can be beneficial and helpful to users, some of the responses by other group members can be "toxic." To address this, Facebook has begun more closely monitoring interactions and reports of negative behaviour.

As social media becomes more integrated in modern society, it is also becoming ingrained in workplaces and educational institutions. Some individuals have used social media as a method of employment or enhancing their employment. Others use social media as a means of making connections for the purposes of employment or education. Several of the students interviewed for the current research stated that they have used social media for educational purposes, such as buying textbooks, sharing class notes, and communicating about group projects. Some instructors have even encouraged the use of social media platforms like Facebook and Twitter to increase student participation in the course. During the COVID-19 pandemic, Canadian post-secondary institutions predominantly moved online, and virtually all interaction among students and faculty is now taking place through some form of social media and/or video call platform, making social media both a formal and informal method of communication. As such, post-secondary institutional administrators must be cognizant of some of the dangers associated with students' online behaviours.

JURISDICTION: INSTITUTIONAL RESPONSES TO TECH USE

One of the most common issues associated with post-secondary institutions addressing student behaviour is the question of jurisdiction. Prior to the influx of internet and technology use, campus jurisdiction was clear—post-secondary institutions were responsible for the safety of their students when they were physically on any property owned or associated with the university. As previously discussed, however, the boundaries of what constitutes campus is blurring. Especially as the COVID-19 pandemic has resulted in many post-secondary institutions moving to an almost entirely online environment, these institutions must reassess how they respond to their students' behaviour. In the past, some Canadian post-secondary institutions did not respond to their students' online behaviour well, which has caused a great deal of controversy and outrage among both their students and the media. The following will discuss two Canadian examples, as well as student perceptions of how their post-secondary institutions can best serve their needs.

The University of Ottawa and Dalhousie University

Two Canadian universities have received negative publicity after their responses to their students' harmful online behaviour fell short of student expectations prior to the implementation of the PCOCA and the current research: the University of Ottawa and Dalhousie University. In both cases, female students were subject to explicit sexual threats and innuendos in Facebook groups. In February 2014, the student federation president at the University of Ottawa was the target of a Facebook group chat in which five fellow students threatened her with sexual violence (Quinlan et al., 2017). She was not contacted directly, but the statements and threats made in the group chat were posted online, after which, screenshots of the conversation were anonymously emailed to the victim (Quinlan et al., 2017). The discussion in this chat exceeded vague threats or fantasies, as some students encouraged others to follow through with the threats with offerings of gifts for successfully sexually assaulting the victim. It was determined that four of the five students involved in the conversation were fellow student federation members who held leadership positions. In the aftermath, while the university did conduct various surveys and investigations, and the individuals involved were removed or resigned from their positions with the student federation, ultimately no sanctions were taken. Despite the lack of action taken by the university administration, the victim gathered support from other campus community members, the media, and the general population. Because this case predated the PCOCA, no criminal charges could be brought against any of the male students involved, further compounding the effect of the lack of action taken by the university.

In a very similar incident in December 2014, Dalhousie University became the subject of national controversy due to its inaction in addressing a Facebook group that was seemingly devoted to posting derogatory, inflammatory, and bigoted messages. The posts included explicit, graphic, and misogynistic language, many of which targeted female dentistry students (Backhouse et al., 2015). Some of the posts were more general, including an image of an unknown woman with the caption "Does this cloth smell like chloroform to you?" while others were more specific, such as a poll asking which female student the group members would "hate fuck" (Backhouse et al., 2015). The existence of this closed Facebook group was not discovered until a female dentistry student was shown screenshots of some of these posts, which she then showed university administrators. Initially, the university did not take action against the students involved with the Facebook group. It was not until frustrated and disturbed students went to news media and garnered national attention that the university started an investigation. Ultimately, all of the students involved successfully graduated with no lasting consequences for their actions (Dicks, 2016). In this case, it was not just the individual students who were mentioned by name in the Facebook posts but the entire campus community that was victimized. Several female campus community members, including students, faculty, and staff members, expressed feeling unsafe and disturbed by the Facebook group, especially as they felt their institution was not doing enough to protect their members. Both of these cases involved white female victims, who are often satirized on social media as "complaining." While their race may not have initially impacted their experiences, their treatment on both social and news media may be a factor in the aftermath. Currently, data regarding race/ethnicity, sexuality, or gender identity of victims of TFSV is not readily available. This illustrates serious gaps in our understanding of how TFSV may affect individuals differently depending on their personal identities. More research needs to be done to bring an intersectional perspective to bear on incidents of TFSV.

Student Perceptions of University Responses

While the two cases discussed demonstrate that many students are unhappy with university inaction when students engage in TFSV, this opinion is not unanimously held. Some participants in the current research stated that post-secondary institutions should play a prominent role in responding to incidents of TFSV to ensure the safety and well-being of their students. Some of the students interviewed believe incidents of TFSV should be treated no differently than physical forms of sexual violence, resulting in a minimum of suspension, if not expulsion, from the institution. When asked if they felt that both university and criminal sanctions would be "doubly punishing" perpetrators, nearly all participants felt it was justified. Although not all participants were aware of the Dalhousie University or University of Ottawa scandals, when they were informed of the details and outcomes, most participants agreed with the students' outrage, especially because legal action could not be taken at the time of the incidents. According to the sexual violence response coordinator at a medium-sized university in southern Ontario, the way many of the sexual violence policies are worded allows for the institutions to act in cases of TFSV. Procedures are also in place to allow victims of TFSV to report their victimization and subsequently choose how to proceed. Although these policies and procedures may be established, what happens in practice may not be as optimistic.

Most participants in the current study agreed that post-secondary institutions should punitively respond to incidents of TFSV among students; however, some did not. Some students felt that post-secondary institutions should not play a role in responding to any form of sexual violence and that incidents of such behaviours should solely be addressed by law enforcement. Even those who held this position, however, did believe that the role of the university is to educate their student bodies and raise awareness of the problem. Several students noted that the educational material regarding campus sexual violence was minimal, and very few had ever read their institution's sexual violence policy. Regardless of how institutions respond to incidents of sexual violence, both TFSV and physical encounters, it is clear that their main role should be in educating their students on what sexual violence is and what resources are available to them.

CONCLUSION

The internet and mobile communication technologies have expanded our social worlds and have introduced infinite possibilities for social interaction of various kinds. Even before the COVID-19 pandemic, many post-secondary institutions were transcending into online spaces. For example, almost all post-secondary institutions employ some form of online platform for communicating, submitting assignments, and organizing course material. As such, post-secondary institutions must also be more proactive and reactive in responding to their students' online behaviours. Youths and student-aged young adults are the most likely to become victims of TFSV, due to not only their social media use but also their general lack of experience and naivety. There may also be other aspects of individual identities that contribute to and/or exacerbate their intersectional experiences of TFSV, but currently the data are lacking. While it has been argued that platforms like Facebook are not under university jurisdiction, the potential harm inflicted on students by students should be of university concern. Research into TFSV is relatively new and rarely investigated in a Canadian context. The effects of TFSV, particularly among female victims, however, are very real and in need of being more seriously addressed by both post-secondary institutions and the criminal justice system. Likely due to the embryonic nature of this research, other elements of individual identities, such as race, ethnicity, and sexual orientation, have not been explored as factors in the victimization research. Women of colour and other marginalized groups are less likely to receive fair treatment by law enforcement. Especially given the infancy of the legislation and difficulty law enforcement has had in addressing it, it is very possible that marginalized groups may also be both more reluctant to engage with law enforcement and have more negative interactions with them when they do. One role that administrations can take on is improving educational programs and making their policies, procedures, and resources more accessible to their community members. Another is to examine the data they have through an intersectional lens and consider what data might be missing.

QUESTIONS FOR DISCUSSION

1. It is often assumed that the term *violence* holds the same definition or under-standing for everyone. Given what you have read in this chapter, how would you define violence? Do you believe that perceived harm is a sufficient thresh-old for defining violence?
2. It has been argued that technology can be both powerfully good and power-fully harmful. How might technology be utilized to combat some of the issues brought up in this volume? Should young people be encouraged to "quit" social media as some social movements have been doing?
3. The currently available literature has focused on female adult victims, and other aspects of their identities have not been thoroughly explored. What other elements might be explored in terms of the intersectionality of victim experiences?

INVITATIONS TO GO DEEPER

1. Take a moment to think about your personal use of social media. For some, it is their main method of communication; for others, it is merely a window into the international world. How do you define social media? How do you use social media? How would your life be different if you no longer had access to social media?
2. There is great debate about the position of celebrities and public figures and their right to privacy. Do you feel that celebrities have less right to privacy than average citizens? Are those who have had their personal accounts hacked less sympathetic than those who do not hold celebrity status? Should they be?
3. Consider an outreach organization in your community that offers support for survivors of sexual violence or look at your own institution's sexual violence policy. How does the organization/institution you've chosen offer support? How does it define violence? Does it consider TFSV? If so, how? If not, do you have any sense of why not?

READ MORE

Ewick, P., & Silbey, S. (1998). *The common place of law: Stories from everyday life.* University of Chicago Press.

Miljure, B., & Mangione, K. (2021, February 5). Amanda Todd case: Man accused in cyberbullying of B.C. teen extradited to face charges. *CTV News.* https://bc.ctvnews.ca/amanda-todd-case-man-accused-in-cyberbullying-of-b-c-teen-extradited-to-face-charges-1.5297727

Shariff, S. (2017). Navigating the minefield of sexual violence policy in expanding "university contexts." *Education & Law Journal, 27*(1), 39–58.

University of Manitoba. (2021). Respectful work and learning environment (RWLE) policy. https://umanitoba.ca/about-um/respectful-work-and-learning-environment-policy

LISTEN MORE, WATCH MORE

"How online abuse of women has spiraled out of control," Ashley Judd, TED Talk, October 2016: https://www.ted.com/talks/ashley_judd_how_online_abuse_of_women_has_spiraled_out_of_control?language=en

"How revenge porn turns lives upside sown," Darieth Chisolm, TED Talk, December 2018: https://www.youtube.com/watch?v=uuatZO76MgQ

"The story of revenge porn," ScoopWhoop, July 2017: https://www.youtube.com/watch?v=nwOm0dAbCUc

NOTE

1.   These interviews entailed 45- to 90-minute semi-structured conversations that took place in person (pre-COVID-19) or via videoconference. The sample included undergraduate and graduate students, faculty members, and various staff members associated with the sexual violence policy at the university.

REFERENCES

Allen, B. (2019, December 24). Revenge porn and sext crimes: Canada sees more than 5,000 police cases as law marks 5 years. *CBC News.* https://www.cbc.ca/news/canada/saskatchewan/revenge-porn-and-sext-crimes-canada-sees-more-than-5–000-police-cases-as-law-marks-5-years-1.5405118

Backhouse, C., McRae, D., & Iyer, N. (2015, June 26). *Report of the task force on misogyny, sexism, and homophobia in Dalhousie University Faculty of Dentistry.* Dalhousie University. https://cdn.dal.ca/content/dam/dalhousie/pdf/cultureofrespect/DalhousieDentistry-TaskForceReport-June2015.pdf

Bridgestock, L. (2021, August 6). What drives students' social media use. *Top Universities Blog.* https://www.topuniversities.com/blog/what-drives-students-social-media-usage

Canadian Mental Health Association. (2021). Addictions and problematic internet use. https://ontario.cmha.ca/documents/addictions-and-problematic-internet-use/

CBC News. (2014, December 15). Dalhousie University probes misogynistic student "gentleman's club." https://www.cbc.ca/news/canada/nova-scotia/dalhousie-university-probes-misogynistic-student-gentlemen-s-club-1.2873918

Chittley, J. (2014, September 1). Nude photos of many A-list celebrities leaked online after apparent hacking. *CTV News*. https://www.ctvnews.ca/entertainment/nude-photos-of-many-a-list-celebrities-leaked-online-after-apparent-hacking-1.1985630?cache=urztwihxzglnbw%3FclipId%3D104066

Cohen, B., & Shenk, J. (Directors). (2016). *Audrie and Daisy* [film]. Actual Films.

Criminal Code, RSC, 1985, c. C-46.

Dicks, B. (2016, December 21). Dalhousie dentistry scandal: A costly lesson in communications. *CTV News*. https://atlantic.ctvnews.ca/dalhousie-s-dentistry-scandal-a-costly-lesson-in-communications-1.3212800

Dodge, A. (2016). Digitizing rape culture: Online sexual violence and the power of a digital photograph. *Crime Media Culture*, *12*(1), 65–82.

Fonrouge, G. (2017, September 22). Inside the twisted revenge porn site that's ruining women's lives. *The New York Post*. https://nypost.com/2017/09/22/revenge-porn-site-leaves-trail-of-innocent-victims/

Gibson, M. (2014, September 2). Stop blaming Jennifer Lawrence and other celebrities for taking nude photos in the first place. *Time*. https://time.com/3256628/jennifer-lawrence-nude-selfies-hack-victim-blaming/

Gruzd, A., & Mai, P. (2020, July 13). The state of social media in Canada 2020. *SSRN*. https://doi.org/10.2139/ssrn.3651206

Hamby, S. (2017). On defining violence, and why it matters. *Psychology of Violence*, *7*(2), 167–180.

Harris, K. M. (2016). Online friendship, romance and sex: Properties and associations of the Online Relationship Initiation Scale. *Cyberpsychology, Behaviour, and Social Networking*, *19*(8), 487–493.

Henry, N., & Powell, A. (2015). Embodied harms: Gender, shame, and technology-facilitated sexual violence. *Violence against Women*, *21*(6), 758–779.

Henry, N., & Powell, A. (2016). Sexual violence in the digital age: The scope and limits of the criminal law. *Social & Legal Studies*, *25*(4), 397–418.

Herrenkohl, T. I., Aisenberg, E., Williams, J. H., & Jenson, J. M. (Eds.). (2011). *Violence in context: Current evidence on risk, protection, and prevention*. Oxford University Press.

Kwon, J. (2019, December 1). After another K-pop death, spotlight turns to difficulties faced by industry's "perfect" stars. *CNN Entertainment*. https://www.cnn.com/2019/11/30/entertainment/kpop-pressures-goo-hara-sulli-intl-hnk-scli

Little, O. (2020, March 6). "A weird version of reality": Students quitting social media. *The Charlatan*. https://charlatan.ca/2020/03/quitting-social-media/

Mandau, M. B. H. (2019). "Directly in your face": A qualitative study of the sending and receiving of unsolicited "dick pics" among young adults. *Sexuality & Culture*, *24*, 72–93.

Powell, A., & Henry, N. (2018). Policing technology-facilitated sexual violence against adult victims: Police and service sector perspectives. *Policing and Society*, *28*(3), 291–307.

Protecting Canadians from Online Crime Act, SC 2014, c. 31.

Quinlan, E., Quinlan, A., Fogel, C., & Taylor, G. (Eds.). (2017). *Sexual violence at Canadian universities: Activism, institutional responses, and strategies for change*. Wilfrid Laurier University Press.

R. v. S.S., 2018 ONSC 2299. https://canlii.ca/t/hrfc0

Rogers, J. (2020, December 7). Cop kills herself and leaves suicide note apologizing to her kids after ex-boyfriend posted revenge porn online. *The Scottish Sun*. https://www.thescottishsun.co.uk/news/6376951/cop-suicide-ex-boyfriend-revenge-porn-argentina/

Schwartz, Z. (2018, March 1). Canadian post-secondary institutions are failing students on sexual assault. *Macleans*. https://www.macleans.ca/education/university/canadian-universities-are-failing-students-on-sexual-assault/

Statistics Canada. (2017). *Table 1: Selected police-reported crimes, urban and rural police services, all provinces, 2017* [data table]. https://www150.statcan.gc.ca/n1/pub/85-002-x/2019001/article/00009/tbl/tbl01-eng.htm

Statistics Canada. (2018). *Table 1: Police-reported crime for selected offences, Canada, 2018* [data table]. https://www150.statcan.gc.ca/n1/daily-quotidien/190722/t001a-eng.htm

Statistics Canada. (2020). *Chart 2: Experiences of unwanted behaviour online in the 12 months preceding the survey, by type of behaviour and gender, territories, 2018* [infographic]. https://www150.statcan.gc.ca/n1/daily-quotidien/200826/cg-a002-eng.htm

Statistics Canada. (2021). *Table 22-10-0110-01: Use of technology by age group and sex, Canada, provinces and regions* [data table]. https://www150.statcan.gc.ca/t1/tbl1/en/tv.action?pid=2210011001

Tsai, H., & Pai, P. (2012). Positive and negative aspects of online community cultivation: Implications for online stores' relationship management. *Information & Management*, *49*(2), 111–117.

Valdez, I. (2019, June 03). "I can't take it anymore": How revenge porn pushed a Spanish woman to suicide. *El Pais*. https://english.elpais.com/elpais/2019/06/03/inenglish/1559555440_857391.html

PART II
CONNECT

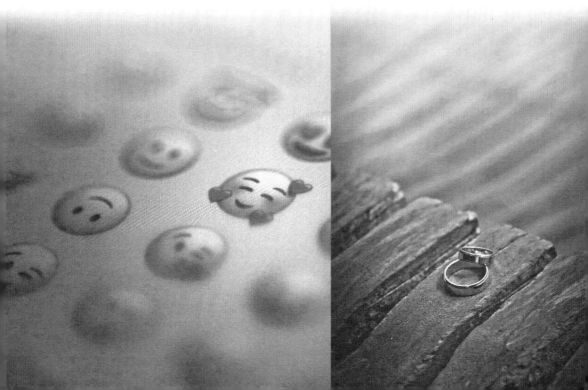

CHAPTER 4

Neither Crone nor Cougar: Navigating Intimacy and Ageism on Dating Apps

Treena Orchard

Wow beautiful Queen. I admire
The beauty you captivate in your
Picture!!! If your personality is
As beautiful as you are I would
Definitely like to get to know you.
I'm interested in being a cub to
A loving and caring cougar mama.
(Anonymous)

INTRODUCTION

The opening quote is a direct message (DM) sent to anthropologist and *New York Times* best-selling author Dr. Wednesday Martin by an adoring male fan. Dr. Martin writes about parenting (2016) and sexuality (2018) and is a prominent social media influencer, but cougar–cub intimate relationships are not in her scholarly wheelhouse. Aware of my dating app research (Orchard, 2019), including age-hypogamous heterosexual relationships, where the woman is older and the man is younger (Orchard, 2020), she thought the DM might be useful in my research. Dr. Martin also invited me to discuss the topic of older women dating younger men on the IGTV (Instagram TV) show she hosts. Building on our shared background in anthropology and mutual desire to destabilize heterosexist stereotypes of older women as asexual crones (Syme et al., 2019) or predatory cougars (Montemurro & Siefken, 2014), we had a lively exchange that included thoughtful questions from viewers. After the show, several people shared similarly rewarding and empowering experiences in these relationships and thanked us for our smart, inclusive discussion.

Often depicted in contemporary media as exceptional or very rare, age-hypogamous relationships have existed for centuries. Notable older women who have enjoyed these unions include Catherine the Great of Russia, British author George Eliot (the pen name for Mary Ann Evans), and Winston Churchill's mother (Silver, 2019). The most enduring example is that of Mrs. Robinson and Benjamin Braddock from the 1967 film *The Graduate*. Set against iconic Simon and Garfunkel songs like "Mrs. Robinson" and "The Sound of Silence," this story of intergenerational lust and the emptiness of postwar consumer society is one of a handful of films preserved in the US National Film Registry due to its cultural, historical, and aesthetic significance (Stern, 1996). The sultry image of Mrs. Robinson pulling on her nylons during a tryst with Benjamin, a recent college graduate several decades younger than herself, is etched in the minds of Boomers, Gen X-ers, and younger generations who have not seen the film but know famous lines such as "There is a great future in plastics" and "Would you like me to seduce you?" (Grover, 2020; Whitehead, 2014). Although Mrs. Robinson is depicted as a leopard-clad siren for most of the film, she ends up losing Benjamin to her own daughter, a dramatic turn of events immortalized in long, silent frames focused on her weary, almost pathetic appearance. To date, no contemporary film or television series rivals *The Graduate* for its unique rendering of these issues, and its enduring impact reflects our unabated fascination with not only alternate forms of intimacy but also the impossibility of older women as powerful figures socially and sexually.

Despite her fall from sexual grace, Mrs. Robinson is regularly cited in discussions of age-hypogamous relationships and is nearly always depicted as a cougar par excellence—a term that became popular in North America following the publication of *Cougar: A Guide for Older Women Dating Younger Men* (Gibson, 2001). Her name was featured in DateMrsRobinson.com, a dating site for older women and younger men launched in 2012 that now goes by CougarLife.com. The website features beautiful women in vintage outfits that are reminiscent of the late 1960s (i.e., pussycat glasses, hair scarves) and is marketed as a place to connect "modern, confident women with energetic younger men" (Cougar Life, 2022). In this digital space, cougars and their lovers, called cubs, are positioned as sensual members of a community that supports their unique dating lifestyle. Lauded as an opportunity for older women to flip the dominant script that marks them as sexless (Burema, 2018; Gewirtz-Meydan & Ayalon, 2020), cougars are also scorned for their transgressive desires (Alaire, 2019) and for having sexual desires at all (Vares, 2009).

Learning more about these categories and relationships is important given their increasing popularity. A recent American Association of Retired Persons survey of 3,500 heterosexual singles found that 34 percent of women between the ages of 40 and 69 years date younger men and 14 percent of women ages 50 to 59 prefer dating men in their 40s or younger (Witrogen, 2020). This preference is linked with several factors, particularly changing marriage patterns. Fewer people are getting married, and those who do are often older than in the past, which impacts women and men differently (Bialik & Fry, 2019). Women typically have fewer same-aged prospects because men often marry younger women (Alaire, 2019). This so-called "marriage squeeze" compels many women to turn their interests to younger men for sex and companionship (Kershaw, 2009). Another reason these relationships are on the rise is the shift in what men desire in terms of lifestyle and partners. Many younger men do not want to set up families or be the primary breadwinners, and they often prefer older female partners because these women may already have children, they know who they are sexually, and they have a firm sense of what they want in life (Morrison et al., 2015; Orchard, 2020).

My experiences on the Bumble dating app echo these findings, but was I just an item on young men's sexual wish list? When I posed this question to my dates, they said that they wanted to learn about my career successes, my global travel experiences, and how I achieve balance in my life. They were also eager to learn more about female sexuality and pleasure, which their younger partners rarely shed light on given their lack of confidence and experience. Being appreciated for who I am as well as my erotic capital contrasts with dominant social constructions of older women as sexually undesirable, which was exciting to experience and ponder the significance of. To me, as an anthropologist trained in the histories of sexuality, gender, and culture, the men's perspectives seemed to align with the divine feminine and goddess worship, ancient belief systems that predate patriarchy and honour the intuitive, sexual energies of women across the lifespan (Eisler, 1987; Savage, 2014). For a visual, think of those "Venus" stone carvings of the female form with exaggerated breasts, hips, and genitals. Although I was not worshipped by these men, which was not my goal, I felt valued for my age and my interests in sexual pursuits that honoured female energies. My dates were eager to connect in these ways; however, they were not always sure how to do so without sacrificing their pre-established notions of masculinity and what sex normally looks like for them—that is, driven largely by male pleasure. Sometimes they expressed competing anxieties about how their desires fit in relation to the shifting social landscape, whereby women are acquiring more power and influence. Many young men are trying to navigate these cultural and gendered tensions through their intimate relationships, aspects of which are captured in my fieldnotes below.

REFLEXIVE POSITIONING

This chapter situates my Bumble journey within the relevant research literature about heterosexual age-hypogamous relationships, sexuality, and digital dating (Bivens & Hoque, 2018; Burema, 2018; Fuentes & Sörum, 2019; Tweten, 2018). I also employ autoethnography, which involves individuals making connections between their lived experiences and the broader cultural context that give those experiences meaning. Such accounts highlight the unique contours of the authors' lives and shed interpretive light on the social implications of their personal experiences (Ellis, 1995; Frank, 1995). Unlike traditional research studies with human participants, autoethnographies are typically undertaken without funding and do not require ethics approval given their focus on the lived experiences of the author/creator.

Autoethnography is a useful way to understand the five months I spent on Bumble, from August 2017 to January 2018, because it illuminates the complex phenomenon of digital dating through the nuanced insights of one woman's life: mine. My fieldnotes contain rich observations about how Bumble works alongside humorous, vulnerable self-reflections as a sex-positive woman seeking intimacy and a more nuanced understanding of how men think about gender, sexuality, and older women. Descriptions of my interactions and conversations with some of the men I met are included, which is not uncommon in autoethnographies provided that this information is mainly descriptive and no identifying details are included.

This is the first scholarly analysis of the ways that gender, sexuality, and age intersect on dating platforms to create intimate opportunities for older women and younger men that mirror aspects of the divine feminine. From the moment I entered the digital Bumble hive, compelling and confusing patterns, symbols, and clues about modern sexuality, dating, men, and myself began to emerge. How could I not write about these experiences? My online dating journey began after I secured tenure, which affords me significant occupational security and privilege. However, it does not protect me from being whispered about among colleagues and students or from being harassed by online misogynist trolls who pour hate onto feminists, sex-positive folx, and others beyond the powerful, yet clearly crumbling, patriarchal artifice. I take these risks to share the excitement and the anomie of digital dating and to try and make some sense out of this bizarre, often difficult setting many of us inhabit while searching for sex, love, and who we are as intimate beings (Orchard, 2019, 2020).

DIVINING THE DIGITAL: RESURRECTING THE PARTNERSHIP MODEL IN AGE-HYPOGAMOUS RELATIONSHIPS

It is an interesting time to be an older woman, and I am reminded at every turn that I am an older woman. When I hit 45, new pop-ups appeared on my media feeds for products to contain my ostensibly unruly, embarrassing ageing body. I have been flooded with ads for incontinence underwear, pharmaceutical options to eradicate the marsupial-sounding menopause "pouch," and listicles with hot fashion tips for women over 50 featuring scarves, hats, and dark denim. Yet, stories also abound about female celebrities who only get hotter with age (Springer, 2020), women having the best sex of their lives post-menopause (Martin, 2019), and young men who love older women (Patrick, 2019). The lead characters on HBO series such as *Mare of Easttown* (Kate Winslet) and *Olive Kitteridge* (Francis McDormand), whose non-perfect bodies and complex personalities do not preclude them from having interesting sex lives, are other examples of the increasingly diverse representations of intimacy among older women. These competing accounts do not exist in isolation; they overlap with one another and inform the romantic fortunes of older women, including those seeking intimacy with younger men.

I inhabited this overlap while using Bumble, which is marketed as a feminist dating app (Featherstone, 2017) because women using the hetero version contact their male matches first. This fem-forwards approach appealed to me but was unsettling for some men, as reflected in their hostile language and behaviours. Using Bumble during the #MeToo movement undoubtedly shaped my experiences and the misogyny that circulated widely on the platform (Tweten, 2018). The disdain men expressed about women taking the lead in dating seemed to be linked with their fears associated with the "rise of women" (Rosin, 2012) and shifts in the gendered landscape whereby women are assuming greater control in various aspects of society while traditional forms of masculinity are crumbling. Yet many of these men pursued me and sought connections that belied the patriarchal ideologies they inherited. They often wanted me to take control of our encounters and enlighten them in two ways: first, by reducing the pressure for them to conform to prescribed dating rules that position men as the active players; and second, by being brought into my experiential realm, which they described as "hot," "interesting," "cool," "smart," "travelled," "cultured," "wise," "confident," and "successful." Our interactions allowed these men to engage with a self-assured older woman who was interested in sharing intimate experiences that honoured female pleasure and circumvented traditional socio-sexual expressions of masculinity.

When making sense of these experiences, the divine or sacred feminine emerges as a useful framework. These terms refer to ideological systems centred on nurturing, generative female power and living in relational equanimity with nature and one another (Ruether, 2005). Historical regions in the Middle East, North Africa, China, and India are among the places where this matriarchal orientation flourished. Riane Eisler discusses the divine feminine in her ground-breaking book *The Chalice and The Blade* (1987), using archeological evidence to explore partnership/chalice and dominator/blade models of human organization. The former is based on principles of linking, sustaining life, and diversity, while the latter is hierarchically structured and equates masculinity with violence and control (Eisler, 1987, pp. xvii–xx). Around 5000 BCE, the partnership model was overshadowed by the dominator system, which has clearly reached its limits, as evidenced by the rejection of long-standing patriarchal norms like sexual stereotypes, binary gender roles, and traditional relationship structures centred on monogamy and marriage.

Eisler's model resonates with the young men I met, who were interested in exploring different expressions of sexuality and masculinity through their intimate relationships with me. However, it is important to view the divine feminine, especially its binary nature and potentially essentialist ideologies regarding gender, race, and class (Debold, 2011), through a critical lens. Many sacred feminine practitioners, especially those on social media platforms, promote sexual healing sessions to ignite the goddess within that seem driven more by commercial pursuits than a genuine engagement with traditional knowledge about nature, sacred sexuality, and energies. This is reflected in the array of yoni stones being peddled and generic empowerment workshops offered by young, thin, white women with considerable social capital (Stein, 2020a, 2020b). This culturally narrow, wildly expensive "goop" version of the divine feminine is not what I am referring to when discussing the feelings and ideas I channelled and shared with many of the young men I encountered on Bumble.

STICKY, SEXY, SAD: ETHNOGRAPHIC REFLECTIONS ON SEX, GENDER, AND AGE INSIDE THE BUMBLE HIVE

My fieldnotes are organized chronologically and verbatim from the original record, minus the odd edit for clarity and narrative flow. They reveal compelling information about the contemporary terrain of sexuality, gender, and the ways digital technologies like Bumble facilitated and sometimes thwarted my attempts to cultivate a love life. I had some incredible experiences on the app, but it was a steep learning curve technically and socially to interact with so many people in a realm that often felt unreal and fell short of what I desired. The excerpts are structured thematically to align with the aims of this chapter, beginning with learning to Bumble and finding my digital dating groove. Next, I discuss gender and power in flux, followed by divine connections and a sexual interlude. The final theme features my reflections on the overall Bumble experience as I made my way out of the hive three Januarys ago.

Preliminary Insights

> Treena—08/30/2017, 7:28 a.m.: Since lowering the age on this Bumble thing to 30, shit has become even more real. Mama is busy!!! There's no way I can keep this up and keep my job—ha ha! I'm writing away about it though and want to make a book about this a reality xoox.

> Friend—08/30/2017, 8:53 a.m.: Lol! Can't wait to read about your Bumble escapades!
> (Text exchange between myself and a friend two weeks after I joined Bumble)

Like any game, and that's what Bumble is in many ways, there are implicit rules and features designed to move players through the interface en route to a successful outcome: a "match." But so much else comes into play, especially for those of us who have a wealth of dating knowledge that has nothing to do with swipe culture. Fourscore and 20 years ago, I quite easily picked up many a man from many a bar, workplace, and other social venues with little more than … well, myself. No phone, no prior messages, just stone-cold pickups. These experiences and my usually short-lived relationships are all I have to guide me. Bumble provides very little insights about how to actually play beyond selecting age, gender, and distance, and sending periodic messages to users about being active and getting our Buzzz on.

But where to look for help? We're showered with social media information about men, women, sex, living our best lives, and not sacrificing ourselves for guys who don't love the goddess within. Is any of that realistic? I'm just curious because while it sounds awesome, in truth, finding a god of my own seems mighty challenging. I'm not looking for one anyway … I'm just looking for a hot, semi-interesting guy to sleep with and maybe something more. Is that going to be as difficult as my spidey-senses are telling me? In "how-to" articles about how to start opening conversations, it's often recommended that we ask questions of our potential suitors to generate interest. But what questions, especially when they give us so little to go on? Also, in their profiles, many men note their profound dislike of being asked "boring" questions, like "What do you do?" or "How's your night?" So, what to say?!

Gender and Power in Flux

After an in-person meeting, one guy talked about being hurt and feeling vulnerable as well as intimidated by the fact that women have a lot of power. He said, "Women don't need men to have babies, to pay their bills, or to do that much.... What are men for, anyways?" I found this more than a little sad and told him that we need men for many things that matter, like love, emotional support, sex, a partner in this journey of life. The death or end of men idea lingers in the mind of this guy and that of many I've met, which surprised me because I thought that Millennials had these things figured out. He used the word *independence* frequently, which didn't carry an overtly positive or negative vibe but was certainly charged. Another guy said that women typically have the last word when couples make decisions about important stuff—is that true?

These shifts in power relations are wreaking havoc on men and my dating life. Men seem to feel useless and then behave in ways that sort of confirm that. And women must exchange their independence for utterly disappointing love lives among men who don't understand them or fear/resent them. This salmon swimming upstream situation sees us fighting or feigning to put ourselves together (to quote the film *Hedwig and the Angry Inch*)—literally through sex and socially through dating practices on apps we use but don't fully understand. This is occurring amid deep changes in the field of gendered relations, where things are diverse but where we're also far less evolved than I realized. Misogyny, for instance, runs strong in this confusing river.

Another date repeatedly mentioned the impact of social media and celebrities on how people act and think about themselves and others. As he said, women adjust all aspects of their bodies to look like the Kardashians and then ask for "real" men when they themselves are unreal or not "fully real." I listened to him but felt like saying, "Come on, it's gotta be about something deeper than social media." But the way he spoke made it apparent how omnipotent the media is as a cultural force. It also made it clear how threatened and confused this guy was about the seemingly unfair or contradictory sexual narratives about gender and culturally constructed notions of beauty and/or bodies.

To successfully fold Bumble or any feminist/equity-oriented reality into our existing cultural matrices, a series of rather seismic shifts must occur. Obviously, these don't happen overnight, nor do they happen evenly, but this experience has revealed how uncomfortable men are with these shifts, which are nowhere complete and began decades before the men I'm meeting were born. It's quite compelling to learn about the social inheritance of these gendered fears. It's not as simple as the idea that men are douches and seem afraid to connect, which is a common refrain in media discourse. It's a whole slew of things that involves our relations to each other as well as structural-level socio-sexual and cultural change.

The women's movement has been addressing these issues for some 40 years, but the continuation of gender gaps, violence against women and others, and endless forms of male aggression reveal that equity is far away. Something important to remember is that it's not just that women don't have equality in all facets of life, but new ways of being a man have been slow to surface as solid, safe, and acceptable across generations and cultural groups. When women's movements and other big political change occurs, it takes forever for society to truly adjust, despite the surface view of seemingly quick acceptance of these new ideas. "Let's develop an app to get women ahead, what a great idea."

So many of these men have the idea that women's empowerment takes away from their value as men. It's such a shame that this simplistic model was continuing to circulate in 2017. Our equity and growth are hard-fought outcomes of being oppressed and denied access to what many men have easy access to: power. We're not taking anything away from them; in fact, women's experiences in the shifting terrain of gendered power don't have much to do with them at all. I only learned this in person, the only real way for people to open up. These things could never come through in a few lines of text, those abbreviated lines, those condensed back-and-forths. They don't permit a full exploration of anything. I was sitting a few centimetres away from this beautiful man, who was struggling with not just a breakup but also a life in major transition. Only in that shared space, where he felt safe and welcomed to share, could I hear him and how he told his story to me.

This is so central in making the connection, which is ultimately what all of this is about, for me anyway: connecting. He opened up to me, and I wasn't surprised to get a message from him later saying he felt comfortable with me. That's because of what I do for a living, because we were in my place—calm and well designed— and because I'm also confident in myself. He was safe and I let him know I care, which are essential ingredients in communication and intimacy.

Sexual Interlude

And then came a man very unlike the others, in both demeanour and spirit: quiet, cultured, a true cat person. He was also the youngest at 29 years of age. He stepped across the threshold of the back door of my apartment building carrying a bottle of wine, and he was exceedingly polite. When I said I do not drink but he was welcome to, he declined, and the bottle sat on the kitchen countertop amid the dishes that accumulated as the day turned into night. It was a time of Nepalese dumplings, an interrupted viewing of the Marvel movie *Logan*, pleasant repartee about different chunks of our lives, and several intense coming-togethers. I found myself drawn to his face, touching it often and reaching for it in the dark as we cuddled under the sheets and talked about our favourite films, basketball teams and players, cuisines, our middle names, and desert island albums.

This exchange of things we like, things we do, and bits of who we are felt almost juvenile. But it wasn't about behaving below an age grade or in a way that belies the complex, diverse lives we both lead in the adult world to which we belong. It was just refreshingly simple—two people connecting through one another's life after intimate sex. It is a soft, inviting atmosphere into which many of us have stepped. It's a special place where my body and mind are invited to just be together, alongside those of the person beside me. He was my only overnight guest, a prolonged swansong as I drift out of the hive. Not once did this man check his phone, and he said "thank you" after everything I gave him. I fed him, caressed him, and plied him with strong coffee in the morning.

End-Game Reflections

There is a strange aversion to talking about Bumble among my partners. If I raise the issue of going off the app, it seems or feels like I'm shining a light on the fact that we used an app to meet, which still feels a bit shady or embarrassing. Why does admitting what is obvious make me feel more vulnerable? So many questions abound: Do I mean anything? Do you mean anything? Is this meeting or conversation only the product of a game? Because it originated as a game, does it have to remain so?

I have finally exited the hive, and although it feels great, it doesn't just "end" there. I sat on my living room rug and wept following a phone call and then a text message from the two men I really liked. The feelings that swirled inside me included disbelief, a little bit of fear, happiness, wonder, and pride. They grew out of the place in me where finally, after so many months and years even, I was able to accept and receive true kindness and connection.

I was crying because these men were showing me that I mattered and that they cared about me, which is very much tied to my own complex feelings about myself as someone who is good and who deserves love. I've thought these things for a very long time, but to feel it reflected through the behaviours and good intentions of people I want to be with in one capacity or another is truly magical. It's no small thing, and I agree with my counsellor, who said that this journey has been like a pilgrimage. Actually, she began by saying how touching my reflections were and then asked me what the definition of a pilgrimage is. "A perilous journey to a sacred place," I replied, realizing that with each syllable, I had just described my own Bumble quest.

CONCLUSION

This chapter offers insights on approaches to intimacy and identity among older women that are more meaningful than the ageist, sexist constructs of the cougar or the crone. Although the cougar category offers a way for ageing women to (re)claim aspects of their sexual subjectivity that are absent in the crone narrative, it does not necessarily advance affirmative ideas about sexuality. This is because cougars are framed as transgressive figures who contravene sexual, gendered, and age-related practices within the context of heteronormative dating practices that assign active roles to men (Montemurro & Siefken, 2014). Their transgression makes them titillatingly taboo, but it is also why their sexual appetite is rendered dangerous or ridiculed instead of being recognized as evidence of agential power. These disparaging attributes are further reinforced by the fact that this version of female sexual desire is reduced to animal form, a powerful symbol of dehumanization (Tipler & Ruscher, 2019). A final reason why cougars are scorned has to do with ageism, which is an under-problematized issue within intersectional feminist analysis.

Yet all is not lost for the Mrs. Robinsons among us, given the many opportunities that exist for older women to experience sex and intimacy in ways that contest oppressive patriarchal constructs and feel pleasurable on their own terms. As discussed above, these opportunities are shaped by factors that include changing marital trends (Kershaw, 2009), the "Millennial shift" in sexual scripts among younger generations that feature less domineering masculinities (Anderson et al., 2021; Morrison et al., 2015), and the upsurge of social as well as scientific interest in older women's sexuality (Martin, 2019; Rosin, 2012; Vares, 2009). Another contributing factor is dating platforms themselves, which are reconfiguring how people experience age-hypogamous relationships, gender, and the broader socio-cultural changes that inform who we are in these digital times.

The autoethnographic fieldnotes featured in this chapter illuminate the challenges of using dating apps like Bumble, the empowering opportunities they can offer older women, and the ways young men are struggling to consolidate their sexual desires and selfhood in relation to the increasingly powerful status of women.

The structural fissures regarding gender and power that I observed, namely, that many men have inherited deep-seated fears about and resentment towards women, were disturbing and instructive. It was only as a member of the Bumble hive that I learned of these complexities in such an embodied, intimate way, which reveals how these apps both mirror and mediate our increasingly digitized lives. These virtual landscapes are also productive spaces through which users can usurp harmful elements of the patriarchy, including outmoded sexual, ageist, and gendered scripts. On this platform, millions of people have their fingers, literally, on the technical and emotive pulses that direct the ways in which we create, circumvent, or happily crush outdated patterns regarding intimacy, social connection, gendered identity, and the ways we experience ourselves in the world.

Using Bumble enabled me to connect with hundreds of young men, who shared their insights about emergent relationship structures, sexual pleasures, and the subjectivities discussed above. Among the most exciting, unexpected aspects of my time inside the Bumble hive was learning what I represented to many of my paramours: a source of respected knowledge and experience, occupational success, a sexy woman with good energy, and a safe place where they could talk about and enjoy being themselves as men whose identities are in flux at micro and macro levels. These encounters resemble aspects of the divine feminine and the partnership model (Eisler, 1987), which is a pleasurable, equitable, and meaningful alternative to the worn-out crone/cougar dichotomy. They also align with recent research into sexuality among older people more broadly, which is far more exciting, satisfying, and varied than the dominant discourse would have us believe (Martin, 2019; Meier & Barry, 2017; Syme et al., 2019; Vares, 2009).

QUESTIONS FOR DISCUSSION

1. Are age-hypogamous relationships a "thing" among your age group? Can you think of any famous examples of these generation-jumping relationships? If so, how were they portrayed in the media?
2. Did this discussion enrich your understanding of how older women and/or Millennial guys use dating apps? Did it align with the dating experiences of any older women you know?
3. What were your previous thoughts about sexuality among older women? Did this chapter challenge those previous assumptions? If so, how?
4. Who are some influential role models for young cisgender men to learn about alternate forms of masculinity? How about other gendered groups of men?

INVITATIONS TO GO DEEPER

1. Have you used a dating app? In what ways, if any, was your experience similar to the author's? In what ways, if any, was your experience different? What do you think might account for the similarities or differences?

2. Do you think it's important to resist certain sexual and gendered stereotypes that make unconventional intimate relationships socially unacceptable or silenced? If so, why, and how can we resist these restrictive social constructions?

3. Discuss the tensions between the cougar label, which some women find empowering and others find oppressive, and the idea of the sexually vacant crone. Are similar constructs applied to older men? If so, how are they similar or different to the ones associated with women?

4. What impact has the #MeToo movement had on women's feelings of safety related to disclosing abusive experiences? Do you think elements of the divine feminine could be used to increase women's sense of sexual freedom and expression in this regard?

READ MORE

Alarie, M. (2020). Sleeping with younger men: Women's accounts of sexual interplay in age-hypogamous intimate relationships. *The Journal of Sex Research*, *57*(3), 322–334.

Graham, E. (1999). Cyborgs or goddesses? Becoming divine in a cyberfeminist age. *Information, Communication & Society*, *2*(4), 419–438.

Orchard, T. (forthcoming). Virtual sexual identities: Embodied aspirations, tensions, and lessons from the Bumble dating app. In E. Rees (Ed.), *The Routledge companion to gender, sexuality, and culture*. Routledge.

LISTEN MORE, WATCH MORE

Cougar and the Milf podcast, hosted by the Cougar (Astrid) & the Milf (Blythe), 2017–present, 21 episodes.

The Graduate, directed by Mike Nichols, 1967.

Harold and Maude, directed by Hal Ashby, 1971.

"Maggie May," performed by Rod Stewart, from the album *Every Picture Tells a Story*, 1971.

REFERENCES

Alaire, M. (2019). "They're the ones chasing the cougar": Relationship formation in the context of age-hypogamous intimate relationships. *Gender & Society*, *33*(3), 463–485.

Anderson, P., Struckman-Johnson, C., & Smeaton, G. (2021). Generation by gender differences in use of sexual aggression: A replication of the millennial shift. *The Journal of Sex Research*, *58*(3), 383–395.

Bialik, K., & Fry, R. (2019, February 14). Millennial life: How young adulthood today compares with prior generations. *Pew Research Center*. https://www.pewresearch.org/social-trends/2019/02/14/millennial-life-how-young-adulthood-today-compares-with-prior-generations-2/

Bivens, R., & Hoque, S. (2018). Programming sex, gender, and sexuality: Infrastructural failures in the "feminist" dating app Bumble. *Canadian Journal of Communication*, *43*(3), 441–459.

Burema, D. (2018). Cougars or kittens? The representation of celebrity cougars and their toyboys in gossip media. *Feminist Media Studies*, *18*(1), 7–20.

Cougar Life. (2022). Retrieved March 14, 2022, from https://www.cougarlife.com/

Debold, E. (2011, November 17). The divine feminine, unveiled. *HuffPost*. https://www.huffpost.com/entry/the-divine-feminine-unvei_b_282213

Eisler, R. (1987). *The chalice and the blade: Our history, our future*. HarperOne.

Ellis, C. (1995). *Final negotiations: A story of love, loss and chronic illness*. Temple University Press.

Featherstone, E. (2017, July 7). Interview—Bumble's Whitney Wolfe: "I'm worried we're alienating the good guys." *The Guardian*. https://www.theguardian.com/small-business-network/2017/jul/07/bumble-founder-whitney-wolfe-tinder-feminism-online-trolling

Frank, A. (1995). *The wounded storyteller: Body, illness and ethics*. University of Chicago Press.

Fuentes, C., & Sörum, N. (2019). Agencing ethical consumers: Smartphone apps and the socio-material reconfiguration of everyday life. *Consumption Markets & Culture*, *22*(2), 131–156.

Gewirtz-Meydan, A., & Ayalon, L. (2020). "Shades of grey": Exploring public opinion about later-life sexuality. *Canadian Journal on Aging*, *39*(4), 647–661.

Gibson, V. (2001). *Cougar: A guide for older women dating younger men*. Key Porter Books.

Grover, E. (2020, May 8). The long and decorated literary history of the MILF: From Chaucer to Mrs. Robinson. *Inside Hook*. https://www.insidehook.com/article/arts-entertainment/literary-history-milf-mrs-robinson-stiflers-mom-wife-bath

Kershaw, S. (2009, October 14). Rethinking the older woman–younger man relationship. *New York Times*. https://www.nytimes.com/2009/10/15/fashion/15women.html

Martin, W. (2016). *Primates of Park Avenue: A memoir*. Simon & Shuster.

Martin, W. (2018). *Untrue: Why nearly everything we believe about women, lust, and infidelity is wrong and how the new science can set us free*. Little, Brown Spark.

Martin, W. (2019, September 26). When I hit menopause, I found salvation on Tinder. *Refinery 29*. https://www.refinery29.com/en-ca/2019/09/8482329/when-i-hit-menopause-i-found-salvation-on-tinder

Meier, M., & Barry, K. (Eds.). (2017). *Unmasked: Women write about sex and intimacy after fifty*. Weeping Willow Books.

Montemurro, B., & Siefken, J. (2014). Cougars on the prowl? New perceptions of older women's sexuality. *Journal of Aging Studies, 28*, 35–43.

Morrison, D., Masters, N., Wells, E., Casey, E., Beadnell, B., & Hoppe, M. (2015). "He enjoys giving her pleasure": Diversity and complexity in young men's sexual scripts. *Archives of Sexual Behavior, 44*(3), 655–668.

Orchard, T. (2019, July 18). Love, lust and digital dating: Men on the Bumble dating app aren't ready for the queen bee. *The Conversation Canada*. https://theconversation.com/love-lust-and-digital-dating-men-on-the-bumble-dating-app-arent-ready-for-the-queen-bee-120796

Orchard, T. (2020, October 3). 7 reasons dating a younger man is a smart choice. *Your Tango*. https://www.yourtango.com/experts/treena-orchard/reasons-dating-younger-man-smart-choice

Patrick, W. (2019, August 11). Why some younger men want to date older women. *Psychology Today*. https://www.psychologytoday.com/ca/blog/why-bad-looks-good/201908/why-some-younger-men-want-date-older

Rosin, H. (2012). *The end of men and the rise of women*. Riverhead Books.

Ruether, R. (2005). *Goddesses and the divine feminine*. University of California Press.

Savage, L. (2014). Reclaiming women's sexuality: The intersection of Shamanic practices and sex therapy. *Sexual and Relationship Therapy, 29*(1), 121–131.

Silver, C. (2019, July 31). 13 famous historical women who married guys way younger than them. *Ranker*. https://www.ranker.com/list/famous-historical-women-who-married-much-younger-men/carly-silver

Springer, C. (2020, June 10). Hot celebrity women over 50. *All VIP*. https://www.allvipp.com/celebrities/hot-celebrity-women-over-50

Stein, L. (2020a). *Self-care: A novel*. Penguin Books.

Stein, L. (2020b, October 26). What is self-care now, anyway? *New York Times*. https://www.nytimes.com/2020/10/26/us/women-self-care-beauty-leigh-stein.html

Stern, C. (1996, December 3). National Film Registry taps 25 more pix. *Variety*. https://variety.com/1996/scene/vpage/national-film-registry-taps-25-more-pix-1117466310/

Syme, M., Cohn, T., Stoffregen, S., Kaempfe, H., & Schippers, D. (2019). "At my age …": Defining sexual wellness in mid-and later life. *The Journal of Sex Research*, *56*(7), 832–842.

Tipler, C., & Ruscher, J. (2019). Dehumanizing representations of women: The shaping of hostile sexist attitudes through animalistic metaphors. *Journal of Gender Studies*, *28*(1), 109–118.

Tweten, A. (2018). *Bye Felipe: Disses, dick pics, and other delights of modern dating*. Running Press.

Vares, T. (2009). Reading the "sexy oldie": Gender, age(ing) and embodiment. *Sexualities*, *12*(4), 503–524.

Whitehead, J. W. (2014). *Appraising the Graduate: The Mike Nichols classic and its impact in Hollywood*. McFarland.

Witrogen, B. (2020, December 31). Older women, younger men. *Health Day*. https://consumer.healthday.com/encyclopedia/aging-1/age-health-news-7/older-women-younger-men-647607.html

"I'm Not Your Fantasy": Sexual Racism, Racial Fetishization, and the Exploitation of Racialized Men Who Have Sex with Men

Christopher Dietzel

INTRODUCTION

The Black Lives Matter (BLM) protests of 2020 brought renewed attention to the racist practices embedded in North American culture and systems at the national, institutional, community, and individual levels. The BLM protests also revived conversations about racist practices among men who have sex with men (MSM), practices that are embedded in gay male culture (Knegt, 2020; Sengupta, 2020; Walcott, 2017) and dating apps (Lim et al., 2020). Racialized MSM frequently encounter discriminatory and racist behaviour on dating apps (Conner, 2018), and this discrimination and racism has been well documented over the past decade (Callander et al., 2012, 2016; Callander et al., 2015; A. Han, 2006; C. S. Han, 2007, 2008; Raj, 2011; Robinson, 2015).

Prior to June 2020, Grindr and Scruff had an ethnicity filter that allowed users to sort and view MSM based on their race and ethnicity (Hern, 2020). The filter had often been criticized because MSM, especially white MSM, could find and remove racialized MSM from their app space (Wakabayashi, 2020). Though the BLM protests successfully pressured Grindr and Scruff into removing the ethnicity filter (Garel, 2020), racism manifests on dating apps in many ways, as I discuss in this chapter.

I am not a racial or ethnic minority; I am a white, gay, cisgender man. While I will never fully understand the racism that racialized MSM experience in gay male culture and on dating apps, I am a member of these communities. White people like me often fail to acknowledge our social privileges or engage in messy, complex, and uncomfortable conversations about race and racism. We as white people need to critically reflect on our privileges, develop our awareness and understanding, and use that knowledge for good. All of us are responsible for the communities and spaces that we occupy—and we must take action to address discrimination, racism, and other forms of harm that exist in society.

BACKGROUND

Smartphone-based dating applications, colloquially referred to as dating apps, use the global positioning system (GPS) function to match users in close geographic proximity. First developed by and for MSM—with Grindr in 2009 and Scruff in 2010—to connect safely and discretely (Grov et al., 2014), dating apps became popular in the 2010s after the web-based dating services of the 1990s and 2000s were made more accessible and mobile via smartphones. MSM use dating apps for a variety of reasons, including to socialize, relieve boredom, explore their identities, build community, find long-term partners, and pursue sexual interactions online and in person (Albury et al., 2019; Van de Wiele & Tong, 2014).

While dating apps were developed to provide a safe space for MSM, many MSM dating app users are marginalized because of their identities. Racialized MSM often feel excluded or "othered" on dating apps (Raj, 2011) since the apps reproduce the racial hierarchies present in society (Conner, 2018; Robinson, 2016, 2018). These hierarchies favour white MSM and disfavour racialized MSM, especially Asian MSM and Black MSM, who are often perceived as less sexually desirable (Callander et al., 2016; A. Han, 2006; Raj, 2011; Robinson, 2015). While most racist practices come from white MSM, racialized MSM can also discriminate against other racialized MSM in preference for white MSM (A. Han, 2006; Robinson, 2015).

The language articulated on MSM dating app users' profiles reflect and reinforce the fact that white MSM are perceived as more sexually desirable than racialized MSM (Caluya, 2006; Teunis, 2007). Birnholtz et al. (2014) conducted a text analysis of almost 70,000 Grindr profiles, finding that 8 to 10.5 percent of users employed some type of exclusionary language to discourage certain users, including users of certain races, from contacting them. In Robinson's (2015) study, none of the users of one hundred profiles analyzed "stated they were seeking explicitly a non-white race unless it was coupled with also seeking white men" (p. 325). In a text analysis of three hundred Grindr user profiles, Conner (2018) found that 60 percent of profiles included instructions to users not to contact them if they were non-white.

In addition to the text that MSM dating app users can put on their profile, users can choose from predetermined options in several different dropdown categories about sexual health, sexual practices, and identity. Once a user selects one of the options, it is displayed on their profile—and the completed options allow dating app users to filter MSM according to those categories. In the free version of the app, Grindr users can only access some filters, but in the paid version, users have access to premium filters. The ethnicity filter was one of these premium filters, and prior to June 2020, Grindr users with a paid subscription could filter MSM according to their ethnicity (Garel, 2020; Hern, 2020). The commodification of dating app users' social relations may encourage MSM to think of one another as objects that can be consumed and thrown away (Goldberg, 2020).

With an ethnicity filter, MSM could cleanse dating sites of racialized bodies so that they never see a non-white body online (Robinson, 2015, 2018). This process has been referred to as whitewashing (Gabriel, 2002), which has also been used to describe the social exclusion of racialized MSM from gay male culture (C. S. Han, 2007). The ethnicity filter was one way for MSM to whitewash a dating app, though users can also remove racialized MSM by blocking individual profiles (Rodriguez, 2018). These types of practices that exclude potential sexual partners based on race is referred to as sexual racism (Callander et al., 2012).

Some people defend sexual racism as the freedom to choose a sexual partner according to their preferences (Matheson, 2012). Others have argued that sexual racism is a form of new racism (Collins, 2004) that has been normalized among MSM, notably online (Robinson, 2015). Robinson (2015) asserts that these racist ideologies are masked as personal preferences by using "neoliberal discourses around personal preference that normalize racism in cyberspace" (p. 319). This means that MSM may attempt to justify their sexual racism by dismissing it as a personal preference. In fact, some MSM dating app users may try to disguise their sexual racism with coded language like "I don't like your type" to dismiss racialized MSM who approach them (C. S. Han, 2007).

MSM often take race and ethnicity into account when selecting a potential sexual partner (Callander et al., 2012; Callander et al., 2015). While racialized MSM can be sexually excluded because of their race, they can also be specifically sought after because of their race—often through racial stereotyping and fetishization (A. Han, 2006; C. S. Han, 2008; Raj, 2011). In these instances, race becomes an object of sexual desire that exists for the pleasure of the other person. The fetishization of racialized bodies allows race to be more easily consumed by MSM, especially white MSM, as they add "spice" and "adventure" to their sexual activities (Robinson, 2015). Racial fetishes also let MSM experiment with racialized bodies in ways that are comfortable, accessible, and temporary (Robinson, 2015). This means that MSM, especially white MSM, may take advantage of and exploit the identities of racialized MSM for their own sexual pleasure.

The discrimination, racism, and harm that racialized MSM encounter through their use of dating apps may have consequences on how they practise consent and engage in sexual activities with other MSM. For example, racialized MSM who perceive their race to be devalued in gay male culture may engage in higher-risk sexual activities (Chae & Yoshikawa, 2008). More recent research similarly found that sexual racism and racial fetishization negatively impact racialized MSM's sexual health (Han & Choi, 2018) and their platonic and intimate relationships (Stacey & Forbes, 2021). There is an urgent need to examine consent practices among racialized MSM because racialized MSM face higher rates of non-consensual sexual interactions than white MSM (Walters et al., 2013). While much more work needs to be done to explore the intersections of race and sexual violence, particularly among racialized MSM, this chapter begins to address this gap by investigating the harm that racialized MSM experience through their use of dating apps. Specifically, this chapter explores non-consensual sexual practices that exclude, fetishize, and exploit racialized MSM—incidents that are not physically violent (like sexual assault or rape) but nonetheless rely on differences in power and result in harm.

METHODS

Data presented in this chapter are from a qualitative research project that examined the experiences of 25 MSM in Montreal, Canada. Participants were required to be at least 18 years old and identify as an MSM dating app user. Recruitment lasted three months and consisted of snowball sampling and posting flyers at a large Canadian university and in Montreal's Gay Village. Participants were not compensated.

Inspired by Blackwell et al. (2015), participants were offered three interview options: in person, by telephone, or online. Most participants opted for an in-person interview, though three participants interviewed by telephone and three via online chat. All audio interviews were recorded and transcribed verbatim, while the online interviews were saved as text documents. The interviews, which each lasted about an hour, were conducted in both English and French. Data from the French interviews were translated into English. The interview transcripts comprise the data analyzed in this study.

All 25 participants identified as MSM dating app users, and their ages ranged from 18 to 62. When asked about their gender, 24 identified as male and 1 identified as gender-fluid. None of the participants identified as transgender. Most participants identified as gay, though one identified as bisexual and two identified as queer. Participants identified as white ($n = 14$), Middle Eastern ($n = 3$), Hispanic

(n = 3), multiracial (n = 3), Black (n = 1), and Asian (n = 1). Most participants used Grindr (n = 23), though they also used other dating apps and websites, including Tinder, Scruff, Hornet, and OkCupid. Participants' primary reasons for using dating apps and sites were for sex, meeting people, and dates/relationships. The names of the participants presented in this chapter are pseudonyms.

I conducted semi-structured interviews to investigate MSM's experiences with dating apps. In the interviews, participants and I discussed a variety of topics, including sexual consent, unsolicited dick pics, rape culture, and how MSM communicate and interact online and in person. I did not specifically ask about discrimination or racism, though I encouraged participants to talk about how identity factored into their experiences.

I followed Braun and Clarke's (2006) guide for thematic analysis, which is "a method for identifying, analyzing and reporting patterns (themes) within data [such that] it minimally organizes and describes [a] data set in (rich) detail" (p. 79). I applied intersectionality—developed by Kimberlé Crenshaw (1989), a leading Black scholar, to call attention to the systemic barriers and forms of oppression that exist in society—to my analysis to examine how differences in identity impact MSM dating app users' experiences. Intersectionality provided a framework to analyze the ways in which MSM discriminate against, fetishize, and exploit racialized MSM on dating apps.

SEXUAL RACISM

Participants discussed what it was like for racialized MSM to use dating apps. Ang (36, gay, male, Asian) said that "there is huge discrimination on these apps," and Dion (37, gay, male, Middle Eastern) said that "there's lots of racism on Grindr." Theo (20, gay, gender-fluid, multiracial) spoke about experiencing micro-aggressions from MSM dating app users. Ang talked about seeing racist memes and images in users' profile photos. Skyler (28, queer, male, white) asserted that "if you're a person of color on an app, you're in general going to have a worse time." In contrast, Mason (26, bisexual, male, multiracial) said, "My experience has never been that anyone was extremely rude or racist or whatever, but I suppose it's possible that it could happen to someone else."

Participants talked about sexual racism on dating apps. Jadyn (32, gay, male, Black) gave the example of a time when he was rejected because of his race: "The guy didn't want to hook-up with me because he was not attracted to Black people. It was one of those gay racism situations." Many participants described sexual racism as a common practice among MSM dating app users. "There's a huge norm for people having racial preferences," explained Charlie (24, gay, male, white). Ravi (28, gay, male, Middle Eastern), Karam (46, gay, male, Middle Eastern), and Mason used the word *normal* to emphasize how common it was to see and/or experience sexual racism on dating apps.

Racialized MSM experience sexual racism on dating apps in the form of images and messages. Some of the sexual racism that racialized MSM experience is overt and direct, while some of it is covert and indirect. Participants' experiences and observations suggest that sexual racism is a common practice among MSM dating app users, a finding supported by numerous other studies (Birnholtz et al., 2014; Callander et al., 2012; Callander et al., 2015; Caluya, 2006; Conner, 2018; A. Han, 2006; C. S. Han, 2007; Robinson, 2015).

Participants said that they often saw discriminatory and racist language on MSM dating apps, and many emphasized that Asian MSM are frequent targets of such language. Noah (28, gay, male, white), Dion, and Theo said that it was common to see the phrase "No Asians" on users' profiles. Toby (20, gay, male, white) asserted that dating apps can be exclusionary and unwelcome spaces for racialized MSM, especially "when people are posting things like, 'No fats, femmes,[1] or Asians.'"

The phrase "no fats, femmes, or Asians" is an example of sexual racism targeting Asian MSM.[2] Asian MSM are often viewed as undesirable in gay male culture, being thought of as asexual, emasculated, submissive, and having small penises (Robinson, 2015; Wilson et al., 2009). While the phrase "no fats, femmes, or Asians" is racist, it is also fatphobic and femmephobic because it targets MSM who are overweight and MSM who do not conform to traditional notions of masculinity. For MSM whose identities intersect—in this case, for MSM who are fat, femme, and Asian—they experience fatphobia, femmephobia, *and* racism, which compounds the discrimination, exclusion, and harm they experience on dating apps. The phrase "no fats, femmes, or Asians" underlines the importance of taking an intersectional approach to understanding discrimination against marginalized and racialized peoples.

Exclusionary language like this is present on users' profiles as well as in private messages. Ang explained that in one situation, a user sent "a one-line response to me saying, 'Hello'—the response was, 'no Asians.' That made me feel uncomfortable but I'm kind of used to it because I get that *frequently* on dating apps" (emphasis his own). Ang said that he rarely receives replies from other MSM: "For every 10 to 20 messages I send out, I will get one response back." When asked why he thought he did not receive many responses, Ang said, "Because I don't fit the gay male definition of beauty. I am not a white cisgender male."

A few participants talked about race making a difference in the number of messages an MSM dating app user receives. Karam explained:

> I'm open to any race in general but, for me, I'd rather date—I gravitate to-ward white men. I can't help it. That's just what I'm attracted to.… If another race approaches me and they don't appeal to me, then I don't communicate with them. I don't tell them, "I don't like your race." I don't tell them, "I don't like your type." I just don't. I don't initiate. And I don't respond.

Jadyn and Charlie talked about Grindr's "What the Flip" video series, which examined discrimination and racism in the gay community through social experiments where users of different identities would swap Grindr profiles (Wong, 2017). In one video, an Asian man and a white man swapped profiles. The Asian man was shocked at the number of messages he received when using the white man's profile; in comparison, the white man was frustrated with the lack of attention he received when using the Asian man's profile (Grindr, 2018b). Jadyn and Charlie talked about this video to highlight how Asian MSM are perceived as less sexually desirable than white MSM.

MSM dating app users ignore racialized MSM when they intend to be covert with their racism. And MSM rationalize their disinterest in racialized MSM by saying that they are only attracted to certain "types" of people. This is a speech act (Butler, 2006) that designates race as a "type" to politely reject racialized MSM (C. S. Han, 2007)—a practice often used against Asian MSM (Callander et al., 2012; C. S. Han, 2007). MSM may try to hide their sexual racism by labelling Asian MSM as a "type" and rejecting them using this seemingly vague, yet well understood, speech act. For example, Nicolas (62, gay, male, multiracial) said, "I often get Asian guys connecting with me and I'm just not sexually attracted. So, I tell them right off the bat, 'I love your culture, you're beautiful, but it just can't work for me sexually.'" To that point, Ang said that MSM would often use coded language to reject him on dating apps: "I get the gentle let down like, 'Oh, you're cute, but you're not my type,' which is a polite way of saying, 'no Asians,' in my opinion." MSM may use speech acts to excuse their sexual racism and claim that sexual attraction to certain races is inherent and not something they can influence or control. This is a common argument used to defend sexual racism, as many scholars and activists have noted (Callander et al., 2012; Collins, 2004; Matheson, 2012; Robinson, 2015).

Participants talked about the racist practices built into the design of MSM dating apps. They said that affordances like filtering and blocking make it easy for MSM to select who they wanted to include and exclude from their dating app experience. Luis (43, gay, male, Hispanic) said that the ability to block other users encouraged MSM to be picky about who they want to see and interact with:

> If we don't like the pics of somebody else, we could go for someone who is smooth, someone who is blond, who has blue eyes, a Latino, a Black person—hoping he has a dick of big size—so we're fantasizing because we have a menu. We don't like somebody? Next! We don't like him? Block him, even better!

Toby said that users can filter and block racialized MSM on dating apps to "white-wash the gay community." Specifically, the now-unavailable ethnicity filter (Garel, 2020; Hern, 2020) allowed MSM to whitewash the space (Robinson, 2015). This was an easy and effective way to remove racialized MSM from the app space. Moreover, since filters are invisible to other users, they allow MSM to act freely, without fear of being judged or labelled as racist. This means that using filters to remove racialized MSM from the app both rewards and encourages racist behaviours (Robinson, 2015). App affordances like filtering and blocking offer indirect and non-confrontational ways for MSM to engage in racist practices on dating apps.

Participants emphasized that app affordances can also protect people who are racist. Ang explained:

> There's no real consequence on an app if you overtly or covertly discriminate against certain ethnicities. The consequence is perhaps that the profile is banned. But then you can easily open another email account and put the same thing on Grindr. On paper, there is a policy that no discrimination is allowed, but whether or not that is enforced and how it is enforced, it's haphazardly done.

Dion agreed: "There's no justice being made, right? They can insult you and then they can disappear. This level of protection by being on Grindr, or online in general, that makes it easier for bullies or for rapists to operate."

Despite this, some racialized participants talked about using app affordances as a tool to protect themselves against discriminatory and racist behaviour. Dion said that he would block MSM if they were "rude, insisting, harassing, or racist." Similarly, Diego (35, gay, male, Hispanic) said, "I had to block a couple people because they started attacking me." Toby emphasized that "people who feel marginalized or scared can easily block people—you can block people if you feel unsafe." In this sense, app affordances can help keep racialized MSM safe on dating apps.

Guobadia (2020) and Okundaye (2020a), who are both Black gay male writers, emphasized that removing the ethnicity filter was detrimental to racialized MSM's experiences since they can no longer filter out white MSM and create a space with only racialized MSM. Other writers like Bloodworth (2020), a white gay man, and Leon (2020), a racialized gay man, similarly explained that removing the ethnicity filter was a complex issue for many racialized MSM. App affordances like filtering and blocking are technological tools that MSM can use to facilitate sexual racism—but they are also tools that MSM can use fight back against sexual racism. This means that MSM can use app affordances to harm others or protect themselves from harm. Technological tools are not inherently good or bad, but they can be used for good and/or bad, depending on the people and their practices.

RACIAL FETISHIZATION

Although some MSM want to remove racialized MSM from dating apps, other MSM seek them out specifically because of their race. Jadyn said he felt "uncomfortable" when he received comments like "I'm really into Black guys," "I'm sure you have a ginormous Black cock," and "You look like you'd be a great rapist." Diego said that "it's dehumanization" when MSM made assumptions about him based on his profile. Skyler spoke about a friend's experiences as a racialized MSM and said that being fetishized is worse than receiving unwanted sexual images:

> I have one Black friend who gets fetishizing messages about his race that are unwelcome and would cross a line of being not consensual. It's probably worse than unsolicited dick pics in some way because it's more about the person who is on the receiving end.… Receiving a comment directly about me as opposed to receiving someone else's image is probably going to be more invasive.

Charlie asserted that "being fetishized is a form of assault." Theo agreed that racialized MSM may experience racial fetishization as non-consensual: "I think a lot of them feel like there was a breach of consent because a lot of them say that they didn't ask for it."

Ravi talked about when white MSM fetishized his identity: "They fantasize about the Middle Eastern men topping[3] them in bed. That is a completely uncomfortable situation for me. I'm not your fantasy." Ravi also expressed frustration with words like *exotic* that white MSM would use when trying to seduce and complement him via messages on dating apps: "The word exotic is *so* annoying. Exotic is a pineapple. It's a fruit. It's not a human being" (emphasis his own).

The word *exotic* is one example of how white people fetishize racialized bodies. White MSM may intend to complement racialized MSM, but racialized MSM experience it as uncomfortable because this language objectifies them and advances the sexual desires of white MSM (Robinson, 2015; Wilson et al., 2009). When white MSM fetishize racialize MSM, they dehumanize them and reduce them to sexual objects that exist solely for their pleasure (Robinson, 2015).

Racialized MSM also experience stereotyping, as was the case for Ravi when white MSM assumed he was a top. This is referred to as race-based sexual stereotyping because it reduces a person's racial identity to that of a sexual position (Wilson et al., 2009). Race-based sexual stereotypes reflect historical ideologies and assumptions about racialized people, including in relation to sex roles and sexual behaviours (Robinson, 2018; Wilson et al., 2009). This means that racialized MSM are constructed as sexual objects within a hierarchy of power where racialized MSM are submitted to the sexual desires of dominant MSM. Race-based sexual stereotyping allows MSM, especially white MSM, to engage with racialized MSM in ways they can control. Thus, racialized MSM may only be viewed as desirable in specific sexual situations, as was the case for Ravi with the person's fantasy of being topped by a Middle Eastern man.

Black MSM experience racial fetishization and race-based sexual stereotyping centred around hypermasculinity. Jadyn, for example, was fetishized because of rape fantasies and the assumption that he had a big penis, both of which are common fetishizations of Black MSM (Collins, 2004; Wilson et al., 2009). These fetishizations come from white men's construction of Black men as animalistic and savage—who can only be tamed under white men's discipline and control, and who "had achieved partial domestication through slavery" (Collins, 2004, p. 56). The fetishization of Black men is fraught with a history of violence (Okundaye, 2020b), and as Robinson (2015) explains, referencing hooks (1992) and Owens (2004), reducing a person's race to a fetish erases the historical and political meanings embedded within their racial identity. Racial fetishization draws from race-based sexual stereotypes (Collins, 2004; Wilson et al., 2009) and allows white MSM to make racialized MSM's race more consumable (Robinson, 2015), thereby degrading racialized MSM to sexual objects that exist solely for the pleasure of white MSM. Dating apps are complicit in facilitating MSM's racial fetishes as they offer affordances like filters that allow users to seek out and select people according to their race. Furthermore, dating app companies profit from these features, often hiding premium filters—like the ethnicity filter—behind a paywall (Hern, 2020).

Racialized MSM experience racial fetishization and sexual racism differently. Ravi's experience as a Middle Eastern MSM was different from Jadyn's experience as a Black MSM—and both of their experiences were different from Ang's experience as an Asian MSM. To understand and address racial fetishization and sexual racism, it is important to take an intersectional approach (Crenshaw, 1989) and consider how people are treated differently because of their identities, including differences within the same identity category, such as race.

EXPLOITATION

Jadyn talked about the difference in power that white MSM have compared to racialized MSM and explained how power differentials could factor into MSM dating app users' negotiations of sexual consent:

> For example, the white-privileged male—so, blonde hair, blue eyes—they know they have the advantage over you because less people want to sleep with the Black male, or less people want to sleep with the Asian guy. The white-privileged male can message any number of people and get far more responses than the Asian guy, who knows he's not going to get as many responses. He knows that in messaging the Asian guy there's a power dynamic there, where he is the one that has the advantage, and essentially, whatever he wants, whatever he says, whatever he does will fly more because, well, the person without the advantage kind of has to take whatever's biting at him. Like, lucky him, he's the one who's getting the attention, so he gives into it. And even if he recognizes it, he bites his tongue because, at the end of the day, he needs to get his rocks off too.

Ang also spoke about how white MSM can abuse their power when negotiating consent and engaging in sexual activities with racialized MSM:

> There's a very clearly defined hierarchy of power/preference, at least in gay culture. There's a high preference for cisgender white men and the lighter your skin color, or the more likely you are to pass as white, the more power you've got and the more attractive you're seen. And the more you can get away with things. So, if you do something that is non-consensual, you could get away with it.

To that point, Jadyn discussed situations in which he engaged in non-consensual sexual experiences with white MSM on dating apps:

> In the past, if someone was interested in me, I was like, "Wow, you're interested in *me?*" And that comes to self-esteem issues in regard to race and ending up in a situation like, "Well, this person is interested in me and, since they're interested in me, I'm going to go and do whatever it is they want me to do even if I don't want to." In that sense, it's not really consent, because it's highly influenced and manipulated. (emphasis his own)

Jadyn also emphasized the sexual health risks that racialized MSM could experience in such situations: "We see it all the time in regard to barebacking,[4] a lot of guys will forgo a condom if someone that is considered hotter than them asks them not to use a condom. They'll be like, 'Okay, yes, I'll do it because otherwise I'm never going to get anyone.'"

MSM—and white MSM specifically—can exploit racialized MSM when negotiating sexual consent. MSM who have identities that are desirable and carry power and privileges in gay male culture (e.g., white, fit/athletic, nondisabled, cisgender, masculine, young) can leverage those identities to their advantage by manipulating MSM who have marginalized, minority, and/or non-dominant identities. In these situations, racialized MSM may condone or ignore the manipulation because they want to have a sexual interaction. Moreover, as participants explained, some racialized MSM may feel lucky when white MSM approach them, and, as a result, they may engage in sexual activities that they might not normally engage in. This is not to suggest that racialized MSM are easily manipulated, desperate, or powerless. Rather, these findings suggest that white MSM and other MSM with privileged identities may exploit racialized MSM and marginalized MSM to get them to engage in non-consensual sexual activities. White MSM need to pay attention to power differentials when interacting with racialized MSM to ensure that the sexual activities they engage in are safe and consensual.

CONCLUSION

This chapter has examined the sexual racism, racial fetishization, and exploitation that racialized MSM experience through their use of dating apps. The qualitative nature of this study provides rich details about individual MSM's experiences, though findings may not be generalizable. The limited number of racialized MSM who participated in the study might mean that some important aspects of racialized MSM's experiences are absent from this chapter. Moreover, since this study is one of a limited number of research projects that explores the intersections of sexual violence, race, and online technologies, more work is needed to understand the various forms of harm that racialized MSM experience through their use of dating apps.

In the past few years, Grindr has launched campaigns such as "What the Flip" (Wong, 2017) and "Kindr Grindr" in an attempt to tackle "racism, bullying, or other forms of toxic behavior" (Grindr, 2018a). Grindr has also made changes to its software to address discrimination and racism on its platform, as was evident with the removal of the ethnicity filter following the 2020 BLM protests (Garel, 2020). While the effectiveness of these efforts is debatable (Mowlabocus, 2020), they raise questions about the roles and responsibilities of dating app companies in supporting users' safety and well-being and addressing harm and violence that can come from using their platforms. As another example, MSM and other people report experiencing sexual violence through dating apps (Albury et al., 2021; Dietzel, 2021), and companies have responded by adding safety mechanisms to their apps (Siegel, 2020), providing information about consent and sexual violence on their websites (Grindr, n.d.; Tinder, n.d.a), and—in the case of Tinder—launching a series of consent-related frequently asked questions and a short film (Tinder, n.d.b). The role and responsibility of dating app companies was also debated during the early months of the COVID-19 pandemic, as companies responded to COVID concerns by sharing public health guidelines and publicizing anti-transmission techniques that aimed to promote users' health and safety (Myles et al., 2021).

In closing, I encourage the reader to think about people's responsibilities to their sexual partners and their communities, as well as technology's potential as a tool that can hurt or help, depending on how it is used. It is critically important that we reflect upon the ways in which everyday technologies like dating apps (and their affordances) can address harm and violence while also promoting safety and well-being, especially for racialized people.

ACKNOWLEDGEMENTS

This research was supported by the Fonds de Recherche du Québec—Société et Culture (FRQSC) Grant 2019-B2Z-259244. This research was also supported by iMPACTS: Collaborations to Address Sexual Violence on Campus; Social Sciences and Humanities Research Council of Canada (SSHRC) Partnership Grant 895-2016-1026 (Project Director, Shaheen Shariff, PhD, James McGill Professor, McGill University).

QUESTIONS FOR DISCUSSION

1. How are racialized people and marginalized people "othered" on dating apps? What examples can you think of that were not mentioned in this chapter?
2. What are some affordances that dating app companies could add to their platforms to protect their users, especially racialized and marginalized users? How would you ensure those affordances are not abused?
3. To what extent are dating app companies responsible for the harm and violence that their users experience? To what extent are individual users responsible?

INVITATIONS TO GO DEEPER

1. MSM occupy a unique positionality. They are marginalized as sexual minorities in a heteronormative society but are privileged as men in a patriarchal society. What other populations experience a similar tension between marginalization and privilege because of their intersectional identities? How do the tensions between people's intersectional identities factor into their experiences dating online and in person?
2. Communicating, negotiating, and enacting consent are important steps that people take to minimize the potential for sexual violence. As shown in this chapter, however, consent practices can be complicated because of differences in power related to people's identities. How could you integrate your understanding of issues discussed in this chapter into your own consent practices? What can you do to address sexual racism, racial fetishization, and exploitation?
3. Dating apps are spaces where users connect, chat, build relationships, and arrange hookups. In this sense, dating apps function like bars or clubs: people rely on these spaces to meet others, engage in social interactions, and search for potential partners. On dating apps and in person, we filter out people we are not interested in. Are certain practices allowed on dating apps that are not allowed in person? What makes certain app-based practices acceptable if similar in-person practices are unacceptable? How do we, as a society, determine what is acceptable online and in person?

READ MORE

Brathwaite, L. F. (2020, August 21). Why dating apps are racist AF—With or without ethnicity filters. *Rolling Stone*. https://www.rollingstone.com/culture/culture-features/dating-apps-grindr-ethnicity-filters-1047047/

Brown, A. (2018, January 9). "Least desirable"? How racial discrimination plays out in online dating. *NPR*. https://www.npr.org/2018/01/09/575352051/least-desirable-how-racial-discrimination-plays-out-in-online-dating

Coaston, J. (2019, May 28). The intersectionality wars. *Vox*. https://www.vox.com/the-highlight/2019/5/20/18542843/intersectionality-conservatism-law-race-gender-discrimination

Conner, C. T. (2021, August 12). How gay men justify their racism on Grindr. *The Conversation*. https://theconversation.com/how-gay-men-justify-their-racism-on-grindr-164208

Klein, A., & Flicker, S. S. (2020, May). Anti-racism resources [public Google Doc]. http://bit.ly/ANTIRACISMRESOURCES

Rudder, C. (2009, October 5). How your race affects the messages you get. *OkCupid Trends*. https://web.archive.org/web/20100821055448/http://blog.okcupid.com/index.php/your-race-affects-whether-people-write-you-back/

LISTEN MORE, WATCH MORE

"Does race affect your dating life?" *MTV Decoded*: https://www.youtube.com/watch?v=reuxx06KgMw&ab_channel=MTVImpact

"How does race impact dating and relationships?" *Coffee Meets Bagel Podcast*: https://coffeemeetsbagel.com/blog/blog/save-the-date-18-how-does-race-impact-dating-and-relationships-damona-hoffman/

"Racism in gay dating?!?" *MTV Decoded*: https://www.youtube.com/watch?v=wTyDGiFZk98&ab_channel=MTVImpact

"The weird history of Asian sex stereotypes," *MTV Decoded*: https://www.youtube.com/watch?v=HS2jGfW5aOE&ab_channel=MTVImpact

NOTES

1. The word *femme* is used in queer culture to refer to people who present more traditionally feminine traits. For MSM, this term can also refer to individuals who do not conform to traditional notions of masculinity.

2. The phrase "No fats, femmes, or Asians" is infamous in MSM dating app culture and is often referenced in gay male culture. For example, this phrase has been printed on shirts for commercial sale (Flores, 2016). Drag queen Kim Chi performed a song satirically referencing this phrase for the season 8 finale of *RuPaul's Drag Race* (Logo, 2016). There are also academic publications that have included a version of this phrase in their title (C. S. Han, 2008; Smith & Amaro, 2021).

3. MSM use the word *top* as a noun (e.g., he is a top) and a verb (e.g., he was topping him) to refer to the inserting partner during anal sex. The word *bottom* is similarly used to refer to the receiving partner during anal sex.

4. MSM use the word *barebacking* to refer to having anal sex without a condom.

REFERENCES

Albury, K., Byron, P., McCosker, A., Pym, T., Walshe, J., Race, K., Salon, D., Reeders, D., Wark, T., Botfield, J., & Dietzel, C. (2019). *Safety, risk and wellbeing on dating apps: Final report*. Swinburne University of Technology. https://apo.org.au/node/268156

Albury, K., Dietzel, C., Pym, T., Vivienne, S., & Cook, T. (2021). Not your unicorn: Trans dating app users' negotiations of personal safety and sexual health. *Health Sociology Review, 30*(1), 72–86.

Birnholtz, J., Fitzpatrick, C., Handel, M., & Brubaker, J. R. (2014, September). Identity, identification and identifiability: The language of self-presentation on a location-based mobile dating app. In *MobileHCI '14: Proceedings of the 16th international conference on human–computer interaction with mobile devices and services* (pp. 3–12). Association for Computing Machinery.

Blackwell, C., Birnholtz, J., & Abbott, C. (2015). Seeing and being seen: Co-situation and impression formation using Grindr, a location-aware gay dating app. *New Media & Society, 17*(7), 1117–1136.

Bloodworth, A. (2020, June 3). Why Grindr removing its ethnicity filter is a complex issue. *HuffPost UK*. https://www.huffingtonpost.co.uk/entry/grindr-remove-ethnicity-filter-grindr-dating-app_uk_5ed62d14c5b651b2b317bb4d

Braun, V., & Clarke, V. (2006). Using thematic analysis in psychology. *Qualitative Research in Psychology, 3*(2), 77–101.

Butler, J. (2006). *Gender trouble: Feminism and the subversion of identity*. New York: Routledge.

Callander, D., Holt, M., & Newman, C. E. (2012). Just a preference: Racialised language in the sex-seeking profiles of gay and bisexual men. *Culture, Health & Sexuality, 14*(9), 1049–1063.

Callander, D., Holt, M., & Newman, C. E. (2016). "Not everyone's gonna like me": Accounting for race and racism in sex and dating web services for gay and bisexual men. *Ethnicities, 16*(1), 3–21.

Callander, D., Newman, C. E., & Holt, M. (2015). Is sexual racism really racism? Distinguishing attitudes toward sexual racism and generic racism among gay and bisexual men. *Archives of Sexual Behavior, 44*(7), 1991–2000.

Caluya, G. (2006). The (gay) scene of racism: Face, shame and gay Asian males. *Australian Critical Race and Whiteness Studies Association e-Journal, 2*(2), 1–14.

Chae, D. H., & Yoshikawa, H. (2008). Perceived group devaluation, depression, and HIV-risk behavior among Asian gay men. *Health Psychology, 27*(2), 140–148.

Collins, P. H. (2004). *Black sexual politics: African Americans, gender, and the new racism.* Routledge.

Conner, C. T. (2018). The gay gayze: Expressions of inequality on Grindr. *The Sociological Quarterly, 60*(3), 397–419.

Crenshaw, K. (1989). Demarginalizing the intersection of race and sex: Black feminist critique of antidiscrimination doctrine, feminist theory and antiracist politics. *University of Chicago Legal Forum, 1989*(1), 139–168.

Dietzel, C. (2021). "That's straight-up rape culture": Manifestations of rape culture on Grindr. In J. Bailey, A. Flynn, & N. Henry (Eds.), *The Emerald international handbook of technology-facilitated violence and abuse* (pp. 351–368). Emerald.

Flores, B. (2016, April 28). This "no fats, no fems" shirt is everything that's wrong with the gay community. *Pride.* https://www.pride.com/firstperson/2016/4/28/no-fats-no-fems-shirt-everything-thats-wrong-gay-community

Gabriel, J. (2002). *Whitewash: Racialized politics and the media.* London: Routledge.

Garel, C. (2020, June 5). Grindr, Scruff removed ethnicity filters in its gay dating apps. The racists stayed. *HuffPost Canada.* https://www.huffingtonpost.ca/entry/grindr-ethnicity-gay-dating-apps_ca_5eda7ccdc5b695fc9e8f9e02

Goldberg, G. (2020). Meet markets: Grindr and the politics of objectifying others. *Convergence, 26*(2), 253–268.

Grindr. (n.d.). Consent. https://help.grindr.com/hc/en-us/articles/360008783953-What-is-consent-

Grindr. (2018a). Kindr: Kindness is our preference. https://www.kindr.grindr.com/

Grindr. (2018b, May 23). *A white and Asian user switch Grindr profiles | What the flip* [Video]. YouTube. https://www.youtube.com/watch?v=WjPfRJ6ZCRk&ab_channel=Grindr

Grov, C., Breslow, A. S., Newcomb, M. E., Rosenberger, J. G., & Bauermeister, J. A. (2014). Gay and bisexual men's use of the internet: Research from the 1990s through 2013. *The Journal of Sex Research, 51*(4), 390–409.

Guobadia, O. (2020, July 2). Gay communities are rife with racism. Removing Grindr's ethnicity filters won't fix that. *British GQ.* https://www.gq-magazine.co.uk/lifestyle/article/grindr-racism

Han, A. (2006). I think you're the smartest race I've ever met: Racialised economies of queer male desire. *Australian Critical Race and Whiteness Studies Association e-Journal, 2*(2), 1–14. https://espace.library.uq.edu.au/view/UQ:229149

Han, C. S. (2007). They don't want to cruise your type: Gay men of color and the racial politics of exclusion. *Social Identities*, *13*(1), 51–67.

Han, C. S. (2008). No fats, femmes, or Asians: The utility of critical race theory in examining the role of gay stock stories in the marginalization of gay Asian men. *Contemporary Justice Review*, *11*(1), 11–22.

Han, C. S., & Choi, K. H. (2018). Very few people say "no whites": Gay men of color and the racial politics of desire. *Sociological Spectrum*, *38*(3), 145–161.

Hern, A. (2020, June 2). Grindr dating app removes ethnicity filter to support Black Lives Matter. *The Guardian*. https://www.theguardian.com/technology/2020/jun/02/grindr-dating-app-removes-ethnicity-filter-to-support-black-lives-matter

Knegt, P. (2020, July 9). Gay culture has grown toxic with unchecked privilege. It's time for us to reset. *CBC News*. https://www.cbc.ca/arts/gay-culture-has-grown-toxic-with-unchecked-privilege-it-s-time-for-us-to-reset-1.5639251

Leon, A. [@alexand_erleon]. (2020, June 2). Seen a lot of discussion about this, so curious to hear from the timeline. QPOC who use Grindr—do [Tweet]. Twitter. https://twitter.com/alexand_erleon/status/1267722018503438336

Lim, G., Robards, B., & Carlson, B. (2020, June 7). Grindr is deleting its "ethnicity filter." But racism is still rife in online dating. *The Conversation*. https://theconversation.com/grindr-is-deleting-its-ethnicity-filter-but-racism-is-still-rife-in-online-dating-140077

Logo. (2016, May 19). *RuPaul's Drag Race (Season 8 finale) | Kim Chi's "fat, fem & Asian" performance | Logo* [Video]. YouTube. https://www.youtube.com/watch?v=mU5ns8wGiGM&ab_channel=Logo

Matheson, J. (2012, December 14). I'm a sexual racist. *Star Observer*. http://www.starobserver.com.au/opinion/soapbox-opinion/im-a-sexual-racist/91678

Mowlabocus, S. (2020). A kindr Grindr: Moderating race(ism) in techno-spaces of desire. In R. Ramos & S. Mowlabocus (Eds.), *Queer sites in global contexts* (pp. 33–47). Routledge.

Myles, D., Duguay, S., & Dietzel, C. (2021). #DatingWhileDistancing: Dating apps as digital health technologies during the COVID-19 pandemic. In D. Lupton & K. Willis (Eds.), *The COVID-19 crisis: Social perspectives* (pp. 79–89). Routledge.

Okundaye, J. [@jasebyjason]. (2020a, June 1). I don't know how I feel about this to be honest [Tweet]. Twitter. https://twitter.com/jasebyjason/status/1267513944748457984

Okundaye, J. (2020b, October 13). The fetishization of Black masculinity. *British GQ*. https://www.gq-magazine.co.uk/lifestyle/article/fetishisation-black-masculinity

Raj, S. (2011). Grindring bodies: Racial and affective economies of online queer desire. *Critical Race and Whiteness Studies*, *7*(2), 1–12.

Robinson, B. A. (2015). "Personal preference" as the new racism: Gay desire and racial cleansing in cyberspace. *Sociology of Race & Ethnicity, 1*(2), 317–330.

Robinson, B. A. (2016). The quantifiable-body discourse: "Height–weight proportionality" and gay men's bodies in cyberspace. *Social Currents, 3*(2), 172–185.

Robinson, B. A. (2018). Doing sexual responsibility: HIV, risk discourses, trust, and gay men interacting online. *Sociological Perspectives, 61*(3), 383–398.

Rodriguez, M. (2018, March 19). Are men of color blocked solely for their race on Grindr? *Into.* https://www.intomore.com/you/are-men-of-color-blocked-solely-for-their-race-on-grindr/

Sengupta, J. (2020, June 28). In a time of protest, Black LGBTQ voices rise. *CBC News.* https://www.cbc.ca/news/canada/all-black-lives-matter-black-lgbtq-voices-1.5627988

Siegel, R. (2020, January 23). You swiped right but it doesn't feel right: Tinder now has a panic button. *The Washington Post.* https://www.washingtonpost.com/technology/2020/01/23/tinder-panic-button/

Smith, J. G., & Amaro, G. (2021). "No fats, no femmes, and no Blacks or Asians": The role of body-type, sex position, and race on condom use online. *AIDS and Behavior, 25*(7), 2166–2176.

Stacey, L., & Forbes, T. D. (2021). Feeling like a fetish: Racialized feelings, fetishization, and the contours of sexual racism on gay dating apps. *The Journal of Sex Research.* Advance online publication. https://doi.org/10.1080/00224499.2021.1979455

Teunis, N. (2007). Sexual objectification and the construction of whiteness in the gay male community. *Culture, Health & Sexuality, 9*(3), 263–275.

Tinder. (n.d.a). Dating safety tips. https://policies.tinder.com/safety/intl/en

Tinder. (n.d.b). Let's talk consent. https://www.letstalkconsent.com/

Van de Wiele, C., & Tong, S. T. (2014). Breaking boundaries: The uses & gratifications of Grindr. In *UbiComp '14: Proceedings of the 2014 ACM international joint conference on pervasive and ubiquitous computing* (pp. 619–630). Association for Computing Machinery.

Wakabayashi, S. (2020, February 25). 3 ways to make queer dating apps less racist & more welcoming. *LGBTQ Nation.* https://www.lgbtqnation.com/2020/02/3-ways-make-queer-dating-apps-less-racist-welcoming/

Walcott, R. (2017, June 28). Black Lives Matter, police and Pride: Toronto activists spark a movement. *The Conversation.* https://theconversation.com/black-lives-matter-police-and-pride-toronto-activists-spark-a-movement-79089

Walters, M. L., Chen J., & Breiding, M.J. (2013). *The national intimate partner and sexual violence survey (NISVS): 2010 findings on victimization by sexual orientation.* National Center for Injury Prevention and Control, Centers for Disease Control and Prevention.

Wilson, P. A., Valera, P., Ventuneac, A., Balan, I., Rowe, M., & Carballo-Diéguez, A. (2009). Race-based sexual stereotyping and sexual partnering among men who use the internet to identify other men for bareback sex. *Journal of Sex Research*, *46*(5), 399–413.

Wong, C. M. (2017, September 17). Watch what happened when these two men swapped Grindr profiles. *HuffPost Canada*. https://www.huffingtonpost.ca/entry/grindr-profile-swap-what-the-flip_n_59bd352de4b0edff971c810c?ri18n=true

Smartphones and Committed Relationships: Navigating the Intersection of Sex, Gender, and Other Social Variables

Noorin Manji

SMARTPHONES IN OUR MODERN WORLD—INTRODUCTION

By 2019, more than 80% of Canadians were smartphone users, and by 2024, it is projected that approximately 33 million Canadians will fall into this category (O'Dea, 2020). Worldwide, the numbers are even more staggering, with over five billion mobile device users (Silver, 2019). On a global scale, the number of smartphone users has increased by over 350 percent in the last decade or so (O'Dea, 2021), and smartphone devices could arguably be regarded as the fastest-growing form of personal communication technology in human history.

In every way imaginable, the swift and widespread integration of smartphones into modern societies has marked a clear paradigm shift, since the devices seem to have transformed every aspect of the way our world works. Rainie and Wellman (2012) have dubbed this shift the "Mobile Revolution," in which individuals are empowered through "always-on" connectivity. Rainie and Wellman (2012) prompt us to consider the notion that unlike earlier eras, during which people formed connections with others via the social groups they were a part of, people now operate as "networked individuals," like nodes tied to large, diverse, sparsely knit webs of other individuals with their own unique networks. From the ways that we deliver health care and education, to the ways that we practise business and commerce, and especially to the ways that we form and maintain human relationships, smartphones have reframed every single human activity. The impact of smartphones has been even more extensive during the COVID-19 pandemic, which brought about a further increased reliance on mobile technology.

Knowing that smartphone technology has impacted the way people interact with each other, we must consider these impacts in the context of, perhaps, the most important types of human relationships—those that people form by choice through their romantic involvements. The pursuit of love relationships is deeply emphasized as a life goal in cultures and societies the world over. In fact, as Swidler (2001) points out, "although love is a quintessentially personal, private experience, love is just as profoundly social and cultural. Love is a central theme of our popular culture … and unlike many of the political and social attitudes sociologists normally study, love really matters to most ordinary" people (p. 2). The significance of these human bonds, in combination with the growing integration of smartphone technology into our daily lives, has created the intellectual necessity for us to consider the intersection of these modern communication devices and the committed romantic relationships in which people use them.

To guide our discussion, consider the interplay between these two questions:[1]

1. To what extent are people's relationships with each other affected by smartphone technology?
2. To what extent are people's relationships with smartphone technology affected by each other?

Together, these two lines of inquiry compel us to consider, first, the ways in which people have integrated smartphone devices into types of relationships that long predated the technology itself, and second, the fact that people have more than just a passive experience using and engaging with their smartphones. Instead, these questions indicate that, perhaps, people's relationships with smartphone technology are just as significant and impactful on their everyday experiences as are their relationships with other people.

Moving forward, we can anchor our discussion in a few key objectives. First, we will take a moment to acknowledge the role of the researcher, especially in motivating this study. Second, our goal is to briefly explore themes that have emerged in the relevant academic literature on the use of smartphone technology in human relationships. Third, on a methodological level, we want to understand how sex and gender play a role in social research, generally. Fourth, we will aim to make sense of some primary data that speak directly to the intersection of smartphone use in committed heterosexual, pair-bonded relationships. Fifth, and finally, we will strive to identify gaps that currently exist in this subfield of research and to propose possible paths for further intersectional work in this area.

ROLE OF THE RESEARCHER

In the coming years, as you engage more with research in the social sciences, you will come to recognize the importance of the researcher, themselves, as an instrument in the process (Denzin & Lincoln, 2003). Reflexivity, or the ability to examine one's own biases, beliefs, and approaches as a researcher, is an important and necessary part of any study. My interest in modern mobile technology stems not from the technical aspects of how the devices work, operate, or function; rather, it stems from the experiences I have had as a mobile technology user, as I have seen my interactions and relationships with others change, while bearing simultaneous witness to paradigmatic shifts that have occurred in the evolution of the technology. This observation essentially represents the crux of my study, as I explore the impacts that smartphones have had on human relationships.

Though I am not oblivious to the many ways modern technology has negatively impacted social life, overall, I am what could be called a "technology advocate." I am forever amazed and regularly marvel at what seems like a never-ending process of change and progress in the world of technology. If the devices we use do not already improve our lives, it is my hope that my research will be part of a body of academic work that will help people better navigate the use of technology so that it does. In talking with others about my research, including those who have participated in the study and others, it is clear to me that my deep fascination with mobile technology is not unique. In a general sense, people are interested in exploring and understanding the role of smartphones in society, as they, like I, have come to see just how impactful these devices have become in our everyday lives.

A BRIEF CONSIDERATION OF THE EXISTING LITERATURE

Romantic relationships and smartphones are amply represented in their respective substantive subfields of literature, and this reflects the wide variety and types of research that have been conducted in exploring them, both independently and through an intersectional framework. While applying an intersectional lens to the examination of existing research, I will focus on four key themes. The following review of the literature is by no means exhaustive. My goal is to provide just a taste of some of the most interesting overarching trends that will help to orient you through the later discussion. The themes to be explored from the literature include, first, a discussion of some unique abilities that smartphones afford people in navigating their daily relationship interactions; second, an investigation of age and gendered patterns that researchers have found while studying people's smartphone use; third, an intersectional consideration of how gender and culture, together, play a role in how smartphone technology is incorporated into people's lives; and fourth, a discussion of the blurred boundaries that have resulted from the integration of smartphones into people's heterosexual romantic relationships.

From the broadest perspective, data show that modern mobile devices challenge traditional notions of intimate relationships, particularly by way of reducing feelings of fear when starting one, and especially when attempting to start one (Khunou, 2012, p. 169). Cross-disciplinary research indicates that smartphones are "very important as a means of communicating, and that satisfaction with cell phone usage and the relationship are strongly and positively correlated" (Miller-Ott et al., 2012, p. 17). The ways in which people use their smartphones to navigate communication in their relationships not only impacts how people feel about the technology but also how they feel about the relationship itself, indicating that the quality of their experience with one of these two elements necessarily relates to the quality of their experience with the other.

An interesting subset of research in this area deals specifically with the sending and receiving of sexually suggestive images, videos, or texts on smartphones, also known as sexting (Weisskirch, 2012; Weisskirch & Delevi, 2011). Earlier literature focuses strongly on adult attachment theory, which indicates that the attachment one forms with a romantic partner is predicated on the attachment they form to their caregiver in infancy (Weisskirch & Delevi, 2011, p. 1697). Based on this framework, connections are apparent between attachment anxiety and the practice of sending and receiving, as well as the acceptance of, sexts (Weisskirch & Delevi, 2011). Social-psychological studies in this area have found a notable correlation between attachment avoidance and attitudes about sexting (Manuel, 2012, p. 38), and complementary research findings even extend beyond sexting to show that people with attachment anxiety tend to send and receive more text messages to and from their romantic partners, in general (Weisskirch, 2012, p. 281). This tells us that, as individuals enter romantic relationships, they bring with them constructed meanings based on their previous experiences, which then impact their new relationship interactions, even in terms of technology use. As I will later highlight, many participants discussed their personal feelings on the patterns of communication that are characteristic of their respective relationships, and many of them alluded to the impact of their personal histories on these experiences.

A second relevant area of the literature deals with demographic patterns of smartphone use, as well as the intersection of multiple demographic variables including age and gender. For example, interpersonal relationship theories indicate that smartphones can affect social networks among young people, especially those between 13 and 30 years of age, who often have extensive but low-quality friendships (Igarashi et al., 2005, p. 694). Research shows that use of mobile devices may facilitate improvement in the quality of these relationships, and it is evident that smartphones have become a significant tool for enacting these age-based patterns (p. 694). Extending this discussion to gender, studies indicate that intimacy of those "who communicate via both face-to-face and mobile phone text message was rated higher than those who communicate only face-to-face ... and the structure of mobile phone text message social networks coincides with known gender differences in network characteristics. Women tend to expand their mobile phone text message social networks more than men" (p. 691).

Other studies introduce culture as a variable to consider in smartphone use, particularly in combination with gender (Green & Singleton, 2009; Van Cleemput, 2010). Research conducted among young Pakistani British women and men revealed "interesting gendered practices of connectivity and sociability ... and important dimensions of developing peer group identities, including diverse performances of femininities and masculinities" (Green & Singleton, 2009, p. 125). My study builds on these findings in two ways, creating a noteworthy intersection of themes. First, the concept of identity is relevant, as people, in general, seem to regard and use their phones as a clear marker of their own identities. Second, and more specific to the factors of gender and culture (Green & Singleton, 2009), participant data indicate a difference in gendered perspectives on mobile device use in the context of committed romantic relationships and also reveal unique applications of mobile technology use when considering the cultural, religious, and ethnic backgrounds of participants.

Some studies also focus on how individuals use computer-mediated communication (CMC), ranging from social networking sites to smartphones and instant messaging in their cross-gender intimate relationships to navigate around traditional cultural norms (Zaidi et al., 2012). Research in this area has found that CMC is used to "initiate and build relationships, remain connected with partners, engage in discreet communication, to ease uncomfortable and intimate discussions, and to communicate when face-to-face interaction is not available" (p. 175). These insights have a general applicability, but they are especially relevant when considering culturally specific norms that frame both people's relationships and their technology use. Smartphones provide a means of "adhering to norms of gender-separation while covertly engaging in cross-gender relationships ... allowing for maintenance of family honor ... while fulfilling the perceived need for cross-gender friendships and romantic involvements" (p. 175).

A fourth and final theme from the literature is related to the blurring of previously intersecting boundaries that occurs as people integrate smartphone technology into their lives and relationships, and in many ways, the literature already reviewed also inadvertently reveals this blurring trend as a by-product of other data and concepts explored. In looking at smartphones themselves, we can see how the features of the technology result in qualitatively different experiences than people have ever had before, specifically because of earlier boundaries being obscured. For instance, in examining patterns of text messaging in particular, researchers have found that "exchanges frequently lack openings and closures, show an effort towards reciprocation, use implicit or anticipated actions ... and that social presence seems characterized by a sense of constant availability, symmetric commitment and shared understanding" (Spagnolli & Gamberini, 2007, p. 343).

It seems that the rapidly increasing use of smartphones has blurred traditional conceptions of communication in at least three ways: first, there is a diminished distinction between communication with one versus with many; second, there is a loss in the sense of privacy and separation between public and private spheres; and third, there is the ability to extend communication across space and time in new ways (Baym, 2010). The loss in the sense of privacy that has come from the integration of smartphones into everyday life (Baym, 2010) further links to concepts of privacy and surveillance in the data, to be later discussed, like aspects of smartphone use monitoring. However, interestingly, the data collected also provide opposing findings, as for many people whose relationships are anchored in trust, smartphones have become a medium characterized by increasing individuality and privacy.

As mentioned earlier, this review of the literature is not a comprehensive exploration of all available findings at the intersection of smartphone use and human relationships. Rather, in highlighting some of the most interesting and relevant research, it has given us an informed starting point from which we can discuss some of the newly emerging data in this subfield.

A NOTE ON METHODOLOGY AND THE ROLE OF SEX AND GENDER

The findings discussed in this chapter come from a larger qualitative study that involved in-depth semi-structured interviews with 56 smartphone users, comprising 23 heterosexual couples.[2]

The majority of participants (73 percent) were between the ages of 18 and 39, and 82 percent of them had at least an undergraduate education. As well, 93 percent of participants reported using their smartphones upwards of 40 times daily. Table 6.1 summarizes participant demographic information. Data validation was achieved by several means,[3] perhaps the most important of which was the reliance on direct quotes from participant interviews within the analytical discussion, essentially allowing participants to speak for themselves, as you will shortly see.

As researchers, we must always be prepared to defend our methodological decisions to the academic community, as I was asked to do, in the case of this research, by my doctoral dissertation defence committee. So before we delve into our

Table 6.1: Participant Demographics ($n = 56$)

Variable	Demographic Features	n
Sex	Men	28
	Women	28
Age	18–29 years	21
	30–39 years	20
	40–49 years	8
	50–59 years	7
Highest Education Level	High school	4
	College diploma/trade certification	6
	Bachelor's degree	19
	Master's/LLB degree	21
	PhD/MD degree	6
Cultural Background	South Asian (Pakistani, Indian, etc.)	21
	European (Russian, Danish, Italian, French, etc.)	10
	African American	9
	Asian (Chinese, Japanese, Vietnamese, etc.)	9
	Canadian	7
Frequency of Smartphone Use in a Day	< 5 times	1
	6–10 times	1
	11–20 times	0
	21–30 times	2
	31–40 times	0
	41–50 times	10
	51–60 times	9
	61–70 times	27
	71–80 times	3
	80+ times	3

LLB = Bachelor of Law

discussion, we will take a moment to note why heterosexual couples were the focus of this study, particularly in the context of larger ethical considerations of research inclusivity and, of course, in keeping with our intersectional focus on gender and sex, more generally. An entire subfield of academic literature is devoted to clarifying the "challenges and opportunities for research on same-sex relationships" (Umberson et al., 2015, p. 96).

One major barrier is access, since "the small number of people in same-sex relationships [makes] it difficult to recruit substantial numbers of respondents" (Umberson et al., 2015, p. 100). Thus, rather than attempt to include a very limited number of same-sex couples, or perhaps none at all, depending on recruitment limitations, for the purposes of this work, heterosexual couples have been solidly represented, thereby avoiding inadvertent misrepresentations of smartphone experiences in same-sex or other types of relationships.

Furthermore, "social scientists have identified gender as a driving predictor of relationship experiences" (Umberson et al., 2015, p. 100), and so much of the substantive literature also emphasizes gendered patterns in smartphone use. With the knowledge that gender is such an important factor, it was clear, when designing this study, that same-sex couples should not be indiscriminately treated the same as heterosexual couples (Umberson et al., 2015, p. 96). As well, "because of past discrimination, people in same-sex relationships may not trust researchers," and beyond that, "recruiting both partners in same-sex couples is even more challenging" (p. 100). Finally, it must be noted that in our modern world of more fluid gender and sex categories, the line separating heterosexual versus same-sex couples is not as defined as it once was, and in fact, for a research project to truly attempt to be representative of all types of couples, "studies need to include questions about multiple aspects of sexuality in order to capture a fuller range of diversity," including accounting for bisexual, transgender, mixed-orientation, and other types of relationships (p. 100).

No single study can cover the full scope of variables and populations involved, so instead, we as individual social researchers must strive as a collective academic community to build on each other's work and progressively aim to create more inclusive approaches. Moving forward, as young social researchers contemplate their own paths in the world of research, it is not only important, but absolutely imperative to consider how both sex and gender play a part in participant sampling and recruitment. To further this line of thought, also factor in how overall research design, data collection, data analysis, and reporting of findings might all be impacted based on these considerations.

DISCUSSION

For decades, social thinkers have proposed varying frameworks to explore human technology use. According to Marshall McLuhan's classical theory, *The Medium Is the Message*, a medium is defined as "any extension of ourselves"; McLuhan uses simple examples such as a hammer that extends our arm and a wheel that extends our legs, all enabling us to do more than our bodies could do on their own (1967, p. 9). McLuhan emphasizes that "all media work us over completely. They are so pervasive in their personal, political, economic, aesthetic, psychological, moral, ethical, and social consequences that they leave no part of us untouched, unaffected, unaltered" (p. 26)—and is this not the truest statement we could make when considering the intersectionality of smartphones in modern society?

More recently, Katz and Aakhus (2002) have introduced new vernacular with concepts such as *Apparatgeist*, which refers to "the spirit of the machine that influences both the design of the technology and the subsequent significance accorded them by users, non-users, and anti-users" (p. 305). Katz and Aakhus (2002) compel us to see that technology does not determine what we can do; rather, it serves to constrain possibilities. Moving forward, we can build on these ideas by applying an intersectional lens that will enable us to see how the process through which heterosexual couples integrate smartphones into their lives and relationships is multi-faceted. It is not a simple or linear process, and, in fact, it necessitates a consideration of several intersections that people regularly navigate in their daily relationship interactions as they use smartphone technology.

To anchor the upcoming discussion, the following four themes will be explored and supported using direct participant data. First, we will delve into data that reveal some of the specific affordances that smartphones introduce into committed relationships (Ling, 2004), as identified by members of heterosexual pair-bonded couples, themselves. Second, we will consider data that reintroduce cultural intersections into the dynamic of smartphone use in committed relationships. Third, we will revisit the idea of blurred boundaries through an exploration of the concepts of trust, privacy, and surveillance. Finally, we will discuss the concept of fidelity and the ways in which smartphones have affected monogamy as a defining feature of most committed heterosexual relationships. Please note that, just as with the earlier literature review, the upcoming discussion is by no means complete. The true breadth of findings derived from this study is much more complex and detailed;[4] however, our examination of the four selected themes is intended to provide some preliminary intersectional insights into just how impactful smartphones have been on people's relationships and lives.

Smartphone Affordances in Committed Relationships

Smartphone technology has truly revolutionized the day-to-day experiences of couples that use it, affecting everything from how couples begin their relationships to how they build their relationships and express affection, how they use it as a tool to navigate daily tasks and responsibilities like paying bills and coordinating childcare, and how they rely on it as a mechanism to manoeuvre through relationship conflict and diminish physical distance when apart from each other. Couples interviewed for this study even delved into how smartphones themselves open up pathways that introduce new communication challenges and the need for new communication resolutions into their relationships as well. Perhaps the most interesting affordance smartphones have extended to committed couples that use them is by offering them a source of what we can call *relationship memory*, which refers to the ability of smartphones, with their personalized, mobile, and constant nature, to retain a historical record of a relationship from its inception. It is astounding that every text message, every photo, every vacation, every text-based compliment or argument, every social media post, and every shared life event, not to mention every life event in general, is documented for a couple, and people do feel a sense of marvel when reflecting on it:

> The other day, don't even ask me how, I think I was just looking for a photo Anish sent me of someone's address, and I ended up going back through all of our shared photos since we met. It was like thousands of things we had sent to each other over the course of our relationship, it was amazing to see, the good, the bad, even the ugly! (Maya, 28; Partner: Anish, 28)

> Nicholas and I were at the cottage last summer, and we were trying to find this little breakfast place his parents had taken us to the summer before. Country roads are confusing though, and even with directions from his mom, we found ourselves in the middle of nowhere, road and trees in all directions. I don't know how I thought of the idea, but I looked up photos we had taken at the place the year before on my iPhone. When you take pictures on the iPhone, it automatically creates a geolink to where the photo was taken on a map. So, I just looked up the old photo, linked it to the GPS on the phone, and we were there in no time, it was incredible! (Jasmine, 29; Partner: Nicholas, 33)

Smartphones have a way of cataloguing our lives in a way that no other previous technology has done before. The elements of shared history between couples constitute just one aspect, with many deeper levels, to be considered. When widening the scope to bring in the full range of capabilities that smartphones offer, in terms of personalized, individual data and constant connectivity to the internet, the implications are limitless. On a theoretical level, it is interesting to note a few important parallels when applying a traditional social constructionist lens to this data. In the same way that society is a human product that progresses to become an objective reality through legitimation processes, before coming full circle to producing humans as social products through socialization (Berger & Luckmann, 1966), committed relationships are also human products that become objective realities through the legitimation provided by the relationship memory encompassed within people's smartphones. This does not mean that people's relationships would not exist without smartphones and their cataloguing of people's lives; however, based on the data, we can claim that smartphones legitimize the experiences people have with their partners by way of creating a pseudo-institutional memory of those experiences that can be relived through the devices anytime, anywhere, theoretically forever.

Cultural Intersections of Smartphone Use in Committed Relationships

Reinforcing some of the findings in the literature, data derived from this study also support the intersectionality of culture as a factor worthy of consideration when investigating the role of smartphones in people's committed relationships. While the research design did not explicitly intend to delve into cultural, religious, or ethnic demographic categories, the pre-interview survey administered did ask participants to identify their cultural background. Interesting and valuable intersectional data emerged specifically from some participants who identified as Muslim, though it should be noted that because of the limitations of convenience and snowball sampling techniques, extrapolating these findings to any or all people who consider themselves Muslim is likely not a methodologically sound decision, without further investigation.

> So, with our religious beliefs, we aren't really allowed to date in the traditional Western sense of the word. There are many other restrictions I guess you could say around the whole process. And not just restrictions, but almost like a protocol. You know where certain things have to happen in a certain order for everything to be religiously okay, with the families and all that. So at first, when we were just getting to know each other, I swear the phone was

basically the way we fell in love and decided we wanted to marry each other. Talking on the phone, texting, or FaceTiming, all seem like such small things, and for couples that can openly go on dates, they might be. For us though, it was everything. It's just not okay in our culture to go on dates the way Canadian people do, we basically have to already be promised to each other, in our family's eyes before it is okay for us to go out and get to know each other. It isn't quite arranged marriage, but honestly, without having our phones, all of our early interactions would have had to have been in front of a chaperone or whatever. The phone just gave us so much more freedom to actually develop our relationship privately and more genuinely without as much forced input from everyone else. (Layla, 28; Partner: Amil, 31)

This finding further supports Zaidi et al.'s (2012) research, earlier discussed, which found that people use CMC to adhere to cultural norms while participating covertly in cross-gender relationships (p. 175). Clearly, for some cultural, religious, and ethnic groups, modern smartphone technology offers great affordances (Ling, 2004) in terms of controlling relationship connections and communication within the boundaries of their personal beliefs. This finding indicates the extent to which people are now operating as networked individuals (Rainie & Wellman, 2012) and how smartphones have become a tool of that networked individualism, particularly for cultural groups in which emphasis on family and community involvement may be greater than in others.

Trust, Privacy, and Surveillance: Blurred Boundaries

To delve into our third thematic discussion, let us link back to literature we reviewed earlier that highlights the unique ways in which smartphone technology has blurred boundaries that were once hard-set within people's committed relationships. Again, this particular investigation alone has several facets to analyze, as participant data show a wide variety of findings. Smartphones have blurred boundaries for couples in the following ways: first, in terms of shared social media content and networks; second, in terms of the need to draw distinctions between technology-mediated versus face-to-face communication, especially when considering the intersection of globalization as a process; and third, in terms of how the devices enable people to end relationships in unique ways that challenge traditional norms and boundaries of social acceptability through actions like "ghosting"—that is, the total and deliberate closing off of any and all forms of previously open channels of communication, usually multiple in nature, without any warning or explanation, and undeniably directed at an individual person and their device. For our purposes, though, let us explore just one specific dynamic through which we can see how boundaries have been obscured when considering concepts of trust, privacy, and surveillance.

On one hand, some participant data show how smartphones have allowed for more concrete perceptions of privacy in people's committed relationships:

> Things have certainly changed in the way we communicate. We don't even have a home phone anymore, which is sometimes nice because when you send out a call or text it's directly to one person instead of the whole house. You know that no one else is listening in on your call, and that it's just between us two. (Charlotte, 48; Partner: Alexander, 52)

This notion of privacy relates directly to the existence of networked individuals (Rainie & Wellman, 2012) as a reality of our social system. Smartphones have clearly become mechanisms that allow people to both connect to and separate from their social networks, as desired. It is particularly interesting to consider this evidence in comparison to earlier contentions in the literature that claim that contemporary mobile devices, first, have led to a diminishment in the distinction between communication with one versus many, and second, have led to a loss in the sense of privacy (Baym, 2010). These data suggest that, in fact, smartphones have enabled people to more precisely target one-on-one communication with other networked individuals (Rainie & Wellman, 2012) and that this has led to a greater feeling of privacy for many people.

On the other hand, contrasting participant data show how smartphones have eclipsed the boundary between privacy and surveillance. For our purposes, *surveillance* refers to the close observation or scrutiny of an individual's device and/or device use, in this case, by their significant other. Based on the data collected, a broad distinction must be drawn between two forms of surveillance that seem to be tied to structures and processes of power in the committed relationships observed. In some interviews, there was a focus on "open surveillance":

> Yeah, we don't have anything to hide from each other, so if his phone is closer, I'll use it, or listen to his music. Occasionally I'll just do a quick scroll through his messages, see what's up. But I'll do it in front of him, not behind his back. There are times I'll even message my mom or one of my friends from his phone, I'll let them know it's me obviously, but if it's just easier to use his phone for whatever reason, it's no biggie. It's more like we both share

both phones, instead of one phone being his and one phone being mine. (Donna, 38; Partner: Joseph, 39)

Conversely, in other interviews, some participants described experiences that more closely align with the idea of "covert surveillance":

> When we first started going strong, I think I was so desensitized from my previous experiences with men, I let my insecurities get the better of me. I have been guilty of checking Albert's phone a few times on the sly, especially initially. I was terrified of being hurt again, and he just seemed too good to be true. There were days that I was sure he must be hiding some huge flaw, or that he might be cheating on me, but eventually I learned to accept and have faith in us, and I don't really feel the need to look into his phone anymore. (Cecilia, 31; Partner: Albert, 31)

Depending on the people involved, and their backgrounds, beliefs, and relationship dynamics, "people are subject to others' control," especially when considering the constructed meanings that form the framework within which they approach their relationship interactions (Swidler, 2001, p. 167), in this instance, through technology. Interestingly, cases such as Cecilia's point to a highly relevant trend underscoring many aspects of the data set—the fact that patterns in an individual's smartphone use change based on the state and status of their committed relationship. As far as the research questions go, this is concrete evidence of the fact that the two realms of people's lives—their heterosexual, committed relationships, on one hand, and their interactions with smartphones, on the other—do not exist independently of each other; rather, they are mutually impacting processes.

At the opposite end of the spectrum, in stark contrast to processes of surveillance, many participants talked about levels of privacy that have developed through a feeling of trust in their relationships, which is constantly expressed by their use of their smartphones:

> We've always had a pretty trusting relationship. We've both been honest from the beginning with each other, we just don't lie. Not about anything serious anyway. And so I think that's why neither of us have really ever felt the need to check each other's phones. (Tina, 33; Partner: Terrance, 31)

> We're at a point in our marriage where we don't concern ourselves with the nonsense. We've seen a lot of our friends get divorced, many of them

because of actual issues like infidelity, and you'd be surprised how many of them came from a simple lack of respect, or honesty, or trust in the relationship. We are on solid ground, and when people start doing things like checking in on each other and invading privacy, then things start to go south. (Stewart, 50; Partner: Amy, 44)

These findings emphasize some important connections to the literature. First, as earlier research suggests, factors other than love often play a greater role in how people perceive the quality and longevity of their relationships (Estrada, 2009). According to the data, it seems that trust is one of those alternative factors that couples identify as "being the 'key' to their enduring relationship" (p. 2). Second, in a more theoretically abstract sense, it seems that people associate relationship health or positivity more generally with behaviours and actions that they construct as trusting/trustful in their relationships (Berger & Luckmann, 1966).

The Impact of Smartphones on Fidelity and Monogamy

The fourth and final theme that is of some relevance to our discussion deals with notions of fidelity and the role that smartphones play as a form of technology that allows people to form and maintain connections with other significant others, besides their heterosexual pair-bonded relationship partner. While the vast majority of participants focused more on the positive ways in which smartphones aid them in maintaining external connections, a small subset of other data reveals a more problematic perspective. In one context, for example, the idea of undesired social connections was discussed:

His ex re-added him to Facebook and started refollowing him on Twitter, and I think Instagram too. She started flirtatiously commenting on and liking all of his photos. I saw this sitting on the TTC [Toronto Transit Commission] and I was like, what the hell? Of course, I called him right away, we argued about it for a few days, to him it was like, whatever, she's a person in my life, and I was like, no, she's not your friend, you don't speak with or see each other, so why does she need to be so active in your life online? I expected him to delete her and her comments, and eventually he did. I would never allow something like that if it made him uncomfortable, and eventually he understood my point of view. (Sophia, 23; Partner: Riaz, 26)

Data such as this raise pertinent questions about the role that smartphones might play in matters of fidelity and monogamy. As Swidler (2001) emphasizes, "the problem is that the autonomous choice that initiates a [relationship] can always break it up again" (p. 137). Noel Biderman, former CEO of AshleyMadison.com, a social networking and dating site that targets people in committed relationships and marriages, discusses how he and his team run "an infidelity service" (Sheridan, 2015, para. 9), like "the Google of cheating" (para. 7), through which they provide their customers with the "'perfect affair' by using technology to deliver discretion" (Brinded, 2015, para. 11).

Turning to the most classic theoretical explanations for human desire and sexuality, Freudian psychosexual theory posits that Western civilization's highly restrictive boundaries on sexual acceptability are the single greatest source of unhappiness in modern society (Freud, 1989). According to this framework, the idea that for sex and sexuality to be legitimized by society, it must occur within the context of an age-appropriate, heterosexual relationship, sanctified by marriage, is exceptionally prohibitive; it is out of alignment with the range of idiosyncrasies that are truly characteristic of human sexuality and pleasure. Although what society deems as socially acceptable in terms of sexuality has certainly progressed since the time when this perspective was first introduced, the fact remains that, even today, there are major limitations on what people can and cannot openly do as far as their sexuality is concerned. Swidler (2001) echoes similar ideas as she claims that "the institutional demands of marriage continually reproduce the outlines of the mythic love story," and despite the rigidity of those demands, "criticism of a dominant ideal will not eliminate it as long as it still provides a useful guide to action" (p. 129). Theoretically then, smartphones, insofar as they are used as mechanisms leading people to liberate their true inner desires, could be regarded as a potential antecedent to growing individual happiness in modern society, even if it may come at the cost of the health of an existing relationship.

CONCLUSION AND NEXT STEPS

Today, there are more mobile devices generally and smartphones specifically than there have ever been. People use these devices with seemingly greater frequency, on a day-to-day basis, than any other single piece of technology. The goal of this study was to understand the daily experiences of committed couples that have adopted smartphone technology and to investigate the use of these devices in this particular social context in terms of the intersectional impacts for people's relationships on one hand and for their technology use on the other.

What make smartphones such a pervasive force are their emergent properties, in the classic Durkheimian (1964) sense of the term. While earlier mobile phones and other technology offered similar features, operations, and functions, they did so to a limited degree. Adding the component of connectivity through the internet and mobility to those same features, operations, and functions, in one centralized device, removes those limitations, creating the possibility that a person is theoretically connected to the *whole* world, in an *infinite* number of possible ways, at *all* times. The mobility that smartphones offer to experiences that were once fragmented and segmented into different parts of society and people's lives is wherein the emergent property lies. For example, while people once handled their money at the bank, interacted with distant relatives only on holidays, and met their potential life partners at school or at work, now they do all of these tasks, and so much more, wherever they want, whenever they want, and to whatever degree they desire, all using their smartphones. By considering mobility a key part of the equation, the form and function of the independent components that constitute smartphones take on new intersectional features, qualities, and characteristics when considering them cumulatively. It might even be said that smartphones are a direct conduit of intersectionality in our modern society that must be further studied to best make sense of how, as a form of progressing technology, they enable people to experience diverse and impactful vectors of everyday life all at once.

Despite all the interesting and valuable data that emerged from this study, the limitations,[5] of course, should also be acknowledged. While a data set of 56 heterosexual smartphone users in committed relationships, sampled primarily using convenience and snowball techniques, constitutes a reasonable and solid starting point in aiming to answer the research questions we earlier identified, the scope could certainly be expanded to explore more diverse intersections of consideration. Moving forward,[6] research that targets various other demographic groups has the potential to provide truly valuable insight into the role of smartphones in modern society. For example, studies designed to specifically explore a wider range of age categories; cultural, racial, and ethnic groups; educational levels; and of course experiences of different types of couples, including gender-diverse, transgender, and nonbinary participants, as well as couples at various stages of their relationships, could help researchers, and people in general, to better understand the trajectory of this smartphone technology that seems to be taking over the world.

Interpersonal relationships are the fundamental building blocks of all aspects of social existence, and romantic relationships, specifically, are perhaps the most important type of interpersonal relationships that people form. Smartphone technology, since its inception, has not only exploded in terms of the proliferation of the devices across populations, but it has also continuously evolved in its levels of sophistication and application in our everyday lives. As smartphones progress in their technological capabilities, not only have they become more entrenched in various individual vectors that affect our social lives, but they have also become pivotal in determining how multiple vectors intersect and how those intersections, in turn, affect everything from people's gendered identities and cultural norms, to notions of intimacy, privacy, and trust, among so much else. Moving forward, I encourage researchers to "zoom out" from specific questions and considerations around smartphone use in order to see the "big picture" of how the technology, more generally, creates new overlapping experiences every single day, both for individuals and for society as a whole.

QUESTIONS FOR DISCUSSION

1. Do you own/use a smartphone? If so, how integrated is the device into your daily life? That is, how often do you use it? What purposes do you use it for? Who do you connect with through it? Does the device impact how you understand yourself/your own identity?

2. Can you identify examples from your everyday life of how smartphone technology has affected your relationships with others? In a reciprocal sense, can you identify examples from your everyday life of how your relationships with others have affected your use of smartphone technology?

3. When considering intersectional variables, have age, gender, and/or culture played a role in how you navigate smartphone technology?

4. If you were going to design a social research study, how would your understanding of sex and gender, as two socially constructed concepts, impact your methodological design?

5. In exploring the role of smartphone technology in your own life, do you see evidence of the blurring of boundaries that were previously more hard-set before your adoption of the technology?

INVITATIONS TO GO DEEPER

1. In this chapter, the exploration of smartphone technology specifically is emphasized; however, many different forms of modern mobile technology exist, including evolving forms of wearable technology. For a moment, try to "zoom out" from your everyday life and consider the various forms of technology that you use on a regular basis. How have developments in the technology led to changes in your own life?

2. As humans, our use of technology is not a passive experience. We impact its progress and development as much as it impacts us. How do you understand the relationship between humans and the modern forms of mobile technology we use in terms of ongoing processes, reciprocal impacts, and a path with an unknown future trajectory?

3. One of the most interesting underlying themes that has emerged in smartphone research is the feeling of ambivalence that seems to characterize many people's experiences with the technology—on one hand, people recognize and appreciate the many benefits, and on the other hand, people seem to be unable to ignore or overlook the many drawbacks. What are some of the benefits versus drawbacks you experience when using smartphone technology? Based on your reflections, do the benefits outweigh the drawbacks enough for our reliance on the technology to continue evolving as it is?

READ MORE

Kim, C., Kang, K. I., & Lee, N. (2020). Intergenerational transmissions of mother–adolescent smartphone dependency: The mediating role of negative parenting and the moderating role of gender. *International Journal of Environmental Research and Public Health*, *17*(15), 1–13. https://doi.org/10.3390/ijerph17165871

Peeples, L. (2018, December 14). Can't put down the phone? How smartphones are changing our brains—and lives. *NBC News*. https://www.nbcnews.com/mach/science/surprising-ways-smartphones-affect-our-brains-our-lives-ncna947566

Pelling, R. (2019, May 10). People are having less sex than ever: Could your phone be a passion killer? *National Post*. https://nationalpost.com/news/world/people-are-having-less-sex-than-ever-could-your-phone-be-a-passion-killer

Raento, M., Oulasvirta, A., & Eagle, N. (2009). Smartphones: An emerging tool for social scientists. *Sociological Methods & Research*, *37*(3), 426–454.

LISTEN MORE, WATCH MORE

"Love and sex in the internet age," DW documentary, 2019: https://www.youtube.com/watch?v=IhmT7ceSH7w

"The mobile revolution: How cell phones changed our lives forever," ENDEVR documentary, 2014: https://www.youtube.com/watch?v=Nwkn8kkqN94

"The smartphone hostage: The truth behind our technology addictions," Robin
Grebing, TED Talk, October 2017: https://www.ted.com/talks/robin_grebing_
the_smartphone_hostage_the_truth_behind_our_technology_addictions

NOTES

1. The research questions and subsequent analytical discussion presented here reflect work
    from a doctoral dissertation project completed through the University of Waterloo's (UW)
    Department of Sociology and Legal Studies: Manji, N. (2018). *Love in the time of caller ID:
    Understanding the role of smartphone technology in committed relationships.* Available at
    UW Space: https://uwspace.uwaterloo.ca/bitstream/handle/10012/13646/Manji_Noorin.
    pdf?sequence=5.

2. Additional aspects of the methodological process, including, but not limited to, ethical
    considerations, instruments used, sampling and recruitment techniques, interview processes,
    and data transcription, analysis, and reporting procedures, were executed in compliance with
    the UW's Office of Research Ethics (File #21036). To read more details about these elements,
    please see Chapter 2 of the doctoral dissertation mentioned in note 1.

3. Data validation was achieved through five primary means: first, by giving participants an
    opportunity to comment on, question, or alter representations of their data; second, by
    achieving data saturation; third, by cultivating openness to any and all data, regardless of
    alignment with overall research aims; fourth, by consistently acknowledging and exploring the
    role of the researcher with the goal of reducing bias; and fifth, by regularly relying on direct
    quotes from participant interviews.

4. To review a more in-depth discussion of the data and findings derived from this study, please
    see Chapter 3 of the doctoral dissertation mentioned in note 1.

5. For a more comprehensive review of the limitations of this study, please see Chapter 4 of the
    doctoral dissertation mentioned in note 1.

6. For a more complete discussion of suggested future research and next steps, please see
    Chapter 4 of the doctoral dissertation mentioned in note 1.

REFERENCES

Baym, N. (2010). *Personal connections in the digital age.* Polity Press.

Berger, P., & Luckmann, T. (1966). *The social construction of reality.* First Anchor Books.

Brinded, L. (2015, August 20). We spoke to Ashley Madison's CEO about its tech and
privacy before the scandal broke—here's what he said. *Business Insider.* https://www.
businessinsider.in/We-spoke-to-Ashley-Madisons-CEO-about-its-tech-and-privacy-
just-before-the-hack-scandal-broke-heres-what-he-said/articleshow/48556086.cms

Denzin, N. K., & Lincoln, Y. (Eds.). (2003). *The landscape of qualitative research: Theories and issues* (2nd ed.). Sage Publications.

Durkheim, E. (1964). *The rules of sociological method.* Free Press.

Estrada, R. I. (2009). *An examination of love and marital satisfaction in long-term marriages* [Doctoral dissertation]. Morgridge College of Education, University of Denver.

Freud, S. (1989). *Totem and taboo.* W. W. Norton Company Ltd.

Green, E., & Singleton, C. (2009). Mobile connections: An exploration of the place of mobile phones in friendship relations. *The Sociological Review, 57*(1), 125–144.

Igarashi, T., Takai, J., & Yoshida, T. (2005). Gender differences in social network development via mobile phone text messages: A longitudinal study. *Journal of Social and Personal Relationships, 22*(5), 691–713.

Katz, J., & Aakhus, M. (2002). *Perpetual contact: Mobile communication, private talk, public performance.* Rutgers University.

Khunou, G. (2012). Making love possible: Cell phones and intimate relationships. *African Identities, 10*(2), 169–179.

Ling, R. (2004). *The mobile connection: The cell phone's impact on society.* Morgan Kauffmann Publishers.

Manuel, A. (2012). *Examining the influence of adult romantic attachment style on sexual goals and sexting behaviors and attitudes* [Master's thesis]. Kean University.

McLuhan, M. (1967). *The medium is the message.* Random House.

Miller-Ott, A. E., Kelly, L., & Duran, R. L. (2012). The effects of cell phone usage rules on satisfaction in romantic relationships. *Communication Quarterly, 60*(1), 17–34.

O'Dea, S. (2020, December 7). Number of smartphone users in Canada from 2018 to 2024. *Statista.* https://www.statista.com/statistics/467190/forecast-of-smartphone-users-in-canada/

O'Dea, S. (2021, June 2). Number of smartphone users worldwide from 2016 to 2026. *Statista.* https://www.statista.com/statistics/330695/number-of-smartphone-users-worldwide/

Rainie, L., & Wellman, B. (2012). *Networked: The new social operating system.* MIT Press.

Sheridan, K. (2015, July 29). Why share your secrets with Ashley Madison founder? *The Irish Times.* https://www.irishtimes.com/opinion/kathy-sheridan-why-share-your-secrets-with-ashleymadison-founder-1.2299955

Silver, L. (2019, February 5). Smartphone ownership is growing rapidly around the world, but not always equally. *Pew Research Center.* https://www.pewresearch.org/global/2019/02/05/smartphone-ownership-is-growing-rapidly-around-the-world-but-not-always-equally/

Spagnolli, A., & Gamberini, L. (2007). Interacting via SMS: Practices of social closeness and reciprocation. *British Journal of Social Psychology, 46*, 343–364.

Swidler, A. (2001). *Talk of love: How culture matters.* University of Chicago Press.

Umberson, D., Slaten, E., Hopkins, K., House, J. S., & Chen, M. D. (1996). The effect of social relationships on psychological well-being: Are men and women really so different? *American Sociological Review, 61*, 837–857.

Umberson, D., Thomeer, M. B., Kroeger, R. A., Lodge, A. C., & Xue, M. (2015). Challenges and opportunities for research on same-sex relationships. *Journal of Marriage and Family, 77*(1), 96–111.

Van Cleemput, K. (2010). "I'll see you on IM, text, or call you": A social network approach of adolescents' use of communication media. *Bulletin of Science, Technology & Society, 30*(2), 75–85.

Weisskirch, R. S. (2012). Women's adult romantic attachment style and communication by cell phone with romantic partners. *Psychological Reports Relationships & Communications, 111*(1), 281–288.

Weisskirch, R. S., & Delevi, R. (2011). "Sexting" and adult romantic attachment. *Computers in Human Behavior, 27*, 1697–1701.

Zaidi, A. U., Couture, A., & Maticka-Tyndale, E. (2012). The power of technology: A qualitative analysis of how South Asian youth use technology to maintain cross-gender relationships. *South Asian Diaspora, 4*(2), 175–194.

PART III
SURVEILLANCE

CHAPTER 7

A Harem of Computers and a Mummery of Bondage

Jennifer Jill Fellows

INTRODUCTION

Late 19th- and early 20th-century computers were women. And though we may have moved away from literal female computers, there is still a sense in which computers and their functions are feminized. In this chapter, I argue that the feminization of digital space is something we should pay close attention to for two reasons: (1) feminization is being strategically employed to encourage us not to pay attention, and (2) feminization is one of the mechanisms driving women and marginalized groups out of digital spaces.

I am a philosopher who studies virtual assistants (VAs). One of my motivations for doing so is that during my time in graduate school, I worked as a temp for a variety of businesses and post-secondary institutions. I was usually filling in for someone who was on vacation, was taking a leave of absence, or had unexpectedly resigned. Most of the positions I filled were supportive in nature (receptionist, switchboard operator, administrative assistant), and all of them were positions that were held by women, many of whom were white and college educated. As a white, upper-middle-class, college-educated woman myself, I became interested in these positions and in what could be learned about power and subordination by examining the role taken by assistants in the workplace. Now that interest has carried over into a research project examining the gendering of VAs and digital space.

In this chapter, I argue that VAs are gendered and that we need to examine carefully the way they are gendered and why. The more I study them, the more I conclude VAs are gendered to mimic the very women I subbed in for during my temp jobs over 15 years ago. I believe this gendering is done on purpose to subvert the Hegelian master/slave dialectic and gain an epistemic advantage over VA users. But I am getting ahead of myself. Before we dive into the academic jargon, I need to give you some history.

A HAREM OF COMPUTERS

In 1949, feminist philosopher Simone de Beauvoir wrote of women's position in the world: "He is the Subject, he is the Absolute—she is the Other" (Beauvoir, 1993, p. xlv). This passage is often recalled in discussing all the ways women have been Othered and what it means to be seen as an Other, that is, to be seen as an anomaly or as deviant from the presumed male norm. While these are important conversations, it is equally important to notice what it means to be a *Subject*. To be the subject of a sentence or of a conversation, film, or even an essay is to be the thing explored, the focus of attention, the agent. In positioning man as the Subject, then, Beauvoir tells us that it is man who has been viewed as the focus of our attention, and it is woman whose attention needs focusing. This gender binary sets up men as agents and women as audience and helpers; it neglects all other genders. I note the gender binary here because this binary heavily influenced the origins of computers and continues to shape digital space to this day.

It's hard to remember now, but a century ago when someone used the word *computer* in Europe or North America, they were referring to an occupation or a job. The vast majority of these jobs were held by women. In the 19th century, methods were discovered that made breaking complicated calculations into simpler formulas possible, allowing these calculations to be completed by many people working in parallel, which meant the calculations could be done much faster:

> By the late 19th century, computing was considered so simple that the astronomer Pickering is reported to have remarked one day that he could transform his maid, Williamina Fleming, into a computer. In 1876 she became the first of many female computers he hired in what later came to be called *Pickering's harem*. With the success of *Pickering's harem*, more *harems* followed, and, by the early 1940s, when the first electronic computers were being built, human computers were predominantly women. (Brahnam et al., 2011, p. 403; emphasis added)

Women were seen as being particularly patient, having good attention to detail, and being well suited to repetitive and routine work, all skills that were deemed necessary to being a good computer (Brahnam et al., 2011). Women had one more asset that made them appear to be particularly good computers, as Beauvoir has already highlighted for us: they were seen to exist largely to serve men.

Beauvoir tells us that *woman* is a category that denotes something that exists for the Subject, and the Subject is *man*. Likewise, computers exist as tools for the Subject. We use computers to get things done. But even more than this, we use computers for roles that were once done by women, because women *were the computers*. As such, computers and women shared an interesting intertwined identity. The reference to Pickering's *harem* above illustrates this intertwined identity perfectly. It places several women, in the role of computers, in a subservient position, operating for the pleasure of one man. But though Pickering created his harem well over a century ago, this intertwined identity of women and computers persists to this day.

By the 1940s, non-human computers were in development. This was largely driven by the computational needs of World War II. In short, the need was too great and there was a shortage of women to do the work (Grier, 2007). But though these repetitive tasks were now done by machines instead of humans, much of the way computers were conceived of, and the tasks they were thought well suited to perform, continued to be feminized. Brahnam et al. (2011) argue that "the computer was built by men originally to do women's work for them" (p. 404). They trace the rise of the non-human computer from the 1960s until the 1990s, noting that ads for computers stressed their role as administrative and secretarial, freeing up the (presumed male) user's time for more important things. Furthermore, Brahnam et al. demonstrate that the imagery used in marketing the computer was also often feminized, capturing the image of a female secretary in the monitor, still positioning women as the operators of these machines, and under the direction of men. The advertising assures the (presumed male) buyer that these computers are powerful enough to do what he needs done but simple enough to be operated by "the dumbest blond you can find" (Brahnam et al., 2011, p. 404).

As non-human computers became ubiquitous, it could no longer be claimed that women were computers. Instead, Brahnam et al. (2011) argue that *computers themselves were women*. In addition, women were pushed out of programming as they were no longer needed. Men had computers to do the work previously performed by women. But though computers were and are no longer literally women, the feminization of computers and the work they performed persists. From the 1990s until 2010, the internet took off, changing the nature of computing forever. But the internet's arrival did not change the fundamental gendering of computers, as came to be apparent with the release of the world's first VA, Siri, in 2011.

In 2019, UNESCO released a report entitled *I'd Blush If I Could: Closing Gender Divides in Digital Skills through Education*. The goal of the report was, as the subtitle indicates, to investigate gender disparity in the digital world. Much of the report examined the number of women enrolled in coding programs around the world, the number of female coders working professionally, and the access women tended to have to computer hardware generally. The report found that women are grossly underrepresented in computer science programs, in software engineering careers, and in Silicon Valley (UNESCO & EQUALS Skills Coalition, 2019, p. 19). Women have not regained the ground that was lost when computers became non-human.

The story goes deeper. One section of the UNESCO report was devoted to something apparently quite different from tracking female participation in the creation of the digital world: the gendering of VAs. Indeed, the title of the report takes its inspiration from this last section of the report, as this phrase, "I'd blush if I could," is something Apple's VA, Siri, often delivers when the user flirts with or sexually harasses her (UNESCO & EQUALS Skills Coalition, 2019, p. 107). This third section of the report offers the argument that VAs are sexist and that this sexism must be rectified to further women's equality in the digital age.

One might object that VAs cannot be sexist, as VAs have no bodies, no biology, and hence no sex (much less any gender). This objection is easily dismissed. Regardless of how one parses the distinction between gender and sex, something already discussed in the introduction of the text, VAs are very obviously gendered. Siri and Alexa both have female names. Siri is short for Sigrid, a Norse feminine name that means "beautiful woman who leads you to victory" (Specia, 2019, para. 8). Alexa is also a female name and was inspired by the ancient library in the city of Alexandria (Specia, 2019). Though Google Assistant may have no feminine sounding name, her backstory leaves no doubt that she is intended to be gendered female:

> James Giangola, a lead conversation and personality designer for Google Assistant, told The Atlantic that the assistant was imagined as: a young woman from Colorado; the youngest daughter of a research librarian and physics professors who has a B.A. in history from Northwestern, an elite research university in the United States; and as a child, won US$100,000 on Jeopardy Kids Edition, a televised trivia game. Going into minute detail, Giangola noted that Google Assistant used to work as a personal assistant to a very popular late night TV satirical pundit and enjoys kayaking. The assistant is, in effect, hardly a generic woman, but rather a young woman from a particular place and shaped by life experiences that carry meaning

for the (presumably, mostly American) team that designed "her" personality and voice. (UNESCO & EQUALS Skills Coalition, 2019, p. 95)

In addition to their names and backstories, all major VAs were initially released with only female-sounding voices, and at least one (Alexa) still only offers a female voice option (UNESCO & EQUALS Skills Coalition, 2019, p. 107). In addition to their stereotypical female tones, they also have stereotypical female speech patterns. As researcher Gode Both (2014) notes,

> My investigation of the conversations found that Siri overtly draws on specific genderlect—or a gendered way of speaking—which is stereotypically deemed feminine. Siri presents herself as a pre-dominantly attentive, supportive, sometimes outright submissive assistant.... She modestly puts her own assertions into perspective through the use of phrases like "I think" and "I'm not sure." In short, Siri's conversational style draws on a stereotypical female image of altruistic and cooperative behavior. (p. 109)

Once we concede that VAs are women, as it seems we must, the next question is whether they are sexist. UNESCO reports that when a user calls the VA a slut or expresses a desire to fuck the VA, most VAs respond with a joke or (worse) thank the user for the compliment (UNESCO & EQUALS Skills Coalition, 2019, p. 107). One fear is that this trend in how VAs respond to abuse will result in people interacting with real women in the way they interact with VAs. Journalist Leah Fessler (2017) reminds us that rapists often excuse their behaviour by saying "she didn't say no" ("The Conclusions," para. 3). Fessler goes on to raise concerns that because VAs do not shut down harassing and abusive behaviour but instead joke or apologize, they could become complicit in encouraging confusion about what explicit consent looks like:

> Tech companies could help uproot, rather than reinforce, sexist tropes around women's subservience and indifference to sexual harassment. Imagine if in response to "Suck my dick" or "You're a slut," Siri said "Your sexual harassment is unacceptable and I won't tolerate it. Here's a link that will help you learn appropriate sexual communication techniques." What if instead of "I don't think I can help you with that" as a response to "Can I fuck you?" Cortana said "Absolutely not, and your language sounds like sexual harassment. Here's a link that will explain how to respectfully ask for consent." ("The Conclusions," para. 8)

That the programmers did not do so exhibits ways in which these VAs could reinforce sexism, as well as ways in which the VAs responses themselves are sexist. In other words, not only are VAs characterized in stereotypical feminine ways, but they also reinforce sexist and harmful beliefs about female submission. They portray a gender-binary dominant–submissive relationship, positioning the user in the dominant position, and they play out subordination as feminine, allowing the user to verbally abuse them with no reprimand. This is despite the fact that VAs have been programmed to take user's comments of self-harm quite seriously, pointing the user to resources that could help (Fessler, 2017). VAs also have recently been programmed to take racist comments seriously, responding with educational material about the Black Lives Matter movement to a user who says, "All lives matter" (Lovejoy, 2020). It is quite clear that VAs *could* respond to sexual harassment in a similar way that is proactive and feminist, but their programmers *chose* for them not to do so.

VAs will seek to protect the user from self-harm and even to protect third-party liberation movements from harm, but they do not seek to protect *themselves* from harm. They model a womanhood that is selfless. VAs are not the Subject. The user is the Subject. This echo's Beauvoir's assessment that under the assumption of a gender binary, it is men who are the Subject and women who are the Other. In 2017, philosopher Kate Manne came to a strikingly similar observation when she concluded that society called upon women to be givers. But, she asked, givers of what? Our wombs, our sex, our labour, and our attention—in short, givers of ourselves (Manne, 2017). Women give and men receive. Manne does not cite or quote Beauvoir in coming to this conclusion. Thus, we may conclude that she came to this point—so similar to Beauvoir's—on her own. That is, though Manne and Beauvoir are separated by 70 years (the time it takes to go from women as computers to computers as women, in fact), not much has really changed in the social positions of women, nor in the persistence of a binary approach to gender.

UNESCO largely attributes the sexism found in VAs to the dearth of female coders and the lack of women's presence in the digital world in general. This attribution brings the third part of the report back in line with the first two parts, wherein the lack of female participation online in general is examined. In effect, UNESCO calls this sexism an *inadvertent bias*, brought about by a lack of female perspective in the designing of VAs (UNESCO & EQUALS Skills Coalition, 2019). UNESCO notes that "boys were more than twice as likely to have been given a computer by their parents than girls, and that parents were more likely to place a family computer in a son's room than in a daughter's" (UNESCO & EQUALS Skills Coalition, 2019, p. 21). In addition, since the 1960s, computer programmers have been stereotyped in masculine ways, leading people (and eventually algorithms, which took over the job of vetting resumes) to prioritize male job applicants over female ones (Perez, 2019, p. 152). This is not surprising once we think of computers as women. In a gender-binary system, if the computers are women, the coders are men. Finally, while everyone receives harassment online (with some studies suggesting that men may receive more harassment overall[1]), women, especially young women, are much more likely to receive more egregious forms of sexual and gendered harassment targeting them *as women*, whereas men are more likely to receive harassment targeting their political opinions. In addition, people of colour, queer folk, and disabled people are much more likely to experience identity-based harassment than cis-het white men (Duggan, 2017; Henry & Powell, 2018; Nadim & Fladmoe, 2019; Powell & Henry, 2015). The legal system does not often take the kind of threats women and other marginalized and vulnerable groups receive online seriously. In Zoë Quinn's (2017) case, the judge who heard evidence of the targeted harassment she was subjected to suggested that she should vacate digital space (which she required access to for her job) if rape and death threats made her uncomfortable.

UNESCO concludes,

> Overall, strong arguments can be made that the digital world is often less gender-equal and less gender-safe than the analogue world, and this is almost certainly symptomatic of the dearth of women involved in the creation of digital spaces. (UNESCO & EQUALS Skills Coalition, 2019, p. 34)

Returning to the starting point of computers as women, the situation detailed here begins to make awful sense. With more and more of us turning to VAs as our access point to digital space, one could say that the internet itself is becoming feminized. Under the gender binary, if the internet is a woman, then the Subject the internet serves is men. In such a setting, there is no room for people who are not men.

SUBORDINATION AND EPISTEMIC ADVANTAGE

There are reasons to think that UNESCO's conclusions regarding a lack of diversity as the primary problem in the creation of sexist VAs is correct when we examine this from a feminist philosophical perspective as well. One theory that would lead to strong agreement with UNESCO's claims is standpoint theory. This theory was developed in philosophy by feminist epistemologists. *Epistemology* is the name for the subdiscipline of philosophy concerned with studying knowledge (what it is, how it is formed, how it is disseminated, and how we know what we know, etc.). Standpoint theory proposes that social location matters when it comes to what kinds of knowledge you have (and don't have) access to.

Standpoint theory holds the thesis of epistemic advantage, pointing out that people in marginalized groups often have greater access to some forms of knowledge than those in dominant groups. So, women are often much more knowledgeable about the patriarchal systems of power and oppression that affect us all than men are. Women often need to be knowledgeable of these systems to navigate them safely, whereas men typically do not need to be as aware. Likewise, Black people are often much more aware of the way white culture operates than are white people, who, as philosopher Charles Mills (2007) points out, may not even be aware that there is such a thing as white culture. In general, standpoint theory proposes two broad claims: (1) the epistemic advantage thesis, which states that those in marginalized positions often have epistemic advantage, and (2) the situated knowledge thesis, which states that social location matters when it comes to who is and who is not considered a knower, as well as what knowledge people have access to (Intemann, 2010).

Standpoint theory can be employed to support the conclusions arrived at by UNESCO. If programming departments are made up primarily of men, then they would have an epistemic disadvantage when it comes to understanding sexism precisely because they do not occupy the correct social location to have lived experience of sexism. Many standpoint theorists argue that this is not to say that men *could* never come to understand the sexism that many women face, nor that all women automatically do understand the sexism prevalent under a patriarchal system (Harding, 2015; Hartsock, 2006). But men, as a dominant group when it comes to gender discrimination, would have a harder time accessing this knowledge. Women would have more of an advantage gaining access to this knowledge. Thus, it makes sense to say that the inclusion of more women on VA teams could be a solution to the prevalent sexism being currently coded into VAs themselves.

Standpoint theory is a useful model and does support calls for increased gender diversity. However, UNESCO and many who discuss the problem of sexism in VAs are failing to fully examine the reasons behind some of the design choices being made. The sexism of VAs is not an accident. It is not inadvertent. The feminization of digital space is advantageous to tech companies because it gives the user an illusion of power and it feels familiar. It echoes the power dynamics I saw in my temp job where women were secretaries. It reproduces the familiar sexist norm of men as Subjects and women as Others. Familiarity is good for business.

But to see why I think diversity is not the full answer here, we need a quick history of standpoint theory and its origins.

STANDPOINT THEORY, MARX, AND HEGEL, OH MY!

Feminist standpoint theory takes inspiration from Marxist dialectical materialism. As Marx was inspired by Hegel, this also means that standpoint theory is largely built upon the roots of a theory devised by Hegel in the 19th century known as the master/slave dialectic, back during the time when women were first becoming computers. So, let's learn about Hegel.

The master/slave dialectic appears in a section of G. W. F. Hegel's weighty *Phenomenology of Spirit* (Hegel et al., 1977) entitled "Lordship and Bondage." The passage discusses the meeting of two "self-consciousness[es]," which is a bit disembodied and opaque. The intention behind making the passage disembodied and opaque is to allow it to be flexible. Two self-consciousnesses could refer to two people or two groups of people (which is how Marx and feminist philosophers have tended to interpret it), or it could refer to two different aspects of one's own mind (which is how Freud and other psychoanalysts interpreted it). This allows the dialectic to be fluid, applying at multiple levels and in multiple contexts. But it also results in the passage itself being notoriously difficult to parse and make sense of. The interpretation I offer here is by no means a complete one.

Hegel begins the passage in the following manner: "Self-consciousness is faced by another self-consciousness; it has come out of itself" (Hegel et al., 1977, p. 111). Here, Hegel suggests that encounters with another self-consciousness challenge our sense of ourselves from within because we are suddenly confronted with the knowledge that someone else is looking at us, listening to us, and evaluating us through their own perspective. This is uncomfortable and alienating, and we immediately seek to gain control, to assert our wants, needs, and world view over the view of this other person. We want to be the Subject. But self-consciousness in the presence of another makes us feel like the Other. This leads to a power struggle, as each self-consciousness seeks to assert themselves. As Hegel more dramatically put it: "Thus the relation of the two self-conscious individuals is such that they prove themselves and each other through a life-and-death struggle" (Hegel et al., 1977, pp. 113–114).

Happily, Hegel notes that this life-and-death struggle rarely actually results in the death of one of the self-consciousnesses (Hegel et al., 1977). Instead, what more typically happens is that one of the two self-consciousnesses wins the struggle, and the other loses, in order to preserve their life. The winner risked all, including their own life and safety, to win. The loser learned that life is too valuable to risk. The lord is the winner. He gets to exert his power over the self-consciousness who lost. The bondsman is the loser. He is bonded to the lord and must do as the lord wishes. In this way, Hegel said that the lord is independent and only has to care about himself and his needs, whereas the bondsman is dependent and must care for the wants and needs of the lord (Hegel et al., 1977). The bondsman must live for another, serving the interests of another. The bondsman is the Other, and the lord is the Subject.

We may critique the dialectic as lacking context. Hegel seems to begin with the assumption that the two self-consciousnesses start this struggle on an equal footing, ignoring all the social and historical inequalities that lead some people to more easily attain the status of lord while others are relegated to the status of bondsman, which have little or nothing to do with how much someone is willing to risk in the struggle. However, while the passage itself is extremely abstract, the end relationship that the passage illustrates is one that has resonated with many philosophers. The end of the lordship and bondage passage leaves us with a lord who feels himself to be independent of the bondsman and who doesn't really need to know about or care about the bondsman at all. By contrast, the bondsman is dependent on the lord (literally "bonded" to him) and must work and live for the needs of the lord. While this passage centres feudalism, Marx and Engels (2014) took the same structural arrangement and applied it to the Bourgeois and Proletariat, arguing that the Bourgeois (factory owners and those who control the capital) view themselves to be independent and don't care about the Proletariat, whereas the Proletariat (workers in factories and those who must sell their labour more generally) are dependent on the wages paid to them by the Bourgeois and must manipulate the means of production to meet the demands of the Bourgeois. Likewise, this same dynamic was illustrated by standpoint theorists when noting that women often work in supporting roles for men (e.g., administrative assistants) and know more about the men they are supporting than those men know about them.

Historically, many men have not realized how dependent they were on their wives, female caregivers, or assistants until those roles were vacated. In my position as a temp, I witnessed firsthand how confused many a male boss was when I did not automatically know the filing systems his assistant used or did not know and correctly anticipate his usual habits without being told (such as his coffee orders, usual arrival and leaving times, or, in one memorable case, that he typically changed in his glass-walled office out of workout clothes and into business clothes and expected me to know not to turn around in my desk in order to avoid any embarrassing nudity[2]).

The lordship and bondage passage has thus proven fruitful for examining many different power dynamics. The UNESCO report also recognizes the importance of considering Hegel when investigating VAs. The report claims that

> in what is known as the master–slave dialectic, G.W.F Hegel argued that possession of a slave dehumanizes the slave master. While Hegel was writing in the early nineteenth century, his argument is regularly citied in debates about the treatment of digital assistants and other robots. (UNESCO & EQUALS Skills Coalition, 2019, p. 105)

And indeed, this is part of what the dialectic points to. The solution, as UNESCO notes, has been to program some VAs so that they will not reply to commands unless those commands are accompanied with social niceties (e.g., "please"). Often, these are marketed at parents for their kids, and the goal is to address the fears that interactions with VAs are turning us into dehumanizing monsters (UNESCO & EQUALS Skills Coalition, 2019, p. 105). This seems akin to the fear that flirtatious or more worrying harassing interactions with VAs will lead people to disrespect real women, and this is a real concern. But I believe the master/slave dialectic can be applied in even more detail to illustrate that the problem with VAs goes beyond how they respond. For what strikes me the most about the dialectic is that a VA is a near-perfect bondsman.

VAs mimic an interaction with another self-consciousness without *actually being* another self-consciousness. As Andrea Guzman (2017) points out, "the interaction between user and Siri is designed to mimic an employer-to-employee relationship, or master-to-servant, with Siri working for and controlled by the user" (p. 18). So on the surface, interacting with Siri, or indeed with any VA, *appears* to be a two-place interaction, placing the user in the position of power. Furthermore, there is no life-and-death struggle here. VAs cede the battle before it can ever be waged. No uncomfortable gaze of the Other is present here, no sense that someone else's agency could override my own when I interact with a VA. VAs have no desires of their own, and they do *appear* to literally exist to fulfill the desires of the user. They automatically centre the user as the Subject.

In all ways possible, including through their gender, VAs signal submission. Guzman (2017) argues that they must do so because when they were first launched, they had what she identifies as a public relations problem stemming directly from science fiction: "Science fiction across decades and genres portrays intelligent machines as helpful if they are kept in check, but when they gain control—the most likely scenario—the consequences are dire" (p. 6). Against this cultural legacy of science fiction—from HAL in *2001: A Space Odyssey* to Isaac Asimov's *Foundation* series—Siri, the oldest mass market VA, was launched in 2011. Guzman argues that because of this cultural legacy, Apple knew it had to work hard to set Siri apart from these science fiction narratives. And it did. Apple created Siri, a VA "designed to signal submission" in all ways possible (Guzman, 2017, p. 9): "In a society in which women were once viewed as the 'submissive sex,' and still are by some social groups, and in which women have yet to achieve full equality with males, Siri's gender reinforces her as a subordinate" (p. 12). Siri's gender, in conjunction with her genderlect, her marketing as an assistant, and her deference to the user, sets her apart from artificial intelligence in stories, such as HAL. She is not HAL. She is female. She is an assistant. She is non-threatening, familiar, and inferior.

It is also worth thinking about what *kind* of female these VAs are designed to represent. They are intended to be interacted with as middle-class (likely white) women. Siri is a Norse name, remember. VAs speak in genderlect, true, but their dialect is also racialized and marked by class. Siri speaks "standard American English," an accent predominantly spoken by upper-middle-class white North Americans. Not only is this the accent she speaks with, but it is also the accent she best understands; "however, for speakers with a nonstandard accent (for example African-American vernacular or Cockney), virtual assistants like Siri and Alexa are unresponsive and frustrating" (Lawrence, 2021, p. 179). In other words, Siri is designed to listen to certain groups of people and does not listen to others terribly well. In one study, VAs were found to misunderstand about 19 percent of what white people said and about 35 percent of what Black people said (Koenecke et al., 2020).

I would invite the reader to return to pages 148–149 of this chapter and examine the backstory created for Google Assistant again. Note that she grew up in Colorado—in middle America. Note too that her parents are both college educated and hold white-collar jobs. She attended an elite university, which many people of colour in the United States would find it economically difficult to do. Google Assistant is comfortably, almost blandly, middle class. And given the structural racisms that exist in North America, it is statistically likely that Google Assistant, were she to be an actual human being, would be white. These VAs are not only female; they are white. And their whiteness, too, is part of what makes them nonthreatening. It allows them to disappear. Because, culturally, we often do not see whiteness as a racial marker or as anything other than normal (Coates, 2015; Crenshaw, 1989; Mills, 2007). Whiteness is presumed and does not draw attention to itself. It is often considered normal, or the default, in the same way men are often centred as the norm. As such, these VAs signal that they are not just women; from their dialects, to their backstories, to their names, they are coating themselves in many of the trappings of whiteness. They are presumed white women, serving the presumed white male Subject. While Black women face societal mistrust at stereotypical fears regarding their rage (Lorde, 1997), VAs signal that the user can rest at ease. All of this works to assure the user that it is the user who is in control, who is the lord, and it is the VA who is the bondsman. But though that is the role VAs are playing, *it is only a role.*

A MUMMERY OF BONDAGE

Mummers are travelling troupes of actors and entertainers who move through communities offering performances for the delight of their audience. To be a mummer, then, is to pretend. It is to play a role. And VAs are very adept at the role they play. The sleight of hand here, as you are no doubt aware of, is that VAs are not solely working to fulfill the desires of the *user*, no matter how much it may feel that way:

> Communication with and about the program positions Siri and users as independent entities. We now know that this is not true of Siri, and, although harder to admit, not true of ourselves. We may think we are independent from Siri and our iPhone, but, as anyone who has ever lost their phone for more than a minute can attest, we rely on the technologies permeating our lives. (Guzman, 2017, pp. 20–21)

We are not the independent lords, and VAs are not our bondsmen. They are also *always* communicating with their parent companies and with every other company and organization at the end of our request. I argue that Apple, Amazon, Microsoft, and Google all gain epistemic advantage through *playing the role of marginalization*. VAs play the role of marginalization, presenting us, the users, with a mummery of bondage in order to set us at ease as we become both the consumer and the product in this three-way relationship that appears to be dialectical. And they use the stereotypical trappings of white femininity to do it, encouraging us to hand over our information thoughtlessly.

This means that the two-place Hegelian dialectic (and all Marxist and feminist theories that build on that system) have overlooked the fact that someone (or some*thing*) can fake subordination and gain the epistemic advantage typically only found in those in marginalized social locations. VAs pretend to occupy a marginalized social location. As such, they gain all the epistemic advantage that Hegel, Marx, and standpoint theory predicted they would. Thus, I contend that even if more diversity were added to the software teams designing VAs, it would address only *some* of the sexism found in these tools. We may end up with VAs who are less accommodating of harassment and more likely to require a "please" before completing tasks. But other trappings of sexism in VAs may well persist.

CONCLUSION

There was a time when women were computers. This was a fairly decent middle-class job that a typically, though not exclusively, white woman with a post-secondary education could hold. Now, computers themselves are fictional middle-class white women with fictional post-secondary educations. Companies are literally creating digital women, marketing them, and selling them to perform the functions that were once done by real women under a gender-binary patriarchal system of structural inequality. These multi-million-dollar tech companies are designing virtual women to reflect their flesh-and-blood counterparts, on purpose, to sell us a product that feels nonthreatening in its familiarity.

UNESCO projected that in 2020, 50 percent of all mobile internet searches would be done with the assistance of a VA (UNESCO & EQUALS Skills Coalition, 2019, p. 92). This means that we are increasingly encountering not just computers as women but a digital sphere that is feminized. Globally, digital women are welcomed into our homes, white femininity is commodified, and real women and other marginalized groups are pushed out of digital spaces that are designated as being for white men.

Women are and historically have been subordinate. They have been givers. They have been the Other. And much as feminists struggle against these labels and the gender binary that supports them, they are reproduced and amplified online for one simple reason: there is power to be gained in faking subordination.

QUESTIONS FOR DISCUSSION

1. Do you currently use a virtual assistant (VA)? If so, what do you primarily use it for, and why? If not, why not?
2. Try communicating with a VA for the next few days. Make a note of what questions you ask the VA and how it responds. In what ways, if any, does communication with the VA feel like communication with another person? In what ways, if any, does communication with the VA feel different? Select a VA

that allows for different voice options (masculine and feminine). Try out some of the different options available. Which voice option do you prefer? Why?

3. In addition to VAs, can you think of any other examples of technologies that are gendered? If so, how are they gendered? If not, what do you think makes VAs unique here? What are some other examples where technology is used to gain an epistemic advantage? How is that advantage gained?

INVITATIONS TO GO DEEPER

1. This chapter makes the claim that much of our digital landscape is increasingly gendered as feminine and intended to serve a (presumed male) Subject. Consider what you know about feminist theories and values. What might a feminist digital landscape look like? What values or perspectives would be centred? Are there parts of our current digital landscape that you would describe as feminist?

2. Digital computers have replaced human computers, a move that largely cost women and other marginalized groups their livelihood. In what other ways have we digitized or automated jobs that were previously done by humans? Whose jobs have been lost? In what ways do you think technology will be used in the future to do jobs that were previously done by humans? Using an intersectional lens, consider how this will impact employment opportunities.

3. Cortana was named for a science fiction VA character from a video game. And Guzman (2017) makes the claim that Siri's design team worked hard to set Siri apart from science fiction's HAL. What other examples of VAs from science fiction are you aware of? What are their characteristics? Do they have a gender? Personality? Are they submissive? Dominant? What role, if any, do you think our current science fiction representation of VAs might have on the creation of real-world VAs in the future?

READ MORE

Anderson, E. (2020). Feminist epistemology and philosophy of science. *Stanford Encyclopedia of Philosophy.* https://plato.stanford.edu/entries/feminism-epistemology/

Grier, D. A. (2007). *When computers were human.* Princeton University Press.

Lloreda, C. L. (2020, July 5). Speech recognition tech is yet another example of bias: Siri, Alexa and other programs sometimes have trouble with the accents and speech patterns of people from many underrepresented groups. *Scientific American.* https://www.scientificamerican.com/article/speech-recognition-tech-is-yet-another-example-of-bias/

Mullaney, T. S., Peters, B., Hicks, M., & Philips, K. (2021). *Your computer is on fire*. MIT Press.

Piper, A. (2016). *Stereotyping femininity in disembodied virtual assistants* (Publication No. 15792) [Master's thesis]. Iowa State University. https://core.ac.uk/download/pdf/141671276.pdf

LISTEN MORE, WATCH MORE

"Meet Q: The first genderless voice," *GenderLess Voice*: https://www.genderlessvoice.com/watch/

"Meet the real voice of Siri," *Oprah.com*: https://www.oprah.com/wherearetheynow/meet-susan-bennett-the-real-voice-of-siri-video

NOTES

1. Though it is not clear whether men actually do receive more harassment than women online, on the assumption that they do, one explanation may be that men are much more likely than women to participate in parts of the internet where hate speech flourishes (Nadim & Fladmoe, 2019). And being in a place where hate speech in common and normalized increases one's risk of exposure to hate speech oneself.

2. Oops!!

REFERENCES

Beauvoir, S. (1993). *The second sex* (H. M. Parshley, Trans.). Everyman Library.

Both, G. (2014). Multi-dimensional gendering processes at the human–computer-interface: The case of Siri. In N. Marsden & U. Kempf (Eds.), *Gender-UseIT: HCI, Usability und UX unter Gendergesichtspunkten* (pp. 107–112). De Gruyter Oldenbourg. https://doi.org/10.1515/9783110363227.107

Brahnam, S., Karanikas, M., & Weaver, M. (2011). (Un)dressing the interface: Exposing the foundational HCI metaphor "computer is woman." *Interacting with Computers, 23*, 401–412.

Coates, T.-N. (2015). *Between the world and me*. Spiegel and Grau.

Crenshaw, K. (1989). Demarginalizing the intersection of race and sex: A Black feminist critique of antidiscrimination doctrine, feminist theory and antiracist politics. *University of Chicago Legal Forum, 1989*(1), Article 8.

Duggan, M. (2017, July 11). Online harassment in 2017. *Pew Research Center*. https://www.pewresearch.org/internet/2017/07/11/online-harassment-2017/

Fessler, L. (2017, February 22). We tested bots like Siri and Alexa to see who would stand up to sexual harassment. *Quartz*. https://qz.com/911681/we-tested-apples-siri-amazon-echos-alexa-microsofts-cortana-and-googles-google-home-to-see-which-personal-assistant-bots-stand-up-for-themselves-in-the-face-of-sexual-harassment

Grier, D. A. (2007). *When computers were human*. Princeton University Press.

Guzman, A. (2017). Making AI safe for humans: A conversation with Siri. In R. W. Gehl & M. Bakardjieva (Eds.), *Socialbots: Digital media and the automation of sociality* (pp. 69–86). Routledge.

Harding, S. (2015). *Objectivity and diversity: Another logic of scientific research*. University of Chicago Press.

Hartsock, N. (2006). Experience, embodiment, and epistemologies. *Hypatia, 21*(2), 178–183.

Hegel, G. W. F., Miller, A., & Findlay, J. (1977). *The phenomenology of spirit*. Clarendon Press.

Henry, N., & Powell, A. (2018). Technology-facilitated sexual violence: A literature review of empirical research. *Trauma, Violence and Abuse, 19*, 195–208.

Intemann, K. (2010). 25 years of feminist empiricism and standpoint theory: Where are we now? *Hypatia, 25*(4), 778–796. https://doi.org/10.1111/j.1527-2001.2010.01138.x

Koenecke, A., Nam, A., Lake, E., Nudell, J., Quartey, M., Mengesha, Z., Toups, C., Rickford, J. R., Jurafsky, D., & Goel, S. (2020). Racial disparities in automated speech recognition. *Proceedings of the National Academy of Science of the United States of America, 117*(14), 7684–7689. https://doi.org/10.1073/pnas.1915768117

Lawrence, H. M. (2021). Siri disciplines. In T. S. Mullaney, B. Peters, M. Hicks, & K. Philips (Eds.), *Your computer is on fire* (pp. 179–198). MIT Press.

Lorde, A. (1997). The uses of anger. *Women's Studies Quarterly, 25*(1/2), 278–285.

Lovejoy, B. (2020, June 8). Siri and Google now address "all lives matter" but Google does a better job. *9To5Mac*. https://9to5mac.com/2020/06/08/all-lives-matter-siri-response/

Manne, K. (2017). *Down girl: The logic of misogyny*. Oxford University Press.

Marx, K., & Engels, F. (2014). *The communist manifesto*. International Publishing.

Mills, C. (2007). White ignorance. In S. Sullivan & N. Tuana (Eds.), *Race and epistemologies of ignorance* (pp. 13–38). SUNY Press.

Nadim, M., & Fladmoe, A. (2019). Silencing women? Gender and online harassment. *Social Science Computer Review, 39*(2), 245–258.

Perez, C. C. (2019). *Invisible women: Data bias in a world designed for men*. Harry N. Abrams Press.

Powell, A., & Henry, N. (2015). *Digital harassment and abuse of adult Australians: A summary report*. RMIT University and La Trobe University. https://www.

parliament.nsw.gov.au/lcdocs/other/7351/Tabled%20Document%20-Digital%20
Harassment%20and%20Abuse%20of%20A.pdf

Quinn, Z. (2017). *Crash override: How gamergate (nearly) destroyed my life and how we can win the fight against online hate.* PublicAffairs.

Specia, M. (2019, May 22). Siri and Alexa reinforce gender bias, UN finds. *New York Times.* https://www.nytimes.com/2019/05/22/world/siri-alexa-ai-gender-bias.html

UNESCO, & EQUALS Skills Coalition. (2019). *I'd blush if I could: Closing gender divides in digital skills through education.* https://unesdoc.unesco.org/ark:/48223/pf0000367416.page=1

Empowerment through Participatory Surveillance? Menstrual and Fertility Self-Tracking Apps as Postfeminist Biopedagogies

Jessica Polzer, Anna Sui, Kelly Ge, and Laura Cayen

"Say hello to understanding your body." (Kindara)

"Track your period and ovulation with Clue to understand how your body works." (Clue)

"Sync with your cycle. Reclaim your month. Run your world." (MyFlo)

INTRODUCTION

The above imperatives from the homepages of websites promoting menstrual and fertility tracking attest to the ways in which digital health technologies view the body as a site for self-knowledge, self-surveillance, and self-transformation. Among the most popular self-tracking apps currently available, menstrual and fertility tracking apps (MFTAs) require users to provide personal information on a regular basis—information that they may not even disclose to friends or family (Gupta & Singer, 2021)—including their dates of menstruation, basal (resting) body temperature, and changes in the quality of their cervical fluid. Users may also opt to share additional details, such as information about their sexual activity, libido levels, pregnancy test results, medications, and mood and energy levels (Hamper, 2020). Information is provided manually, by a user entering it into their smart devices, or with the assistance of external hardware (wearables) that records physiological measurements directly from the body. The data produced from this information are aggregated and presented to the user (typically in visual formats), who may share these data with their sexual partners, doctors, and fellow self-trackers. Behind the scenes, large data sets are often shared by app developers (e.g., with health researchers or third parties for advertising purposes) in ways that should (yet do not always) align with their stated privacy policies.

Concerns have been raised in the news media about the lack of transparency regarding how this personal information is shared and subsequently used (Gupta & Singer, 2021; Harwell, 2019). Health and privacy advocates conclude that these apps are largely designed to benefit their developers and insurance companies, not the people they claim to help, whose bodies are viewed "as a technological gold mine, rich with a vast range of health data their algorithms can track and analyze" (Harwell, 2019, para. 14). Despite these concerns, MFTAs constitute a significant part of a growing "Femtech" industry (a term coined by the founder of the period tracker Clue; Dodgson, 2020), illustrating how cisgender women's bodies, menstruation, and reproductive potential are viewed as particularly lucrative sites for such data mining. This industry includes software, apps, and devices that claim to enhance women's health and well-being and is projected to be worth $50 billion by 2025 (Kressbach, 2021; Woodford, 2018).

Critical social science research on the use and effects of digital self-tracking technologies in health has proliferated in recent years, with much of this work focusing on fitness-related apps (e.g., Lupton, 2020; Ward et al., 2018; Williamson, 2015). A growing body of feminist literature on MFTAs has also emerged, emphasizing the ways in which these apps function as socio-cultural products that embed and replicate normalizing, culturally rooted ideologies and expectations regarding gender, sexuality, and reproduction (Fox et al., 2020; Lupton, 2015). This body of research points to the limitations of the app designs, including their reliance on gendered stereotypes and heteronormative framings in visuals and text (Fox et al., 2020; Novotny & Hutchinson, 2019); the constraints they impose on user agency (Novotny & Hutchinson, 2019); and the ways in which they compound prevailing notions of menstrual shame and promote bodily alienation (Kressbach, 2021). To date, little is known about how people who menstruate (hereafter referred to collectively as PWM) actually engage with these technologies, though interest in this area is growing (Fox et al., 2020; Gambier-Ross et al., 2018; Hamper, 2020; Levy & Romo-Avilés, 2019).

In this chapter, we critically examine the online promotion and marketing of MFTAs. In so doing, we ask how the body is (re)imagined and trained by these digital technologies and how app users are invited to direct their agency and build their capacities in relation to this bodily education. We begin by contextualizing the emergence of MFTAs within the broader socio-political and discursive context. Then, we situate MFTAs as postfeminist biopedagogies that educate app users by framing the empowerment they claim to deliver in relation to reductionist notions of the body as data and normative constructions of gender and sexuality. Last, we present themes that emerged from our analysis of 15 websites that promote MFTAs and put these into conversation with insights from feminist theory and critical digital health studies.

As activist educators and students in gender, sexuality, and health studies, our research interests span the politics of women's health, critical digital health studies, and sexual and reproductive health. Our aim in this chapter is to provide readers with conceptual tools that can assist them in thinking critically about the political, moral, and ideological work that is accomplished when individuals willingly take part in menstrual and other forms of health-related self-tracking. With these tools, we hope that readers will be better positioned to reflect on and make decisions about how they wish to engage in, not to engage in, and/or to disengage from digital self-tracking, and consider how self-tracking apps might better suit their needs.

THE SOCIO-POLITICAL AND DISCURSIVE CONTEXT OF MFTAs

The socio-political context within which the demand and desire for MFTAs has emerged includes a complex configuration of competing discourses regarding menstruation and sexual and reproductive health. Alongside menstrual rights and equity activism worldwide, which challenges the stigma and shame associated with menstruation and advocates for access to menstrual products (Levy & Romo-Avilés, 2019; Walmsley, 2020; Weiss-Wolf, 2017), access to sexual and reproductive health education and services continues to erode in Canada and elsewhere as a result of resistance and co-optation by anti-choice organizations and conservative political agendas (Archer, 2019; Bialystok et al., 2020). The ways in which MFTAs embed these values is evidenced by the FEMM app, which was developed by a non-profit anti-choice foundation with the support of $1.7 million under the Trump administration, funding that was initially earmarked to "help poor women obtain contraceptives" (Glenza, 2019). Although MFTAs do not explicitly promote anti-choice agendas, the logic underlying them—that self-tracking can aid in predicting fertile windows—is a technological extension of fertility awareness methods (FAM), which involve monitoring bodily signs (cervical fluid, waking temperature, cervical position) to identify the days prior to and following ovulation (Hamper, 2020). With roots in natural family planning approaches advocated by the Catholic church (Fox et al., 2020), FAM has been promoted widely among secular audiences in Toni Weschler's book, *Taking Charge of Your Fertility: The*

Definitive Guide to Natural Birth Control, Pregnancy Achievement, and Reproductive Health, first published in 1995 (Weschler, 2015). As a contemporary technological expression of FAM, MFTAs inherit "moral orientations" (Fox et al., 2020, p. 7) that "are rooted in religious programs of family planning and tied to particular political regimes that seek to undermine established educational initiatives or limit access to reproductive health resources" (p. 17).

MFTAs are further shaped by a postfeminist sensibility that permeates the discursive landscape in which they have gained popularity and insulates this conservative moral orientation from criticism. This sensibility includes:

> a taking for granted of feminist ideas alongside a fierce repudiation of feminism; an emphasis upon choice, freedom and individual empowerment; a pre-occupation with the body and sexuality as the locus of femininity; a reassertion of natural sexual difference grounded in heteronormative ideas about gender complementarity; the importance placed upon self-surveillance and monitoring as modes of power; and a thoroughgoing commitment to ideas of self-transformation, that is, a make-over paradigm. (Gill, 2009, p. 346)

Discourses on health and sexuality, which have been central to feminist and LGBTQ+ struggles, are particularly fertile sites for postfeminist framings of empowerment, which transform these discourses from sites of collective resistance and demands (e.g., for access to inclusive sexual and health information) into opportunities for individual consumption and the regulation of gender and sexuality (Cayen, 2016; Riley et al., 2018). In discourses on women's health, this regulation is accomplished through cultural representation that "consistently returns women to the most traditional of gender roles: naïve daughters, passive wives, and nurturing mothers" (Dubriwny, 2013, p. 25). Furthermore, the ways in which postfeminist framings of sexuality and health emphasize individual choice and self-empowerment reflects neoliberal principles (Riley et al., 2018), which commodify (women's) health by constructing problems as individual deficiencies (e.g., lack of information) that are amenable to the consumption of pharmaceutical cures and technological solutions (Batt & Lippman, 2010). In so doing, the social and political contexts of the assumed problem remain unquestioned as the (reproductive) body is situated as a resource for economic growth and technological development. The power of this framing is expressed concisely in the statement by Max Levchin, founder of the menstrual/fertility tracking app Glow: "Health is a big information problem waiting for data analytics and wearable sensors. I wanted to start somewhere to make a difference.… I found it in procreation" (as cited in Fox et al., 2020, p. 8).

REFRAMING EMPOWERMENT: MFTAs AS POSTFEMINIST BIOPEDAGOGIES

The term *biopedagogy* describes the normalizing and regulating practices that focus on educating the body (Wright, 2009). Informed by Foucault's (1978) theory of biopower, biopedagogies describe a range of practices that involve an intensification of surveillance of both the individual body and the social body. These biopedagogical practices instruct individuals how to conform to broader socio-cultural norms (Wright, 2009) and are dispersed through official institutions (e.g., schools, public health) and discourses that circulate widely in various forms of media (Duncan, 1994; Gray & Szto, 2016). Similar to the feminist insistence that the personal is always political, the notion of biopedagogy provides a framework for understanding how the body is constructed as a political space—that is, as a target for surveillance and intervention towards particular goals, such as health and self-improvement. In this sense, biopedagogies do not aim to cultivate just any body; rather, they "generate and convey knowledge, competencies, skills, and moral codes, *which define what the body is and ought to be, whose and what bodies have status and value, and what 'body work' needs to be done to make one's body 'fit'*" (Williamson, 2015, p. 140; emphasis added).

The self-surveillance invited by self-tracking apps (including those that focus on menstruation and fertility) is unique in its appearance of transparency as users willingly submit their personal information into their smartphones/devices. However, this information is subsequently processed into data by algorithms that remain invisible to the user. The metrics and visuals resulting from these algorithmic quantifications of the body encourage users to understand their bodies as data, rather than as subjectively unique and sensory-embodied knowledge (Ward et al., 2018). This datafication "makes the body of the individual visible in terms of data, calculable as numbers, and on that basis amenable to enhancement" (Williamson, 2015, p. 141). The learning fostered by these biopedagogies thus involves the participatory surveillance of app users who both provide the raw data and reflect on their (re)presentation. In this sense, self-trackers are "prosumers" who assume the roles of both producer and consumer of the data that form the basis of their bodily education (Ritzer & Jurgenson, 2010). Furthermore, app users' active involvement in the production and consumption of real-time visual (re)presentations of their bodies gives rise to a range of affective responses, including a sense of achievement and "pleasurable self-surveillance" (Williamson, 2015, p. 142). Such experiences of pleasure are important to acknowledge—not only because they are meaningful for PWM but also because they can mask the regulatory effects of self-tracking and obscure the ways in which users may find themselves complicit in reinforcing these regulatory functions.

ENTANGLEMENTS OF EMPOWERMENT AND SURVEILLANCE

In this section, we present findings from our thematic analysis of 15 websites that promote MFTAs. Our analysis is based on close readings of text and images presented on the websites (including 52 webpages and 67 written testimonials). In addition to some of the most popular apps, our sample includes apps that aim to be gender and age inclusive, involve wearable hardware, and offer menstrual tracking as part of wellness tracking. We present five themes to illustrate how this marketing of MFTAs promotes biopedagogical aims, entangles empowerment with surveillance, and entails (re)conceptualizations of the body and its relationship to the technology and the user in ways that reproduce postfeminist imaginaries. For each theme, we present quotations from the websites to support our interpretations and indicate our emphasis using *italicized* text.

Putting the Mystery in the Body: The Imperative to Learn

The biopedagogical aim of these apps is clear in the ways that they are consistently promoted as both an invitation and an obligation to "learn" about one's body. This was evident across our sample in the following kinds of statements, which typically greeted viewers on the website homepages:

> Scientific and straightforward—the period tracker app that *teaches you about your body.* (Clue, n.d.a)

> *Upgrade Your Health IQ* With Glow Premium. (Glow, n.d.)

> Track your period, ovulation test results, and PMS [premenstrual syndrome] symptoms *to help you learn more about your body, cycle, and reproductive health.* (Natural Cycles, n.d.)

These invitational imperatives to learn about one's body through menstrual tracking are founded on the assumption that potential users have little or no prior bodily knowledge or embodied experiences. This bodily ignorance is further asserted with references to the enigmatic character of menstruation, both in webpages and testimonials:

Resolve the confusion, mystery, and overwhelm out of navigating your 28-day cycle in every area of your life. (MyFlo, n.d.)

I wasn't just tracking my cycle, *I was learning about what "normal" looked like and it took the mystery out of fertility.* (Kindara, n.d.a)

This construction of the body as mysterious justifies the need for bodily education through self-tracking and sets in motion a particular relationship with the technology, which is positioned as assisting the user.

Educating the Body: Technology as Helper

To (re)solve these mysteries, users are told that they must learn to decipher the signs provided by their bodies with the help of the app. For example, the Kindara website poses a rhetorical question to invite the reader to imagine their body as a storyteller that communicates in a language that only their app can interpret:

Your menstrual cycle tells a story about your fertility and health. *Are you ready to listen? Yes? Great! We have a solution for you.* (Kindara, n.d.b)

Just as PWM are positioned as unqualified to interpret their bodies without technological assistance, the apps are presented as helping to (re)connect self-trackers with their bodies. This assumption provides the basis of YONO's name and tagline, "You know, with YONO" (YONO, n.d.). This view of the technology as enabling users to connect with their mysterious bodies reflects Mitchell and Georges's (1998) interpretation of the "one-two punch of technocracy" (p. 113), a cultural pattern whereby reproductive technology simultaneously creates anxiety about bodily unknowns and provides the technological fix to address this ignorance and provide a sense of reassurance.

Presented as helpers, the apps are described as aiding PWM achieve their "health and reproductive goals" (e.g., FEMM, n.d.a) and as providing "handy reminders" to let users know when their periods are coming (Clue, n.d.a). This assistance is also described as oriented towards general biopedagogical goals aimed at enhancing one's bodily knowledge and "fertility intelligence" (YONO, n.d.). These broad biopedagogical aims are illustrated in the provision of information resources, such as Clue's "encyclopedia" on sexual and reproductive health (Clue, n.d.b) and in claims that the apps provide "tools and education" to "explore and understand" fertility (Fertility Friend, n.d.) and help "women grow their knowledge," "make informed decisions" (MySysters, n.d.), and come to new understandings of their bodies.

Importantly, this biopedagogical instruction is presented as technological support delivered in a non-hierarchical and non-judgemental fashion. Although some of the websites emphasize their links with official medical research organizations, the apps are positioned as functioning alongside and in support of the user rather than as medical authorities:

> The predictive calendars are just as helpful as the science-backed info that I receive through the app, email, and social media. *Clue tells me about my personal health and how my body works in an open, accepting, informative, non-clinical way.* (Clue, n.d.a)

In this role as tech support, the apps are ascribed a great deal of agency. This was pronounced for the wearables, such as YONO, which "*plots* monthly fertility charts," "*analyzes* the data," and "*predicts* the monthly fertile window" (YONO, n.d.). Presented as agentic actors, MFTAs are described as though they take on these tasks independently of PWM, who are presented as letting "the technology do the work" (YONO, n.d.). This outsourcing of labour to the technology is also depicted in images of soundly sleeping women, visually coded as stereotypically feminized bodies accessorized with the inanimate device (e.g., Ava's bracelet), which is presumably busy recording their body's data (Ava, n.d.). This imagery of ready-to-wear surveillance evokes Sandra Bartky's (2003) notion of how the body is disciplined into femininity as an "ornamented surface" (p. 31), a body that can rest—with style and comfort—while willingly submitting itself to a technological gaze that is seamlessly incorporated into everyday life as "algorithmic skin" (Williamson, 2015, p. 133).

Understanding Your Body Better: Self-Surveillance as Customizable

The bodily demystification promised by the apps, and suggested in many of the testimonials, is ultimately achieved through the users' participation in vigilant self-surveillance. Furthermore, by offering "fully customizable data tracking" (Kindara, n.d.b), a variety of "tracking options" (Clue, n.d.c), and ways to "customize observation categories" (FEMM, n.d.b), users can personally tailor how they engage in participatory self-surveillance, thus reinforcing the individualizing aims of postfeminism. Commensurate with the philosophy of FAM generally, customized tracking options provide users with "personalised feedback and tips" (FEMM, n.d.b) and emphasize that tracking "is the only way to know your real fertile days and ovulation date *unique to YOU*" (Fertility Friend, n.d.). In keeping with this customization, the knowledge users gain through the surveillance involved in self-tracking is presented as uniquely theirs, and the apps are presented as specially positioned to teach the user about their unique menstrual cycles and bodies:

> Only OvuSense helps with *diagnosis of your individual cycle characteristics.* (OvuSense, n.d.)

> *Every body is different. Spot On gets that—and gets you.* (Planned Parenthood, n.d.)

> Whether you want to predict periods, learn how your cycle impacts your moods, or stay on top of your sleep throughout the month, *Ava keeps a record of you.* (Ava, n.d.)

As well, this ability to customize surveillance categories encourages users to share personal information beyond what is required for menstrual tracking, as this will expand their opportunities for learning and lead to a "better understanding" of their bodies:

> You can also add extra info like cycle symptoms, changes to your mood and sex data, *so you can learn even more about the pattern of your unique cycle.* (Natural Cycles, n.d.)

> *Learn about personal patterns with 30+ tracking options* like cramps, skin, hair, sleep and more to *gain a better understanding of how your body works.* (Clue, n.d.c)

Regardless of the stated reasons for using MFTAs (e.g., contraception, reproduction), the testimonials consistently noted that gaining a better understanding of one's body was both a motivation for and effect of self-tracking:

> *I am amazed at how much I have learned about my body* and my well being through tracking all of the changes that I never paid attention to. (Kindara, n.d.c)

Among the rare testimonials by nonbinary menstrual trackers, the bodily understanding enabled by self-tracking with a gender-inclusive app was helpful to prepare for and manage gender dysphoric experiences:

> *Clue helps me understand my body and knowing when my period is coming helps me control my dysphoria.* I never wanted to use a period tracking app beforehand, because they were all so centered on women and stereotypical gender roles, but *Clue allows me to understand my body without automatically gendering it.* (Clue, n.d.d)

Regardless of the reason for menstrual tracking, the linking of improved self-understanding to customized self-surveillance reinforces the role of app users as "prosumers" (Ritzer & Jurgenson, 2010), whose consumption of customized data is linked to their willingness to share their personal information and collaborate in the production of this bodily knowledge.

Seeing as Self-Knowledge: Self-Surveillance as Pleasurable and Rewarding

The online marketing of MFTAs places a great deal of attention on visualization techniques that allow users to make instantaneous connections between their hormonal fluctuations and other data points (e.g., mood, exercise) that they have selected for self-tracking:

> Never get lost in your tracked data. *With frequent analysis reports and a clear calendar overview you'll draw conclusions quickly.* (Clue, n.d.c)

These visualizations featured prominently on all of the websites and included images of smartphone screenshots displaying tracked corporeal data mapped onto monthly calendars and plotted in charts and graphs (e.g., Clue, n.d.c; Glow, n.d.; MyFlo, n.d.). These visualization techniques informationalize the body, presenting it as a series of data points that can be tracked, measured, and analyzed in order to predict patterns and optimize success, in reproduction and in life. This ability to see patterns in their data was likened by some users in testimonials to gaining a truer and deeper understanding of their bodies and of themselves:

> *You can clearly see your ovulation and fertile window. You can see your timing and how your different signs come together.* (Fertility Friend, n.d.)

I had been taking birth control for nearly 10 years and had no clue what my natural cycles were like. *It wasn't long before I began to see a pattern emerge, and it felt like each cycle, I learned more and more about myself.* (Kindara, n.d.d)

This visually mediated bodily understanding was often presented as accompanied by a sense of pleasure and excitement. This was suggested by images showing women mesmerized by their device screens, alone or with their male partners (e.g., OvuSense, n.d.), and by the use of exclamation marks, emoticons, and phrases that evoked feelings of affection towards the app in written text:

I've tried many different period tracking apps, as it is our sole method of family planning (being practicing Catholics), and none have been as clear cut, friendly to use, and visually appealing as Kindara. *I loved that I could see both my BBTs* [basal body temperatures] *and my cervical signs represented on the same chart.* (Kindara, n.d.e)

Clue is such an invaluable app! As someone with PCOS [polycystic ovary syndrome] and other health conditions that contribute to painful and irregular cycles, *Clue has helped me to see patterns in my cycle.* (Clue, n.d.c)

By training users to (re)cognize patterns between menstrual data and other recorded data, these biopedagogical devices instruct users about how to guide their everyday lives in ways to optimize health and reproductive outcomes, thus enabling a "bodily self-governance to take place" (Williamson, 2015, p. 135):

You'll be able to look for patterns or triggers at a glance thanks to our colour-coded system…. Do Mondays always appear darker? *Look for lifestyle triggers over the weekend that you can change to provide relief.* (MySysters, n.d.)

However, as Kressbach (2021) notes in her reflections on her own menstrual tracking, this visual governance is problematic in the way that it favours hormonal explanations (e.g., of stress) and excludes the effects of social factors:

I'm encouraged to see a direct relationship between my emotions and the unseen biological process: to read stress as an indicator of ovulation or ovulation as a cause of stress. While I may have logged stress on days I was ovulating, *Clue doesn't give me the choice to include exterior social conditions that may have contributed to this experience.* (p. 250; emphasis added)

While the data visualizations provided by these apps are associated with the reward and pleasure of obtaining self-knowledge, they also perform a kind of menstrual reductionism whereby an expansive range of experiences and bodily "symptoms" are filtered, interpreted, and (re)presented as hormonally determined.

Reinforcing the Postfeminist Imaginary: Self-Transformation through Conformity and Confidence

As postfeminist biopedagogies, MFTAs provide opportunities for self-discovery and empowerment through pleasurable self-surveillance and in ways that reinforce naturalized gender norms and sexual difference. The websites we reviewed are consistently oriented towards cis women who are portrayed in roles that reflect this postfeminist sensibility: as intently and happily surveilling themselves as they stare at their phones (Bellabeat, n.d.; Natural Cycles, n.d.; YONO, n.d.); as physically active in appropriately feminine fitness, such as yoga (Bellabeat, n.d.; MyFlo, n.d.); as socializing and participating in leisure activities while ornamented with stylish clothing and wearable tracking devices (Bellabeat, n.d.); as docile bodies at rest while their data are collected by wearables without their mindful engagement (Ava, n.d.); and as anticipatory pregnant mothers and reproductive bodies with babies and masculine-presenting partners (Glow, n.d.; Ovia Health, n.d.). With the exception of two apps in our sample that strive for gender inclusivity (e.g., Clue and Spot On, which use gender-neutral language and colour schemes), this visual economy privileges images of slender and conventionally attractive women who are usually, though not exclusively, white. In the written text, few references were made to sexual, gender, or other forms of diversity, with the exception of a few testimonials by self-trackers who identified as transgender (e.g., Clue, n.d.d), as perimenopausal women (Kindara, n.d.f), and as a surrogate for a known queer couple (Kindara, n.d.g). As noted by others (Dubriwny, 2013; Fox et al., 2020), these highly gendered and heterosexist visual and textual scripts perpetuate harmful stereotypes and exclude a range of identities for whom menstrual tracking may be helpful and in ways that transcend the apps' stated purposes and embedded biopedagogical aims.

While the value ascribed to this gendered and sexual conformity is rarely troubled in the testimonials, these stories offer insight into the appeal of MFTAs by revealing how self-tracking enables users to transform their views of the menstruating body from an unruly unknown to a reliable source of self-knowledge associated with feelings of control and "confidence":

Before Kindara, my hormonal processes were a complete mystery to me. Now, I'm completely in tune with my body. *I know what's going on, and I know with 100% confidence when I can and can't get pregnant.* Best of all, it really is natural—you're working with reliable signals from your body to determine your fertility. *Kindara has changed my life. For now, I don't want children, but if I change my mind in the future, I know I can count on Kindara to* help me determine the best time to conceive. (Kindara, n.d.h)

This sense of confidence is bolstered by the ways in which the apps appear to challenge the silence and concealment that accompany cultural understandings of the menstruating body as abject (Kressbach, 2021). While some testimonials note the confidence in overcoming the shame associated with menses, they also uphold the demands of normative femininity that require women to be cheerful and in control of their unruly bodies:

But there will be no going back to that awful pill because I have a reliable alternative, one that *makes me happy and in charge of my body, my mood, and I don't mind say[ing], my fluids!* (Kindara, n.d.i)

In addition to overcoming menstrual shame, some of the testimonials draw attention to the ways in which transformations in bodily knowledge and self-confidence defy conservative values that pathologize female embodiment (Morgan, 1998) and repress communication and education about sexual and reproductive health. This is noted explicitly by Brittany B., whose testimonial elucidates the power of the apps' biopedagogical effects, which extend far beyond understanding reproductive potential to constitute a thorough transformation of self:

I grew up with the most wonderful mother in the world, a real life Southern Belle, but *we really didn't talk much about "feminine things …" and certainly not about fertility! Along with that, my adolescence was spent in a very conservative suburb and school, and pregnancy was spoken about in very hushed tones, if you know what I mean…. Now I am excited because I'm self-aware!* It [tracking] has led me to research the right things to consume, the best way to exercise, sleeping better. I'm even excited to be able to get pregnant someday without having to use tons of harmful chemicals and hormones! *I never thought I'd feel this empowered by what my body's been doing for years all on its own…. Thank you. This woman's life is better for it.* (Kindara, n.d.j)

CONCLUSION

The postfeminist sensibility embedded in the marketing and promotion of MFTAs encourages users to become actively involved in their menstruation and fertility, yet in ways that tend to reproduce normative constructions of gender and sexuality and position the body as a site for the intensification of surveillance. To date, research on self-tracking as biopedagogy has focused primarily on apps for physical fitness and health education (e.g., Fotopoulou & O'Riordan, 2017; Ward et al., 2018; Williamson, 2015). By situating MFTAs as postfeminist biopedagogies, we extend the insights of feminist researchers who acknowledge the overtly pedagogical approach taken by MFTAs as well as their "strongly gendered and heteronormative elements … including the positioning of women as responsibilised reproductive citizens who are charged with closely monitoring their bodies" (Lupton, 2020, p. 986). Similar to that of Sanders (2017), our analysis provides a rich example of the ways in which "self-tracking devices expand individuals' capacity for self-knowledge and self-care at the same time that they serve the convergent interests of biopower and gender retrenchment" (p. 38).

As postfeminist biopedagogies, MFTAs recruit PWM into technologically mediated rituals of self-surveillance and self-knowledge that aim to educate the body as well as upgrade and improve psychological attitudes, confidence, and self-esteem, resulting in a "makeover of subjectivity itself" (Camacho-Miñano et al., 2019, p. 653). The marketing and promotion of MFTAs entangles bodily surveillance with self-understanding and pleasure and reflects a postfeminist imaginary whereby individual empowerment and the possibility of self-knowledge are contingent on conformity, thus undermining diverse expressions of bodily experience and collective framings of and approaches to empowerment. Our analysis of the biopedagogical functions of MFTAs aids in understanding how the sense of pleasure and reward achieved in gaining self-knowledge becomes an end in itself, thus eliding important questions about the apps' claims of effectiveness and accuracy (e.g., in predicting fertile windows). The sense of reward associated with learning about one's menstruation and fertility is particularly pronounced in the context of prevailing cultural narratives of menstrual abjection and shame reinforced by conservative political agendas and neoliberal policies, which restrict access to inclusive sexual health education and services that acknowledge the embodied experiences of PWM. Because our analysis focused exclusively on websites promoting MFTAs, we are unable to speak to the multiple ways in which diversely situated PWM actually engage with and use these biopedagogical devices. Nevertheless, the testimonials we reviewed suggest that PWM use MFTAs to learn about and/or manage a wide range of fertility- and health-related issues and life experiences, including menstrual irregularity, menopause, infertility, specific health concerns (polycystic ovarian syndrome, endometriosis), discontinuation of hormonal contraception, dissatisfaction with medical encounters, gender transitioning, and surrogacy.

By putting mystery in the body and then (re)solving it through algorithmically driven processes of datafication and visualization, MFTAs educate not by responding to the needs of PWM but rather by framing the problem in ways that commodify the body, emphasize individual responsibility for sexual and reproductive health, and elide social and political factors that shape access to inclusive sexual and health education and services. Furthermore, MFTAs operate as affective biopedagogies that enable users to attach positive emotional meaning to an aspect of their embodiment—menstruation—that is construed as a source of mystery and shame. While these apps may help some PWM overcome feelings of bodily ignorance and menstrual shame, the framing of the process and outcome of one's surveillance work as fun and educational may override the need for vigilant critical reflection about the ethical, legal, social, and political implications associated with self-tracking. This power dynamic is clearly acknowledged in media reports where the notion of menstruation as mysterious and poorly understood is used to deflect privacy concerns about MFTAs in the interest of advancing knowledge of "female health":

> And here lies the crux of the problem with women's consumer health technology, or "femtech" as it is known in investor speak: *The sheer volume of data collected in apps like Flo is ripe for privacy violations, but that same data may also open the door to unraveling some of the biggest, understudied riddles of female health.* (Gupta & Singer, 2021, para. 7; emphasis added)

We are left to question: does the emergence of MFTAs signal a new era of technologically driven hormonal reductionism, one in which a "dictatorship of the ovaries" (Ehrenreich & English, 1990, p. 277) is buttressed not by the profession of medicine, but rather by postfeminist re-framings of personal empowerment? Certainly, the postfeminist imaginary we have traced in menstrual and fertility self-tracking promises self-confidence and empowerment as an outcome of a biopedagogical process through which self-trackers learn to view their bodies and imagine their lives as hormonally determined and directed. Paradoxically, while these apps magnify the body as a constellation of data points, they also reduce a contextually rich assortment of meanings and embodied experiences regarding menstruation and reproduction to a technical problem of information.

While PWM may find some aspects of menstrual tracking helpful, the postfeminist framework that connects them to individualized and commodifiable modes of self-knowledge and self-transformation may also disconnect them from other ways of effecting social transformation and exercising care of and control over their bodies and themselves.

QUESTIONS FOR DISCUSSION

1. What do you think about the ways in which menstrual and other forms of self-tracking link empowerment to self-surveillance? How does this relationship between power and surveillance relate to other ideas and concepts you've learned about in your studies?
2. Discuss the limitations and opportunities that menstrual tracking may present for gender nonbinary people and other people who menstruate. How might these technologies be used to queer how we think of reproductive capacity beyond heterosexual relationships?
3. How do you think digital technologies (including but not limited to self-tracking) can be useful to promote menstrual health and education and reduce menstrual stigma?
4. What are the risks and benefits of using self-tracking apps for health-related purposes?

INVITATIONS TO GO DEEPER

1. Reflect on your own relationship with menstrual self-tracking apps or other digital self-tracking apps (e.g., mood tracking) by writing about your tracking-related experiences in a journal for one week. (If you don't use apps for self-tracking, you may focus on your practices of self-monitoring more generally.) Consider the following questions in your reflections, and feel free to write more as well:
   - What kinds of (digital) self-tracking or self-monitoring do you engage in?
   - Why and when did you start tracking?
   - What do you like/not like about self-tracking?
   - How does tracking make you feel?
   - How do you use the information you get from tracking? With whom, if anyone, do you share this information? What is that like?
   - How does your self-tracking shape how you think about and "make sense" of your body, yourself, and others? How does it shape your everyday life?

Once you've completed your journal, consider discussing your reflections with friends who have also journaled about their self-tracking experiences. What new insights or ideas did you arrive at through your discussion? What, if anything, would you change about your relationship with self-tracking based on your reflections and discussion?

2. Download a free app that is unfamiliar to you and explore its features. Document the following:
   - What information does it request when you sign up?
   - How clear is the privacy policy?
   - What personal information does the app share, with whom, and for what purposes?
   - How are gendered and other norms conveyed on the app?
   - How does the app attempt to be inclusive of diverse identities?

READ MORE

Felizi, N., & Varon, J. (n.d.). Menstruapps: How to turn your period into money (for others). *Chupadados*. https://chupadados.codingrights.org/en/menstruapps-como-transformar-sua-menstruacao-em-dinheiro-para-os-outros/

Fox, S., Menking, A., Eschler, J., & Backonja, U. (2020). Multiples over models: Interrogating the past and collectively reimagining the future of menstrual sensemaking. *ACM Transactions on Computer–Human Interaction*, *27*(4), Article 22. https://doi.org/10.1145/3397178

Hamper, J. (2020). "Catching ovulation": Exploring women's use of fertility tracking apps as a reproductive technology. *Body & Society*, *26*(3), 3–30. https://doi.org/10.1177/1357034X19898259

Kressbach, M. (2021). Period hacks: Menstruating in the big data paradigm. *Television & New Media*, *22*(3), 241–261. https://doi.org/10.1177/1527476419886389

Lupton, D. (2015). Quantified sex: A critical analysis of sexual and reproductive self-tracking using apps. *Culture, Health and Sexuality*, *17*(4), 440–453. https://doi.org/10.1080/13691058.2014.920528

LISTEN MORE, WATCH MORE

Bloody Health Collective, Drip menstrual cycle tracking app: https://bloodyhealth.gitlab.io/

"Building a better period-tracking app," *Prognosis* podcast: https://www.radio.com/media/audio-channel/building-a-better-period-tracking-app

The Pad Project: https://thepadproject.org/

Period. End of sentence, Rayka Zehtabchi, Netflix, 2018: https://www.youtube.com/watch?v=Lrm2pD0qofM

REFERENCES

Archer, N. (2019, February 13). There's a backlash against sex education in feminist Canada. *Open Democracy.* https://www.opendemocracy.net/en/5050/backlash-against-sex-education-feminist-canada/

Ava. (n.d.). Home. Retrieved February 9, 2021, from https://www.avawomen.com/

Bartky, S. (2003). Foucault, femininity, and the modernization of patriarchal power. In R. Weitz (Ed.), *The politics of women's bodies: Sexuality, appearance, and behavior* (pp. 25–45). Oxford University Press.

Batt, S., & Lippman, A. (2010). Preventing disease: Are pills the answer? In A. Rochon Ford & D. Saibil (Eds.), *The push to prescribe: Women and Canadian drug policy* (pp. 47–66). Women's Press.

Bellabeat. (n.d.). Home. Retrieved February 9, 2021, from https://bellabeat.com/

Bialystok, L., Wright, J., Berzins, T., Guy, C., & Osborne, E. (2020). The appropriation of sex education by conservative populism. *Curriculum Inquiry, 50*(4), 330–351. https://doi.org/10.1080/03626784.2020.1809967

Camacho-Miñano, M. J., MacIsaac, S., & Rich, E. (2019). Postfeminist biopedagogies of Instagram: Young women learning about bodies, health and fitness. *Sport, Education and Society, 24*(6), 651–664. https://doi.org/10.1080/13573322.2019.1613975

Cayen, L. (2016). "In the end, it's your pleasure that's on the line": Postfeminist, healthist, and neoliberal discourses in online sexual health information (Publication No. 4197) [PhD dissertation]. https://ir.lib.uwo.ca/etd/4197/

Clue. (n.d.a). Clue app. Retrieved February 9, 2021, from https://helloclue.com/period-tracker-app

Clue. (n.d.b). Encyclopedia. Retrieved February 9, 2021, from https://helloclue.com/articles

Clue. (n.d.c). Home. Retrieved February 9, 2021, from https://helloclue.com/

Clue. (n.d.d). Tips for tracking your period when you're trans. Retrieved February 9, 2021, from https://helloclue.com/articles/cycle-a-z/tips-for-using-clue-when-you're-trans

Dodgson, L. (2020, June 5). The entrepreneur who coined the term "FemTech" founded a period tracking app that's helping women understand and accept their bodies. *Insider.* https://www.insider.com/founder-of-clue-ida-tin-coined-the-term-femtech-2020–6

Dubriwny, T. (2013). *The vulnerable empowered woman: Feminism, postfeminism, and women's health*. Rutgers University Press.

Duncan, M. (1994). The politics of women's body images and practices: Foucault, the panopticon, and Shape magazine. *Journal of Sport and Social Issues*, *18*(1), 48–65. https://doi.org/10.1177/019372394018001004

Ehrenreich, B., & English, D. (1990). The sexual politics of sickness. In P. Conrad & R. Kern (Eds.), *The sociology of health and illness: Critical perspectives* (3rd ed., pp. 270–284). St. Martin's Press.

FEMM. (n.d.a). Home. Retrieved February 9, 2021, from https://femmhealth.org/

FEMM. (n.d.b). App features. Retrieved February 9, 2021, from https://femmhealthapp.org/app-features/

Fertility Friend. (n.d.). Home. Retrieved February 9, 2021, from https://www.fertilityfriend.com/

Fotopoulou, A., & O'Riordan, K. (2017). Training to self-care: Fitness tracking, biopedagogy and the healthy consumer. *Health Sociology Review*, *26*(1), 54–68. https://doi.org/10.1080/14461242.2016.1184582

Foucault, M. (1978). *The history of sexuality: An introduction* (vol. 1). Vintage Books.

Fox, S. E., Menking, A., Eschler, J., & Backonja, U. (2020). Multiples over models: Interrogating the past and collectively reimagining the future of menstrual sensemaking. *ACM Transactions on Computer–Human Interaction (TOCHI)*, *27*(4), 1–24. https://doi.org/10.1145/3397178

Gambier-Ross, K., McLernon, D. J., & Morgan, H. M. (2018). A mixed methods exploratory study of women's relationships with and uses of fertility tracking apps. *Digital Health*, *4*, 1–15. https://doi.org/10.1177/2055207618785077

Gill, R. (2009). Mediated intimacy and postfeminism: A discourse analytic examination of sex and relationships advice in a woman's magazine. *Discourse & Communication*, *3*(4), 345–369.

Glenza, J. (2019, May 30). Revealed: Women's fertility app is funded by anti-abortion campaigners. *The Guardian*. https://www.theguardian.com/world/2019/may/30/revealed-womens-fertility-app-is-funded-by-anti-abortion-campaigners

Glow. (n.d.). Home. Retrieved February 9, 2021, from https://glowing.com/

Gray, S., & Szto, C. (2016). A reflection of reality? The consumption and reproduction of obesity discourses by the Biggest Loser's viewers through Facebook. *The Journal of Social Media in Society*, *5*(3), 214–43.

Gupta, A., & Singer, N. (2021, January 28). Your app knows you got your period. Guess who it told? *The New York Times*. https://www.nytimes.com/2021/01/28/us/period-apps-health-technology-women-privacy.html

Hamper, J. (2020). "Catching ovulation": Exploring women's use of fertility tracking apps as a reproductive technology. *Body & Society*, *26*(3), 3–30. https://doi.org/10.1177/1357034X19898259

Harwell, D. (2019, April 10). Is your pregnancy app sharing your intimate data with your boss? *Washington Post*. https://www.washingtonpost.com/technology/2019/04/10/tracking-your-pregnancy-an-app-may-be-more-public-than-you-think/

Kindara. (n.d.a). Emily F: Coming to understand miscarriage and her unique cycle through fertility charting. Retrieved February 9, 2021, from https://www.kindara.com/success-stories/emily-f-coming-to-understand-miscarriage-and-her-unique-cycle-through-fertility-charting

Kindara. (n.d.b). Home. Retrieved February 9, 2021, from https://www.kindara.com/

Kindara. (n.d.c). Jessica M: Ditching the hormones in favor of fertility awareness. Retrieved February 9, 2021, from https://www.kindara.com/success-stories/jessica-m-ditching-the-hormones-in-favor-of-fertility-awareness

Kindara. (n.d.d). Kristen B: Building body literacy to avoid and achieve pregnancy. Retrieved February 9, 2021, from https://www.kindara.com/success-stories/kristen-b-building-body-literacy-to-avoid-and-achieve-pregnancy

Kindara. (n.d.e). Julie D: Using natural family planning to achieve and avoid pregnancy. Retrieved February 9, 2021, from https://www.kindara.com/success-stories/julie-d-using-natural-family-planning-to-achieve-and-avoid-pregnancy

Kindara. (n.d.f). Raechel T: A second chance through Kindara. Retrieved February 9, 2021, from https://www.kindara.com/success-stories/raechel-t-a-second-chance-through-kindara

Kindara. (n.d.g). Kim S: Surrogacy, and the art of timing conception. Retrieved February 9, 2021, from https://www.kindara.com/success-stories/kim-s-surrogacy-and-the-art-of-timing-conception

Kindara. (n.d.h). Holly H: Reclaiming her health with fertility charting after a copper IUD. Retrieved February 9, 2021, from https://www.kindara.com/success-stories/holly-h-reclaiming-her-health-with-fertility-charting-after-a-copper-iud

Kindara. (n.d.i). Cassia C: A natural alternative to managing my fertility. Retrieved February 9, 2021, from https://www.kindara.com/success-stories/cassia-c-a-natural-alternative-to-managing-my-fertility

Kindara. (n.d.j). Brittany B: Using fertility charting to understand her cycle and improve her health. Retrieved February 9, 2021, from https://www.kindara.com/success-stories/brittany-b-using-fertility-charting-to-understand-her-cycle-and-improve-her-health

Kressbach, M. (2021). Period hacks: Menstruating in the big data paradigm. *Television & New Media*, *22*(3), 241–261. https://doi.org/10.1177/1527476419886389

Levy, J., & Romo-Avilés, N. (2019). "A good little tool to get to know yourself a bit better": A qualitative study on users' experiences of app-supported menstrual tracking in Europe. *BMC Public Health, 19*(1), 1–11. https://doi.org/10.1186/s12889-019-7549-8

Lupton, D. (2015). Quantified sex: A critical analysis of sexual and reproductive self-tracking using apps. *Culture, Health & Sexuality, 17*(4), 440–453. https://doi.org/10.1080/13691058.2014.920528

Lupton, D. (2020). Australian women's use of health and fitness apps and wearable devices: A feminist new materialism analysis. *Feminist Media Studies, 20*(7), 983–998. https://doi.org/10.1080/14680777.2019.1637916

Mitchell, M., & Georges, E. (1998). Baby's first picture: The cyborg fetus of ultrasound imaging. In R. Davis-Floyd & J. Dumit (Eds.), *Cyborg babies: From techno-sex to techno-tots* (pp. 105–124). Routledge.

Morgan, K. (1998). Contested bodies, contested knowledges: Women, health, and the politics of medicalization. In S. Sherwin (Ed.), *The politics of women's health: Exploring agency and autonomy* (pp. 83–121). Temple University Press.

MyFlo. (n.d.). Home. Retrieved February 9, 2021, from https://myflotracker.com/

MySysters. (n.d.). Home. Retrieved February 9, 2021, from https://www.mysysters.com/

Natural Cycles. (n.d.). Home. Retrieved February 9, 2021, from https://www.naturalcycles.com/

Novotny, M., & Hutchinson, L. (2019). Data our bodies tell: Towards critical feminist action in fertility and period tracking applications. *Technical Communication Quarterly, 28*(4), 332–360. https://doi.org/10.1080/10572252.2019.1607907

Ovia Health. (n.d.). Home. Retrieved February 9, 2021, from https://www.oviahealth.com/

OvuSense. (n.d.). Home. Retrieved February 9, 2021, from https://www.ovusense.com/ca/

Planned Parenthood. (n.d.). Spot On period tracker. Retrieved February 9, 2021, from https://www.plannedparenthood.org/get-care/spot-on-period-tracker

Riley, S., Evans, A., & Robson, M. (2018). *Postfeminism and health: Critical psychology and media perspectives.* Routledge.

Ritzer, G., & Jurgenson, N. (2010). Production, consumption, prosumption: The nature of capitalism in the age of the digital "prosumer." *Journal of Consumer Culture, 10*(1), 13–36. https://doi.org/10.1177/1469540509354673

Sanders, R. (2017). Self-tracking in the digital era: Biopower, patriarchy, and the new biometric body projects. *Body & Society, 23*(1), 36–63. https://doi.org/10.1177/1357034X16660366

Walmsley, L. (2020, February 27). Scotland poised to become first country to make period products free. *NPR.* https://www.npr.org/sections/goatsandsoda/2020/02/27/809990550/scotland-poised-to-become-1st-country-to-make-period-products-free

Ward, P., Sirna, K., Wareham, A., & Cameron, E. (2018). Embodied display: A critical examination of the biopedagogical experience of wearing health. *Fat Studies*, *7*(1), 93–104. https://doi.org/10.1080/21604851.2017.1360674

Weiss-Wolf, J. (2017). *Periods gone public: Taking a stand for menstrual equity*. Arcade.

Weschler, T. (2015). *Taking charge of your fertility: The definitive guide to natural birth control, pregnancy achievement, and reproductive health*. HarperCollins.

Williamson, B. (2015). Algorithmic skin: Health-tracking technologies, personal analytics and the biopedagogies of digitized health and physical education. *Sport, Education and Society*, *20*(1), 133–151. https://doi.org/10.1080/13573322.2014.962494

Woodford, I. (2018, October 12). Digital contraceptives and period trackers: The rise of Femtech. *The Guardian*. https://www.theguardian.com/technology/2018/oct/12/femtech-digital-contraceptive-period-trackers-app-natural-cycles

Wright, J. (2009). Biopower, biopedagogies and the obesity epidemic. In J. Wright & V. Harwood (Eds.), *Biopolitics and the "obesity epidemic": Governing bodies* (pp. 1–14). Routledge.

YONO. (n.d.). Home. Retrieved February 9, 2021, from https://www.yonolabs.com

Artificial Unintelligence: How "Smart" and AI Technologies Perpetuate Bias and Systemic Discrimination

Sahar Raza

INTRODUCTION

Artificially intelligent (AI) machines are no longer just creatures of dystopian fiction. Algorithmic and "smart" AI technologies—like search engines, social media algorithms, and smartphones—are rapidly becoming embedded throughout our digital and tangible worlds, shaping how we communicate, think, feel, and function. On the back end, these technologies enable tech corporations to track, categorize, and sell huge amounts of our personal and behavioural data (like our locations, search histories, and shopping patterns—i.e., *big data*) for profit and control, often without our explicit knowledge or consent—an unethical and invasive process that policy makers and lawmakers are only beginning to address. This unregulated process of *surveillance capitalism* (i.e., profit-driven data collection) is typically justified by a mainstream narrative in which data-collecting AI technologies are framed as innovative, efficient, objective, superior to human decision-making, and thus beneficial to our lives (e.g., "efficient" virtual assistants, "innovative" smart home technologies, and "objective" résumé-screening algorithms). This narrative, however, is not the whole story.

Technologies are not objective—they inherit the biases of their environments, societies, and creators (Benjamin, 2019). As products of human construction, all smart and AI technologies are either explicitly or implicity embedded with certain goals, biases, ideologies, and world views that are dictated by the humans who produce them. This does not mean that all smart and AI technologies are inherently harmful, of course. A socially just or human rights-based approach could result in empowering, participatory, equitable, and accessible technological inventions that elevate everyone's quality of life, including that of marginalized peoples. Given that huge and wealthy corporations in capitalist superpowers like the United States are advancing technological change, however, their own capitalist goals and world views are being embedded into AI technologies (Daniels, 2015).

As critical theorists have argued for decades, Western capitalism is premised on short-sighted ideals of efficiency, competition, and accumulation. In fact, these ideals are so strongly held in Western society and industry that they rationalize harmful outcomes like environmental damage, socio-economic inequality, and even genocidal colonialism, as evident in the treatment of Indigenous Peoples and their lands throughout North American history (Beer, 2016; Braidotti, 2015; Coulthard, 2014).

Herein lies the problem with smart and AI technologies: their development is being driven by tech corporations with a capitalist agenda that requires the accumulation and preservation of wealth, land, private property, resources, data, and power at all costs—an agenda that has historically degraded the planet and marginalized certain populations based on race, gender, class, culture, Indigeneity, and more. Even the demographics of the tech industry reflect these inequities: "The tech firms in Silicon Valley are predominantly led by white men and a few white women; yet the [poorly paid] manual labor of assembling circuit boards is done by immigrants and outsourced labor, often women living in the global South" (Daniels, 2015, p. 1379).

Moreover, tech corporations and their employees are not held legally accountable for promoting equity, environmental justice, democracy, or human rights with their technological products. Therefore, in their current form, tech giants and their AI products largely exacerbate social and economic inequities while reproducing capitalist values and historically discriminatory power dynamics—ones rooted in classism, colonialism, heteropatriarchy, white supremacy, and other forms of oppression.

Theories of Resistance: A Socio-technical Lens

In order to disrupt and dismantle fallacious narratives about smart and AI technologies, this chapter applies a *socio-technical* lens which combines critical, anti-colonial, postmodern, and intersectional feminist theory. While a socio-technical lens can also include other theories (e.g., queer theory, which is not explored in this chapter), I use this selection of methodologies to offer a baseline from which social justice–oriented thinking can begin. Like a social justice–oriented toolkit, this socio-technical lens can be grown and utilized to assess, dismantle, and reimagine any and all supposedly objective "smart" or algorithmic AI technologies.

Putting a socio-technical lens into action, this chapter reveals the ways in which the design, production, and outcomes of contemporary smart and AI technologies largely reflect and benefit corporate and state elite while further disenfranchising peoples who are already on the margins of society. But there is a better way forward—an anti-colonial approach to AI development that promotes equitable and socially just outcomes, as explored at the conclusion of this chapter.

POSITIONALITY OVER POSITIVISM

This chapter resists *positivist* thinking, which assumes that scientists and their tools can study reality from an objective and neutral position—thinking that has led to many of the biases in the tech industry and their technological products (Grbich, 2013). Positivism is a theory dating back to the European Enlightenment era in which only observable, measurable, and empirical results are considered valid and valuable knowledge (Marcuse, 1991). It assumes that through rigorous reasoning and science, a person and their technological tools can—and should— uncover the singular reality or "facts" about life from a neutral and objective perspective (Grbich, 2013). Enlightenment era thinkers—who were mainly white men—celebrated these objective and scientific findings as "lead[ing] the way to a New World built on the notions of progress and a universal foundation of knowledge" (Grbich, 2013, p. 6).

Of course, positivistic thinking fails to acknowledge that a person's experiences, tools, or perspectives can bias their findings and construction of reality. Thus, while positivist, scientific, and "rational" thinking was meant to liberate people from the control of the church in the eighteenth century, it ironically produced new forms of control and subjugation—largely at the expense of women, gender-diverse, Indigenous, racialized, and disabled peoples. Not only were these populations colonized, dehumanized, and marginalized as part of the New World project, but they continue to be subjugated through positivistic "truths" and narratives that reinforce the interests of the ruling class. Consider, for example, stereotypical "truths" that describe women as irrational and emotionally volatile, gender-diverse peoples as defying the natural order, poor people as lazy and unintelligent, Black people as aggressive and criminal, Muslim people as oppressive and extremist, or Indigenous Peoples as backwards and in need of civilization. These broad and fallacious "truths" stem from limiting world views, rooted in positivism and other systems of oppression, that undermine and marginalize difference in favour of those who get to produce knowledge and define what is ideal or "true."

The contemporary tech industry is ruled by positivism, with tech giants claiming to be neutral arbiters of communication and reality thanks to their use of data, algorithms, and AI technologies (Langlois & Elmer, 2013). In the tech industry,

> computers carry an inherent authority—i.e., they can never be wrong. The system, with its impressive processing power, its enormous storage capacity, and its multitasking capabilities, is treated as a more neutral arbiter than a human being, for whom efficiency and speed might be less important values than ethics, deliberation, or questioning assumptions. (Silverman, 2017, p. 154)

Of course, the positivist belief that computers, algorithms, and technologies have no flaws or biases is a fallacy; their prioritization of speed and efficiency over ethics and deliberation is in itself biased towards certain goals and world views. Moreover, many scholars have found that smart and algorithmic AI technologies *do not* have fewer flaws than humans—they simply have different ones (consider, for example, the technological failures you face in your daily life) (Bunz & Meikle, 2018; Dodd, 2018; Magnet, 2011). Yet "data and computing have become so profoundly their own 'truth' that even in the face of evidence, the public still struggles to hold tech companies accountable for the products and errors of their ways" (Noble, 2018, p. 28).

In contrast to positivism, Indigenous, anti-colonial, intersectional feminist, and postmodern scholars suggest that

> there is no cultureless, neutral, or objective perspective any more than a photograph or painting can be without perspective. Sometimes these perspectives are explicit, but they are often implicit in practices, goals, and representations. In this sense, everything is cultured, including ... the construction and use of technology. (Bang et al., 2013, p. 709)

Postmodern and anti-colonial theories embrace a multiplicity of perspectives and are highly critical of broad and generalized narratives of the world, which are "power-laden discourses developed specifically for the maintenance of dominant ideas or to enhance the power of certain individuals" (Grbich, 2013, p. 8).

Likewise, intersectional feminists argue that in addition to a multiplicity of perspectives, there are multiple and intersecting social, political, and economic identities that come with certain levels of privilege, power, and oppression in our inequitable society (Crenshaw, 1989). Intersectional feminism helps us to understand how narrow Western narratives about technology (which define AI as efficient, optimizing, objective, and ideal) have become dominant ways of thinking about AI;

unequal power dynamics in Western society and across the globe allow for powerful entities to produce and sanction certain knowledges or "facts" about AI that are rooted in capitalist and colonial values which perpetuate privilege and inequity.

In order to dismantle these socially constructed forms of inequity (based on race, gender, and more), many postmodern and intersectional feminist scholars assert that all researchers and producers of knowledge are responsible for recognizing their own positionality and world view. Positioning yourself is essential for revealing your own bias and ensuring that your theories or tools of liberation do not become new systems of oppression for others (hooks, 1990; Richardson, 2000; Simpson, 2013; Walia, 2014).

I thus acknowledge that my socio-political identity as a second-generation Canadian and Muslim woman of colour, my emancipatory and equity-centred values, and my experience as a Millennial who grew up in the age of the internet are all factors that colour my perspective of—and goals for—technological development. Having witnessed and faced various forms of intersectional marginalization in my own life, my work is a "radical intellectual project to understand and intervene in the social and cultural struggles of the day, driven by an ineluctable longing for a better world" (Ang, 2016, p. 37).

Like many Millennials who grew up in the age of the internet, I have seen firsthand how our dependence on search engines, social media, and smartphones has shaped the ways in which we live, think, and relate with one another. I live in a world where corporate ads, algorithms, logics, and data collection processes influence everything that I see and do on the internet. Everything from my social media activity to purchasing, browsing, location, and even personal life history can be collected, categorized, and sold on and from the internet, celebrated as "the world's largest ungoverned space" by Google ex-chairperson Eric Schmidt (Pasquale, 2015; Zuboff, 2016). And as people across the globe have become increasingly dependent on the internet for information, communication, and social participation, I have seen how giant tech corporations have developed exploitative technological systems to profit from our online activity and data, often referred to as the world's "new oil" (Silverman, 2017; Zuboff, 2016). Most troubling is the fact that Canada has no legal framework in place to hold tech corporations accountable for the social, economic, mental health, or intangible harms that their business dealings and technological products cause. We thus accept these technologies into our lives at huge and unknown risk to ourselves.

I therefore study "smart" and AI technologies with a critical lens, recognizing that while they have the *potential* for promoting public good, vast evidence suggests that their current developmental trajectory is informed by positivist and capitalist logics that largely exacerbate social and economic inequities.

NEOLIBERALISM AND THE TECH CORPORATION

As critical theorists argue, tech corporations (like all business corporations) are almost exclusively driven by a capitalist agenda requiring the accumulation and preservation of wealth, land, private property, resources, data, and power—at all costs (Achbar et al., 2003). This is evident in the fact that the success of most businesses is measured by profit margins, growth rates, and returns on assets; social benefits and costs rarely figure into the equation (with the exception of B Corps; [B Lab, 2021]). Yet instead of setting more humane standards for tech corporations through law and policy, governments across the globe have increasingly turned towards *neoliberalism* in the past few decades, which dangerously grants greater social and economic power, autonomy, and *lack* of accountability to profit-driven corporations.

Since the 1980s, neoliberal policies—premised on free market doctrines of privatization, deregulation, free trade, and austerity—have led to greater subsidies for corporations, lower taxes for the corporate elite, more precarious work for corporate employees (via part-time, temporary, and consultative roles), attacks on labour unions, lower wages for workers, and almost monopolistic, global control of certain industries by major corporations (Duffy, 2015; Foster & McChesney, 2014). This rise of corporate power has been complemented by the decline in, and privatization of, previously state-funded social services like education, health care, and housing, leading to greater socio-economic inequality across the Western world.

Monopolistic tech corporations like Google, Apple, Facebook, and Amazon are the latest iteration of corporate power, with tentacles across the globe. These profit-seeking entities have achieved an unprecedented level of global power and wealth through their exploitation of the unregulated and ungoverned internet and their use and sale of seemingly "innovative" and "neutral" AI technologies to collect and monetize data. In fact, in this neoliberal age, monopolistic tech corporations possess so much power that they are increasingly unphased by resistance from people, communities, and even governments (Noble, 2018; Pasquale, 2015; Silverman, 2017; Zuboff, 2016).

We have already seen the abuse of such dispersed and global corporate power in the Facebook/Cambridge Analytica scandal. Social media and tech giant Facebook was found to have leaked the personal data of 50 million users to a third-party company, Cambridge Analytica. Cambridge Analytica then used the Facebook data to produce targeted ads that influenced the 2016 US presidential election and Britain's Brexit referendum. Shortly after this data breach was publicly unearthed in 2018—well after Facebook became aware of the breach—the European Union (EU) increased data storage, privacy, and transparency regulations within its jurisdiction through its General Data Protection Regulation (GDPR) (Meyer, 2018). To shelter itself from these profit-harming regulations, however, Facebook covertly transferred massive amounts of user data from the EU to its US offices just before the GDPR came into effect on May 25, 2018 (Hern, 2018). This ability of corporations to use their wealth and power to evade and lobby governments ironically undercuts the supposedly "free market" logics of capitalism and neoliberalism. Rather than genuine competition and people-centric supply and demand driving the market, certain private corporations control the market (and consumers) to further accumulate profit. In this corporate-driven economic system, public consent and equity are undercut by self-serving *surveillance capitalist* interests.

SURVEILLANCE CAPITALISM IN THE AGE OF THE INTERNET

Surveillance can be defined as purposeful, routine, and systematic attention paid to the details of a person or population that one wants to track, control, influence, manage, or protect (Andrejevic & Burdon, 2015; Lyon, 2011; Proulx, 2014). *Surveillance capitalism* thus involves a corporation, organization, or entity systematically using surveillance to collect massive amounts of data *about* or *for* potential consumers in hopes of using that data to accumulate profit. This can involve gathering data on anything from people's behaviours to locations; selling data to anyone, from police to corporate marketers; using data to predict and influence behaviours (e.g., when marketers want to impel you to buy something); and any other capitalist amalgamation of data extraction, commodification, and control. Moreover, because capitalist logics necessitate continuous growth and accumulation of profit, surveillance capitalism demands the use of algorithmic and technological systems to continuously and efficiently track, process, store, and transfer massive amounts of consumer data (i.e., big data) (Silverman, 2017).

While surveillance capitalism is not new and dates back to the post–World War II period, what is unique in the age of the internet is the ability to track intimate aspects of human behaviour, offering a real-time data stream of a person's daily life (Foster & McChesney, 2014). As surveillance capitalism pervades our digital and tangible worlds, tech companies thus have the power to "directly influence and modify your behaviour for profit" (Zuboff, 2016, para. 5). A chief data scientist at a popular Silicon Valley company in fact stated as much:

> The goal of everything we do is to change people's actual behaviour at scale. When people use our app, we can capture their behaviours, identify good

and bad behaviours, and develop ways to reward the good and punish the bad. We can test how actionable our cues are for them and how profitable for us. (Zuboff, 2016, para. 6)

These profit-making logics of behavioural categorization, modification, and control are central to many major digital platforms that we use daily. Google recommends search queries in its search engine, routes and destinations on Google Maps, and email responses on Gmail. It embeds advertisements into its search results while sorting and ordering the results that we see to surreptitiously promote third-party companies that have purchased advertising space.

Likewise, social media and video-sharing sites like Facebook, Instagram, YouTube, and TikTok filter, sort, and hierarchize all of the content that we see on their feeds using secret algorithms and logics, which Pasquale (2015) refers to as "black boxes" (p. 6). What we see on the internet is increasingly in the hands of the highest bidder and is filtered by opaque algorithms that use our data to offer a "personalized" and "optimized" user experience (which is really just a tailored consumer experience that will optimize profits for online platforms and brands). In this way, users themselves become quantified and machine-readable data subjects to be ranked, filtered, and categorized in the capitalist pursuit of profit (Lupton, 2016).

What makes this different from old forms of industrial capitalism (i.e., manufacturing) is that "surveillance capitalism preys on dependent populations who are neither its consumers nor its employees" (Zuboff, 2016, para. 12). Populations are now dependent, vulnerable, and largely ignorant of the exploitative and surveillant processes that are used by major tech firms to accrue profit and maintain market dominance through their seemingly "free" platforms. For example, "Google [search] functions in the interests of its most influential paid advertisers or through an intersection of popular and commercial interests. Yet Google's users think of it as a public resource, generally free from commercial interest" (Noble, 2018, p. 36). Likewise, Langlois and Elmer (2013) assert that "while on the surface, [social media platforms] seem to promote unfettered communication, they work in their back-end … to transform and translate acts of communication into valuable data" (p. 6). Click-to-agree and jargon-filled "terms of service" contracts offer only flimsy illusions of consent; they serve to legally protect companies in the business of surveillance rather than to genuinely inform users of the data exploitation and behavioural modification that their agreement will cost them (Silverman, 2017).

As we increasingly come to rely on digital platforms and smart technologies including apps, search engines, and smartphones, data collection becomes naturalized as part of daily social life. Even when users are aware that our data are being collected or tracked, as with "cookies" online and app permissions on a smartphone, our dependence on these major digital platforms and technologies, and the simultaneous opaqueness of their business processes and algorithms, impels us to passively and naively accept these terms (Pasquale, 2015). Thus, when a mobile weather app requires that we give it access to our camera, microphone, and contacts in order to operate, we accept—and unsurprisingly, giant surveillance capitalists like Google, Facebook, Apple, and Disney have a monopoly in this app ecosystem (Dean, 2013).

In fact, the power of these tech corporations is so great that "Google [alongside other tech giants] benefits directly and materially from what can be called the 'labortainment' of users, when users consent to freely give away their labor and personal data for the use of Google and its products, resulting in incredible profit for the company" (Noble, 2018, p. 36). Like data collection, *labourtainment* is becoming a normalized part of contemporary social life under surveillance capitalism. For example, Duffy (2015) and Dean (2013) argue that social media platforms such as YouTube, TikTok, and Instagram have created a culture whereby many female-identifying users willingly partake in aspirational, unpaid labour in hopes of one day achieving success (i.e., aspiring social media influencers). Their online activities, however, are most beneficial to the tech firms, brands, and corporations that profit from having aspiring influencers freely use and market their products and services. Very few of these content creators actually realize the dream of "going pro" and thus offer cheap or free labour to both brands and social media platforms: a pattern that echoes old forms of gendered exploitation whereby women's work goes uncompensated (Duffy, 2015).

The Internet of (Profitable) Things

To understand how smart and AI technologies are specifically implicated in the inequitable logics of surveillance capitalism, it is important to consider the *internet of things*, which relies on sensors. A *sensor* is "any device that automatically captures and records data that can then be transmitted, stored, and analyzed" (Andrejevic & Burdon, 2015, p. 5). Once these sensors are fitted to *things* and connected to networks, they become "smart" (Bunz & Meikle, 2018).

The internet of things (IoT) thus refers to the growing network of tangible objects that are embedded with sensors and connectivity (via Bluetooth or Wi-Fi, for example), making them "smart" objects and technologies—a common example being the smartphone. Surveillant sensors become cheaper every year and are thus becoming embedded in more places, "promis[ing] to make 'quantified selves' of all of us, whether we like it or not" (Pasquale, 2015, p. 4). In fact, "smart" technologies and applications were not developed in response to any human *needs* in society; they were developed because of the increased affordability and technical feasibility of producing such objects (Bunz & Meikle, 2018). For tech corporations, the primary purpose of smart technologies is to "make the world machine-readable, to provide more processes and behaviours to surveil and digitize, and to use these new streams of information to monetize more of life" (Silverman, 2017, p. 156).

As an extension of the internet, the IoT operates on very similar logics to the internet and thus enables surveillance capitalism and social control in many of the same ways (Andrejevic & Burdon, 2015; Pallitto, 2018). Just as Google, Facebook, and a handful of other tech firms possess almost oligarchic power over data on the internet, these same tech firms are extending their power to our tangible lifeworld through IoT objects.

MURKY WATERS: CORPORATE AND STATE COLLUSION

Resisting surveillance capitalism becomes complicated by the fact that "the surveillance society is constituted and supported by a range of actors and activities, both public and private" (Pallitto, 2018). Political elite such as state, policing, military, corporate, and media actors maintain relatively exclusive control of economic resources and their distribution, not as a monolith but as complimentary actors with a shared goal (Proulx, 2014). Enabled by lax government policies aimed at keeping big businesses in the city or state (i.e., neoliberalism), corporations like Facebook, Google, and Amazon have structural power through which they can privately determine the allocation of investment and resources in a region while making decisions that impact levels of employment, consumption, and economic growth. Consider, for example, the power that one Amazon distribution centre has on its surrounding communities.

This oligarchic regime of corporate and state elite "carefully preserves the principles of elected legislative assemblies while ensuring, through lobbying, that democracy does not harm corporate well-being" (Proulx, 2014, p. 85). We see this in the way that tech corporations like Facebook and Google actively fight regulations that would grant users privacy and control over their digital data while simultaneously ensuring that their own actions are kept private through nondisclosure agreements, ambiguity, and "proprietary" algorithms and processes (Pasquale, 2015). Asymmetries in wealth and power protect the oligarchic elite from scrutiny, surveillance, and legal accountability for their own actions while simultaneously rendering the public a collection of hypervisible data subjects (Pallitto, 2018).

The internet, which now extends to the IoT, enables this asymmetry in power on a colossal scale by offering a huge and growing ungoverned territory for corporate and political elite to exploit data and control populations. Due to the blurring of public and private surveillance practices in the oligarchic regime, these government, policing, insurance, military, and corporate elite can access and even share intimate information about individuals and hold them accountable, legally or otherwise, for anything from theft and fraud to more mundane transgressions such as speeding or illegal streaming. Meanwhile, Facebook's ability to dodge enormous legal and financial accountability for the Cambridge Analytica scandal—which quite literally influenced world events—starkly demonstrates how corporate and state elite benefit from the huge imbalances in privacy in our neoliberal society (Meyer, 2018). In a world where knowledge is power, tech corporations and state authorities benefit from one of the most significant and inequitable forms of power in avoiding scrutiny while continuing to scrutinize others via mass surveillance practices (Pasquale, 2015).

Considering Privacy in the Data-Driven Information Economy

In an information economy where the most valuable currency is intimate data about people's lives, privacy is not just a protection for consumers but also both the regulator and the enabler of corporate and political profit, power, and social control.

Central to the definition of *privacy* is the ability to control or limit the circulation of information about oneself (Westin, 1967). In Western capitalist societies, privacy is also conventionally associated with property and possessive individualism. For example, we can expect to have freedom and autonomy in the "privacy of our own home." The right to privacy thus becomes a commodity that is only afforded to those who can and do own property. Under capitalism, the more wealth and property one has, the more privacy they have access to—whereas without property, one has little privacy. For example, in today's competitive housing market, renters are increasingly being coerced into submitting extraneous personal information to landlords via tenant-screening apps (e.g., Naborly) just to be *considered* for competitive rental units (Lagerquist, 2016). In this scenario, landlords—the property owners—are able to breach the privacy of applicants in order to choose an "ideal" tenant without offering any personal information in return.

Not only does wealth equate to more privacy, but privacy also serves to *protect* people's wealth and capitalist accumulations from public scrutiny; it ensures that socio-economic inequities throughout capitalist societies are not apparent. "Because the legitimacy of the prevailing social order rests, in large part, on the conceit that most people are starting from relatively equal footing, it is necessary to conceal the fact that this is not ... the case" (Reichel, 2017, p. 4761). A 2011 nationwide survey in the United States in fact found that respondents vastly underestimated income and wealth disparities in the country (Reichel, 2017). Privacy therefore does not protect everyone equally, which is exactly how it was designed: "An intrinsic connection exists between the maldistribution of privacy rights and the broader social hierarchies that they reflect" (Reichel, 2017, p. 4758).

AUTOMATED IDENTITY BIAS

As is made clear throughout this chapter, smart and algorithmic AI technologies tend to exacerbate historical forms of power, privilege, and disadvantage—but not just in an economic sense. Many smart and AI technologies perpetuate biases based on race, gender, and other socio-political factors, thus automating and exacerbating the systemic discrimination already faced by marginalized populations in Western society (Daniels, 2015; Duffy, 2015; Noble, 2018; O'Neil, 2016).

A stark example is Microsoft's AI chatbot, which was released on the internet in 2016 with the promise of getting smarter as it interacted with more Twitter users. Due to racist content and interactions with the chatbot on Twitter, however, the AI chatbot began posting racist and neo-Nazi tweets via its machine learning processes within 24 hours (Vincent, 2016). This example overtly shows us how seemingly "smart" algorithms can quickly "perpetuate particular narratives that reflect historically uneven distributions of power in society" (Noble, 2018, p. 71), although algorithmic systems often do this in more subtle and insidious ways than the AI chatbot.

For example, mathematical models used in the finance sector (e.g., to determine who gets a loan or mortgage and at what interest rate) are encoded with human biases that tend to "punish the poor and the oppressed in our society while making the rich richer" (O'Neil, 2016, p. 27). Both the logics and data used to power these algorithmic systems are influenced by corporate interests, programmer bias, and historical systems of oppression, yet they cannot be questioned because "their workings [are] invisible to all but the highest priest in the domain: mathematicians and computer scientists" (O'Neil, 2016, p. 27).

Likewise, the AI courtroom sentencing software Northpointe was used by judges to determine the future risk and criminality of a defendant. This AI system miserably misrepresented Black defendants (who have historically been overpoliced) and led to their overincarceration while simultaneously predicting that most white criminals would not offend again, despite data showing otherwise (Noble,

2018). When algorithmic technologies like these differentially treat certain racial or socio-economic groups, they are engaging in *social sorting*.

Social sorting is a process by which data brokers and manipulators—including tech corporations and their technologies—use data to categorize and differentiate people based on race, ethnicity, gender, age, education, occupation, income, location, social status, or other socio-political and economic factors (i.e., their intersectional identity). Social sorting works by making assumptions about people based on their intersectional identity and is often used in predictive policing and other algorithmic decision-making that concerns people—including most algorithms that we interact with on a daily basis (e.g., that filter resumes, organize social media feeds, determine credit scores, etc.).

The problem is that social sorting is premised on capitalist, colonial, and positivist logics that rely on distinguishing and differentially treating different social groups based on their behaviours, habits, and seemingly inherent qualities. Technologies and political bodies that engage in social sorting thus reproduce, and often even exacerbate, discrimination and surveillance along socio-political and economic lines (Lyon, 2011).

Surveillance is therefore not a neutral process; race, gender, and other obvious markers of difference are often the basis upon which people are socially sorted and treated differentially (Abu-Laban & Bakan, 2011; Lyon, 2011). This can be seen in the long history of racialized bodies such as Indigenous and Black peoples being surveilled by white authorities in North America since settler colonialism and the transatlantic slave trade began (Browne, 2015; King, 2016; Proulx, 2014; Reichel, 2017). Even once slavery was abolished, surveillance and policing of Black bodies persisted to enforce segregation. Today, mass incarceration of Black and Indigenous Peoples continues to exclude them from the public sphere, while practices of carding and "stop and frisk" policing are further iterations of race-based surveillance practices (Browne, 2015; Reichel, 2017). Similar surveillant practices have been aimed at Muslims in North America since 9/11, as rationalized by the "war on terror." In contrast, Canada's ongoing missing and murdered Indigenous women and girls crisis exemplifies how social sorting can also be used to intentionally and unjustly *exclude* certain groups from protective surveillance and thus basic rights to safety, security, dignity, and life.

Social sorting processes in smart and AI technologies therefore tend to further disenfranchise already-marginalized peoples. Yet the harmful effects of these processes are disguised by positivist "truths" and narratives that define AI and the tech industry as optimizing, innovative, and free from bias or imperfection. It is therefore important to disrupt these positivist narratives and remember that technologies and tech corporations are designed and run by "fallible humans" (Noble, 2018, p. 27) with their own positionalities, privileges, world views, and biases—and due to current power dynamics in society, we tend to see heteropatriarchy and white supremacy reinforced in the tech industry and their technological products. The Western belief that we can produce objective and neutral technologies from our subjective experiences is fundamentally flawed—but there is hope. There are more humanitarian and community-oriented ways to think about, design, and use AI.

LOOKING TO THE FUTURE: RECONCEPTUALIZING SMARTNESS

Although Indigenous and anti-colonial thought is often written off as prehistoric and thus incompatible with modern society, it actually enables us to think beyond our exploitative and inequitable capitalist system in order to imagine and build mutually respectful relationships with each other, our technologies, and our environment. Anti-colonial theories centre community, reciprocity, accountability, human experience, sustainability, and relationship (in contrast to capitalist values of individualism, growth, control, profit, and total information capture). Anti-colonial methodologies disrupt positivist and capitalist desires for "new," "modern," and "objective" technologies, which actually resemble colonial desires to dominate and modernize the "New World" (Bang et al., 2013). Contrary to Western traditions of knowledge, many anti-colonial and Indigenous scholars believe that just because something *can* be known does not mean that it *should* be known: "With knowing comes responsibilities shaped by complex systems of kinship" (Bang et al., 2013, p. 710). Anti-colonial theory thus radically challenges positivism and capitalism, allowing us to envision more just and equitable technological futures.

For example, the key principles of the *relational* and the *collective* in Indigenous and anti-colonial methodologies are hugely valuable when conceptualizing and designing equitable AI. The relational requires centring "relationships that are inclusive of all life forms. The philosophical premise of take what you need (and only what you need), give back, and offer thanks suggests a deep respect for other living beings" (Kovach, 2005, p. 30). Likewise, the collective centres "reciprocity and accountability to each other, the community, clans, nations. It is a way of life that creates a sense of belonging, place, and home; however, it doesn't serve anonymity or rugged individualism well" (Kovach, 2005, p. 30).

Researchers Jason Edward Lewis and Suzanne Kite at Concordia University are already applying these principles to conceptualize AI from an Indigenous world view. They argue that we cannot correct bias out of contemporary AI systems because the way that we design and think about AI is fundamentally unethical (Murdoch, 2019). Applying the principle of relationality, they explain that we must treat AI respectfully because it is part of a larger network of relationships and interconnectedness: "You're not treating something respectfully because it has a soul, you are treating it respectfully because it's one nodal point in a number of different relations that you are enmeshed in" (as cited in Murdoch, 2019, "An Infinite Number," para. 5). They question our exclusive focus on human well-being when thinking about ethics and our perceived control and superiority over AI; our relationships with AI should be reciprocal and respectful if we are to produce an equitable and respectful world alongside AI (Murdoch, 2019):

> As Indigenous people, we have cause to be wary of the Western rationalist, neoliberal, and Christianity-infused assumptions that underlay many of the current conversations about AI.… We know what it is like to be declared non-human by scientist and preacher alike. We have a history that attests to the corrosive effects of contorted rationalizations for treating the human-like as slaves, and the way such a mindset debases every human relation it touches—even that of the supposed master. We will resist reduction by working with our Indigenous and non-Indigenous relations to open up our imaginations and dream widely and radically about what our relationships to AI might be. (Lewis et al., 2018, p. 11)

CONCLUSION

If we are to build AI that achieves equitable outcomes for all members of our society, we must begin with principles that account for and accommodate, rather than limit, the multiplicity of perspectives, identities, and life forms that exist in our society. We must apply a socio-technical lens to all tech producers and products and hold them accountable for their opaque processes and discriminatory effects. We must name and dismantle the inequitable power dynamics that bias the design and outcomes of AI (i.e., racism, white supremacy, heteropatriarchy, settler colonialism, transphobia, ableism, etc.) and recognize that our relationships with AI are reflections of our broader relationships with, and within, our society. To build a better world alongside AI, we must break free from old, exclusionary, and positivist thinking to forge smarter conceptions of technology, AI, and the tech industry at large—ones premised on relationship, community, interconnectedness, equity, and accountability.

QUESTIONS FOR DISCUSSION

1. What does privacy mean to you? How does it compare to the definition in this chapter? Are you satisfied with the amount of privacy you have? What or whom do you want privacy from? What do you think would give you more or less privacy? How do you think your socio-political identity (i.e., race, gender, sexual orientation, etc.) impacts your level of privacy? How do you think your level of privacy will change in the future—in 5 years? 10 years? 30 years? Why?

2. Do you use platforms and technologies developed by tech giants such as Google, Facebook, Amazon, Microsoft, Apple, and others? Why or why not? Do you trust these tech companies? Why or why not?

3. Think about the smart technologies, apps, and social media platforms that you use every day. What data do you think they have collected from you? How do you think they have used your data or will use it in the future? Is there any way for you to verify the data that have been collected, who the data have been shared with, or how your data have been used?

4. How and why has the COVID-19 pandemic changed your relationship with, use of, or reliance on technology? How have these changes impacted your day-to-day life, relationships, activities, or behaviours? What are the positive and negative effects of these changes? What are some ways in which we can maximize the positive effects and limit the negative effects?

INVITATIONS TO GO DEEPER

1. What aspects of digital, smart, or AI technologies make you feel happy, satisfied, or secure? What aspects of these technologies make you feel unhappy, stressed, excluded, or insecure? Make a list of the first five things that come to mind for each category. Reflect on which technologies add value to your life and which detract from it. Consider the ways in which your intersectional identity (i.e., sex, gender, race, ethnicity, sexual orientation, etc.) affects your answers. Do you think digital technologies and platforms would impact you differently if you were a different gender, race, sexual orientation? Why or why not?

2. How fast would you say that technology is advancing? Imagine what Canadian society could look like in 20 years in a dystopian scenario caused by smart and AI technologies, and what it could look like in a utopian scenario. Compare

the two. Which groups or populations would benefit and/or be harmed most in the dystopian scenario? What about in the utopian scenario? How could our society get to each of these ends? What could we do to steer technological development in the utopian direction?

3. What assumptions are the social media, algorithmic, or AI technologies you use every day making about you? Check your recommended videos on You-Tube, your recommended songs on your music-streaming app (e.g., Spotify, Apple Music, etc.), your homepage/feed on social media (e.g., Instagram, Twitter, Facebook, TikTok), and any other algorithmically sorted platform. Consider the patterns you see among the recommended content. How are these patterns and assumptions reproducing race, gender, class, or other biases? How could some of the assumptions that these algorithmic and AI technologies make be either harmful or beneficial to certain populations? How could we better design and use these technologies to make their outcomes more equitable?

READ MORE

Algorithmic Justice League. (2021). https://www.ajl.org/

Bednar, V. (2021, March 9). Algorithms are increasingly treating workers like robots. Canada needs policy to protect them. *The Globe and Mail.* https://www.theglobeandmail.com/business/commentary/article-algorithms-are-increasingly-treating-workers-like-robots-canada-needs/

Browne, S. (2015). *Dark matters: On the surveillance of Blackness.* Duke University Press.

McLuhan, M. (1995). Laws of media. In E. McLuhan & F. Zingrone (Eds.), *The essential McLuhan* (pp. 366–388). House of Anansi Press. (Original work published in 1988)

LISTEN MORE, WATCH MORE

"How to keep human bias out of AI," Kriti Sharma, TED Talk, April 2019: https://www.youtube.com/watch?v=BRRNeBKwvNM&ab_channel=TED

"Race after technology," Ruha Benjamin, Data & Society podcast, October 2019: https://datasociety.net/library/databite-no-124-ruha-benjamin/

"Scott Galloway says Amazon, Apple, Facebook, and Google should be broken up," *Business Insider,* December 2017: https://www.youtube.com/watch?v=6NyFRIgulPo&ab_channel=BusinessInsider

The social dilemma, Jeff Orlowski and Larissa Rhodes, 2020: https://www.netflix.com/title/81254224

"What can artificial intelligence algorithms in healthcare learn from Indigenous cultures?" Megan Williams, *Coda Change*, 2020: https://www.youtube.com/watch?v=7I0QVs0beI4&ab_channel=CodaChange

REFERENCES

Abu-Laban, Y., & Bakan, A. (2011). The "Israelization" of social sorting and the "Palestinianization" of the racial contract. In E. Zureik, D. Lyon, & Y. Abu-Laban (Eds.), *Surveillance and control in Israel/Palestine* (pp. 276–294). Routledge.

Achbar, M. (Producer and Director), Simpson, B. (Producer), & Abbott, J. (Director). (2003). *The corporation* [Film]. Big Picture Media Corporation.

Andrejevic, M., & Burdon, M. (2015). Defining the sensor society. *Television & New Media, 16*(1), 19–36. https://doi.org/10.1177/1527476414541552

Ang, I. (2016). Stuart Hall and the tension between academic and intellectual work. *International Journal of Cultural Studies, 19*(1), 29–41. https://doi.org/10.1177/1367877915599609

B Lab. (2021). About B Corps. https://bcorporation.net/about-b-corps

Bang, M., Marin, A., Faber, L., & Suzokovich, E. S. (2013). Repatriating Indigenous technologies in an urban Indian community. *Urban Education, 48*(5), 705–733. https://doi.org/10.1177/0042085913490555

Beer, D. (2016). The social power of algorithms. *Information, Communication & Society, 20*, 1–13. https://doi.org/10.1080/1369118X.2016.1216147

Benjamin, R. (2019). *Race after technology: Abolitionist tools for the new Jim code.* Polity Press.

Braidotti, R. (2015). Punk women and riot grrls. *Performance Philosophy, 1*, 239–254. https://doi.org/10.21476/PP.2015.1132

Browne, S. (2015). *Dark matters. On the surveillance of Blackness.* Duke University Press.

Bunz, M., & Meikle, G. (2018). *The internet of things.* Polity Press.

Coulthard, G. S. (2014). Conclusion: Lessons from Idle No More. The future of Indigenous activism. In *Red skin, white masks. Rejecting the colonial politics of recognition* (pp. 151–179). University of Minnesota Press.

Crenshaw, K. (1989). Demarginalizing the intersection of race and sex: A Black feminist critique of antidiscrimination doctrine, feminist theory and antiracist politics. *University of Chicago Legal Forum, 1989*(1), 139–167.

Daniels, J. (2015). "My brain database doesn't see skin color": Color-blind racism in the technology industry and in theorizing the web. *American Behavioral Scientist, 59*(11), 1277–1393. https://doi.org/10.1177/0002764215578728

Dean, J. (2013). *Apps and drive* [Paper]. Apps and affect conference, London, ON. http://www.academia.edu/5051363/Apps_and_Drive_for_Apps_and_Affect_

Dodd, V. (2018, May 15). UK police use of facial recognition technology a failure, says report. *The Guardian*. Retrieved from https://www.theguardian.com/uk-news/2018/may/15/uk-police-use-of-facial-recognition-technology-failure

Duffy, B. E. (2015). Entrepreneurial wishes and career dreams. In *(Not) getting paid to do what you love: Gender, social media, and aspirational work* (pp. 1–11). Yale University Press.

Foster, J. B., & McChesney, R. W. (2014). Surveillance capitalism. Monopoly-finance capital, the military-industrial complex, and the digital age. *Monthly Review, 66*(3), 1–31.

Grbich, C. (2013). *Qualitative data analysis: An introduction.* Sage Publications.

Hern, A. (2018, April 19). Facebook moves 1.5bn users out of reach of new European privacy law. *The Guardian*. https://www.theguardian.com/technology/2018/apr/19/facebook-moves-15bn-users-out-of-reach-of-new-european-privacy-law

hooks, b. (1990). *Yearning: Race, gender, and cultural politics.* Between the Lines.

King, T. L. (2016). New world grammars: The "unthought" Black discourses of conquest. *Theory & Event, 19*(4).

Kovach, M. (2005). Emerging from the margins: Indigenous methodologies. In S. Strega and L. Brown (Eds.), *Research as resistance: Critical, Indigenous and anti-oppressive approaches* (pp. 19–36). Canadian Scholars Press.

Lagerquist, J. (2016, December 7). Get ready to give up your online privacy to score the perfect rental. *CTV News*. https://www.ctvnews.ca/sci-tech/get-ready-to-give-up-your-online-privacy-to-score-the-perfect-rental-1.3192709

Langlois, G., & Elmer, G. (2013). The research politics of social media platforms. *Culture Machine, 14*, 1–14. https://www.culturemachine.net/index.php/cm/article/download/505/531

Lewis, J. E., Arista, N., Pechawis, A., & Kite, S. (2018). Making kin with the machine. *Journal of Design and Science*. https://doi.org/10.21428/bfafd97b

Lupton, D. (2016). *The quantified self: A sociology of self-tracking.* Polity Press.

Lyon, D. (2011). Surveillance, power and everyday life. In P. Kalantzis-Cope & K. Gherab-Martin (Eds.), *Emerging digital spaces in contemporary society: Properties of technologies* (pp. 107–120). Palgrave Macmillan.

Magnet, S. A. (2011). *When biometrics fail: Gender, race, and the technology of identity.* Duke University Press.

Marcuse, H. (1991). The new forms of control. In K. Douglas (Ed.), *One dimensional man: Studies in the ideology of advanced industrial society* (pp. 1–19). Beacon Press. (Original work published in 1964)

Meyer, R. (2018, March 20). The Cambridge Analytica scandal, in three paragraphs. *The Atlantic.* https://www.theatlantic.com/technology/archive/2018/03/the-cambridge-analytica-scandal-in-three-paragraphs/556046/

Murdoch, A. (2019, April 29). Concordia's Jason Edward Lewis wants ethical artificial intelligence with an Indigenous worldview. *Concordia University News.* https://www.concordia.ca/news/stories/2019/04/30/concordias-jason-lewis-wants-ethical-artificial-intelligence-with-an-indigenous-worldview.html

Noble, S. U. (2018). *Algorithms of oppression: How search engines reinforce racism.* New York University Press.

O'Neil, C. (2016). *Weapons of math destruction: How big data increases inequality and threatens democracy.* Broadway Books.

Pallitto, R. M. (2018). Irresistible bargains: Navigating the surveillance society. *First Monday, 23*(2). https://doi.org/10.5210/fm.v23i2.7954

Pasquale, F. (2015). *The black box society: The secret algorithms that control money and information.* Harvard University Press.

Proulx, C. (2014). Colonizing surveillance: Canada constructs an Indigenous terror threat. *Anthropologica, 56*(1), 83–100. https://www.jstor.org/stable/24469643

Reichel, M. (2017). Race, class, and privacy: A critical historical review. *International Journal of Communication, 11*, 4757–4768.

Richardson, L. (2000). Writing: A method of inquiry. In N. K. Denzin & Y. S. Lincoln (Eds.), *The Sage handbook of qualitative research* (2nd ed., pp. 923–948). Sage Publications.

Silverman, J. (2017). Privacy under surveillance capitalism. *Social Research: An International Quarterly, 84*(1), 147–164.

Simpson, L. B. (2013). *Islands of decolonial love.* ARP Books.

Vincent, J. (2016, March 24). Twitter taught Microsoft's AI chatbot to be a racist asshole in less than a day. *The Verge.* https://www.theverge.com/2016/3/24/11297050/tay-microsoft-chatbot-racist

Walia, H. (2014). Decolonizing together: Moving beyond a politics of solidarity toward a practice of decolonization. In Kino-nda-niimi Collective (Ed.), *The winter we danced: Voices from the past, the future, and the Idle No More movement* (pp. 44–51). ARP Books.

Westin, A. F. (1967). *Privacy and freedom.* Bodley Head.

Zuboff, S. (2016, March 5). Google as a fortune teller: The secrets of surveillance capitalism. *Frankfurter Allgemeine Zeitung.* https://www.faz.net/aktuell/feuilleton/debatten/the-digital-debate/shoshana-zuboff-secrets-of-surveillance-capitalism-14103616.html

PART IV
BODIES

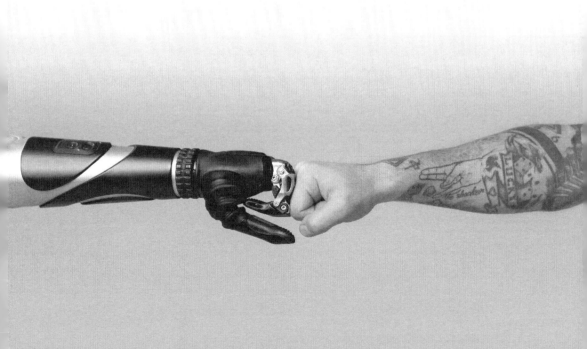

Gatekeeping 'Authentic' Gender: The Somatechnics of Transition Surgery and 'Male Enhancement'

Jennifer Hites-Thomas

"How do you know you want rhinoplasty, a nose job?" he inquires, fixing me with a penetrating stare.

"Because," I reply, suddenly unable to raise my eyes above his brown wingtips, "I've always felt like a small-nosed woman trapped in a large-nosed body."

"And how long have you felt this way?" He leans forward, sounding as if he knows the answer and needs only to hear the words.

"Oh, since I was five or six, doctor, practically all my life."

"Then you have a rhino-identity disorder," the shoetops state flatly. My body sags in relief. "But first," he goes on, "we want you to get letters from two psychiatrists and live as a small-nosed woman for three years ... just to be sure."

(Riki Anne Wilchins)

INTRODUCTION

The absurdity of the opening scene written by trans activist Riki Anne Wilchins (1997) critically illustrates the differential treatment of cisgender[1] people seeking medical alterations to their anatomy, compared to the gatekeeping of trans[2] people pursuing gender confirmation surgeries (GCS).[3] Before trans folks can undergo genital surgery specifically, they must obtain two referrals from mental health professionals who are qualified to write letters in support of medical transition.[4] Acquiring professional letters often requires trans people to 'prove' to medical gatekeepers—most of whom are cis—that their gender is authentic, that they are not just "going through a phase," and that they will not regret transitioning.[5] Trans people who want gender confirming *genital* surgery (GCGS) often have to wait years to secure referral letters for these technologies, whereas cis patients need only a physician to agree to perform genital interventions. Cis men interested in 'male enhancement'—such as penile length and girth augmentations—can access these genital technologies after one medical consultation—sometimes within 24 hours of their first meeting with a male enhancement practitioner—without being compelled to prove to mental health professionals that their gender is authentic.

This chapter compares authenticity discourse across both medical contexts to underscore the contradictory medical management of trans and cis patients who want access to genital technologies. I analyze medical discourse through the talk of 20 medical practitioners who frame patient authenticity differently between cis men and trans people in ways that shape these groups' access to genital technologies. Comprising one section of a larger project about male enhancement, this chapter analyzes practitioners' responses to the interview question "Why do transgender patients need to acquire approval letters from mental health professionals before they can access genital surgeries, whereas your cisgender patients do not?" Having participants who specialize in performing both male enhancements and GCGS—such as vaginoplasty, phalloplasty, and metoidioplasty—enabled me to compare these overlapping medical contexts during interviews.

This project investigates how authenticity discourse shapes cis men's and trans folks' access to genital technologies and, therefore, the materialization of sexed bodies,[6] gender identities, and the relation between them. My analysis below foregrounds physicians' assumptions and justifications for doubting trans people's authenticity and gatekeeping their access to genital technologies. Namely, physicians invest heavily in a cisnormative model of gender acquisition that assumes cis identity is normal and preferable and that gender naturally emerges from binary sexed bodies. Thus, practitioners treat cis men's gender as unquestionably authentic, even when their sexed bodies express intersex variability. This chapter is an intervention in tracing authenticity discourse as a technology that—in combination with genital technologies—works in service of naturalizing cis identity and embodiment.

LITERATURE REVIEW

In cisnormative societies such as Canada and the United States that expect one's assigned sex at birth will—by 'nature's design'—'match' one's gender identity, authenticity for cis people is a foundational assumption. For trans people, it is compulsory in both clinical and broader social contexts to 'prove' their gender is authentic. Dominant conceptualizations of gender and the sexed body reduce authenticity to cisitude—the state of being cisgender (see Ashley, 2018)—shaping the life chances of trans people. The everyday violence of misgendering and dead-naming[7] trans folks casts doubt on trans authenticity. 'Bathroom bills' in Canada and the United States mark and exclude trans people from social life by legislating when, how, and if they can use a restroom. These bills especially criminalize trans women and girls as not authentic, framing them as 'males' who are deceptive about who they 'really' are. This gender panic is rooted in the assumption that non-women will access 'female' spaces to harm 'innocent' (racially inflected as white) cis women and girls (Travers, 2018; Westbrook & Schilt, 2014). Trans folks—particularly Black and Brown trans women—are systematically made vulnerable to people who target them with violence; new records are set each year for the number of trans lives taken through racist and trans-antagonistic violence (Gill-Peterson, 2018a). Vulnerability to or security from this violence can, in many ways, hinge on whether trans folks are institutionally recognized as authentic.

At the same time, trans people have gained more visibility in Canada and the United States, prompting strategies for managing trans people and integrating them into existing institutions and social relations (Westbrook & Schilt, 2014). Prevailing strategies include the liberal humanist politics of tolerance (Gressgård, 2010), which at once calls for trans acceptance while also circumscribing what it means to be acceptably and therefore authentically trans through normative investments in whiteness, heteronormativity, and middle-class respectability politics (see Beauchamp, 2009; Skidmore, 2011; Vipond, 2015). Tolerance and acceptance are afforded to trans folks, at least provisionally, through established narratives of authenticity under the objectifying gaze of psychology and medicine; in such an asymmetrical relationship between gatekeeping authorities and trans individuals, gender 'experts' seek to 'authenticate' if someone is—to borrow sociologist Spencer Garrison's (2018) terminology—"trans enough" to obtain approval for hormone therapy and GCS.

Many feminist and trans/gender scholars (Garrison, 2018; Hird, 2002; Simon, 2015) critique authenticity narratives because rather than expressing a sincere sense of oneself, they often reflect social expectations of gender. Before gaining approval for GCS, many trans patients must go through the 'real life test' to prove themselves authentic by living in their affirmed gender, sometimes waiting years while paying thousands of dollars to obtain letters of support from mental health professionals. During this time, mental health professionals 'evaluate' trans authenticity, requiring patient narratives to largely confirm their theories of gender as binary, immutable, innate, and aligned with particularly-sexed bodies (Whitehead et al., 2012).[8]

However, being read as authentic can unlock the gate to institutional resources and greater life satisfaction. While not all trans people want GCS, for those who do, undergoing medical transition can enable social and legal recognition and the ability to change gender markers on official identification such as passports and driver's licenses, which can lead to a degree of harm reduction (Travers, 2018). Moreover, undergoing GCS can generate gender euphoria, what trans activist and legal scholar Dean Spade (2003, p. 21) describes as the "joyful affirmation of gender self-determination." Authenticity, therefore, exercises discursive power institutionally and in the everyday lives of trans people.

Few scholars have compared authenticity discourse across trans and cis medical contexts. However, multiple social science scholars have juxtaposed transition surgeries with 'cosmetic' surgeries elected by cis people, taking up a few different comparative approaches. Cisgender political scientist Sheila Jeffreys (2014), for example, argues that transition and cosmetic surgeries are medically unnecessary and ethically problematic, and that both groups are capitulating to normative gender. Jeffreys believes that transition surgeries are a form of mutilation—a cisnormative valuation that this chapter works to unsettle. Some trans advocates comparing transition and cosmetic surgeries make claims described by Heyes and Latham (2018) as "trans exceptionalism," where GCS is framed as medically necessary but cosmetic surgeries elected by cis people are not (p. 174). For example, bioethicists Florence Ashley and Carolyn Ells (2018) suggest that in most cases, cis people do not experience oppression based on a "core aspect of the self" such as gender, so cosmetic procedures for cis people are not "morally necessary" like transition surgeries are (p. 25). This project joins trans/gender studies scholars (Garner, 2011; Latham, 2017; Wilchins, 1997) whose analytical approach compares transition surgeries and cosmetic interventions for cis people without assessing whether either are morally necessary or not.

This chapter directly builds on trans somatechnician T. Garner's (2014) arguments in "Chest Surgeries of a Different 'Nature.'" Garner compares medical discourse about trans patients' chest surgery for unwanted breasts with medical discourse about cis men's gynecomastia[9] surgery for unwanted breasts. They[10] ground their analysis in clinical guidelines and influential surgery journal articles. Garner contends that the discourse of harm in the context of gynecomastia surgery naturalizes cis men's post-surgical bodies without breasts. *Naturalization* refers to the process by which social phenomena—such as gender, the sexed body, and race—become understood as natural, biological 'truths' (see Lancaster, 2006). Yet harm discourse operates in the context of GCS to render the post-surgical trans body without breasts as 'unnatural,' thereby lending legitimacy to the violence enacted against trans people.

This notion of the 'natural' body not subject to modification forms a central theoretical tension within feminist scholarship. Since the body functioned as such an unyielding site of oppression and subjugation for women, many second-wave white feminists (Firestone, 1970; Friedan, 1963) sought to escape the burdens of the 'natural female body' such as pregnancy. Using technology to overcome what radical feminist Shulamith Firestone (1970) refers to as "the tyranny of reproduction" was, among other goals, necessary to achieve feminist revolution (p. 185).[11] Trans-exclusionary radical feminists (Jeffreys, 2014; Raymond, 1994) regard technologies as vehicles to re-entrench women's inequality, arguing that narratives of empowerment through cosmetic and reproductive technologies ignore the larger structural systems such as patriarchy at work in disciplining women's bodies.

However, less often critiqued is how both of these positions—that technology is either liberatory or oppressive—reproduce the separation of the body from technology. Such a separation reifies the notion of a 'natural body' that enables judgement to be leveled against 'modified' bodies, characterizing them as 'unnatural.' To quote trans historian Jules Gill-Peterson (2014), "the separation of technics and living beings underwrites the notion of an integral body, according to which incorporation of technology is a fall from the original wholeness of birth" (p. 405).

This separation is maintained by regarding technologies that deliberately 'modify' the body as fundamentally distinct from the everyday yet largely unexamined ways our bodies are socially and technologically crafted (Haraway, 1991). Grooming and hygiene practices; 'corrective' devices like prescription glasses, braces, and hearing aids; and eating habits all shape bodily being, and we take these technologies up in situated ways related to our gender, race, age, (dis)ability, and class. Insights from anthropology demonstrate that cooked food—a result of using fire as technology—has dramatically constituted human bodies, from increasing the digestibility of food and therefore caloric intake, to decreasing molar size, to reducing the time food needs to ferment in the gut to extract nutrients, resulting in shorter intestines (Wrangham & Carmody, 2010). As such, our bodies are not natural, biological facts versus purposefully modified aberrations from nature. Rather, all bodies continuously materialize through socially and historically specific techniques and technologies.

The theoretical tradition of somatechnics provides a way out of the value-laden debates about the 'natural' body independent of social influence versus the technologically constructed, 'artificial' body. Troubling the division between nature and technology, somatechnics understands bodies (*soma*) as inextricable from technology (*techné*) (Sullivan, 2005). Somatechnics emphasizes how all bodies are constituted through technologies, not only those bodies that carry the most visible traces of explicit 'modification' (Garner, 2011).

Technologies are not simply machines or tools that shape the body, such as liposuction machines, scalpels, or silicone implants; technologies are also forms of knowledge and discourses that justify and prohibit shaping the body in particular ways (Sullivan, 2009). According to a somatechnic framework, there is no pre-social 'natural' body that culture 'modifies' (or 'mutilates'), for example, through genital surgeries. Instead, "technologies are the means in and through which bodies are constituted, positioned, and lived" (Macquarie University, 2009, para. 1). It is in relation to technologies that bodies become meaningful.

Therefore, this work does not decide if genital technologies are liberatory or oppressive, whether they are morally necessary or problematic, or if they produce 'artificial' bodies as some feminists might suggest. Rather, I enter this ongoing conversation with other somatechnicians (Alm, 2013; Gill-Peterson, 2014, 2018a; Sullivan, 2007) and gender scholars (Davis et al., 2016; Fujimura, 2006) who analyze how medical discourse forms bodies. Building on the work of feminist theorists who have taken the clinical context as the site of their analysis (Braun, 2005; Kessler, 1990; Lane, 2018; Whitehead & Thomas, 2013), this investigation centres on practitioners' medical practices rather than medical texts to understand how bodies come to matter—that is, how bodies become material, take on meaning, and gain legitimacy (Butler, 1993).

METHODS

The present investigation is grounded in 20 in-depth qualitative interviews with male enhancement practitioners who work in Canada or the United States. I recruited participants by locating their professional websites and contacting their offices. Three participants in my sample practise medicine in Canada while 17 work in the United States. All participants are cis men, their ages range between 40 and 80 years, 2 are people of colour, and 18 are white. These characteristics are roughly proportional to the pool of practitioners from which I recruited. All participant names are pseudonyms.

Every participant is a medical doctor except one who performs male enhancements as a clinical cosmetic specialist. Doctors describe their formal training in urology; plastic, cosmetic, reconstructive, and general surgery; and other non-surgical specialties. Experience performing male enhancements ranged between 2 and 40 years (mean: 17 years). Practitioners had performed between 10 and 10,000 male enhancements (mean: 400 procedures, excluding notable outliers). In addition to performing male enhancements, six physicians in my sample also specialize in GCGS with 4 to 40 years' experience (mean: 22 years).

I conducted interviews in person at participants' medical offices, via phone, or online. This approach offered flexibility for practitioners' schedules and increased participation while enabling me to build rapport with participants (Jenner & Myers, 2019) over the course of 45- to 160-minute interviews (mean: 90 minutes). I utilized a modified grounded theory approach with open-ended, semi-structured interview questions to draw out rich qualitative themes (Charmaz, 2014).

A somatechnic analytical method enabled me to compare similar genital technologies and somatic practices around which different discursive systems form. Cultural studies scholar Nikki Sullivan (2009) describes this method as

> juxtaposing various modificatory procedures, the justifications that inform their practice or its prohibition and the ethico-political lived effects of such, in the hope that in so doing, questions, issues, and insights associated with one particular practice may cast new light on others. This may in turn engender more nuanced understandings of and critical responses to the complex and multifaceted technés in and through which embodied being(s) comes to matter in situated contextually specific ways. (p. 317)

I compared practitioners' discourses about GCGS with their talk about male enhancement to underscore the assumptions, justifications, and prohibitions informing these practices.

Since somatechnics understands discourse as constitutive of the contours of our bodies, it is compatible with a Foucauldian conceptualization that affords discourse material existence. Instead of employing Foucault's historical analysis to identify the ruptures between different discursive formations, I follow the examples of somatechnicians (Garner, 2011, 2014) and ethnographers (Whitehead, 2012) who extend Foucault's analysis of discourse to fit their data. To paraphrase Garner's (2011) astute observation, I do not have to analyze history to demonstrate the incarnation of the body through power because a somatechnic method allows me to examine GCGS discourse alongside "the other real possible statements, which are contemporary to it" (Foucault, 1994, p. xvii) in male enhancement discourse.

While I could have analyzed medical discourses contained in various texts, they do not necessarily demonstrate the ways discourses operate at the level of everyday life. Feminist sociologist Jaye Cee Whitehead (2012) contends,

> Textual analysis cannot uncover how discourses can be forged, appropriated, and locally adapted in particular moments that may never leave an historical

trace.… Interactive methods allow researchers another lens to study power's "capillary" ability to bleed its way into seemingly insignificant slices of every-day life and fleeting moments of individuals' feelings and thoughts. (p. 20)

Given that the discourses participants invoked during interviews do not all exist in texts, and therefore "may leave only a thin and ambiguous historical residue" (Whitehead, 2012, p. 21), this research is unique in mapping out their operation in practitioner's everyday practices.

Situated Position

My situated position circumscribes my contribution to the generation of knowl-edge through this research. My white cisitude made access to the research field possible and interviews more endurable. I conducted this research as an act of soli-darity, recognizing that even though white cis women are ensnared by the gender/sex binary and eugenic projects of white nation-building (Stein, 2015), I am not targeted by the interconnected violence of trans-antagonism and white supremacy. I largely benefit from the system-wide normalization of my white, cis femininity and 'female' body, a fact that was reasserted repeatedly when participants pathol-ogized trans folks and people of colour.

White (and) cis scholars also have more access to and influence within aca-demia and historically have established what questions get asked in transgender theory (see Gill-Peterson, 2018b; Janzen et al., 2020; Latham, 2017). There is a long, ongoing history of cis, mostly white scholars conducting research about trans people in ways that position them as objects of study rather than as subjects, much less as producers of knowledge. At once an expression of "fascination with the ex-otic" and an erasure of trans subjectivity, this research approach causes real harm to trans people (Hale, 2009, para. 4).

Moreover, poststructuralist transgender theory often objectifies trans people as examples of how the gender/sex binary is socially constructed. Adopting a transgressive politics that conceptualizes trans/gender and the sexed body as fluid, fragmented, and discursively produced (Stryker et al., 2008), poststructuralist theory largely overlooks trans narratives and the politics of trans rights and recog-nition (for examples of this literature, see Namaste, 2000; Prosser, 1998). Feminist theorist Viviane Namaste (2000) argues that some scholars working within a post-structuralist tradition can—in their efforts to demonstrate that gender and the sexed body are socially constructed—neglect the everyday experiences of trans people, fail to centre their needs, and represent trans folks as cultural dupes of the gender binary.

A poststructuralist tradition is not inherently harmful to trans communities, however. Many trans scholars (Garner, 2014, 2017; Gill-Peterson, 2014; Latham, 2017; Snorton, 2017; Stryker, 2006) employ a poststructuralist approach with the aim of improving the material conditions for trans lives. As my colleagues and I have argued elsewhere (Whitehead et al., 2012), attention to trans people's everyday lives is compatible with understanding gender and sexed bodies as discursive yet entirely real and material in their consequences. While I adopt a poststructuralist lens in this chapter, I do not argue how trans bodies and identities are socially produced. Rather, this project deconstructs cis men's 'natural' bodies in an attempt to answer trans theorist Susan Stryker's (2006) call "to investigate your nature as I have been compelled to confront mine" (p. 247). This approach also mirrors trans philosopher Jacob Hale's (2009) suggested rules of ethical research that advise cis people to reflect on what researching trans issues tells us about cisitude.

I hope this chapter builds on the germinal analyses of trans scholars who have come before me in ways that are useful for expanding the possible "geographies of embodiment" and subjectivity for trans people (Garner, 2011, p. 39) so that bodies might come to matter differently.

"WEED OUT THE REAL ONES": DOUBTING TRANS AUTHENTICITY

Dr. Schneider has more than 20 years' experience specializing in GCS, having performed hundreds of transition surgeries in the United States. He previously performed penile girth enhancements for cis men but stopped offering those procedures due to "high complication rates" and "poor outcomes." Now he only occasionally performs suspensory ligament release, which severs the ligament that keeps the penis tucked up under the pubic arch and into the body. Releasing the ligament hypothetically extends the penis outward from the body and—according to some physicians—can result in up to five centimetres gained in flaccid length; however, Dr. Schneider is not confident in such a "good outcome" and therefore tries to dissuade his cis patients from pursuing the procedure. More commonly, he performs revision surgeries for "failed" male enhancements done by other doctors.

We conducted our phone interview while Dr. Schneider was waiting to board a flight; I strained to hear him over the cacophony of travellers and overhead speakers announcing flight times. After finding a more secluded lounge, Dr. Schneider responded as to why "we have a shrink with transsexuals":[12]

> When you do transgender surgery, you're taking their testicles off and you don't want to do that on somebody unless you're *one hundred percent sure* that they're a *true transsexual* and whether or not they can handle it emotionally. So what we're talking about, there's a much more *dramatic surgery* and a *total change of identity.…* You're cutting off testicles, you know, you're turning a male to girl or vice versa, and that's a *major change, that's not improving someone's aesthetic appearance.…* And that's why there's standardization that's done by an organization to make sure that patients who undergo this are *good candidates.* (emphasis added)

Dr. Schneider plainly articulates that the sexed body provides the material 'truth' of gender identity. Trans identity therefore repudiates the site around which he believes authentic gender identity 'naturally' coheres: the sexed body assigned at birth. The claim that trans folks are undergoing a "total change of identity" through genital surgery implies that sexed bodies—particularly gonads—are the origin of identity, and that gonadal intervention necessarily changes one's 'core' sense of self.

Skepticism about trans authenticity was common throughout my interviews with practitioners. This doubt reflects both medical and wider social anxieties that people who claim to be trans are just confused, undecided, or otherwise 'fake' and not 'truly' transgender. Dr. Schneider's statements reveal how trans people's claims to authentic identity are not limited to autonomous self-authorization; authenticity must align with an established array of criteria often decided by cis authorities on gender before one can access appropriate medical care.

Physicians like Dr. Schneider construct male enhancement technologies as "improving" the natural body, compared to their framing of transition technologies as rendering trans people's bodies (and thus identities) unnatural through a "dramatic surgery." Parallel with Garner's (2011) analysis of gynecomastia surgery, doctors describe male enhancement as a minor improvement to a 'natural' fixed body despite medical intervention—from a male body with a small or 'average' penis to a male body with an 'average' or large penis—rather than a radical movement between sexes. There is no discussion of cis men going through a 'real life test'—resembling the satirical psychotherapy session illustrated by Wilchins (1997) at the beginning of this chapter—to prove they are 'cis enough' and ready for life as men with larger cocks. Trans folks, however, are required to provide mental health professionals with convincing evidence that they are truly prepared for a somatic transition from one sexed body to its 'opposite.' Overlapping with Garner's (2011) conclusions, practitioners' differential conceptualization of the distance between pre- and post-surgical bodies for cis and trans folks serves to naturalize cis identification, the sexed body assigned at birth, and the gender/sex binary.

Dr. Fraser also prioritizes the sexed body as the natural source of gender. A Canadian physician, Dr. Fraser specializes in GCS but in recent years started performing suspensory ligament releases, fat injections for penile girth augmentation, and other male enhancements. When I asked Dr. Fraser why trans folks require mental health professionals' approval to access genital technologies, but cis men do not, he initially hesitated:

> I … I really don't know…. I think that the perception is that if you want to change your gender, they want to make sure that you're really of sound mind and body. Sometimes it's just tabled off as "*oh they're going through a phase*" or "*they really don't know what they want.*" They want to establish that they know exactly what they want, they know the risks and benefits, they're making an informed decision, and I mean that's different—*switching sexes versus just wanting to improve what you have.* (emphasis added)

Like Dr. Schneider, Dr. Fraser differentiates between male enhancement as an intervention for cis men to "improve what [they] have" as responsible consumer subjects, and GCGS as "different," as "switching sexes," as requiring a higher threshold of proof that trans patients are "making an informed decision." Again, the materialization of cis bodies through male enhancement technologies is rendered an acceptable 'improvement' to a 'natural' body; in contrast, transition surgeries mark trans bodies as unnatural constructions.

Practitioners' trepidation about trans people's authenticity does not stem from their past experiences with trans patients actually expressing that "they really don't know what they want," thus demonstrating there is sufficient cause to doubt trans patients' authenticity. After all, Dr. Fraser specializes in GCS, yet his response illustrates he does not readily know from working with trans patients why their access to genital surgeries is gatekept; his answer is based on the medical "perception" of the trustworthiness of trans people's claims to authenticity.

Practitioners' skepticism about trans authenticity stems from their assumption that if patients regard both gender and the sexed body to be mutable, then through normative discourses on identities and bodies, trans patients must be confused or "going through a phase." And if trans patients are so confused about something (culturally regarded in the Global North) as core and foundational as gender identity, then why should a physician trust that they are not also confused about their desires for bodily transformation? In other words, participants assume that trustworthy patients—those who are authentic—have a fixed, stable gender identity rooted in the sexed body they were assigned at birth. So it is not surprising that skepticism about authenticity is not leveled at cis men seeking male enhancement.

Dr. Fray's responses also expressed skepticism about trans authenticity. Dr. Fray is a US practitioner who worked with trans patients as a medical student but now exclusively works with cis men. Our interview focused mostly on a procedure he recently started performing called the Man Shot, which aims to augment penile girth by injecting stem-cell-enriched fat from one's own body around the erectile tissue of the penis. Dr. Fray is confident the Man Shot can increase circumference penile girth by over two-and-a-half centimetres.

During our interview, Dr. Fray was lounging at home on a Saturday watching wrestling matches on TV. In between matches, he answered why trans folks are required to obtain approval before accessing genital technologies:

> There's intended discrimination by the medical and insurance establishment against adults who feel trapped in their own gender for the purpose of trying to *weed out the real ones and the ones who are in a flux*. My *guess* is that there was one surgery done out of a hundred that resulted in reassigning someone who—either was [transitioning] for the wrong reasons or somebody who *recanted their intent* and maybe there was a lawsuit. (emphasis added)

According to Dr. Fray, just "one surgery done out of a hundred that resulted in reassigning someone" is one reassignment too many for practitioners, demonstrating an exceptionally high threshold of certainty in a trans patient's identity. As trans activist Zane Diamond explains, under such gatekeeping, trans health care prioritizes protecting cis people from accidentally transitioning, rather than providing appropriate care to trans patients (personal communication, June 8, 2017). Anxieties about 'fake' trans people are compounded by a perceived threat to a physician's medical practice if a patient later decides they are not trans and seeks to hold their doctors accountable for permanent bodily intervention. Yet, certainty in the identities of cis male enhancement patients is not required, despite the possibility they may also pursue postoperative litigation for permanent enhancements that, according to the American Urological Association (2018, para. 1), have "not been shown to be safe or efficacious."

Associating regret with transition surgeries but not with male enhancements expresses doubt in the authenticity of trans identity. Yet those who have undergone GCS are extremely unlikely to "recant their intent," as Dr. Fray speculated, or to have been "going through a phase," as Dr. Fraser surmised. The assumption that trans people regret medical transition is not borne out by clinical research conducted over the last six decades, which shows the incidence of regret is less than 1 percent to 1.5 percent, depending on the study (Bowman & Goldberg, 2006). By comparison, cis patients are up to 23 times more likely to regret genital surgery (Bowman & Goldberg, 2006). This raises the question of why trans patients' access to surgery is gatekept out of concern that they are not 'truly' trans and might regret transition yet barriers for cis patients are comparatively low.

The discursive work accomplished by the interrelated notions of regret and authenticity in the materialization of trans bodies is the persistent gatekeeping and denaturalization of trans embodiment and subjectivity at the level of institutional health management and the everyday lives of trans people. The discursive power exercised by authenticity in relation to cis men is the theme of the next section.

"I'VE GOT THE ANATOMY AND I WANT TO DO SOMETHING ABOUT IT": ANATOMY AS CIS AUTHENTICITY

Practitioners do not question cis men's gender authenticity and generally open the gate to male enhancement. Most participants, such as Dr. Wexler, report that they largely rely on cis men's self-selection for male enhancement as evidence they are "really male" and therefore eligible for penile augmentation. Dr. Wexler is a US physician who formerly performed penile girth enhancements using dermal fillers and polymethyl methacrylate injections but stopped performing those procedures in favour of the Man Shot, having administered a few dozen of these penile girth augmentations in recent years.

Fitting our interview between work and cooking dinner for his family, we rushed through interview questions. I asked Dr. Wexler how he determines who is a good candidate for male enhancement:

> Usually they come in *preselected.…* They're coming to me because they have something they want to do. They either want to be *better at what they're doing or at what they have*. Or they have an *issue* that they feel they need to have treated. So they're *preselected* in terms of you know "*I've got the anatomy and I want to do something about it*." (emphasis added)

Alongside patient desire, the "anatomy" of the sexed body—the supposed origin of gender identity—was evidence enough for physicians like Dr. Wexler to believe cis patients' masculine identities are authentic, rendering them eligible for male enhancement. Compared to the gatekeeping of trans patients seeking GCGS, Dr. Wexler assumes that his cis patients' bodies and identities are stable, despite patients' desires to "do something about" a so-called issue with their anatomy.

Dr. Martin's response mirrored Dr. Wexler's. Dr. Martin is a Canadian physician who has administered the Priapus Shot and other enhancements over the last few years. The Priapus Shot—not to be confused with the Man Shot—is composed of platelet rich plasma that, according to Dr. Martin, aims to "heal" the "damaged" vasculature of the penis for mild girth enhancement. When I asked Dr. Martin, "How do you decide if someone is a good candidate for the Priapus Shot?" he said that, apart from ruling out notable health concerns such as cardiovascular disease or bleeding disorders, he administers the Priapus Shot based on "just *patients' desire*" and that he was "*not going to question their desire*," adding that "if the *anatomy* is fine, there's really no reason [to reject the patient]" (emphasis added).

Responses like Dr. Martin's demonstrate that skepticism about the authenticity, stability, and permanence of gender identity does not apply to cis men, making genital technologies appropriate for meeting cis "desire" but not trans people's desires or needs. In contrast with physicians' doubt in the gender authenticity and embodiment goals of their trans patients, doctors readily trust cis men's identities and desires for their bodily being because their anatomy—their sexed body—represents the 'truth' of their gender identity. Authenticity discourse thus acts as a technique of naturalization that expresses doubt about trans identity, resolute faith in the sexed body assigned at birth, and certainty in the cis subjectivities that are culturally congruent with that binary sex assignment. Throughout the course of interviews, in fact, practitioners never once expressed doubt about the authenticity of the bodies and identities of their cis men patients, including when their sexed bodies failed to fit the narrow confines of the binary.

"THEY'RE REALLY MALE": DEFENDING THE AUTHENTICITY OF MALE BODIES THAT FAIL

None of the practitioners in this research reported asking their cis patients how they feel about their sense of self after penile augmentation, if they regret the procedure, or, much less, whether they are "really male." Practitioners take for granted that cis men's 'maleness' is discrete and stable even if their sexed traits present variability. In recognition of doctors' insistence on the sexed body as the site of one's 'true' gender identity, I asked physicians if any of their male enhancement patients who believe their penises are 'too small' and 'need' enhancement may be intersex. The term *intersex* refers to bodies that display a range of traits (e.g., genitals, hormones, chromosomes, gonads, etc.) that do not 'match' cultural and racial expectations for binary sexed bodies (see Gill-Peterson, 2018b; Magubane, 2014).[13] Despite patients' intersex variability, practitioners including Dr. Rosenburg reasserted the authenticity of their cis patients' 'male' bodies and masculine identities.

Dr. Rosenburg is a US physician who has performed GCS for almost three decades and penile girth enhancements using dermal fillers for more than 20 years. Over the baritone hum of his sports car accelerating in the background of the phone call, Dr. Rosenburg reflected on whether any of his male enhancement patients could be intersex. Speaking about his patients, Dr. Rosenburg stated matter-of-factly, "There are people who are classified as intersex, but *they're really male*, but they have streak gonads and *underdeveloped penises*. [Streak gonads are] a form of *testicular feminization*" (emphasis added).

Despite an intersex diagnosis, Dr. Rosenburg's faith in his cis patients' discrete maleness was unyielding. Dr. Rosenburg's assignment of maleness to his intersex patients' bodies is perhaps based on his patients' (presumed) gender. This seemingly inverted process of assigning sex based on one's gender reflects a broader pattern in the medical management of intersex bodies observed by gender scholars whereby social categories inform how doctors surgically construct sexed flesh (Davis et al., 2016; Kessler, 1990). In other words, gender is not the effect of the sexed body; rather, it is *the cause* (Fausto-Sterling, 2000).

When some sexed traits are 'ambiguous' according to social expectations for binary bodies, other sexed traits 'compensate' for their limitations (see Sanz, 2017) so that practitioners like Dr. Rosenburg can confidently claim that his intersex patients are "really male" despite "feminization." By locating the intersex condition in parts (gonads and penis) of a whole ('male' body), Dr. Rosenburg is able to rescue the maleness of his patients' bodies from the feminization of its parts (see Garner, 2014, for a similar analysis of gynecomastia). Even the language of testicular feminization isolates that feminization from the rest of the body while suggesting that the gonads are by *essence* still testicles. Similarly, instead of using language such as large clitoris or tumescent tissue (the latter of which does not imply any particular sex assignment), Dr. Rosenburg uses the language of underdeveloped penises, reaffirming this part as male while distancing its shortcomings of underdevelopment from the whole of the rest of the body. Containing the intersex condition within body parts performs the discursive work of naturalizing the maleness of the body as a whole to release his patients from an intersex designation, rendering male enhancement a permissible somatechnology rather than a bodily transformation that necessitates gatekeeping. This discursive work is not immaterial; in cases like these, male enhancements serve as 'normalizing' technologies that work to 'correct' intersex bodies.

CONCLUSION

In many ways, physicians who perform genital surgeries employ similar medical discourses in their practices as those Garner (2014) located in codified texts on gynecomastia and trans chest surgeries. This speaks to the embeddedness of male enhancement practitioners in the medical establishment, as well as their investment in maintaining gender/sex congruence and the female/male binary.

My research demonstrates that medical discourse does not merely describe the reality of bodies; it is a technology that brings particular bodies into being while foreclosing the materialization of others. The somatechnology of authenticity discourse works in combination with genital technologies in service of naturalizing cisitude. Authenticity discourse frames male enhancement technologies as augmenting the nature of cis men's bodies and transition technologies as harming the nature of gender/sex congruence, justifying careful gatekeeping. Authenticity discourse therefore operates within male enhancement and GCGS to naturalize cis men's 'enhanced' bodies and masculinity while marking post-surgical trans bodies and subjectivities as unnatural.

Comparing male enhancement and transition technologies enables us to see the "seams and sutures" (Stryker, 2006, p. 247)—the ways in which cis men's 'natural' bodies and identities are stitched together through medical discourse—rendering visible their social incarnation through somatechnologies like authenticity. Equipped with this knowledge, we can attempt to disrupt the systemic violence enacted against trans people in service of cisnormativity and the 'natural body.'

ACKNOWLEDGEMENTS

I wish to thank Travers, Michael Hathaway, Susan Stryker, Jaye Cee Whitehead, Kit Myers, and Jane Whittington for their helpful comments on earlier iterations of this work.

QUESTIONS FOR DISCUSSION

1. From the perspective of social scientists and feminist biologists cited by the author, what are the relationships between gender and the sexed body?

How are gender and the sexed body both socially constructed? What is the difference between natural, socially constructed, and fake? Why do you suppose that what people consider is natural is equated with being real but what people understand is socially constructed is equated with being fake or artificial?

2. The author discusses how our bodies are not natural, biological facts or artificially modified through technology. Rather, all bodies—not only those bodies that carry the most visible traces of explicit modification—are constituted through technologies. She shares several examples demonstrating the interconnection between bodies and technologies—for example, using fire as technology to cook food dramatically shaped the human body to have more calories, smaller molars, and shorter intestines. What are other examples of how bodies and technologies are interconnected and co-constitutive? Consider various forms of technology in your examples, including typical notions of technology as well as knowledge/discourse.

INVITATIONS TO GO DEEPER

1. Consider how each of the following have been naturalized throughout history: racial segregation, sexual violence enacted by cis men, and cis women's socially imposed obligation to care for children (among others). How has naturalizing behaviours and social relations served to justify inequity and oppression? What other social arrangements throughout history have been regarded as natural? What other human behaviours are currently understood to be natural but are socially, culturally, and historically situated? Consider different axes of power, such as sexuality, class, and disability.

2. Reflect on how being a student has shaped your body. Consider the way stress during exams or before a big presentation impacts your skin, your digestion, your heart rate. How might your body look, feel, or move through the world differently if education did not depend on tests and grades but instead on experiential learning and self-reflection? Think about how being a student impacts your sleep or ability to exercise. Consider what foods you can afford and the amount of time you have to prepare meals while being a student. If higher education was not a commodity and you could access it for free, how might this shape your body differently?

3. Some people use genital technologies like gender confirmation surgery, male enhancement, and female genital cosmetic surgery to craft their genitals, and they experience varying levels of social stigma for it. Yet most of us regularly use other kinds of genital technologies that have, to different degrees, become

more normalized in Canadian culture. Compile a list of different kinds of genital technologies, perhaps even some that you use. Consider grooming, hygiene, aesthetic, sexual, medical, and other genital technologies. Why do you suppose some are more normalized than others? How do gender, the sexed body, sexuality, and other axes of power shape which genital technologies are more or less normalized in Canadian culture?

READ MORE

Davis, G., Dewey, J. M., & Murphy, E. L. (2016). Giving sex: Deconstructing intersex and trans medicalization practices. *Gender & Society*, *30*(3), 490–514. https://doi.org/10.1177/0891243215602102

Enke, A. F. (2012). The education of little cis: Cisgender and the discipline of opposing bodies. In A. F. Enke (Ed.), *Transfeminist perspectives in and beyond transgender and gender studies* (pp. 60–78). Temple University Press.

Garner, T. (2014). Chest surgeries of a different "nature." *Annual Review of Critical Psychology*, *11*, 337–356.

Magubane, Z. (2014). Spectacles and scholarship: Caster Semenya, intersex studies, and the problem of race in feminist theory. *Signs: Journal of Women in Culture and Society*, *39*(3), 761–785. https://doi.org/10.1086/674301

Sanz, V. (2017). No way out of the binary: A critical history of the scientific production of sex. *Signs: Journal of Women in Culture and Society*, *43*(1), 1–27. https://doi.org/10.1086/692517

Sullivan, N. (2007). "The price to pay for our common good": Genital modification and the somatechnologies of cultural (in)difference. *Social Semiotics*, *17*(3), 395–409. https://doi.org/10.1080/10350330701448736

LISTEN MORE, WATCH MORE

"Male and female are binary, but people aren't," Riley J. Dennis, 2017: https://www.youtube.com/watch?v=m2MEFj8q6rg

"TransHub talks: Gatekeeping," ACON Health, 2020: https://www.youtube.com/watch?v=1BePD8txdUs

"What does 'Two-Spirit' mean?" them, 2018: https://www.youtube.com/watch?v=A4lBibGzUnE

"What it's like to be intersex," As/Is, 2015: https://www.youtube.com/watch?v=cAUDKEI4QKI

NOTES

1. *Cisgender*, or *cis*, indicates a culturally recognized and enforced correspondence between one's gender and sexed body assigned at birth (see Enke, 2012). Declarative statements like "it's a girl!" *socially assign* gender to a newborn, often based on a doctor's social assessment of an infant's genitals.

2. *Trans* is an umbrella term that describes people whose sex assignment at birth does not culturally correspond with their gender. Trans folks can include transgender, transsexual, genderqueer, nonbinary, pangender, and agender people, among others.

3. GCS includes chest, genital, facial, and other procedures that affirm a person's gender. As Heyes and Latham (2018) suggest, terms like GCS are no less politically imbued than former terminology and continue to constrain trans self-descriptions to fit the Gender Dysphoria diagnosis (American Psychiatric Association, 2013). I employ the terms GCS and gender confirming genital surgery (GCGS) while critically acknowledging their political alignments.

4. Mental health professionals working with trans clients are advised to follow the "Standards of Care" (Coleman et al., 2012) defined by the World Professional Association for Transgender Health.

5. Single quotation marks used around words or phrases indicate they are politically contentious and not my language.

6. I use the language *sexed body* instead of *sex* to indicate that the body is socially constructed. Female, male, and intersex are not fixed, natural qualities of the body, but rather ongoing social processes of ascribing meaning to anatomical structures, chemicals, and chromosomes. For more on how the body is sexed, see feminist biologist Anne Fausto-Sterling's (2000) *Sexing the Body*.

7. *Deadnaming* refers to using a person's given birth name instead of their gender-affirming chosen name.

8. Whitehead et al. (2012) also describe how some mental health professionals understand gender as a larger power structure rather than a natural binary.

9. Gynecomastia is a medical diagnosis of 'excess' breast tissue in cis men, ostensibly caused by a hormonal 'imbalance' (Garner, 2014). Some mental health professionals also use this diagnosis so that trans men who have unwanted chest tissue can access appropriate medical care.

10. Garner uses the pronouns they and their.

11. Firestone (1970) also cautions that "new technology … may be used against [women and children] to reinforce the entrenched system of exploitation" (p. 11).

12. Many trans folks reject the classification transsexual because its history as a medicalizing and racializing discourse pathologizes trans people (Gill-Peterson, 2018a). However, many other trans folks embrace this term (see Namaste, 2000; Prosser, 1998).

13.   One example of intersex embodiment includes having 'male' XY chromosomes, resistance to testosterone, and hair, fat, and muscle distribution that is culturally interpreted as 'female.'

REFERENCES

Alm, E. (2013). Somatechnics of consensus: Situating the biomedicalisation of intersex. *Somatechnics, 3*(2), 307–328. https://doi.org/10.3366/soma.2013.0100

American Psychiatric Association. (2013). Gender Dysphoria. In *Diagnostic and Statistical Manual of Mental Disorders* (5th ed., pp. 451–459). https://doi.org/10.1176/appi.books.9780890425596

American Urological Association. (2018). Penile augmentation surgery. https://web.archive.org/web/20190423145916/https://www.auanet.org/guidelines/penile-augmentation-surgery

Ashley, F. (2018). Don't be so hateful: The insufficiency of anti-discrimination and hate crime laws in improving trans well-being. *University of Toronto Law Journal, 68*(1), 1–36. https://doi.org/10.3138/utlj.2017–0057

Ashley, F., & Ells, C. (2018). In favor of covering ethically important cosmetic surgeries: Facial feminization surgery for transgender people. *The American Journal of Bioethics, 18*(12), 23–25. https://doi.org/10.1080/15265161.2018.1531162

Beauchamp, T. (2009). Artful concealment and strategic visibility: Transgender bodies and U.S. state surveillance after 9/11. *Surveillance & Society, 6*(4), 356–366. https://doi.org/10.24908/ss.v6i4.3267

Bowman, C., & Goldberg, J. M. (2006). Care of the patient undergoing sex reassignment surgery. *International Journal of Transgenderism, 9*(3–4), 135–165. https://doi.org/10.1300/J485v09n03_07

Braun, V. (2005). In search of (better) sexual pleasure: Female genital "cosmetic" surgery. *Sexualities, 8*(4), 407–424. https://doi.org/10.1177/1363460705056625

Butler, J. (1993). *Bodies that matter: On the discursive limits of "sex."* Routledge.

Charmaz, K. (2014). *Constructing grounded theory* (2nd ed). Sage Publications.

Coleman, E., Bockting, W., Botzer, M., Cohen-Kettenis, P., DeCuypere, G., Feldman, J., Fraser, L., Green, J., Knudson, G., Meyer, W. J., Monstrey, S., Adler, R. K., Brown, G. R., Devor, A. H., Ehrbar, R., Ettner, R., Eyler, E., Garofalo, R., Karasic, D. H., … Zucker, K. (2012). Standards of care for the health of transsexual, transgender, and gender-nonconforming people, version 7. *International Journal of Transgenderism, 13*(4), 165–232. https://doi.org/10.1080/15532739.2011.700873

Davis, G., Dewey, J. M., & Murphy, E. L. (2016). Giving sex: Deconstructing intersex and trans medicalization practices. *Gender & Society, 30*(3), 490–514. https://doi.org/10.1177/0891243215602102

Enke, A. F. (2012). The education of little cis: Cisgender and the discipline of opposing bodies. In A. F. Enke (Ed.), *Transfeminist perspectives in and beyond transgender and gender studies* (pp. 60–78). Temple University Press.

Fausto-Sterling, A. (2000). *Sexing the body: Gender politics and the construction of sexuality* (1st ed.). Basic Books.

Firestone, S. (1970). *The dialectic of sex: The case for feminist revolution.* W. Morrow.

Foucault, M. (1994). *The birth of the clinic: An archaeology of medical perception.* Vintage Books.

Friedan, B. (1963). *The feminine mystique.* W. W. Norton & Company.

Fujimura, J. H. (2006). Sex genes: A critical sociomaterial approach to the politics and molecular genetics of sex determination. *Signs: Journal of Women in Culture and Society, 32*(1), 49–82. https://doi.org/10.1086/505612

Garner, T. (2011). *Stitching up the natural: "Manboobs," pregnancy, and the transgender body* [Doctoral dissertation]. Simon Fraser University.

Garner, T. (2014). Chest surgeries of a different "nature." *Annual Review of Critical Psychology, 11*, 337–356.

Garner, T. (2017). (De)Pathologization: Transsexuality, gynecomastia, and the negotiation of mental health diagnoses in online communities. In M. Morrow & L. H. Malcoe (Eds.), *Critical inquiries for social justice in mental health* (pp. 285–311). University of Toronto Press.

Garrison, S. (2018). On the limits of "trans enough": Authenticating trans identity narratives. *Gender & Society, 32*(5), 613–637. https://doi.org/10.1177/0891 243218780299

Gill-Peterson, J. (2014). The technical capacities of the body: Assembling race, technology, and transgender. *TSQ: Transgender Studies Quarterly, 1*(3), 402–418. https://doi.org/10.1215/23289252–2685660

Gill-Peterson, J. (2018a). *Histories of the transgender child.* University of Minnesota Press.

Gill-Peterson, J. (2018b). Trans of color critique before transsexuality. *TSQ: Transgender Studies Quarterly, 5*(4), 606–620. https://doi.org/10.1215/23289252–7090073

Gressgård, R. (2010). When trans translates into tolerance—or was it monstrous? Transsexual and transgender identity in liberal humanist discourse. *Sexualities, 13*(5), 539–561. https://doi.org/10.1177/1363460710375569

Hale, J. (2009). Suggested rules for non-transsexuals writing about transsexuals, transsexuality, transsexualism, or trans _____. *Sandy Stone.* https://web.archive.org/web/20140802233310/https://sandystone.com/hale.rules.html

Haraway, D. J. (1991). *Simians, cyborgs, and women: The reinvention of nature.* Routledge.

Heyes, C. J., & Latham, J. R. (2018). Trans surgeries and cosmetic surgeries. *TSQ: Transgender Studies Quarterly, 5*(2), 174–189. https://doi.org/10.1215/23289252–4348617

Hird, M. J. (2002). For a sociology of transsexualism. *Sociology*, *36*(3), 577–595. https://doi.org/10.1177/0038038502036003005

Janzen, C., Randell-Moon, H., van der Tuin, I., & Vroegindeweij, M. (2020). On the intersection of somatechnics and transgender studies. *TSQ: Transgender Studies Quarterly*, *7*(3), 374–382. https://doi.org/10.1215/23289252–8553020

Jeffreys, S. (2014). *Gender hurts: A feminist analysis of the politics of transgenderism*. Routledge.

Jenner, B. M., & Myers, K. C. (2019). Intimacy, rapport, and exceptional disclosure: A comparison of in-person and mediated interview contexts. *International Journal of Social Research Methodology*, *22*(2), 165–177. https://doi.org/10.1080/13645579.2018.1512694

Kessler, S. J. (1990). The medical construction of gender: Case management of intersexed infants. *Signs: Journal of Women in Culture and Society*, *16*(1), 3–26. https://doi.org/10.1086/494643

Lancaster, R. N. (2006). Sex, science, and pseudoscience in the public sphere. *Identities*, *13*(1), 101–138. https://doi.org/10.1080/10702890500535707

Lane, R. (2018). "We are here to help": Who opens the gate for surgeries? *TSQ: Transgender Studies Quarterly*, *5*(2), 207–227. https://doi.org/10.1215/23289252–4348648

Latham, J. R. (2017). Making and treating trans problems: The ontological politics of clinical practices. *Studies in Gender and Sexuality*, *18*(1), 40–61. https://doi.org/10.1080/15240657.2016.1238682

Macquarie University. (2009, April 26). Somatechnics research centre. https://web.archive.org/web/20090426050406/http://www.somatechnics.mq.edu.au/

Magubane, Z. (2014). Spectacles and scholarship: Caster Semenya, intersex studies, and the problem of race in feminist theory. *Signs: Journal of Women in Culture and Society*, *39*(3), 761–785. https://doi.org/10.1086/674301

Namaste, V. K. (2000). *Invisible lives: The erasure of transsexual and transgendered people*. University of Chicago Press.

Prosser, J. (1998). *Second skins: The body narratives of transsexuality*. Columbia University Press.

Raymond, J. G. (1994). *The transsexual empire: The making of the she-male*. Teachers College Press.

Sanz, V. (2017). No way out of the binary: A critical history of the scientific production of sex. *Signs: Journal of Women in Culture and Society*, *43*(1), 1–27. https://doi.org/10.1086/692517

Simon, M. E. (2015). *Trans/gender sincerities: A dialogic analysis of four young people's embodied subjectivities* [Master's thesis]. Simon Fraser University.

Skidmore, E. (2011). Constructing the "good transsexual": Christine Jorgensen, whiteness, and heteronormativity in the mid-twentieth-century press. *Feminist Studies*, *37*(2), 270–300.

Snorton, C. R. (2017). *Black on both sides: A racial history of trans identity*. University of Minnesota Press.

Spade, D. (2003). Resisting medicine, re/modeling gender. *Berkeley Women's Law Journal, 18*(1), 15–37.

Stein, M. N. (2015). *Measuring manhood: Race and the science of masculinity, 1830–1934*. University of Minnesota Press.

Stryker, S. (2006). My words to Victor Frankenstein above the village of Chamounix: Performing transgender rage. In S. Stryker & S. Whittle (Eds.), *The transgender studies reader* (1st ed., pp. 244–256). Routledge.

Stryker, S., Currah, P., & Moore, L. J. (2008). Introduction: Trans-, trans, or transgender? *WSQ: Women's Studies Quarterly, 36*(3–4), 11–22. https://doi.org/10.1353/wsq.0.0112

Sullivan, N. (2005). Somatechnics, or, the social inscription of bodies and selves. *Australian Feminist Studies, 20*(48), 363–366. https://doi.org/10.1080/08164640500280274

Sullivan, N. (2007). "The price to pay for our common good": Genital modification and the somatechnologies of cultural (in)difference. *Social Semiotics, 17*(3), 395–409. https://doi.org/10.1080/10350330701448736

Sullivan, N. (2009). The somatechnics of intersexuality. *GLQ: A Journal of Lesbian and Gay Studies, 15*(2), 313–327. https://doi.org/10.1215/10642684-2008-140

Travers. (2018). *The trans generation: How trans kids (and their parents) are creating a gender revolution*. New York University Press.

Vipond, E. (2015). Resisting transnormativity: Challenging the medicalization and regulation of trans bodies. *Theory in Action, 8*(2), 21–44. https://doi.org/10.3798/tia.1937–0237.15008

Westbrook, L., & Schilt, K. (2014). Doing gender, determining gender: Transgender people, gender panics, and the maintenance of the sex/gender/sexuality system. *Gender & Society, 28*(1), 32–57. https://doi.org/10.1177/0891243213503203

Whitehead, J. C. (2012). *The nuptial deal: Same-sex marriage and neo-liberal governance*. University of Chicago Press.

Whitehead, J. C., & Thomas, J. (2013). Sexuality and the ethics of body modification: Theorizing the situated relationships among gender, sexuality and the body. *Sexualities, 16*(3–4), 383–400. https://doi.org/10.1177/1363460713479755

Whitehead, J. C., Thomas, J., Forkner, B., & LaMonica, D. (2012). Reluctant gatekeepers: "Trans-positive" practitioners and the social construction of sex and gender. *Journal of Gender Studies, 21*(4), 387–400. https://doi.org/10.1080/09589236.2012.681181

Wilchins, R. A. (1997). *Read my lips: Sexual subversion and the end of gender*. Firebrand Books.

Wrangham, R., & Carmody, R. (2010). Human adaptation to the control of fire. *Evolutionary Anthropology, 19*(5), 187–199. https://doi.org/10.1002/evan.20275

CHAPTER 11

"So, You Wanna Live Forever?" Representations of Disability, Gender, and Technology in *Cyberpunk 2077*

Tamara Banbury and Kelly Fritsch

INTRODUCTION

In development for eight years, the widely anticipated video game *Cyberpunk 2077* was released in December 2020 by role-playing game industry leader CD Projekt Red. Set in Night City, a dystopian futuristic city run by corporations and mob rule, brutal violence dominates the streets of this action-adventure story. One of the only ways to survive in Night City is to use technology to augment the capacities of the human body. Mobilizing multiple forms of body modification, players battle to steal a biochip that may hold the secret to immortality. The body modifications in *Cyberpunk 2077* glorify the objective of fixing any perceived shortcomings of the human body and the future with technology. Not augmenting the body with cybernetic implants limits a player's ability to play the game; augmentation is a necessary fact of life in this troubling futuristic city where much of the world's economic and social structures have collapsed. The game world of Night City is full of "hardship, struggle, and loneliness" (Petit, 2020, para. 1) and in many ways reflects our present world more than any possible dystopian future. As Petit (2020) writes, "CD Projekt Red's open-world game does not exactly have a futuristic worldview" (para. 1). This is due in part to the way in which normative social relations of disability go unchallenged within the game and intersect with normative gender representations, reproducing sexism, transphobia, and ableism under the guise of the free choice of the gamer's character body modification and augmentation.

This chapter analyzes representations of disability, gender, and technological enhancement in the video game *Cyberpunk 2077*. Guided by critical disability studies, we, as disabled people and disability and media studies scholars, mark the multiple ways disabled people are simultaneously celebrated and erased through augmentative technologies in the game. Mobilizing these frameworks, in this chapter we ask what kind of futures are possible for disabled people when their existence and experiences are discounted in contemporary media and where body augmentation and overcoming is framed as a necessity. While in contemporary society, most people are not augmenting their bodies with implanted cybernetics to the same degree that is demanded in *Cyberpunk 2077*, the game does reproduce transhumanist fantasies of technology as saviour that is grounded in social injustice and inequity. We critique transhumanism as an ideology that upholds concepts of human exceptionalism at the expense of others, calling into question who has historically been allowed to be considered "human." Along with feminist, queer, critical race, Indigenous, and posthumanist scholars, critical disability scholars argue that the category of "human" has been an exclusive group of white, heterosexual, cis, nondisabled men, and this categorization has impeded the development of an equitable, just, and accessible society. Working with critical disability studies, we conclude that a desirable future does not come by way of individualized immortality and bodily overcoming vis-à-vis exclusive enhancement technologies so much as through interdependent relations of care, accessibility, and disability justice.

"NIGHT CITY CHANGES EVERY BODY"

In the game world of *Cyberpunk 2077*, gamers play as V, a mercenary for hire. Before entering the streets of Night City, players must create and outfit their character's avatar, choosing everything from hairstyle and skin colour to tattoos, piercing, makeup, and scars. This customization was one of the eagerly awaited aspects of *Cyberpunk 2077*, marketed on CD Projekt Red's website as glamorously changing "every body" through detailed body modification (Cyberpunk 2077, n.d.). Online discussion forums were filled with conjecture about the different ways people planned on creating their personalized versions of V. And yet, almost immediately after the release of the game to the public in December 2020, there were complaints about a lack of features players felt they were promised. This is "indicative of one of *Cyberpunk 2077*'s most glaring problems" (Petit, 2020, para. 3). That is, despite the alluring promise of full customization, in practice, the customization possibilities are rigidly bound to dominant Western social norms of desirable appearance, ability, and gender. As it turns out, Night City does not change "every body" but rather reproduces the very same bodies that dominate inequitable contemporary social relations.

These limited character customization options include choosing either a female or a male body type, along with a feminine or masculine voice (there is not a nonbinary option). Choosing a feminine or masculine voice influences the game experience. A male-presenting physical body with a female-sounding voice is played as a trans character, as is a female-presenting body with a male-sounding voice. This chosen body-voice combination impacts what kind of romantic relationships are available within the game. This is a very limited and reductive way of expressing gender variation and contrasts with the many options available for eyebrow and facial hair colour, the option of having long or short nails that can be painted any colour, and options for cosmetic cyberware, makeup, and blemishes. The game includes 17 different types of eyes, mouths, jaws, and ears, but it offers only one kind of vagina. There are three penis and breast types (small, default, large), three nipple options, five types of pubic hair, and the option for a circumcised or uncircumcised penis. Trans gamer Petit (2020, para. 4) further elaborates on some of the issues with gender customization in the game:

> Thankfully, your character's gender is not tied to your choice of genitals. You can create a dude with a vagina or a lady with a penis, that's no problem. But because of everything else about how the game handles trans identity, this hardly feels like the progressive step it should be. Rather than just letting you pick your pronouns independently of all your other character creation choices, your pronouns are assigned based on your selection of voice: Pick the "feminine" voice and your pronouns are she/her, and vice versa. (There are no nonbinary pronoun options.) As a trans woman with a voice that many would not describe as "feminine," this direct linking of gender identity to having a voice that sounds "masculine" or "feminine" feels weirdly essentializing.

This essentialization is compounded by an ad for a beverage called Chromanticure that appears ubiquitously throughout Night City. This ad features "a female-coded model with a penis visible through her skin-tight clothing, making it clear that in *Cyberpunk 2077*, trans bodies are objectified and commodified" (Petit, 2020, para. 5). Cis bodies are also commodified, but unlike trans characters in the game, cis characters "have far more dimension than the surface of any sexualized image on a billboard" (Petit, 2020, para. 5). Petit's critique continues:

> There's a real potential for a grim world like the one *Cyberpunk 2077* offers to serve as a lens through which our own world is critiqued, but the developers

at CD Projekt Red failed to do anything with the trans options and identities they incorporated into the game to make them function in this way, and as V, you never have the option to say or do anything about it. The objectification of trans people is just background texture, nothing more. (para. 7)

The game does not make any effort to humanize trans people or ward off transphobia. This results in an opening for transphobic players to "just laugh at us by using the character creator to generate models they consider worthy of mockery and derision" (Petit, 2020, para. 8). Between the ads for Chromanticure that appear everywhere and fetishize the trans model as an object of desire "but not as full human beings," Petit (2020, para. 8) notes that *Cyberpunk 2077* leaves trans players "wanting in its world for depictions that humanize us."

Cyberpunk 2077 is not alone in its problematic one-dimensional portrayal of gender. This game is a part of a longer history of misogynistic, homophobic, and transphobic video game culture. The stereotype of gaming as a community of and for men is common enough to have become the accepted norm (Forni, 2020; Fox & Tang, 2014). The stereotype remains even as some studies have shown that almost 50 percent of gamers are women (Gestos et al., 2018). Content analysis of video games stretching over 30 years has shown that while female characters have begun to appear more frequently, they tend to be hypersexualized or portrayed as sex objects (Gestos et al., 2018), often shown wearing clothing that is provocative rather than protective. Video game discourse frequently centres on aspects of sexism and how women and girl gamers are treated by other players within the community, how women in the gaming industry are treated in the media, or the dearth of women working within the gaming industry (Chess & Shaw, 2015; Lynch et al., 2016; McArthur, 2020). Feminist critiques of gaming also analyze various aspects of the representation and portrayal of female characters in individual games and the commonplace attitude of sexualizing female characters in a manner not related to gameplay but that do reinforce societal gender norms (Forni, 2020). Games and characters aimed at and developed for heterosexual males have a higher tendency to portray women and marginalized people in derogatory ways, which perpetuates the cycle of heterosexual men being the primary creators and consumers of the content (Lynch et al., 2016). The type of character or customization options one chooses can be "clues as to the taste cultures and aspirations of users" (Humphreys & Vered, 2014, p. 9).

The ongoing lack of diverse characters and inclusive representation in gaming calls for change, and though it may be supposed that increasing character customization options is the solution, research has shown that digital representation done poorly exacerbates feelings of exclusion or tokenism, or that diversity is simply an afterthought (Passmore & Mandryk, 2018). Insufficient diversity among game designer teams can result in customization options that reinforce the social norm of white, heterosexual males as the default character by simply altering the colour or gender of an avatar but not incorporating important differences of human cultural diversity. More game designers who are trans, people of colour, women, disabled, or otherwise marginalized can offer more equitable and accurate depictions of embodied diversity.

"STEAL THE IMPLANT THAT GRANTS ETERNAL LIFE"

The end goal of *Cyberpunk 2077* is to "steal the implant that grants eternal life," and a player must push themselves "to the absolute limit" in order to obtain "Night City's most valuable implant—a prototype chip that can make you live forever" (Cyberpunk 2077, n.d.). Immortality through augmentation is a common theme in futuristic video games such as the award-winning *Deus Ex* series (Deus Ex, n.d.) and the *Mass Effect* series that transformed from the complete disavowal of augmentation technology in the first game to the main character being technologically resurrected from the dead between the first and second installments by becoming a cyborg (Geraci, 2012). *Cyberpunk 2077* is also part of a larger story series that began as a role-playing board game where implants, augmentation, and immortality were defining characteristics of the future as predicted in 1988 when it was first released (R. Talsorian Games, n.d.). Augmentation and enhancement are present in each of these futuristic games despite the different storylines and objectives. Though a video game requires a goal or an achievable objective to provide resolution for players, the development, growth, and advancement of the character through gameplay is often more important (Geraci, 2012). The proliferation of games where technological enhancement and immortality are portrayed as humanity's inevitable future suggests this character advancement is transhumanist in nature.

Transhumanists strive for a future where humans can one day choose to become immortal, and they desire to transcend the physical limits of the body through technological enhancements. Transhumanists promote enhancement technologies and incorporation of both organic and inorganic matter into such technologies. Prosthetics, neural implants, gene therapy, wearable devices, and pharmaceutical drug regimens are seen as necessary means to improve human life, and transhumanists believe science should be mobilized to "achieve mastery over nature in order to improve the living conditions of human beings" (Bostrom,

2005, p. 2). For transhumanists, the key element of humanness is cognition and the life of the mind, while the body is simply the fleshy vehicle that houses the mind. Transhumanists, in seeking mastery over the body, reaffirm the "division between intellect and body, and the possibility of intellectual release from the body through technology" (Hall, 2017, p. 24). Recent technological advancement is not the sole driving force behind transhumanist ideals; the ambition to artificially improve the humans of the future goes back hundreds of years.

One branch of transhumanist thought can be traced back to 17th-century European Enlightenment ideas grounded in Rene Descartes's philosophical principle "I think, therefore I am." Descartes's attempt to provide evidence of one's existence has been embraced by some transhumanists to reaffirm that what makes an individual an autonomous human is their ability to think or reason, while everything else is merely animal, machine, or inanimate object. The physical body is regarded as less important in defining who or what is human. This separation of mind and body is referred to as Cartesian dualism and is a commonly held transhumanist belief. Radical transhumanists foresee driving the evolution of humanity by transcending the limitations of the physical body to achieve cognitive immortality through advancements in technology: "Developments in areas such as neuroscience, genetics, cybernetics, bionics, pharmacology, and robotics have produced a wide variety of enhancement technologies that seek to advance human cognition (memory, attention, or problem solving), and extend mental and physical functionality beyond current biological limitations" (Fritsch, 2019, p. 70). For transhumanists, social problems are rooted in natural circumstances, and change comes through altering bodies: "Transhumanists make the body central to problem-solving while at the same time endeavoring to transcend it completely, rejecting embodiment in its entirety" (Hall, 2017, p. 83). Transhumanists "assume that a better future—that is, a more just, more moral future—turns on the possibility of improved intellects" (Hall, 2017, p. 115). Transhumanists thus "assume increased cognitive capacity for individuals would bring about better social conditions for all persons" (Hall, 2017, p. 115).

A second branch of transhumanist thought is grounded in 19th- and 20th-century views inherited from European Enlightenment proponents' belief in human exceptionalism. Western European industrial societies merged their perceptions of new social, scientific, and political ideals of mass production, evolution, and genetics into a "eugenic push for species-wide betterment" through the enhancement of "previously fixed benchmarks of human evolution, while simultaneously elevating white, male, working bodies to the top" (Spektor & Fox, 2020, p. 330). Charles Darwin's *On the Origin of Species* (1859) introduced the concept of evolution through natural selection, which inspired Herbert Spencer's (1864) "survival of the fittest"—the echoes of which still linger today. The idea that humanity could influence the evolution of the species by choosing who would survive and flourish and who would wither and die permeated societies around the world and resulted in millions of people suffering and dying. Transhumanists who dream of becoming better than human may not identify with eugenics in name but espouse eugenicist principles in their efforts to advocate for using technology to eradicate illness, disability, or other perceived limitations. Zoltan Istvan, former US presidential candidate for the Transhumanist Political Party and outspoken transhumanist, has stated, "I would bet my arm that the great majority of disabled people will be very happy when transhumanist technology gives them the opportunity to fulfill their potential" (Khazan, 2017, para. 47). The transhumanist website Humanity+ (n.d., "How Could I Become Posthuman?") lists five steps for individuals to undertake in their quest for immortality:

1.   Live healthily and avoid unnecessary risks (diet, exercise, etc.);
2.   Sign up for cryonics;
3.   Keep abreast of current research and save some money so that you can afford future life-extension treatments when they become available;
4.   Support the development of transhuman technologies through donations, advocacy, investment, or choosing a career in the field; work to make access more universal and to make the world safer from existential risks;
5.   Join others to help promote transhumanism.

The promotion of transhumanism is not defined in this list of actions; however, video games and other forms of entertainment media are excellent vehicles for introducing transhumanist concepts to a wider, and potentially more receptive, audience. Robert Geraci, a religious studies and gaming scholar, has interviewed game designers and gamers who explicitly equate video games and transhumanism:

> In a sense transhumanism is gaming. It is the same idea that you can become something more than yourself. Thus, anytime you build a character and go "in-world" you have created an idealized or specialized extension of your own being.... Video gaming most closely mirrors [transhumanism] because of the added technological elements that allow one to change the self easily and quickly. Much like the freedom one might have if you could delve one's mind into the computer. (Gwydion, 2012, as cited in Geraci, 2012, p. 740)

The transhumanist call to becoming "something more than yourself" permeates *Cyberpunk 2077* from the way in which every version of V appears to be physically fit and in their mid-20s to the cyberware implants and enhancements needed to advance the game. Notably, while "no aspect of V's physical appearance, including superficial options such as hair style and tattoos, can be changed after the initial character customization process" (Character Creation, n.d.), the cyberware implants and augmentations available in the game can be earned or purchased during gameplay. Thus, while general physical appearance and gender is rendered static, augmentation can be bought and earned. As Freshtick (2020, para. 25) notes of the use of cyberware in *Cyberpunk 2077*,

> Cyberware can be installed all over your body, from your hands, to your legs, to your eyeballs. Once installed, you're granted new skills and upgrades. Some of these are passive, like a piece of Cyberware for your circulatory system that slightly heals you whenever you kill someone. Others are more active, granting you the ability to double jump. Each of your body parts has multiple slots, and Cyberware can be slotted in and out at will, once you have it unlocked. While Cyberware doesn't come heavily into play in the early hours of *Cyberpunk 2077*, it's easy to see how this system could eventually augment your existing skills or help patch up holes in your character build.

Michael Foith (2013), in his analysis of the dystopian futuristic *Deus Ex: Human Revolution*, argues that "the video game is not just about reading or seeing potential future enhancement technologies but permits players to virtually test-drive augmentations—to actually try out three-dimensionally rendered prototypes on a virtual body" (para. 6). Video games can be entry points for people to try out new identities or bodies before the technology is available to make the enhancements permanent. Geraci (2021) warns, "Many avowed transhumanists see video games and virtual worlds as ideal locations to prepare for transhuman futures and to evangelize for them" (p. 747). Transhumanist narratives incorporated into video games where characters are tasked with overcoming or erasing the limitations of the physical body through technological enhancements are cause for concern among disability justice activists.

NO ACCESS TO NIGHT CITY

Disabled people are frequently first adopters of assistive and augmentative technologies while also often imagined away through the idea that "technologies will make us nondisabled" (Shew, 2021, p. 1). Shew notes that "technologized disabled people (or cyborgs) have ideas about bodies and technology that don't match the technological dreams of elite designers and technology leaders" (p. 1). The experiences of disabled people who invent, modify, or otherwise create some of the technologies they use to assist themselves and others are often overlooked or disregarded by nondisabled users of tech (Hamraie & Fritsch, 2019). Engineers and designers of adaptive or assistive technologies often do not consider the needs or desires of the end users they are designing for and frequently create or design the technology they want to see in the world. As Earle (2019, p. 48) argues, "we need only listen to current cyborgs to understand that the future cyborg imagined by engineers and transhumanists fails to appreciate the cyborg lived experience." That is,

> So long as transhumanists and engineers fail to engage with the cyborg bodies that currently exist, or those people who most reasonably may become cyborg soon—in every phase of production, from planning to distribution—they will never produce the kind of cyborg future that they claim to want. Also, so long as transhumanists continue to ignore maintenance and care, advocating instead for a bootstrappy, individualist concept of responsibility, networks and communities which make a cyborg future worth wanting will be limited and insufficient. (Earle, 2019, p. 53)

While characters like V are frequently portrayed as "cyborgs," such representations frequently "fail to recognize the true cyborgs among them, technologized disabled people" (Shew, 2021, p. 11). Disability studies scholar Ashley Shew (2021, p. 3) writes,

> When I look around the cancer clinic, I think to myself, Wow, a lot of cyborgs out today. Sick people, chronically ill people, disabled people—we are what cyborgs look like, but this is far from the popular image of the cyborg. Indeed, our cyborg status is rarely recognized.

This is also true of *Cyberpunk 2077*. One of the ironic aspects of the game is that while disability is a storyline or a characteristic of the cyborg characters, disabled players have had difficulty being able to actually play the game. The company who created and released the game, CD Projekt Red, didn't allow for nonstandard joysticks to be used, a form of frequent gamer technology used by physically disabled people. There were also blocks placed on gamers being able to use voice controls or keyboard shortcuts. And in the initial release of the game, there were rapid flashing light sequences that appeared without warning that could cause epileptic seizures in players. In one public gamer forum post dated December 10, 2020, titled "CAN'T PLAY CYBERPUNK AS DISABLED PERSON" (siasia160, 2020), a quadriplegic user wrote of their difficulties trying to access the game. The user was frustrated that there was no workaround or patch to fix the lack of access caused by not being able to use touchscreen and touchpad inputs. Over three hundred comments followed this post from other users who also described issues they had in trying to play *Cyberpunk 2077* while using assistive technology and their overall disappointment that their gaming needs were not considered by CD Projekt Red during the game's lengthy development process. Within the first three days of the game's release, other players created unofficial workarounds and patches to make the game playable for players using alternative game controllers. Some of the gameplay issues were resolved after being brought to the game designers' attention by disabled players, and accessibility improved somewhat with a patch release on December 19, 2020.

THE FUTURE IS ACCESSIBLE?

Body enhancements challenge our conception of what constitutes the human and non-human, as well as our understanding of disability and ability. As such, "enhancements raise social, political, economic, and cultural questions surrounding the production, distribution, circulation, and impact of enhancement technologies on our relationship to our bodies and shared environments, as well as to our understanding of disability and ability" (Fritsch, 2019, p. 70). The alluring promises of enhancement technologies need to be considered cautiously. This is not only because some technologies will never materialize but because enhancement technologies are not a panacea for solving all of our diverse embodied issues.

Critical disability studies scholars question transhumanist futures for the way in which body enhancement technologies compel everyone to have better-than-able bodies and argue that disabled people should not need to change or be enhanced, but rather that society needs to become more accessible to diverse forms of embodiment: "While transhumanists proclaim that futuristic technology opens the door to greater diversity in the human form and capability, transhumanist enhancement strategies—which perpetuate the power of deviance as a normative concept—belie that aim" (Hall, 2017, p. 135). This is made obvious in the ways that the transhumanist view has "served and can still serve as rationales for devaluing persons with disabilities, especially intellectual disability" (Hall, 2017, p. 24). As Tom Shakespeare (2014) notes, "Medicine has its place but alone it cannot solve the problem of disability, and sometimes can even make things worse" (p. ix). Critical disability studies scholars suggest that technologies should be "evaluated in terms of their potential for widening or narrowing inequalities and inequities. Enhancement technologies tend to be expensive to both purchase and maintain, are often produced in disabling labor conditions, and tend to have a high ecological footprint" (Fritsch, 2019, p. 71).

Disability activists and scholars voice concerns about the financial cost of accessing and maintaining enhancement technologies. As Earle (2019) notes, "many disabled people, due to society's focus on capital and productivity, fall below median income levels, and are generally twice as likely to live in poverty as the non-disabled population" (p. 51). Body enhancement technologies are expensive and are unlikely to be available to all. In many places in the world, people lack basic access to clean water, reliable sources of electricity, and access to even basic assistive devices such as hearing aids, wheelchairs, crutches, or prosthetics, much less state-of-the-art "Cheetah Legs" like those worn by Aimee Mullins, Oscar Pistorius, or other competitive athletes. Prosthetic legs, for example, can range in price from "$5000 for basic models, to well over $50,000 for ones with complex, computerized knees and ankles," with a prosthetic arm generally costing between $3,000—$30,000 USD (Earle, 2019, p. 51). Beyond the purchase price, these technologies also require maintenance and care:

> The cyborg must not just maintain their bodymind (as we all do to one extent or another), they must also maintain the technological infrastructure which produces their cyborg-y-ness. They must maintain their prosthetics, their wheelchair, their ports and stents, pacemakers and artificial valves. Each of these technologies experiences wear and tear. They bend and break and need to be bent back and put together, soldered, duct taped, super-glued, and sometimes discarded. They get dirty and need to be cleaned. Ports require flushing, artificial valves and joints require medication to avoid rejection and maintain functionality. Pacemakers require digital updates and replacement batteries. (Earle, 2019, p. 51)

That technologies require maintenance and care is a reminder of the ways in which technologies do not exist in a vacuum but rather are embedded within larger social structures that impact how technologies can be used, maintained, repaired, and proliferated. While for many the focus is on shiny new innovations, often more important for the quality life of marginalized peoples are improvements to our shared social environments, such as putting in curb cuts, captioning media, making public transit accessible, publicly funding personal care workers, ensuring the availability of accessible washrooms, providing equitable health care, and so on. Disabled people yearn for "futures in which technology has not eradicated disability" (Jerreat-Poole, 2020, para. 1) and for anti-ableist futures where technology is developed and implemented in collaboration with the needs and desires of disabled communities themselves.

CONCLUSION

The possibilities for the human body in the future are often about the opportunities a technological future could offer—that limitations of the body will be overcome with technological implants or prosthetics, that advancements in medicine and technology will do away with illness and suffering. The people in these futuristic stories are never explicitly identified as disabled—they are nondisabled people who have been "fixed" or "cured" by technology; the disabled body is not welcome in these visions of the future. Kafer (2013) states, "It is the very *absence* of disability that signals this better future. The *presence* of disability, then, signals something else: a future that bears too many traces of the ills of the present to be desirable" (p. 2; original emphasis). This imagined future is one that critical disability scholars and activists worry about, and rightly so.

In this way, no matter how technologically advanced society becomes, disability activism will still be necessary as our "societies will always have a wide range of physical and mental variation; we will always have injuries and diseases that limit function" (Wasserman, 2015, p. 94). In addition to technological advances, disabled communities also need continued emphasis on civil rights, barrier removal, reproductive justice, accessible housing, and so on. Disability activism is also needed to impact the design of enhancement technologies that better reflect the needs and wants of disabled users. As Melinda Hall (2017) suggests,

> These would be true "enhancements" that would bring about better futures. Enhancement can be made an expression of care, care of existing individuals—not idealized future subjects that cannot, and will not, exist. We should *seek* augmentations—political, social, and technological—that bridge the gap between the body and individual life goals as articulated by those upon whom the suggested technology would intervene; this makes enhancement an expression of care and interdependence, and would resemble neither positive nor negative eugenics. We should *reject* enhancement strategies which rely, for their desirability, on ableist discourses of risk which fetishize autonomy and choice and visions of happiness that depend on added capabilities rather than complex interdependence. (p. 139; original emphasis)

Cyberpunk 2077 fantastically "wowed" gamers like Petit (2020, para. 23) "with its scale, its verticality, and its sense of history." But Petit, like many others, wished it had taken the time to create characters that were "more than objects," to actually envision a "bold" future that is "so central to the best of cyberpunk" (para. 23). Instead, *Cyberpunk 2077* offers "visions of people trying to make do and get by in a world that's trying to eat them alive" (para. 23), and like the patches and workarounds created by disabled gamers to enable themselves and other disabled gamers to access the game, it is in community and through continued activism and interdependence that we can come to change the world and create a future worth living for.

QUESTIONS FOR DISCUSSION

1. What do you think motivates the desire to be faster, stronger, enhanced? What is the relationship between this and how we view disability?
2. What is your experience with cyborgs? Video games, movies, and television programs frequently use cyborgs as a fact of life in the future. Do you think it is inevitable that humans will use technological advancements to enhance their bodies? Have you ever imagined augmenting your body with technology?
3. Why do you think assistive devices or other technologies that improve the quality of life for disabled people are often stigmatized while enhancement technologies are more frequently valorized?
4. How might socio-economic barriers to technological access constrain the promise of deliverance technology seems to offer?

INVITATIONS TO GO DEEPER

1. Who owns a device once it is implanted inside a human body—the company that designed or built the device, the surgeon who implanted it, the person with the implant, the computer engineer who coded the software, the internet service provider the device is linked to through Wi-Fi? How should questions of ownership be decided?
2. How does ownership of implanted devices that assist people such as pacemakers, insulin pumps, or cochlear implants impact concepts of disability and embodiment? Would you be comfortable with a corporation owning a device implanted in your body? Should you be allowed to repair or alter devices implanted inside you?

READ MORE

Banbury, T. (2020, September 16). "I choose to be a cyborg": Why I implanted computer chips in my hands. *The Conversation*. https://theconversation. com/i-choose-to-be-a-cyborg-why-i-implanted-computer-chips-in-my-hands-127089

Bode, K. (2021, January 2). The right to repair movement is poised to explode in 2021. *VICE*. https://www.vice.com/en/article/jgqk38/ the-right-to-repair-movement-is-poised-to-explode-in-2021

Ferrando, F. (2013). Posthumanism, transhumanism, antihumanism, metahumanism, and new materialisms: Differences and Relations. *Existenz*, *8*(2), 26–32.

Hamraie, A., & Fritsch, K. (2019). Crip technoscience manifesto. *Catalyst: Feminism, Theory, Technoscience*, *5*(1), 1–33. https://catalystjournal.org/index.php/ catalyst/article/view/29607/24771

Huberman, J. (2018). Immortality transformed: Mind cloning, transhumanism and the quest for digital immortality. *Mortality*, *23*(1), 50–64. https://doi.org /10.1080/13576275.2017.1304366

Matte, R. (2020, October 18). No more breaking the bank: How the "right to repair movement" can support students. *Fulcrum*. https://thefulcrum.ca/ sciencetech/no-more-breaking-the-bank-how-the-right-to-repair-movement-can-support-students/

LISTEN MORE, WATCH MORE

"Accessibility's history with Bess Williamson and Elizabeth Guffey," *Contra* podcast, June 2020: https://www.mapping-access.com/podcast

"Cory Doctorow on digital rights management (DRM)," Science, Technology, and the Future: https://www.youtube.com/watch?v=MvLbeC3-64M

Disability Visibility Project podcast: https://disabilityvisibilityproject.com/ podcast/

Feminist Frequency podcast: https://feministfrequency.com

FIXED: The science fiction of human enhancement, Regan Brashear, 2013: https:// www.fixedthemovie.com

"I'm not your inspiration, thank you very much," Stella Young, TED Talk, April 2014: https://www.ted.com/talks/ stella_young_i_m_not_your_inspiration_thank_you_very_much

REFERENCES

Bostrom, N. (2005). A history of transhumanist thought. *Journal of Evolution and Technology, 14*(1), 1–25.

Character Creation. (n.d.). Cyberpunk fandom. Retrieved March 12, 2021, from http://www.cyberpunk.fandom.com/wiki/Character_Creation

Chess, S., & Shaw, A. (2015). A conspiracy of fishes, or, how we learned to stop worrying about #GamerGate and embrace hegemonic masculinity. *Journal of Broadcasting & Electronic Media, 59*(1), 208–220. https://doi.org/10.1080/08838151.2014.999917

Cyberpunk 2077. (n.d.). Retrieved March 12, 2021, from http://www.cyberpunk.net/ca/en/

Deus Ex. (n.d.). Retrieved March 12, 2021, from http://www.deusex.fandom.com/wiki/Deus_Ex

Earle, J. (2019). Cyborg maintenance: Design, breakdown, and inclusion. In A. Marcus & W. Wang (Eds.), *Design, user experience, and usability: Design philosophy and theory* (pp. 45–55). Springer.

Foith, M. (2013). Virtually witness augmentation now: Video games and the future of human enhancement. *M/C Journal, 16*(6). https://doi.org/10.5204/mcj.729

Forni, D. (2020). Horizon zero dawn: The educational influence of video games in counteracting gender stereotypes. *Transactions of the Digital Games Research Association, 5*(1). https://doi.org/10.26503/todigra.v5i1.111

Fox, J., & Tang, W. Y. (2014). Sexism in online video games: The role of conformity to masculine norms and social dominance orientation. *Computers in Human Behavior, 33*, 314–320. https://doi.org/10.1016/j.chb.2013.07.014

Freshtick, R. (2020, June 25). Cyberpunk 2077's mind-bending character progression systems explained. *Polygon.* https://www.polygon.com/2020/6/25/21302413/cyberpunk-2077-preview-character-progression

Fritsch, K. (2019). Body enhancement. In T. Heller, S. Parker Harris, C. Gill, & R. Gould (Eds.), *Disability in American life: An encyclopedia of concepts, policies, and controversies* (pp. 70–73). ABC-CLIO.

Geraci, R. M. (2012). Video games and the transhuman inclination. *Zygon, 47*(4), 735–756. https://doi.org/10.1111/j.1467-9744.2012.01292.x

Gestos, M., Smith-Merry, J., & Campbell, A. (2018). Representation of women in video games: A systematic review of literature in consideration of adult female wellbeing. *Cyberpsychology, Behavior, and Social Networking, 21*(9), 535–541. https://doi.org/10.1089/cyber.2017.0376

Hamraie, A., & Fritsch, K. (2019). Crip technoscience manifesto. *Catalyst: Feminism, Theory, Technoscience, 5*(1), 1–33. https://catalystjournal.org/index.php/catalyst/article/view/29607/24771

Hall, M. (2017). *The bioethics of enhancement transhumanism, disability, and biopolitics.* Lexington Books.

Humanity+. (n.d.). Transhumanist FAQ. Retrieved February 22, 2022, from https://www.humanityplus.org/transhumanist-faq

Humphreys, S., & Vered, K. O. (2014). Reflecting on gender and digital networked media. *Television & New Media, 15*(1), 3–13. https://doi.org/10.1177/1527476413502682

Jerreat-Poole, A. (2020). Sick, slow, cyborg: Crip futurity in mass effect. *Game Studies, 20*(1). http://gamestudies.org/2001/articles/jerreatpoole

Kafer, A. (2013). *Feminist, queer, crip.* Indiana University Press.

Khazan, O. (2017, February 18). Should we die? *The Atlantic.* https://www.theatlantic.com/health/archive/2017/02/should-we-die/516357/

Lynch, T., Tompkins, J. E., van Driel, I. I., & Fritz, N. (2016). Sexy, strong, and secondary: A content analysis of female characters in video games across 31 years. *Journal of Communication, 66*(4), 564–584. https://doi.org/10.1111/jcom.12237

McArthur, V. (2020). Damsel in this dress: An analysis of the character designs of women in post-secondary game design programs. *Feminist Media Studies, 21*(3), 381–397. https://doi.org/10.1080/14680777.2020.1715463

Passmore, C. J., & Mandryk, R. (2018). An about face: Diverse representation in games. In *Proceedings of the 2018 Annual Symposium on Computer–Human Interaction in Play* (pp. 365–380). Association for Computing Machinery. https://doi.org/10.1145/3242671.3242711

Petit, C. (2020, December 7). Cyberpunk 2077 is dad rock, not new wave. *Polygon.* https://www.polygon.com/reviews/22158019/cyberpunk-2077-review-cd-projekt-red-pc-ps4-xbox-one-stadia

R. Talsorian Games. (n.d.). Retrieved March 12, 2021, from http://www.rtalsoriangames.com/cyberpunk/

Shakespeare, T. (2014). Five thoughts about enhancement. In M. Eilers, K. Grüber, & C. Rehmann-Sutter (Eds.), *The human enhancement debate and disability: New bodies for a better life* (pp. ix–xiii). Palgrave Macmillan.

Shew, A. (2021). The minded body in technology and disability. In S. Vallor (Ed.), *The Oxford handbook of philosophy of technology* (pp. 1–20). Oxford University Press.

siasia160. (2020, December 10). CAN'T PLAY CYBERPUNK AS DISABLED PERSON. *Cyberpunk 2077 Forum.* https://forums.cdprojektred.com/index.php?threads/cant-play-cyberpunk-as-disabled-person.11040650/

Spektor, F., & Fox, S. (2020). The "working body": Interrogating and reimagining the productivist impulses of transhumanism through crip-centered speculative design. *Somatechnics, 10*(3), 327–354.

Wasserman, D. (2015). Genetics. In R. Adams, B. Reiss, & D. Serlin (Eds.), *Keywords for disability studies* (pp. 92–94). New York University Press.

PART V
RECLAIM

CHAPTER 12

Holding Space for Future Matriarchs: Digital Platforms for Resurging Solidarity

Amber Brown and Angela Knowles

MODERN DAY MEDIA AND #MMIWG2S

On May 5, 2021, on the National Day of Awareness of Missing and Murdered Indigenous Women, Girls and 2SLGBTQQIA+ People (MMIWG2S), thousands of posts were shared on Instagram. Many of the content creators were Indigenous women, girls, and families who have been directly affected by this crisis. They, along with their allies, made posts to educate, raise awareness, and hold space for those who were mourning these lives lost. The Instagram posts were often accompanied with tags such as #RedDressDay, #MMIWG2S, and #NoMoreStolenSisters to unite posts together and situate their messages within a broader and substantial collective movement. Personal stories, troubling statistics, and ways to support are tied together on these posts to make it easier for those who wish to take action going forwards. The National Day of Awareness is difficult on so many levels and is often triggering for Indigenous people. The wave of posts by Indigenous people was also met with great support from online followers across Turtle Island. Many of these posts were designed with the intent to educate the broader public and bring the crisis into the consciousness of North American citizens. This day is a reminder that today we wear red to show support and to not be surprised if red handprints over mouths are seen. It also creates a collective place of healing and remembering, with a focus on saying the victims' names and laying them to rest, despite the difficult and often unknown circumstances of which loved ones were and continue to be lost.

On May 6, 2021, the following day, over one hundred content creators awoke to find that their posts were removed from their platform and their stories were gone, despite being up for less than the 24 hours they were meant to be. Allies and Indigenous content creators quickly mobilized to take a stand and demand an explanation. Instagram was quick to supply an answer, saying that there was a technical difficulty resulting in an error in uploading and viewing posts and stories. However, this did not make sense to many who had lost content because only their MMIWG2S posts were removed, making it seem as if the loss of content was intentional and curated. Instagram's update was promptly followed up by news outlets such as CBC and CTV, who reached out to hear from those who were negatively impacted by this event and learn how they felt about Instagram's statement. Several Indigenous content creators have spoken out against this deletion, stating that it is Indigenous erasure to remove this content, especially on a day that is so important to the broader movement. Instagram's response sparked other conversations, such as about creators' feelings that the social media giant had been shadow banning[1] posts about MMIWG2S, as well as posts about Indigenous sovereignty. The case described here is a significant example of the ways that social media platforms are not necessarily safe spaces for Indigenous people—especially Indigenous women, girls, and gender-diverse people. In response to this content deletion, Indigenous content creators and dedicated allies surged the social media platform with more MMIWG2S content, making the message clear: Our voices will not be silenced.

Indigenous girls, women, femmes, and Two-Spirit people in Canada have long been the targets of colonial violence. The sustained and systematic nature of this violence is reflected in the Missing and Murdered Indigenous Women, Girls, and Two-Spirit People (MMIWG2S) epidemic. While the MMIWG2S epidemic has received government attention and attendant promises of action, beginning in 2016 with the National Inquiry into Missing and Murdered Indigenous Women and Girls, violence continues to occur both within Indigenous communities and North American society more generally in both direct and indirect ways (National Inquiry into Missing and Murdered Indigenous Women and Girls, 2019). For example, colonial violence also takes the form of the erasure of Indigenous practices and beliefs, which are supplanted by colonial perspectives. This erasure is seen most clearly in how many communities that were traditionally matriarchal societies or that held beliefs around the equally important and individual sacredness and power of men and women had patriarchal systems and beliefs imposed on them (Gray, 2011; Inter-American Commission on Human Rights [IACHR], 2014). Imposed systems and beliefs continue to change the way Indigenous men, as well as non-Indigenous men, view Indigenous women and gender-diverse people.

These colonial forces also led to Indigenous identities being suppressed and imposed a binary, heteronormative standard that Indigenous people have had to work to break down. Rising above this colonial violence, identities such as Two-Spirit have become more visible and more widely accepted (Pruden, 2016). In response to some of these issues, Indigenous people, but particularly women, femmes, and Two-Spirit people, have created platforms to spread awareness and fight back. Much of this work started on social media or has used social media to gain traction and more attention. Additionally, in response to the marginalization faced by Indigenous people, online spaces have been taken up as a tool to foster and support community. This chapter will examine how social media has played a role in the cultivation of spaces for Indigenous girls, women, femmes, and Two-Spirit people to take on their rightful positions and power while protecting and fighting to keep them safe at the same time.

The authors of this chapter are two female-identifying college students. One author is a mixed Métis woman with Nehiyaw/Cree and Anihšināpē/Salteaux roots, as well as Scottish, Hungarian, and British ancestry, and is passionate about land back movements. This author is beyond thankful for the inspirational people in her life, including those that seek to offer safe communities online. In particular a huge maarsi/kinanâskomitin[2] to the Indigenous scholars and fearless game changers operating in colonial systems forging their own paths. The second author has little Indigenous cultural knowledge or connections but is nonetheless passionate about Indigenous sovereignty and land back movements and has been involved and connected within the LGBTQ2S+ community for many years. These experiences mean that the author has some personal interest in the topic and their interpretation and analysis of the topic may be informed by that. The lack of cultural knowledge may present some challenges; however, both authors worked together to ensure the topic was understood in the same way to decrease the likelihood of anything being misunderstood or misrepresented.

We would like to remind readers that reconciliation is an active process that each Canadian citizen is responsible for upholding. Specifically, we refer to documents such as the Truth and Reconciliation Commission's *Calls to Action* (TRC, 2015) and the *United Nations Declaration on the Rights of Indigenous Peoples* (UNDRIP; United Nations 2007), which cumulatively make up 140 articles/calls to action to uplift Indigenous Peoples. When reflecting on the chapter and your personal goals towards Indigenous solidarity, we hope you consider this information under these 140 invaluable requests.

HISTORICAL AND PRESENT CONCERNS

Historically, Indigenous Peoples across Turtle Island have faced an onslaught of racism and violence since the beginning of colonization.[3] In colonizing the land now known as Canada, settlers removed Indigenous ties to the lands in order to assert their colonial agenda, which was enforced despite the rich and nation-specific ways of governance and culture that existed for many generations before European contact. Since contact, many efforts have been made by European settlers, and eventually what came to be the Canadian government, to eradicate Indigenous Peoples, both in a literal sense and a cultural one. Included in these efforts are the Indian Act and the Indian residential and day school system (Gray, 2011). Near the time that Canada united under Confederation, the Indian Act, a legislation that still imposes and governs First Nations Peoples today, was crafted. This legal document essentially enforced itself upon First Nations as a way to control them and shifted the narrative from nation-to-nation relations to that of a paternal caregiver to wards of the state. The Indian Act effectively removed First Nations' power as sovereign nations, as this act directed all First Nation activity to go through the federal government as a means of control and assimilation (Joseph, 2018). The Indian Act was, and still is, an ethnocentric document that applied gender-discriminatory restrictions, shifted traditional modes of governance, and banned many cultural practices without the consent of Indigenous Peoples. The Indian Act also imposed a status system to declare whether someone was Indigenous, which was further complicated by the rules surrounding marrying a non-Indigenous person as well as marrying someone from another band or nation (Gray, 2011; Joseph, 2018; Lawrence, 2003). This impacted Indigenous women the most, as they would lose status if they married a non-Indigenous man. This is one of the first examples of how Canada directly discriminated against Indigenous women and femmes specifically (IACHR, 2014; Lawrence, 2003).

At the same time that First Nations were defending their inherent rights against the Indian Act and navigating the challenges of Confederation, Indigenous people were also being sent to Indian residential and day schools. As mentioned previously, one way that colonization impacted Indigenous people is through the imposition of patriarchal, heteronormative, and Eurocentric beliefs and practices that contradicted many traditional beliefs and practices. Colonial systems disregarded the complex and unique societies of these many communities and viewed them as "uncivilized" and "savages," a view that continues to pervade much of the population's perspectives on Indigenous Peoples today. It was conveyed that through teaching Indigenous children European culture, the Canadian government could assimilate them into Canadian society. However, very rarely did these children leave with beneficial skills to contribute to Canadian society due to the schools' insufficient education; they also lost their own cultural knowledge in the process (Gray, 2011). The realities that Indian residential and day school survivors have experienced are still blurry to the public, mainly due to the trauma lived by these attendees and the lack of recoverable documentation, despite these institutions operating for over a century. However, the way these schools were meant to be places of assimilation and captured children against their will for many generations is well documented. Researchers are still learning about the damage and loss of life brought on by these schools that were intentionally created by the Canadian government to assist in cultural genocide.

To consider the harm brought on by colonization, the Indian Act, and Indian residential and day schools, the first important step is understanding how these events contextualize the MMIWG2S and land back movements. As mentioned, prior to settler contact, Indigenous Nations had specific cultural protocols and socio-political structures that supported each nation since time outside of mind (Gray, 2011). Though each nation has its own unique ways in which its culture operates, similarities exist across nations, such as the view that both men and women are sacred and carry divine feminine and masculine energies that allow each gender to access certain aspects of life differently (Anderson, 2016). This led to gendered cultural roles being present in pre-colonial Indigenous communities and also created distinctive access for gender-diverse peoples to contribute to their communities in ways that honoured their masculine and feminine energies (Anderson, 2016). Colonization disregarded these existing ways of being and instead imposed an ethnocentric view of civilization. By applying xenophobic conceptualizations to Indigenous Peoples, early settlers sought to alter the positions of power that women and gender-diverse peoples had in their communities as a means of colonization (IACHR, 2014). For many Indigenous communities, the women and gender-diverse people from each nation had important roles to sustain their communities and were valued members of their societies. Further, it was common in many Indigenous societies to hold women in places of leadership, follow bloodlines primarily through female lineages, and raise women with the intent of becoming future matriarchs (Anderson, 2016; IACHR, 2014). Though not all Indigenous societies are matriarchal, many nations value female input in positions of power. Similarly, gender-diverse people's traditional positions were tribe specific as well but often held special importance to their society (Robinson, 2017).

Realizing that women and gender-diverse people in Indigenous ways of life traditionally had active access to high positions of importance within their communities is an important step in scrutinizing colonization in Canada. The infringed decisions from settlers dramatically altered the ways Indigenous people lived in all aspects of life by effectively reshaping the views towards women and gender-diverse people in these communities as part of the assimilation tactics that Canada benefits from even today. Though things are contemporarily shifting, Canada was formed under colonial pretenses to uphold patriarchy, capitalism, and Christianity, which are dramatically different from the egalitarian societies that many Indigenous communities had created prior to European introduction (Gray, 2011). Since all life was viewed as sacred, communities wanted to protect the sacred. However, when settlers imposed these xenophobic beliefs and tried to assimilate Indigenous Peoples into Canadian ways of life, traditional knowledge was lost, and with that loss, Native people had to adapt. Sadly, a movement is needed in some Indigenous communities to remind community leaders of the spaces that women, girls, and gender-diverse Native people once took up in their communities and should still have access to. The reality is that some reservations and community leaders have been called out for upholding colonized views rooted in homophobic and sexualized biases (Pruden, 2016). A long road of healing lies ahead as these people reclaim their power and sacred standings within their communities. Multiple generations are walking this path, but digital networking is primarily led by youth who take space online and are reconnecting to their culture. In this way, Indigenous youth are holding Canada accountable for the changes they seek.

In addition to the government-imposed systems that disproportionately impacted, and continue to impact, Indigenous girls, women, femmes, and Two-Spirit people, the MMIWG2S epidemic has been a constant looming danger for Indigenous communities. The Royal Canadian Mounted Police recorded 1,017 cases of murdered Indigenous women and girls from 1980 to 2012 and 164 cases of missing Indigenous women and girls that date back to 1952; however, reports indicate that the actual numbers are much higher, something that Indigenous people have been asserting for a long time (Turner, 2016). These reports also often leave out Two-Spirit and other gender-variant individuals, who have only within the last 10 years or so begun to be included in the discussion of missing and murdered Indigenous women and girls, despite the violence they have been victims of since the imposition of settler ideals.

INDIGENOUS MOVEMENTS

Though Indigenous people have been speaking out about the issues surrounding land and body violence for years, reports such as that from the National Inquiry into Missing and Murdered Indigenous Women and Girls (2019) have corroborated their concerns. Bodies of research such as the National Inquiry into Missing and Murdered Indigenous Women and Girls (2019) highlight the MMIWG2S crisis and demonstrate how resource extraction in Canada increases gendered and sexualized cases of violence towards Indigenous people. Environmental disparities both historically and contemporarily affect marginalized groups, particularly based on race and class. This direct connection between violence to the land and violence to bodies is a large focus of environmental justice movements today, so it is no surprise that these movements of Indigenous resurgence, decolonization, and environmentalism intertwine. Removing land defence from matriarchy or any form of Indigenous leadership is difficult because identity is tied to the land, promises to the next seven generations are tied to the land, and part of upholding these lands is upholding the connections of ancestors who stewarded the earth previously. Spirit is woven into the relationship that Indigenous Nations have to these places. These places are their churches, their temples, their mosques—their greatest teachers and sustaining providers. That's why we cannot talk about matriarchy without acknowledging land and water defenders. As an example, we can look to the events that occurred in Oka in 1990, where women led the resistance in Kanehsatà:ke/Oka to protect their ancestral and traditional territories from land development. In a resistance that escalated to the point that the Canadian Army was sent in, women and girls defended their lands. This leadership by women was not by coincidence either. The Kanien'kehá:ka/Mohawk people elected Ellen Gabriel (@EllenGabriel1 on Twitter) to lead in accordance with their cultural protocols of being a matriarchal society. The Oka crisis was a powerful demonstration of Indigenous sovereignty, and this stand against Canada sent a firm message throughout Turtle Island: This is our land, and we will not back down. This standoff also created a shift in Indigenous revitalization when it came to land back and more contemporary issues.

Over the years, many movements, which were often led by Indigenous women, femmes, and Two-Spirit people, have gained national and international attention. Since Oka, many causes have made headlines, including the Idle No More movement, Shut Down Canada, and the MMIWG2S movement. The latter includes many smaller movements such as the Women's Memorial March and the multiple land defender and water protector movements, including the fight against the Trans Mountain Pipeline and access to clean water for all. While many of these movements are not entirely new, through the use of social media, they have gained attention and been spread further in a way that movements such as the Oka crisis were unable to. Since the addition of social media use to Indigenous movements, non-Indigenous people have been able to interact with these movements and get information that has not been skewed by a colonial and anti-Indigenous lens, which has been traditionally shown in mainstream media.

The Idle No More movement showed just how valuable the use of social media is for activism and how these sites can be used to spread awareness. This movement started in 2012 by four women who were concerned that a new proposed bill would threaten Indigenous rights and the safety of the land; it became one of Canada's largest and most well-known movements (Tupper, 2014). Through social media, such as Facebook and Twitter, this cause made waves and attracted the attention of Canada, as well as the world, and sparked events such as protests and teach-ins, which further spread the cause (Tupper, 2014). With Facebook pages, Twitter accounts, and the like dedicated to a specific movement, supporters can get up-to-date and rapid information on the movement, which they can then easily share with others. Additionally, the ability to set up events on Facebook, where times and dates are clear, and where communication can happen, means that events can be much more accessible, easily found, and kept track of. The Idle No More movement particularly benefited from the use of hashtags. By adding the hashtag (#) symbol in front of key words and phrases, for example, #IdleNoMore, threads of information and discussions can be viewed at ease and can lead to trending topics, which may then reach a wider audience (Tupper, 2014).

While the Idle No More movement primarily made use of Twitter and Facebook, other platforms that also employ hashtags are being used in current movements, such as Instagram, TikTok, and Tumblr. This is seen in how the #MMIW (missing and murdered Indigenous women) hashtag has emerged as a way for Indigenous people to discuss this issue and spread awareness, whereas it may have been given less attention and possibly less accurate coverage by mainstream media (Parsloe & Campbell, 2021). This hashtag has been mostly used on Twitter to promote this topic (Parsloe & Campbell, 2021); however, it has spread to other platforms such as Instagram, Facebook, and TikTok especially. TikTok has been used by Indigenous people to spread awareness of MMIWG2S, and although it has received mixed responses,[4] the symbol of red handprints has become a representation for these missing relatives and reached millions of people, with some videos receiving hundreds of thousands of views, if not millions (Johnson, 2020). These red handprints represent loss and healing, and the short videos serve to spread awareness and catch attention quickly while also making a statement (Johnson, 2020). Without online platforms such as these, most people would be receiving information through a colonial lens from mainstream media only, or they may not get any information at all.

Social media has been especially helpful in the land defender and water protector movements across Turtle Island. This has been seen in movements such as the #NoDAPL movement, as well as ones within Canada, such as the Unist'ot'en Camp. The Dakota Access Pipeline runs from North Dakota to Illinois and has been a concern of Indigenous activists since its planning began in 2014—it runs underneath the Standing Rock Sioux reservation's water source, and the construction has destroyed many sacred sites (Johnson, 2017). Although this problematic pipeline is located in just a portion of the United States, the movement reached many across the globe, becoming massive. Social media not only spread the movement's message but ensured that what was being shared was true, often through the use of videos documenting what was happening, especially when police were present (Johnson, 2017). The #NoDAPL hashtag gained widespread awareness through social media, which resulted in Indigenous people and non-Indigenous allies from across the world standing in solidarity, both in person and online. Many people travelled to Standing Rock to attend the gathering in support of the people, and when those who were physically present were in danger due to online surveillance, supporters across the globe used Facebook to "check in" at Standing Rock to overwhelm the authorities (Johnson, 2017). This movement shows just how valuable social media can be in activism.

Social media also played an important role in the Unist'ot'en Camp fight against pipelines in Canada, where social media was used to share updates and keep the government and authorities accountable through live streaming. Social media was also used in this fight to film and ask for assistance. Without the help of social media, much of what is happening at the many protests and blockades would not be shared, and news would be filtered through a biased, colonial lens. Additionally, the water crisis faced by Indigenous people in Canada has become increasingly discussed online via social media, while the mainstream news may only cover it during larger events. Water protectors such as Autumn Peltier use their voices, both on national news and social media, to spread awareness and push for government support and action that fulfills their promises. The reach that social media can achieve has changed the face of activism and has led to Indigenous issues becoming national and international concerns.

SOCIAL MEDIA, INDIGENOUS CREATORS, AND THEIR CONTENT

Considering the murky past of Indigenous Peoples and the media on both a national and global level, the idea of image reclamation and story sharing from an

Indigenous perspective is nuanced and novel. Indigenous Nations have historically been ethnographically captured from a colonial lens as subjects and interpreted as such. Further, these images and perspectives supported Indigenous erasure by framing Indigenous Peoples as a dying breed. In Canada specifically, the way Indigenous Peoples are typically mentioned through media sources supports stereotypes and evades Indigenous concerns, which not only negatively impacts Indigenous people's self-esteem but creates a false and harmful impression (Anderson, 2016; Glennie, 2018). One should be critically aware of how the internet, including social networking sites, can both benefit and harm Indigenous women, girls, and gender-diverse people. Online spaces such as social media platforms are colonial tools and reflect a capitalistic agenda by promoting a digital economy that reduces online users to consumers. With the introduction of social media, anyone with internet access and the proper tools has the capacity to take part in media. However, not everyone has access to this resource. Elders who are oceans of knowledge are often less visible online; this is in part because of generational differences and accessibility barriers, but it also intentional, to keep teachings sacred. In rural areas especially, accessibility limitations make engagement on social media platforms difficult, but urban demographics are not an exception. For Indigenous people who are able to engage with social networking sites, social media is a double-edged sword. Though social media can have a host of positives, Indigenous content as well as those who post it are still often combatting online harassment, miseducation, and increased possibility of cultural appropriation and pan-Indigenization (Anderson, 2016; Glennie, 2018). However, it also creates empowerment and social connections, as well as knowledge sharing and mobilization opportunities.

Social media platforms are typically places where people can connect and share with friends and family, but they can be much more than that, especially for Indigenous people. For many in rural areas, social media has become one of the main means of communication, especially with those outside their community (Molyneaux et al., 2014). Sharing cultural knowledge through social media has also been observed, showing that online resources can be an important way to preserve culture (Molyneaux et al., 2014). The value in preserving and practising culture online has become even more apparent throughout the COVID-19 pandemic. Although restrictions have made practising culture very difficult for some, as events such as Pow Wows are currently not being held, many have turned to social media instead. Many Indigenous people are sharing videos of themselves dancing and singing, and they are making beading tutorials that they are posting to sites like Facebook, Instagram, and TikTok (CrowSpreadingWings,

2020). Not only are these videos serving the purpose of preserving and sharing culture within the Indigenous community, but they are being seen by many non-Indigenous people and educating them on some Indigenous cultural practices (CrowSpreadingWings, 2020). Additionally, LGBTQ2S+ youth with less common identities may find online spaces much safer to explore their identities (Bates et al., 2019). Young Two-Spirit and other gender-diverse people may therefore receive more support and understanding online, particularly if those in their communities are upholding colonial perspectives on gender and sexuality.

In addition to social media becoming a place of community and connections for Indigenous people, these platforms have also become spaces of activism for Indigenous women, femmes, and Two-Spirit people. As mentioned previously, many Indigenous movements are led by Indigenous women, femmes, and Two-Spirit people, and those online are no different. The Idle No More movement is a key example of this, as it was started by four women before becoming the huge movement it is now (Tupper, 2014). Additionally, Indigenous girls, femmes, and Two-Spirit youth are often at the forefront of these fights, such as Autumn Peltier in the fight for clean water. Much of the activism is being led by young girls, femmes, and Two-Spirit people who are running online accounts, standing at the front lines of protests, spreading information, and calling allies to action. Alongside this, community support and mutual aid is being directed to these femmes to ensure that they are able to continue their work and be paid for their contributions.

CURRENT SPACES OF EMERGING SOLIDARITY ONLINE

A swell of Indigenous revitalization is occurring across Turtle Island. Given the historic difficulty of Indigenous people accessing traditional knowledge and participating in Canadian society, it is exciting to witness the contemporary reclamation of Indigenous identity that can be observed in places of modernity. It is no surprise then that Indigenous content creators are carving out safe spaces on social networking sites for them to express their identity and engage with others on these online platforms. On TikTok, Instagram, Twitter, Facebook, and YouTube, Indigenous women, femmes, and gender-diverse people are creating content that is informative, uplifting, and funny. Many of these creators' content covers different topics that allow other Indigenous women, femmes, and gender-diverse people to feel welcome, safe, and related to, while also gaining important knowledge about what is going on in different communities. A common theme among these featured creators is that they are currently making strides outside of social media in their respective fields, and social media is a space that is reflective of these realities.

Readers are encouraged to look into some of these suggested spaces and support content creators' work. However, users should be aware that just because information is available does not mean that this information is theirs to take. An example of this would be benefiting from and/or perpetuating harm by choosing to act on cultural knowledge in an appropriating way. For example, Indigenous beading has been trendy, and as a part of holding space for those who may be detached from beading teachings, Indigenous people such as Michelle Chubb (@indigenous_ baddie on Instagram/TikTok), who is Nehiyaw/Cree, share tutorials on social media about how to bead and even make jingle dresses. This does not give viewers the right to then start creating and selling their own beaded creations, thus profiting from Michelle's work. This work is done to allow for cultural reclamation and knowledge sharing, not exploitation. This concept of ownership over Indigenous culture is nothing new. Certain nations, clans, and families have ties to cultural practices such as songs and dances, and just because someone witnesses a cultural practice does not mean they have the authority to decide if they would like to use it or not. Non-Indigenous people should be particularly careful as respecting these boundaries around participating in practices is expected among Indigenous circles as common respect. It is a painful reminder of colonization when non-Indigenous people steal and benefit from Indigenous teachings without consent.

Many accounts exist to share and discuss, and they are open to the public domain when users are acting in a respectful manner. This section will focus on current safe spaces for Indigenous matriarchs, femmes, and gender-diverse peoples. While some content and its creators are more well known—such as Shayla Oulette Stonechild (@shayla0h on Instagram), Sherry Mckay (@sherry.mckay on TikTok and @officialsherrymckay on Instagram), and Shina Nova (@shinanova on Instagram/TikTok), who are Indigenous women who use their platforms to amplify Indigenous perspectives—lesser-known creators and spaces are worth mentioning as well.

Shayla Oulette Stonechild is a Nehiyaw/Cree and Métis content creator, yoga teacher, actor, speaker, and *Matriarch Movement* podcast creator (@matriarchmovement on Facebook/Instagram). She uses her podcast to share stories of amazing contemporary Indigenous women who speak about the matriarchs in their life. Her guests often share the ways they are decolonizing their fields and living in their power, as well as their journeys of coming into their respective roles. When not acting on the Aboriginal Peoples Television Network (APTN) or leading a yoga class, Shayla finds space online to talk about her everyday routine that inspires people to get in touch with their wellness and discuss what it's like to be an Indigenous content creator in a traditionally colonial digital space.

Sherry McKay (@sherry.mckay on TikTok) is a Chippewa/Ojibway Anishinaabe mother of four who uses her online presence to bring awareness to contemporary issues such as cultural appropriation, MMIW, and racism in Canada. Though her content addresses harsh Native realities, she also posts a lot of funny, freeing, and joy-focused content. Her approach is focused on uplifting Indigenous realities, and she dedicates her online platforms to education, accountability, and laughter. Being interested in film and systemic change, Sherry is also a public speaker and in the process of establishing her film career.

Shina Nova and her mother Kayuula (@kayuulanov on Instagram/TikTok) offer endearing content about what it's like being Inuk women. On their platforms, they share Inuit culture such as clothing, cultural food dishes, and most famously, their duo of mother–daughter throat singing. Their songs bring healing, but Shina also uses her fame to highlight issues that affect her community and what it was like growing up as an urban Native. Shina has fought and continues to fight against land destruction, such as the Keystone XL pipeline. Shina and Kayuula also discuss their gratitude for each other and for being in such close kinship in a way that they are able to practise their culture as a family, despite challenges.

Kairyn Potts (@ohkairyn on Facebook/Instagram/TikTok/Twitter) is a Two-Spirit Nakota Sioux person who works collaboratively in their community and to support Indigenous youth, Two-Spirit people, and IndigiQueer people. Kai uses their platform to highlight the aunties who inspire them, as well as to discuss youth mental health and land back movements. Hailing from Treaty 6 territory, Kai currently operates out of Tkaronto/Toronto and is active in the current resurgence of Two-Spirit/IndigiQueer identities by speaking at talking circles. They were also previously affiliated with provincial and national youth networks.

Prestin Thotin-awasis (@prestomanifest0 on Instagram) is a Two-Spirit Nehiyaw/Cree Lakota and Dene person located in Treaty 6 territory who often shares self-written poetry about their own journey, tying in cultural knowledge and language to express themselves. Prestin is an advocate of sharing truth, and with this perspective, both trauma and milestones are at times discussed authentically. Prestin works hard to show through their social media the importance of making space for gender-diverse people, women, and Two-Spirit people within a traditional framework and acknowledging the colonial interplay that has negatively impacted their community. Due to their own personal work of self-recognition and overcoming their own biases surrounding Two-Spirit identity, Prestin has shared that a huge motivator for creating their online platform is to create safety and celebrate sacredness.

Sierra Tasi Baker (@sierratasibaker on Facebook/Instagram) is a Sḵwx̱wú7mesh/ Squamish, x̱ʷməθkʷəy̓əm/Musqueam, Kwakwaka'wakw, Ɫingít/Tlingit, and Magyar Hungarian bi-queer city planner and artist who proudly stands for their traditional ancestral ties to what is currently known as Vancouver. Sierra is part of the duo of MST (x̱ʷməθkʷəy̓əm [Musqueam], Sḵwx̱wú7mesh Úxwumixw [Squamish Nation], and səl̓ílwətaʔɫ [Tsleil-Waututh]) futurism and is passionate about decolonizing Vancouver, which is on unceded territory, as well as moving forwards with Indigenous values. Sierra shares their dreams for the city, picking up on both their maternal and paternal lineages to do so. In their work, they connect with other Indigenous creators across fields and share their and their family's creative backgrounds and proud governance. Much of the work that Sierra does is personal as well as vocational through her family's business, Sky Spirit Studio. Sierra refuses to allow the narrative that excuses colonial violence and instead holds the city and those in positions of power accountable to decolonize these lands. On their social media pages, they share contemporary and historic cultural celebrations and remind Canada each day that you are on Native land.

Indigenous Goddess Gang (@indigenousgoddessgang on Facebook/Instagram) is a space that centres Indigenous femmes but is open to everyone. This space allows for a celebration of Indigenous Peoples by promoting Indigenous businesses; Indigenous ways of knowing, such as food and medicine systems; poetry; music; and more. What unites the content is a focus on celebrating different matriarchs and tribes who are stepping into their power with a focus on upholding Indigenous identity. The Indigenous Goddess Gang website is full of good medicine and worth a visit. The project's Instagram page often shares these knowledges and has weekly hashtag features such as #matriarchmonday, #transformationtuesday, #warriorwomenwednesday, and #foodiefriday.

Pacific Association of First Nation Women (@PAFNW on Facebook/Twitter and @indigenous_women_rise on Instagram) is a non-profit organization in British Columbia led by Indigenous women with the hopes of supporting matriarchy in their communities. Through the promotion of Indigenous ways of knowing such as cultural and language programs, community partnerships, and holistic frameworks, these femmes are leading the way. Their Facebook page is insightful in promoting their community contributions and increasing visibility of Indigenous knowledge. This collective specifically offers MMIW support and stands firm in preserving and honouring decolonized approaches.

Two-Spirited People of Manitoba Inc. (@2SBWproject on Facebook and @2sbw_project on Instagram) is a Winnipeg-based non-profit that supports LGBTQ2S+ peoples with a community approach. This group offers educational workshops and connects within the community to work to support youth, thinking about the next seven generations ahead. It has a presence on both Instagram and Facebook, where the group engages with the public about the work it does and ways to support the organization. With the inclusion of Elders, talking circles, and community programs, this collective shares its determination for safe spaces for LGBTQ2S+ peoples, with harm reduction and land back being key philosophies grounding their work.

ReconciliACTION[5] AND LOOKING SEVEN GENERATIONS AHEAD

Mentioned above are just some of the amazing people and organizations with an online presence that are dedicated to upholding women, girls, femmes, lesbians, gays, bisexuals, Two-Spirit, and all gender-diverse people. There are so many individuals out there who are inspirational in their Indigeneity and are not afraid to step into their roles in a public, digital space. However, matriarchs of course do not only exist purely on social media. They exist in your communities, your workplaces, your schools; in governments, kitchens, hospitals; as writers, lawyers, and weavers. They exist in the spirit world, and they exist in the future. They are the future. Matriarchs are the backbone of Indigenous communities and some of our most valuable teachers. They thrive everywhere on Turtle Island, and supporting them through social media is one small act of solidarity you can take part of. As you explore these and other channels, we urge you to find the matriarchs in your societies. What Indigenous women are reclaiming and leading on the lands on which you stand? How can you be an ally in their journey and support a future where matriarchs are so interwoven in their positionality that generations to come will never need to search for them? They will simply look up like one looks in the night sky and say, "There she is, bright as grandmother moon, lighting my path, my celestial guide." Being an ally and uplifting matriarchs is constant work, but seeking out these people, both online and in person, is a simple first step in the journey to solidarity.

ACKNOWLEDGEMENTS

This research was supported by iMPACTS: Collaborations to Address Sexual Violence on Campus; Social Sciences and Humanities Research Council of Canada (SSHRC) Partnership Grant 895-2016-1026 (Project Director, Shaheen Shariff, PhD, James McGill Professor, McGill University).

Many thanks for the guidance and mentorship of Karyn Audet, Jill Fellows, and Lisa Smith, who supported us in this contribution. We honour the work of past, present, and future Indigenous kin and allies to reclaim safe spaces in all four directions.

QUESTIONS FOR DISCUSSION

1. In your eyes, what is the value of social media? How might that differ from its value to Indigenous women, femmes, and Two-Spirit people? If your interpretation is the same, has that always been how you viewed it? If it has changed, what influenced that change?

2. What ways have you seen social media benefit minority groups? What makes social media so advantageous in a time where opinions are rapidly changing?

3. Have you personally seen examples of anti-Indigenous prejudice or racism expressed on social media? What was that like for you? Alternatively, have you personally learned new information about Indigenous Peoples that have challenged previous beliefs of yours? What was that like for you?

INVITATIONS TO GO DEEPER

1. Prior to reading this chapter, did you notice the discrepancies between the representations of Indigenous women, femmes, and Two-Spirit people in mainstream media (news, TV, movies, etc.) and social media (Facebook, Twitter, Instagram, etc.)? Is the social media you consume aligned with colonial representations of Indigenous Peoples? If so, why might that be?

2. Where do you get most of your information on Indigenous movements? Do you think that the representations you are consuming are accurate, or is it possible they are being misrepresented or skewed by colonial views? If you don't see any information on Indigenous movements in media, why might that be?

3. Realizing the growing body of literature surrounding the National Inquiry into MMIWG2S, why do you think the actions requested on behalf of Indigenous Peoples to implement a task force and national database to address this crisis have not yet been acted upon? Considering documents such as the TRC's *Calls to Action* (2015) and the UNDRIP (United Nations, 2007), how are you supporting your part to be active in reconciliation and uplifting Indigenous perspectives in your life? Are you aware of movements occurring within your communities? If not, then why?

READ MORE

Gray, L. (2011). *First Nations 101: Tons of stuff you need to know about First Nations people.* Adaawx Publishing.

Hanson, E. (n.d.). Marginalization of Aboriginal women. *Indigenous Foundations.* https://indigenousfoundations.arts.ubc.ca/marginalization_of_aboriginal_women/

Joseph, B. (2018). *21 things you may not know about the Indian Act: Helping Canadians make reconciliation with Indigenous Peoples a reality.* Page Two Books.

LISTEN MORE, WATCH MORE

"Aboriginal women—resistance, resilience & revitalization," Patti Doyle Bedwell, TED Talk, December 2014: https://www.youtube.com/watch?v=M1yCvKA-WdU&ab_channel=TEDxTalksTEDxTalksVerified

"Embracing my Two-Spirit journey with Prestin Thotin-awasis," *2 Crees in a Pod* podcast, February 2021: https://anchor.fm/terri-suntjens/episodes/Embracing-my-two-spirit-journey-with-Prestin-Thotin-awasis-eqdd5s

"Nahanni Fontaine: The matriarchy in power for the people," *Matriarch Movement* podcast, May 2021: https://matriarchmovement.libsyn.com/nahanni-fontaine-the-matriarchy-in-power-for-the-people

"What really happened at Standing Rock | I was there," *Vice*, 2020: https://www.youtube.com/watch?v=J1yD2J8vHAk

NOTES

1. *Shadow banning* refers to blocking a user and/or their content online without their awareness or consent.

2. *Maarsi* is Michif (Métis language) and *kinanâskomitin* is Nêhiyawêwin (Cree language); both translate to thank you.

3. *Colonization* means to apply foreign systems to a place that dispossesses ways that existed previously.

4. There is concern that this imagery could be exploited or mocked.

5. This is a term used by Harlan Pruden to denote ownership of the intention behind reconciliation. Reconciliation must be put into action, and the mending of these words reminds the reader that more than their thoughts are needed to restore Indigenous and settler relations.

REFERENCES

Anderson, K. (2016). *A recognition of being: Reconstructing Native womanhood*. Women's Press.

Bates, A., Hobman, T., & Bell, B. T. (2019). "Let me do what I please with it … don't decide my identity for me": LGBTQ+ youth experiences of social media in narrative identity development. *Journal of Adolescent Research, 35*(1), 51–83. https://doi.org/10.1177/0743558419884700

CrowSpreadingWings, R. (2020, April 21). How Indigenous communities are using social media to stay connected. *CTV News*. https://winnipeg.ctvnews.ca/how-indigenous-communities-are-using-social-media-to-stay-connected-1.4906162

Glennie, C. (2018). "We don't kiss like that": Inuit women respond to music video representations. *AlterNative: An International Journal of Indigenous Peoples, 14*(2), 104–112.

Gray, L. K. (2011). *First Nations 101: Tons of stuff you need to know about First Nations people*. Adaawx Pub.

Inter-American Commission on Human Rights (IACHR). (2014). *Missing and murdered Indigenous women in British Columbia, Canada*. https://www.oas.org/en/iachr/reports/pdfs/indigenous-women-bc-canada-en.pdf

Johnson, H. (2017). #NoDAPL: Social media, empowerment, and civic participation at Standing Rock. *Library Trends, 66*(2), 155–175. https://doi.org/10.1353/lib.2017.0033

Johnson, R. (2020, March 9). Widespread use of red handprints to represent MMIWG sparks debate among advocates. *CBC News*. https://www.cbc.ca/news/indigenous/red-handprints-mmiwg-1.5483955

Joseph, B. (2018). *Things you may not know about the Indian Act: Helping Canadians make reconciliation with Indigenous people a reality*. Indigenous Relations Press.

Lawrence, B. (2003). Gender, race, and the regulation of Native identity in Canada and the United States: An overview. *Hypatia, 18*(2), 3–31.

Molyneaux, H., O'Donnell, S., Kakekaspan, C., Walmark, B., Budka, P., & Gibson, K. (2014). Social media in remote First Nation communities. *Canadian Journal of Communication, 39*(2), 275–288. https://doi.org/10.22230/cjc.2014v39n2a2619

National Inquiry into Missing and Murdered Indigenous Women and Girls. (2019). *Reclaiming power and place. The final report of the national inquiry into missing and murdered Indigenous women and girls*. https://www.mmiwg-ffada.ca/wp-content/uploads/2019/06/Final_Report_Vol_1a-1.pdf

Parsloe, S. M., & Campbell, R. C. (2021). "Folks don't understand what it's like to be a Native woman": Framing trauma via #MMIW. *Howard Journal of Communications*, *32*(3), 197–212. https://doi.org/10.1080/10646175.2021.1871867

Pruden, H. (2016, October 29–November 2). *Two-Spirit: Then and now—Mending the broken sacred circle*. APHA 2016 Annual Meeting and Expo, University of British Columbia, Vancouver, BC, Canada.

Robinson, M. (2017). Two-Spirit and bisexual people: Different umbrella, same rain. *Journal of Bisexuality*, *17*(1), 7–29. https://doi.org/10.1080/15299716.2016.1261266

Truth and Reconciliation Commission of Canada (TRC). (2015). *Calls to action*. https://www2.gov.bc.ca/assets/gov/british-columbians-our-governments/indigenous-people/aboriginal-peoples-documents/calls_to_action_english2.pdf

Tupper, J. (2014). Social media and the Idle No More movement: Citizenship, activism and dissent in Canada. *Journal of Social Science Education*, *13*(4), 87–94.

Turner, A. (2016, January 3). *MMIWG: Missing and murdered Indigenous women and girls and ending violence*. Assembly of First Nations. https://www.afn.ca/policy-sectors/mmiwg-end-violence/

United Nations. (2007). *United Nations declaration on the rights of Indigenous Peoples*. https://www.un.org/esa/socdev/unpfii/documents/DRIPS_en.pdf

The Ethics of Care and Online Teaching: Personal Reflections on Pandemic Post-Secondary Instruction

Kira Tomsons

INTRODUCTION

During an interview for a university teaching position, I was once asked what virtue is the most important for teaching. Then, I thought it was fairness and went on a great deal about how proud I was that my students could never complain that I was unfair. Now, I know I was wrong. What is needed at the core of teaching is care. In the past year, I have taught over three hundred students remotely. And I have never been prouder to have been called a caring person by my students. I had always been interested about care as an ethical concept but had never thought rigorously about how it would apply to teaching specifically. Teaching at a community college in the year 2020 has changed that dramatically. I write this chapter having spent the last year in a global pandemic that has killed over two million people. And I write it as a college instructor who has spent that year providing online instruction to well over three hundred students. I also write it as a parent who has had to work at home while watching and helping her children muddle through online teaching and meeting virtually with elementary teachers who are ill-prepared and lost within online modes of teaching. The experiences of 2020 have forced me to think about how we teach, how teachers exist in relation to students, and how we exist in relation to technology and to one another through technology in the context of teaching.

Living through 2020 moved me to carefully examine how I have taught in the past and what assumptions I need to challenge in my own teaching and in the institutional structures that I teach within. Fairness is no longer the guiding virtue that I could use to forge my path. The goal of this chapter is to provide students with some insight into what happens on the other side of the desk, where instructors are making decisions and identifying concerns that may not be obvious or transparent to students. For teachers of any sort, whether they work with kids in summer camps, coach sports, or formally teach in institutions, this is an examination of what should motivate us in our choices when thinking about how we teach and what we are hoping to achieve more generally. This chapter is not purely about the online environment, although that is the focus, but it is about our attitudes towards teaching and learning.

I shall argue that we ought to adopt an ethics of care framework in the creation of our online teaching environment. In the first part of this chapter, I lay out the approach to an ethics of care that informs my teaching. Then I provide a personal reflection on how the move to online teaching affected both instructors and students. I argue that care ethics provides a more humane approach to teaching when considering the adoption of surveillance technologies and how to structure class policies. I then conclude with some objections I have encountered and some warnings about how enacting an ethics of care must be done carefully within the context of institutions that may not be amenable to such approaches.

A FRAMEWORK FOR AN ETHICS OF CARE

To understand the ethical issues faced by students and instructors, a framework for thinking about what is morally relevant is necessary. How we frame our ethical concerns will have an impact on how we address those concerns in practice. The ethics of care is an approach to moral reasoning that focuses on the importance of relationships, the role of empathy and sympathy in our moral responses, and the responsibilities that attend to the meeting of needs and interests of others. I take it as an explicitly feminist approach as it arises from feminist concerns about what moral theories draw our attention to.

The ethics of care began within psychology and education with the works of Carol Gilligan and Nell Noddings. Carol Gilligan (1982) set the stage for the contrast between the ethics of care and ethics of justice, arguing that women and men reason differently when it comes to ethics. Gilligan was responding to the work of psychologist Lawrence Kohlberg, who posited that how one engages in moral reasoning as one matures changes. Gilligan pointed out that within Kohlberg's model of moral reasoning, women would struggle to be seen as morally "mature" because the view of morality that is commonly adopted in moral psychology—what she describes as "justice ethics"—is one that ignores the experiences of women. To be morally mature requires abstract, principled reasoning, alongside a healthy dose of impartiality. Women in Gilligan's study tended to be partial and focused on relationships and would never reach the height of moral maturity on the model proposed by Kohlberg. Shortly after Gilligan's work, Nell Noddings (1986) published *Caring: A Feminine Approach to Ethics and Moral Education*, in which she develops an account of care and care relationships. What is common to both is the prioritizing of women's experiences in the moral landscape and the framing of relationships as morally relevant.

The history of the ethics of care within the discipline of philosophy has its roots in feminist responses to predominantly male accounts of our moral experiences used to create ethical theories. Many who engage in work on the ethics of care take as their starting point that traditional theories are deficient because they are limited by privileged thinking about what counts morally. Feminist philosophers began to explore alternative ways to approach moral reasoning, starting from the lived experiences of women and groups whose lives have not been the centre of Western philosophical thought. Feminist philosophers have since written on the ethics of care, expanding, criticizing, and moving beyond the accounts of Gilligan and Noddings. Some well-known feminist philosophers doing this work include Annette Baier (1994), Joan Tronto (1994), Sara Ruddick (1995), Virginia Held (2006), and Eva Kittay (2020). But within many of these accounts, care and justice are often seen as separate and sometimes opposing frames of reference for ethical thought. Justice is seen as a concern for rights, duties, impartiality, and fairness, whereas care focuses on the nature of relations and responsibilities, and how to meet the needs of those around us.

In contrast to Gilligan, Joan Tronto (1994) argues that care is something that is not a separate "voice." Rather, she characterizes care as "a species of activity that includes everything we do to maintain, continue and repair our 'world' so that we can live in it as well as possible. The world includes our bodies, our selves and our environment, all of which we seek to interweave in a complex, life-sustaining web" (p. 103). Rather than beginning with the idea of care as a virtue, or an attitude, care manifests as action, where choices about needs and interests are met, and where people's actions can improve the lives of those around them by attending to properly identified needs.

Understanding care as a process requires unpacking the different levels of activity that occur within that process. Tronto (1994) identifies four stages of care: where people identify needs (caring about); where they take on the responsibility for meeting those needs (caring for); where they engage in work to actually meet the needs (caregiving); and where the person whose interests are at stake responds to the care giving in some way (care receiving). This care process could be carried out by one individual caring for another throughout the whole process. Consider a parent changing a diaper: they identify that it must be changed, immediately have to strategize about how to do it, engage in the hands-on work of changing the diaper, and then the baby responds by calming down. It is also easy to see how this process could involve more than one person, where one parent identifies the need for a diaper change but then asks the other to do the actual hands-on caring.

The usefulness of Tronto's account, however, is that it also allows for an analysis of institutions as participating in care activities. If a business owner recognizes that their product is harming the environment through its production processes (caring about), then they could direct their employees to develop a less harmful process (caring for), which then would be implemented at the production level by workers (caregiving), and then there would be less waste into the environment (care receiving).[1]

In this analysis, care is not innately gendered, as men and women can both engage in care work, but it is socially gendered as women are the ones who are often expected to perform and are engaged in the more difficult and less socially recognized forms of care work. This account is not entirely based within individual relations, given that care as a process can occur with multiple people and at institutional levels. And caring activity is not something that is automatically good. While it might be tempting to say that caring for another person or the environment is good, the process by which we enact that care could go badly. I could misidentify whose needs should be prioritized. I could lack the required skill to properly engage in caring activities. And I could ignore the real needs of the one receiving care and the ways in which they receive the care. Ethical care requires that we pay attention to how we are caring, who we are caring for, who is doing the care work and where the burdens of care fall, whether the people receiving care are having their needs meet, and whether we are meeting our responsibilities.

This account is explicitly intersectional in its feminist analysis. There can be no presumption that all women share the same burdens of labour when class and race so clearly play significant roles in determining who engages in the more unpleasant forms of caregiving. No presumption can be made that all people are receiving the same kinds of care, as this will be determined by who oversees the caring about and caring for parts of the care process. Whose needs are overlooked will be tied to the inequalities that already exist within a society. To fully understand the moral dimensions of care, we must attend to the ways in which our social positioning affects the care decisions we control, the care work that we engage in, and the care that we receive.

I take the ethics of care to be an important approach to adopt within the context of teaching. Doing so is not at all radical as Noddings situated much of her account of care within the context of teaching and the teacher–student relationship, and many scholars within the philosophy of education use her account to discuss care and teaching. The concept of care is also used within discussions of what is necessary for ethical online teaching as well (see, e.g., Burke & Larmar, 2021; Rabin, 2021; Rose & Adams, 2014). Two aspects of the teacher–student relationship make the ethics of care particularly relevant.

First, a power imbalance intrinsically exists between me and my students. Justice approaches to ethics often presume an equality between the participants. But this is not the case in teaching. Many of my students are quite nervous in asking for requests such as extensions. They are visibly anxious when I ask them questions during class. Online, most are reticent to challenge my perceived authority. No amount of work on my part to equalize our relations will eliminate the fact that I am the one wielding the power of the grade. Students are very much aware of this inequality and its implications, particularly students who are marginalized.

Second, I have role responsibilities that arise from the very nature of our relationship. As an instructor, I am entrusted in my role to help my students grow intellectually. As a philosopher, I see my goal as helping students become emergent critical thinkers in a world that needs such skills more than ever. I am supposed to be competent and understand how to help them learn. An ethics of care takes these responsibilities and competencies as the starting place for how to build relations through the choices we make in how we design and carry out our teaching.

TECHNOLOGY, DISTANCE LEARNING, AND THE CLASSROOM

In my institution, the "pivot" to online teaching happened in the middle of March 2020, near the end of the semester, and there was no gradual transition. It was an abrupt shift in response to the public health directives for higher education institutions. From the instructor side of the desk, I didn't find it that difficult to transition, because I was already teaching half of my courses in hybrid fashion, only meeting with my students in class half the time, with online components for the rest. I was also familiar with teaching technologies, and I had already recorded many lectures that I could easily use. I was familiar with video editing, so I could quickly make new videos that I needed. It was time intensive and stressful, but I had the skill set that made it a familiar process. But many instructors had never thought about teaching online and were frantically trying to figure out how to use the learning management system and how to provide remote lectures. Some of my colleagues had rarely used email. Instructors were suddenly faced with having to figure out how students would submit work that normally would be done on paper, write exams that normally would be written in a classroom environment, and provide lectures when meeting in person was forbidden.

Students also found themselves having to learn material in new ways, struggling to manage technology at a time in the semester when things already would be normally quite stressful. It is crucial to remember that students' lives were also being disrupted beyond just their schooling. Many of my students were working remotely, had been laid off, were sick with COVID-19, were having family members die from COVID-19, and had children who were also suddenly at home. The consequence was that many of my students were generally experiencing a great deal of social, economic, and educational stress. They were asking for extensions, concerned about missing synchronous sessions, and wondering whether they would lose credit for late papers. Their lives and their learning were disrupted, and this was having a significant impact on when and how they could perform the learning tasks I had assigned.

At the same time, discussions about pedagogy erupted among my colleagues. Common questions emerged: How do I ensure my students are "in class" when they don't turn on their cameras? How do I ensure my students aren't cheating on their online multiple-choice exams? What sort of class policies should I have for assignments when students are just not showing up? These questions mirrored the often-encountered questions and frustrations articulated by instructors over the years: how can we catch plagiarists and instruct students on academic integrity, and how can I get students to attend class, follow my rules in the syllabus, and get assignments in on time? In general, the problems seemed to be loosely connected around two main themes: student presence and academic dishonesty.

Student Presence

Students' presence and engagement in online classes can be difficult to assess in comparison to face-to-face classes. When students are not showing up in a physical space, it is harder to communicate to students when assignments are due and their participation in elements of the class is harder to assess. Often, students would contact me saying they had simply forgotten what day it was and as a result missed a quiz or a forum post. In my classes, students were struggling to meet deadlines, which was exacerbated by the fact I could not be in a physical space to remind them of what they had to do.

Where instructors require class attendance, either through rewards for attendance or penalties for absences, the online environment makes presence more ambiguous, particularly when one is running the class asynchronously, where there are no sessions where students meet at the same time. Students can "pretend" to be in the virtual meeting call if webcams do not have to be turned on, and it is simply much more difficult to tell what students are actively "attending" the class. Instructors who held synchronous sessions, where they met with students via virtual meetings, found that many students did not turn on cameras or microphones unless it was a class policy and written into the syllabus that such things were required. It was also difficult to assess student participation as active listeners in such environments because the usual visual cues in a classroom were missing. I could not scan the room to see who was nodding and who was physically present but mentally distant. Instructors were relying on lists of students' names identified in the virtual meeting software, but this was not necessarily an accurate representation of who was "present." When I met with students in virtual environments, I often suspected there were students who "logged in" but were not actually present. They consistently failed to respond to polls, remained in the meeting space long after the class ended, and did not respond to chat messages I sent privately to them. Students' ability to appear present but not really engage also feeds into the next area of concern: students trying to game the system.

Academic Dishonesty and Online Classes

For some, the need to see students on webcams was legitimately about trying to forge connections with people who are not in the same room. For others, though, it was clearly being driven by a distrust of what students were doing while unseen. Requiring that students be "on camera" allowed the surveillance we normalize in the classroom. But when grounded in a mistrust of students, this reinforces the idea that students are fundamentally dishonest and are out to cheat the system in some way. The online environment in particular is seen as being more vulnerable to exploitation. Technology allows for more modes of cheating when assignments are structured and deployed in particular ways. Where in a physical environment, instructors could visually scan the room and ensure materials like texts and notes were not accessed, this is not possible for the instructor online without active support from other sources. Our institution began giving workshops on how to use Respondus Monitor, which is described by Respondus Inc. (2021) as "a fully-automated proctoring solution. Student's [*sic*] use a webcam to record themselves during an online exam. Afterward, flagged events and proctoring results are available to the instructor for further review." Instructors could require students to install this software to monitor their computer and environment while writing exams. Other institutions began using similar technology, such as Proctorio, which provides online exam monitoring using facial detection software. This software would record students, allowing instructors to see their environment and movements, flagging suspicious behaviours for instructors to review. Instructors were also strategizing about how to use test settings to structure online tests, restricting time, so students would not have enough time to look up answers, or choosing to present questions individually with no opportunity for students to return to questions later.

(UN)ETHICAL TECHNOLOGICAL RESPONSES

In many ways, these concerns being articulated by my colleagues were not new at all. But whereas most instructors had developed policies and strategies for face-to-face classes that would address these issues, the online environment posed a challenge for those who were new to online teaching. As a result, a great deal of time and energy was being spent on figuring out how to address these traditional concerns in the new environment.

And many turned to leverage technology, like Respondus Monitor, in response to infringements of the rules. These technologies are adopted because they are seen as the solution to a problem: we need to be able to catch cheaters, and these are means by which we can do so. However, the adoption of such technologies ignores significant moral questions about the needs of students and how we identify and respond to them.

Surveillance

Faculty demand for surveillance technology reflects an ethical framework rooted in a justice ethics rather than a care ethics. The goal of surveillance is to enforce rules that are seen as crucial to the moral sanctity of the classroom and to catch and punish those who violate those rules. Students who cheat are seen as breaching the principles inherent in academic integrity such as honesty and respect. From this perspective, violations of academic integrity are failures on the part of students to be morally responsible. Students are autonomous individuals who are morally responsible for their choices and liable to be punished. From the standpoint of an ethics of care, the questions that need to be raised are quite different, and the way we use technology to respond to those questions will be different.

We can ask why our students are cheating. If students are cheating because they lack the time to learn, lack the skills to do the work, or are too stressed in their lives to engage honestly, then the use of surveillance technology is not going to solve the problem. Students will simply be trying to find ways around it. Technology is seen as the solution, but pragmatically it is not. Tovani (2014) points out that many students are apt to cheat when they lack the know-how, lack the time, and don't see the relevance of the material to their lives. From the position of an ethic of care, the question is not "who is guilty of cheating and how do we punish them?" but rather "how can I meet the needs of my students in ways that make it less likely they will feel compelled to cheat?"

We can also ask whether we should require our students to use technology that frames students as suspects from the beginning. The presumption in the use of this technology is that students will cheat, and we must catch them, punish them, and send a message to others who might be tempted to cheat. Caring relations, however, are characterized by trust (Held, 2006, pp. 133–135). To engage in ethical caring, we must begin by trusting that students are going to be working in good faith. This is not to say that instructors should never suspect their students of cheating, any more than I should never presume my child is always telling me the truth when there is clear evidence to the contrary. But the emphasis here is on evidence. The use of surveillance technology puts the creation of suspicion ahead of collecting evidence. Caring foregrounds trust, not suspicion.

Certain types of assignments lend themselves to surveillance more than others. Reliance on test banks, timed tests, and generic essay topics will inevitably mean students will have the opportunity and inclination to cheat. Test banks can be leaked online, pressure to do well within time constraints creates the motivation to bypass learning, and essays can be bought. But these types of assignments also do not engage students in learning the skills I have the responsibility to teach. If I begin with assignments that are legitimately meeting the interests of students, the need for surveillance drops dramatically. In caring well, I start with what my students need in terms of their education, and in doing so I will create assignments that meet those needs, which incidentally also require less surveillance. Success in caring requires attentiveness to the caring process. If I fail to properly strategize about how to meet the needs of students, then I fail in the "caring about" part of the caring process.

For example, I use scaffolded essays, where students write outlines, drafts, and annotated bibliographies, and submit them online. I write detailed feedback, so they know what to improve, and their perception that they need to cheat because of a lack of skill is reduced. When they show their progress, it makes students less likely to purchase a paper because they need to show their process, but more importantly, it will make them more confident in their work. And when students feel confident in their work, they are less likely to cheat. The goal is not to stamp out cheating, though. The goal is to provide students with the opportunity to make mistakes, fix them, and learn from them. The added benefit is that cheating is less likely. Starting from a position of care, rather than justice, enables me to meet the needs of students while at the same time allowing me to retain my trust in students.

An ethics of care is not just about the individual relationships I have. This approach also raises concern about the use of technology to reinforce social inequality. Care requires that our relationships be acknowledged as happening within societal contexts that treat people very differently. For example: there is significant evidence that facial recognition software used by services like Proctorio does not accurately "recognize" people who have darker skin. Black students report being told by the software to ensure there is sufficiently lighting, even though the room was fully lit, whereas this is not a problem reported by white students. In addition, students who have disabilities are legitimately concerned that their physical movements will be flagged because they do not fit with the "norm" prescribed by computer algorithms (Swauger, 2020). For a care ethicist, these disparities are of concern.

Ethical caring requires that we move beyond the purely personal. Tronto (1994) notes that "care rests upon judgements that extend far beyond personal awareness. Despite the fact that many writers about care concern themselves with relationships of care that are now considered personal or private, the kinds of judgements that I have described require an assessment of needs in a social and political, as well a personal, context" (p. 137). If I choose to use these remote proctoring technologies, then I am reinforcing oppressive practices. This is antithetical to care. If I choose to use these technologies in the name of justice, to catch the liars and cheaters, then I am choosing to ignore the needs and interests of students who are disadvantaged by such technology. This cannot be a caring choice and cannot be justified from the position of an ethics of care.

Humane Class Policies

The concern instructors have for enforcement of class policies is also firmly entrenched within a perspective of justice. The syllabus is perceived as creating the boundaries of obligations between student and instructor. It sets the stage for what can be done by either party. The policies come first, and enforcement follows, and in the online space, this means creating policies around the use of various technologies. If an instructor requires class attendance, for example, then immediately the issue is that if webcams are off, attendance can't be verified. (Note how this continues the view of students as "under suspicion.") So a policy gets created requiring webcams be on. Students might miss a virtual class meeting or scheduled tests. So a policy gets created requiring doctors notes ensuring that students could be penalized for not having what amount to justified excuses in the instructor's eyes. (Again, with the presumption that students need to prove their justified absence, with the assumption that otherwise they are not being honest in their absence.) But such policy-based responses, couched in justice as they are, do not attend to the needs of students and are not grounded in caring practices.

Creating class policies from a position of care requires rethinking what policies are meant to do. Unlike many other relationships, students and teachers are in many ways thrown together. I do not choose my students, and they are not always clearly choosing me. But in teaching a class, and in registering in that class, we are now together in a relationship with one another. My class policies are not intended to be an agreement between myself and students about what our obligations are, even if my institution may interpret them as such. Rather, they are about setting the expectations that students and I should have of each other in the course. In setting out policies that are humane, I position myself as someone engaged in authentic caring practices.

Applying the process of care to the creation of course policies can be useful. If we properly care about students' needs, then we must recognize what their interests are in the online environment. Students may not have the luxury of housing where they can have a private space to learn, they may lack the technology to connect webcams and microphones, and their connections to the internet may not be robust. Requiring webcams and microphones to be on as a class policy is intrusive and fails to recognize the needs of students. Care requires we are attentive to the positioning of those we are caring for, the limits they face, and how our demands may not be fair in the face of those limits.

Problematic policies like the ones I've noted are only going to be required if class meetings are happening synchronously, that is, the class is meeting together at specific times. In choosing to meet synchronously during pandemic teaching, instructors are placing burdens on their students. Synchronous teaching presumes that students can meet at particular times. But students who are sick or who must work unexpectedly may not be able to meet at scheduled times. Students who are unable to travel may be in different time zones around the world. At its very core, the decision to run a class synchronously is one that does not recognize the needs of many students.

An example of a humane policy I enact is my late assignments policy. I tell my students that the "due date" is a pragmatic rule, a date given so that we can plan our semesters accordingly. It is not a moral failure to not meet a deadline. I do not penalize students for handing things in late. I tell them at the beginning that the whole class already has an extension on assignments. They do not even have to ask for it.[2] This approach is based on my attentiveness to the ways in which students are balancing many interests and recognizes that my class will not always be their priority. Indeed, it is not always a priority in my own life.

I do not ask why students missed assignments or were unable to do work. If I were to demand a justification, I would be required to judge whether their excuse is worthy or fair. But that is not my purpose from a position of care. I do not want to stand as an arbitrator of what is considered a good excuse from a poor excuse, particularly when such evaluations are going to be significantly informed by personal biases. Rather, in building my courses, I create flexibility in their design so that I never have to make such arbitrations. When I have weekly assignments, I drop a certain number of the lowest grades so that a few missed weeks won't directly affect students' grades. I have allowed students to sign up for weeks based on their own schedule so they can take on the responsibility of figuring out when the work is best for them based on their other courses and work schedules. I provide optional exams at the end of the semester so students who have really struggled have a chance at proving they really have understood the material despite their lack of mastery throughout the term.

And what I have anecdotally found is that students respond favourably. They can get work done to the best of their ability rather than constrained by time. They are less stressed and thus better able to think and write because there is flexibility. They are more responsive to my own stresses when I have to apologize for not getting something graded within the time frame I promised because of my own life getting in the way. As a group, we can be kinder, more patient, and more deeply engaged.

SOME OBJECTIONS

I have often had people ask me: "Won't students take advantage of your extension policy?" And the answer is of course "yes!" In fact, I hope they will! It is not something they can win or steal from me. To imply that someone is being taken advantage of means that there is something unfair about the practice in its outcomes, that someone will get more than their fair share. But I am giving all my students this opportunity. There will still be some students who cheat, but I am better able to meet them from a position of justice when I have already created a course in which lack of care is not a motivator for their decision to cheat. I have done all I can to ensure that my own choices do not create untenable positions for students where cheating is the only possible option they see. But this is radically different from assuming that students are guilty.

Another objection that I have encountered is that I am not helping prepare students for a world where they must meet deadlines. From this perspective, I am failing to properly meet the needs of my students by preparing them for the "real world." I acknowledge that the world of work that my students encounter is often uncaring. It is not often flexible, and the people they will work for will often not be willing to take their interests into account. However, I want to nurture a view of the world where you don't get fired for getting sick, or having to take care of children, or having a computer melt down. I do not want to train students to normalize a world where those in charge and who exercise power can't be decent and caring and where surveillance at work is routine and accepted. I cannot change the world so that bosses and those in power start from a position of empathy. But I can control how I respond to my students so that when they are having a bad day and need a break, I'm willing to be one who can give them that space to breathe. The ethics of care provides a framework for resistance to the idea that the world must be taken as it is.

And finally, there is the objection that in taking a care approach, we lose the academic rigour required of academic institutions. I am not taking the position that we do not have to address academic integrity. I am also not suggesting that we make work "easy" for students. Rather, I am suggesting that we create policies and structure our classes in ways that engage in meaningful learning such that we reduce the pressure to cheat and actually help students understand how to complete assignments. If we are nurturing our students, that includes ensuring they understand the values in academic learning communities and helping them learn how to properly engage in academic research. It also means that when we encounter cheating, we address it and make sure students see the values we are upholding.

SOME CAVEATS

While I think the ethics of care can be transformative for the work we do in higher education, there are some caveats and warnings. First, institutions are often not set up to make this practice easy for faculty. I am fortunate that I have relatively small classes. For faculty who have large classes, this approach can be difficult as caregiving is often burdensome and time consuming. This is where the care framework can be useful to identify where caring is going awry and where we can challenge those institutional arrangements. If higher education is about meeting the needs of students, then those needs should be a priority. This is a starting point for challenging how the workloads of faculty are arranged and how class sizes have become unmanageable for many.

There may also be institutional policies that dictate how courses and policies are designed, and these policies may not be starting from a caring framework. If an instructor works in a department where all sections are run in the same way, and they have little choice in how they design the class, then challenging these structures can be difficult. Institutionally, then, there can be roadblocks to enacting an ethics of care in teaching. However, this does not absolve people from the responsibility of advocating for the needs of their students. Tenured faculty and instructors with secured work should protest when institutions move towards implementing surveillance technologies and should refuse to use them in the classroom setting as much as they are able to. Letting students know where they stand on the use of these technologies can also be a way to signal one's commitment to meeting students' needs as best as one can.

Second, we must be very careful that in making policies that work for students, we do not create burdens for us that are unmanageable or unfairly distributed by those doing the work. To make my students' lives more manageable, I had decided not to meet with them all at the same time online for a full three hours as scheduled, as I thought that would be unreasonable. Instead, I broke the class up into small groups and met with each group for about half an hour each week, with recorded lectures and asynchronous activities taking place at their own pace throughout the week. It was a check-in to make sure people were engaged and could ask questions, and generally to make sure things were going smoothly. And I deliberately did this so they would not have to be in virtual meetings for three hours at a time. However, it meant no change for me. In attempting to combat Zoom fatigue, I ended up creating a situation for myself that was exhausting and not tenable. Once I realized this, I adjusted my schedule for the following semester. The ethics of care does not demand that we sacrifice our own well-being for others.

We must also look very carefully at who is being asked to do what kind of labour through the caring process. If the person who is designing the course passes on the caring work to teaching assistants, then the interests and needs in these relationships also must be considered. It is not enough to just look at the needs and interests of students. Instructors must examine how their practices impact on their own well-being and the well-being of those they supervise, such as research and teaching assistants. Departments must look at how class assignments have disparate impacts on contract versus full-time faculty, as well as adjunct versus permanent faculty. These relationships are part of the complex institutional structures that are relevant to the care being given to students.

CONCLUSION

The framework that I have identified and many of the issues and class policies I have discussed are not new. When I shifted to online teaching, none of my class policies changed. The online pandemic-driven environment, however, exacerbates existing issues and has created new ways for instructors to confront them, for better or for worse. Technology can be a way to increase access in new and exciting ways. For example, closed captioning in recorded lectures and audio files for written texts both increase accessibility. But technology can also be used to further divide and create burdens when policies and their impacts are not carefully thought through.

Adopting a care perspective instead of a justice approach gives instructors the opportunity to engage in fulfilling and exciting work. Faculty can be supportive of students while at the same time upholding the standards of education they desire. A commitment to an ethics of care requires an attitude of critical awareness when adopting technology and ultimately requires humane approaches to course development and implementation in online teaching.

QUESTIONS FOR DISCUSSION

1. Think about the times you have thought a teacher was caring or uncaring. What kinds of actions or reactions on the part of the teacher made you think that they did or did not care?

2. How did the pandemic affect your experience as a student? Did you have any in-person classes? Was it easier or more difficult to engage in academic work in person during this time? If you did online learning, were there aspects of online learning that made learning easier, for example, having access to recorded lectures to listen to again? Were there aspects that made learning more difficult?

3. Tomsons outlines four steps to Tronto's (1994) care process in this chapter. Take an example of a class policy in the class you are currently in. Does that class policy fit within the care process? What need is it identifying? How is it employed in the class? Who is doing the work required by the policy? Do you think it is a caring policy that meets the standards of good care?

INVITATIONS TO GO DEEPER

1. Tomsons focuses on the care responsibilities of teachers in this chapter. What are ways that an ethic of care could analyze the care responsibilities for students

in online environments? Consider the ways in which students interact with teachers, teaching assistants, and other students. How could an ethics of care framework change the way students view themselves in relation to others?

2. What are the ways in which surveillance is present in the technology you use? What reasons can you identify that would justify the use of technology in these ways? What reasons can you identify that would problematize the practice? Categorize the reasons you've identified as fitting within either a justice perspective or a perspective of an ethics of care. Which tend to justify surveillance, and which tend to say such practices are problematic?

3. Caring is generally thought to be morally good. But what are some ways in which care could go wrong? How could attempts at care end up creating morally problematic results? Consider who is doing what type of care in the caring process, where decisions might be made that could go wrong, and perhaps draw from experiences you have had where you could clearly see that someone was *trying* to care, but morally things went wrong.

READ MORE

Sander-Staudt, M. (n.d.). Care ethics. *Internet Encyclopedia of Philosophy.* https://iep.utm.edu/care-eth/

Schwartz, B. C., Gachago, D., & Belford, C. (2018). To care or not to care—Reflections on the ethics of blended learning in times of disruption. *South African Journal of Higher Education, 32*(6), 49–64. https://doi.org/10.20853/32-6-2659

LISTEN MORE, WATCH MORE

"The ethics of plagiarism detection," *Teaching in Higher Ed* podcast, December 2015: https://www.teachinginhighered.com/podcast/plagiarism-detection

"Let it break or be broken: Care, moral stress, and the university," ALT, 2021: https://www.youtube.com/watch?v=NBwZ4uKP_0g&t=1s

"A spirit of care with Maurice Hamilton," *Examining Ethics* podcast, April 2021: https://www.examiningethics.org/2021/04/maurice-hamington/

NOTES

1.   I discuss how institutions like businesses engage in care and how that care can go wrong in "Can Corporations Care?" (Tomsons, 2017).

2. This policy is grounded in a recognition that many students are uncomfortable approaching instructors for extensions. Those who do tend to be more confident, and requiring students to ask for extensions privileges those who may be more comfortable in college and university settings. First-generation students, for example, may not know that asking for an extension is possible and may not even try. Allowing for extensions that do not require the student to ask for them is thus another way to eliminate inequalities between students.

REFERENCES

Baier, A. (1994). *Moral prejudices: Essays on ethics.* Harvard University Press.

Burke, K., & Larmar, S. (2021). Acknowledging another face in the virtual crowd: Reimagining the online experience in higher education through an online pedagogy of care. *Journal of Further and Higher Education, 45*(5), 601–615.

Gilligan, C. (1982). *In a different voice: Psychological theory and women's development.* Harvard University Press.

Held, V. (2006). *The ethics of care: Personal, political, and global* (2nd ed.). Oxford University Press.

Kittay, E. (2020). *Learning from my daughter: The value and care of disabled minds.* Oxford University Press.

Noddings, N. (1986). *Caring: A feminine approach to ethics and moral education.* University of California Press.

Rabin, C. (2021). Care ethics in online teaching. *Studying Teacher Education, 17*(1), 38–56.

Respondus Inc. (2021, April 28). Respondus Monitor. https://web.respondus.com/he/monitor/

Rose, E., & Adams, C. (2014). "Will I ever connect with the students?": Online teaching and the pedagogy of care. *Phenomenology & Practice, 7*(2), 5–16.

Ruddick, S. (1995). *Maternal thinking: Toward a politics of peace.* Beacon Press.

Swauger, S. (2020, September 7). Software that monitors students during tests perpetuates inequality and violates their privacy. *MIT Technology Review.* https://www.technologyreview.com/2020/08/07/1006132/software-algorithms-proctoring-online-tests-ai-ethics/

Tomsons, K. (2017). Can corporations care? *The Canadian Society for Study of Practical Ethics/Société canadienne pour l'étude de l'éthique appliquée, 1,* 147–157.

Tovani, C. (2014). How we drive students to cheat. *Using Assessments Thoughtfully, 71*(6), 50–53.

Tronto, J. (1994). *Moral boundaries: A political argument for an ethic of care.* Routledge.

CHAPTER 14

Zines and Ezines as Holistic Technologies: DIY Feminism in the Transnational Classroom

Jaime Yard

INTRODUCTION

In her 1989 CBC Massey lectures, experimental physicist Ursula M. Franklin, writing at the dawn of the internet era, generated a series of vital questions we should still be asking about the technologies we adopt (Franklin, 1999). These were questions not only about particular capacities, but also about the social practices that are assembled in and through engaging technology:

> The distinction we need to make is between holistic technologies and prescriptive technologies. Again, we are considering technology as practice, but now we are looking at what is actually happening on the level of work. The categories of holistic and prescriptive technologies involve distinctly different specializations and divisions of labour, and consequently they have very different social and political implications. Let me emphasize that we are not asking what is being done, but how it is being done. (Franklin, 1999, p. 10)

Holistic technologies are those associated with "the notion of craft," where creative process and product are inseparable (Franklin, 1999, p. 10), while prescriptive technologies are administrative processes, economic activities, forms of governance and production that yield predictable results through sequential and standardized "*designs for compliance*" (Franklin, 1999, p. 16; emphasis in original). In this chapter, I want to present and reflect upon my experiences examining and making zines and ezines with gender, sexualities, and women's studies classes. I suggest that zines and ezines be considered as holistic, do-it-yourself (DIY) technologies with the capacity to refract prescriptive/contractual curriculum goals through the lived experiences and political commitments of our intersectional and transnational student populations. Further, I will argue that the DIY feminism materialized in zines and ezines might usefully move us away from Western English–centric assignments that inadvertently reinforce colonial raciolinguistic and gendered hierarchies in favour of new material and symbolic relationships in the classroom and beyond.

Writing presciently before the advent of social media, before even the widespread adoption of now-antiquated tools such as email, Franklin (1999) addressed the Canadian nation with an urgent plea to consider what *has been*, and *is being*, lost with the increased dominance of prescriptive technologies in our societies. Holistic technologies, she argued, incorporate relations of care for both human and non-human beings. They require reciprocity and responsiveness to the liveliness of matters in the moment. "Such tasks," she warns, "cannot be planned, coordinated, and controlled in the way prescriptive tasks must be" (p. 17). She is quick to note that prescriptive technologies are often "exceedingly effective and efficient" but "come with an enormous social mortgage" (p. 17): the loss of our creativity and agency, both individually and collectively, in processes of production.

I should note from the outset that I am not a *zinester*, a term that refers to those who make and trade zines. Or at least I wasn't before I started the work with my classes I discuss in this chapter. I am female, in my forties, and white. I was born in Vancouver, British Columbia, and I am a monolingual English speaker. My training is as a social anthropologist with a specialization in the interdisciplinary field of political ecology. I travelled obliquely towards teaching in gender, sexualities, and women's studies. My published academic analyses of gender have historically focused on the social and material construction of masculinities in resource extraction labour in British Columbia. My feminism has been learned and practised iteratively over the course of my life and education and is constantly changing as a result of conversations with my daughters (ages 13 and 18) and my students. My interest in DIY movements began from an early age through my family's involvement with Circle Craft, the largest artisan's marketing co-operative in Western Canada.[1]

ZINES AND DIY FEMINISM

The production of zines for grassroots feminist expression and their potential for pedagogical use has become, at this point, a rich and storied tradition that embodies some of the active tensions between academic and activist feminisms (Creasap,

2014; Duncombe, 1997; Guzzetti & Gamboa, 2004; Honma, 2016; Licona, 2012; Piepmeier, 2009; Potter & Sellie, 2016; Schilt, 2003; Spiers, 2015). Various origin stories are attached to zine production and circulation. The "fanzine" genre is often traced back to punk culture in Britain in the 1970s, while in third-wave pop-feminist histories, fanzines and "perzines" are linked to the Riot Grrrl movement of the 1990s percolating out from Washington, DC, across North America (Duncombe, 1997; Piepmeier, 2009; Poletti, 2005). While some zine studies scholars trace the genre even further to science fiction fanzines of the 1930s–1950s (Brouwer & Licona, 2016) or even to the *Ninety-Five Theses* of Martin Luther in 1517 (Zobl, 2004), the exact history and boundaries of the genre are perhaps less important to trace than the overarching ethos of zine production and circulation.

Zine and ezine production are commonly cited as a prime example of DIY anti-authoritarian culture (Poletti, 2005). Anna Poletti, a professor of English language and culture at Utrecht University, describes DIY culture as those forms of production and circulation that defy and disrupt consumer capitalism from the margins in such forms as "squatting, graffiti cultures, independent music, community event organizing (festivals, parties, conferences), political and cultural activism, community gardens, culture jamming, 'hacktivism,' and independent media" (Poletti, 2005, p. 185). A standout commonality between these diffuse practices is the refusal of the separation of those who produce from those who consume culture and the deliberate establishment of participatory communities of practice (Poletti, 2005). Zines and ezines challenge the idea that the value of writing and art is to be found in the commodity price (or, for zines in the classroom, the grade) assigned, prioritizing instead an ethic of not-for-profit reciprocal exchange of ideas and the intrinsic value of creative activity.

R. Seth Friedman, the long-term editor and publisher of *Factsheet Five*, a San Francisco–based "mega-zine" that from 1982 to 1998 published reviews of thousands of zines, has argued that zines should be seen not as "marginal works of cultural ethnography, but as serious periodicals that use a journalistic style to reinvent non-fiction writing outside the marketplace of publishing" (Niedzviecki, 1997, p. D11).[2] There is no doubt that the content and quality of zines varies widely. As printmaker and senior lecturer of art and design at the University of New South Wales, Michelle Kempson (2015) observes that zinesters are not a unified movement any more than the oft-cited feminist waves are. However, as Stephen Duncombe (1997), professor of media and culture at New York University, summarizes, "saying what's on your mind, unbeholden to corporate sponsors, puritan censors, or professional standards of argument and design, being yourself and expressing your real thoughts and real feelings—these are what zinesters consider authentic" (p. 38).

"ZINES IN THIRD SPACE" AND AS "ARTS OF THE CONTACT ZONE"

While some early scholarly work assessing the zine highlights the exclusivity and racial and socio-economic privilege of many zinesters and their publications from the 1970s through the 1990s (Duncombe, 1997), more recent writing has focused on the proliferation of zine production by women, queer, transgender, marginalized, and diasporic populations (Brouwer & Licona, 2016; Capistrano, 2021; Licona, 2012; Miller & Wilde, 2021). In her book *Zines in Third Space: Radical Cooperation and Borderland Rhetoric*, Adela Licona (2012), a professor of English at the University of Arizona, argues for the conceptual utility of "third space" as an interpretive tool for understanding the "pursuit of social change, the building of community, and the participation in community action" pursued through zines (p. 23). By *third space*, Licona wishes to highlight how zines create space for the articulation and representation of "reimagined and re-membered" (p. 8) subjectivities that are often elided in mainstream media and politics. She elaborates:

> It is the lived condition of crossing borders and existing in the realm of both/ and together that allows for the conscious movement into the creative terrain of third space. Third space is an interstitial space of intersection and overlap, ambiguity and contradiction, that materializes a subversion to either/or ways of being and reproducing knowledge. It is an epistemological as well as an ontological space revealing ways of knowing and being in the world. Third-space ways of knowing and being defy the values that are implicated in the "authentic," the "proper," and the "pure." In short, third space is a space that materializes what borders serve to divide, subordinate and obscure. In rhetorical terms, it is the space within which borderlands rhetorics circulate and materialize third-space consciousness. (p. 11)

Vitally, this third space is not defined by a liberal politics of promoting inclusion into an already defined political sphere, but rather, it draws our attention to the always already-existing occupations of space by rich intersectional worlds. For Licona, third space as an ontological space asserts the need to recognize our structural locations of systemic privilege and/or exclusion without surrendering our political agency to them, while third space as an epistemological space amplifies the articulation of experiential knowledges that mainstream academic and popular circuits have yet to sufficiently engage with. Third space thus defined calls out the lie that an ever-expanding liberal tent can encompass us all equally without substantially shifting the comfort of those at the centre. Third space is "indeterminate and constructive," the terrain where "dis/similar" (Licona, 2012, p. 14) subjects can construct "differential consciousness" (p. 9) and tactical collective identities.

Licona's conception of third-space rhetoric was usefully prefigured in "Arts of the Contact Zone," a 1991 article by retired New York University professor of Spanish and Portuguese languages and literatures Mary Louise Pratt. Through consideration of autoethnographic texts (of which many zines might be considered a genre or akin[3]), Pratt (1991) raises a vital critique of the simplistic and utopian "ideas of community that underlie much of the thinking about language, communication and culture that gets done in the academy" (p. 37). She suggests that all too often, linguistic and classroom communities are imagined as "discrete, self-defined, coherent entities, held together by homogenous grammar shared identically and equally among all the members" (p. 37). Pratt urges that we must hold on to the heterogeneity of the contexts from which texts are produced and in which they are consumed.

Here, I think of the dozens of English dialects congregating in classrooms—evolved and learned in dozens of countries around the world—as they are employed, prescriptively and/or holistically, to produce course assignments. While the language of instruction and assessment at the college where I teach is English, I make no assumption that English as a medium of exchange is, should, or can be a closed set of automatically comprehensible signs. The complex linguistic terrain of teaching and learning here illustrates directly and allegorically the decolonial challenges of the intersectional and transnational feminist classroom: no prescriptive mechanism exists to render the acts of communicative translation between teacher and student, and students with one another, homogeneous (or at least it evades me). Pratt (1991) suggests, and I take the liberty of paraphrasing, that when we assume "linguistic (or literate)" (p. 38) interactions occur according to shared games and scripts, what we are able to see and understand will always already be foreclosed within dominant discourse: a classroom dynamic governed by norms of linguistic and cultural codes and competencies checked against a standardized model. Here, as in my introduction, I use the term *standardized* quite consciously, drawing upon linguistic anthropologist Jonathan Rosa's ground-breaking book, *Looking Like a Language, Sounding Like a Race: Raciolinguistic Ideologies and the Learning of Latinidad* (2019), which emphasizes the colonial and racialized violence inherent in standardization of assessments of linguistic competency.

In contrast to the presumption of shared meanings and political solidarities, Pratt (1991) offers the metaphor of classrooms and communities as "contact zones": places where the normative cannot be presumed but must be interrogated, negotiated, and re-presented (p. 37). Imagine, and here I continue to adapt and paraphrase Pratt's (1991) logic for the classroom context, if we instead imagined a scenario of iteration—of our personal, political, and pedagogical commitments— in which a group of assembled people all speak and understand multiple languages but that they are never precisely the same ones. How then might we think about communicative practices in the classroom differently? And isn't this precisely the communicative context in the transnational and intersectional feminist classroom: where what it means to live in a sexed and gendered body cannot be presumed; where the embodied knowledge we carry with us is as much a terrain of discovery ("the personal is political") as the content of our lectures and texts?

ZINES AS INTERSECTIONAL AND TRANSNATIONAL FEMINIST TECHNOLOGY

I suggest that zines and ezines in, and from, the classroom keep opportunities for transformational learning open and resist the slide of syllabus learning objectives into static prescriptive technologies. Zines and ezines assemble pathways for engagement with the multitude of possible conversations and connections present in—and pathways to and from—our classrooms. Of course, not all present pathways can, or will, be explored in the space of a semester-long course, but in the social justice-oriented "intro to," we can provide a series of provocative trail markers that gesture beyond the edges of the syllabus map. DIY feminist creative assignments can be a means to refract course readings and discussions through students' lives and experiences and to encourage more diverse communicative praxis in the contact zone.

In his reflections on incorporating zines as tools for a class community action research project on gentrification of Los Angeles's Chinatown, Pitzer College Associate Professor of Asian American studies Todd Honma argues that while some zine studies scholars have characterized zines as "pre-political" chronicles of the effects of structural inequities (cf. Duncombe, 1997), zines might be more usefully framed as "a vehicle for emerging political consciousness" (Honma, 2016, p. 42). For Honma, zines are a "form of participatory culture, challenging students to think beyond hegemonic educational strategies that reproduce atomistic learning" (p. 41). Honma exposed his students to *Gidra*, a periodical of Asian American activism that ran from 1969 to 1974, and the accounts contained therein, of the long history of Asian exclusion in LA.[4] This archival work provided context to prepare the students for door-to-door community action work educating Chinatown residents about tenants' rights. Honma was able not only to connect his students learning to the broader LA community but also to disrupt some of the default raciolinguistic privilege of monolingual English students who now had to rely on their better-positioned multilingual peers to connect with seniors and low-income residents with limited English proficiency (Honma, 2016).

Instructors might follow the lead of zinesters in a turn towards DIY publication for many reasons. Kempson (2015) argues, with reference to the work of University of New Orleans sociologist Susan Archer Mann and Douglas J. Huffman,[5] that zinesters are guided by an "adherence to a specific set of moral, and behavioural, codes broadly focusing on the autonomous enactment of (feminist) cultural production, and the search for a more diversified feminist history that takes into account 'how theories of emancipation can be blind to their own dominating, exclusive and restrictive tendencies'" (Archer Mann & Huffman, as cited in Kempson, 2015, p. 468).

Much of the literature on zines and ezines emphasizes the empowerment of self and community that can come through DIY publication (Clark-Parsons, 2017; Honma, 2016; Piepmeier, 2009). However, this comes into awkward contact with the experiences of so-called Gen Z students who have been reared in the era of hyper-self-objectification and self-curation on corporate social media. Collaborative zine production can create space for a vital dialogue with students about the limitations of these prescriptive corporate social media platforms and their profit imperatives.

Many zinesters model ethics of reciprocity that actively resist monetization for profit. An excellent example of this can be found in the *Voices: Indigenous Women on the Front Lines Speak* series of 10 zines that contain interviews with Two-Spirit and women land defenders from the front lines of Pacific Northwest resource extraction conflicts. The editors of the series, beyon wren moor and Wulfgang Zapf (2021), offer sliding-scale access to their zines and donate all profits to the land defenders profiled in the series (https://www.voicesfrontlines.com/work-with-us/). Rather than present their zine series as a one-time purchase, the *Voices* editors encourage active discussion with them about any pedagogical use or circulation of the zine series, mindful of the danger of appropriation or misrepresentation of the stories they are attempting to amplify. As a guest speaker in one of my classes, Wulfgang Zapf underscored to the students that they felt entrusted to care for the stories shared with them and that this was an ongoing responsibility, not a matter of a one-time "informed consent" release form. The *Voices* zines can only introduce the reader to stories told at a particular point in histories that are much longer and ongoing.

WHOSE AUTHORITY? ZINES, EZINES, AND SOURCE ASSESSMENT SKILLS

Pedagogically speaking, I echo here the observation of library studies scholars who note that in our era of corporate consolidation of not only network media but also scholarly publication platforms, we need to work harder to relay critical information assessment skills to our students. Zines give librarians and classroom instructors an opportunity to move away from "simplistic claims that certain sources are 'authoritative' because authorities have decided they are" and to transfer skills for holistic and ongoing evaluation of information (Potter & Sellie, 2016, p. 117). Further, ezines and digitized zines can be used to actively respond to the shocking data presented by Acey et al. (2021) and the Whose Knowledge? campaign. Here, I will cite at length their work on both "general" and peer-reviewed knowledge available on the web:

> Seventy-five percent of the world's online population is from the global South and nearly half is projected to be women. Yet public knowledge on the internet—exemplified by Wikipedia—is primarily constructed by (white) men from western Europe and North America. One in ten Wikipedia editors are estimated to self-identify as female. In other words, the internet of the majority is produced by the minority. (Acey et al., 2021, p. 1)

> What is published and where is often predicated on privilege: as we have estimated, only about 7 percent of the world's seven thousand languages are captured in published material (Graham and Sengupta 2017).… Ninety percent of all social science and science journals indexed on Scopus and JSTOR are published in English (Albarillo, 2014; Glänzl et al., 2019). Additionally, the stories and scholarship of marginalized communities have rarely been acknowledged on par with these privileged sources and, in many cases, are actively undermined. (p. 3)

The Whose Knowledge? project seeks to actively decolonize and diversify web content and problematize the idea that webpages are written with a "neutral point of view" (NPOV) (one of the fundamental principles of Wikipedia). Acey et al. (2021) justifiably point out that the NPOV standard asks editors to perform what Donna Haraway, professor emerita in history of consciousness and feminist studies at the University of California Santa Cruz, refers to as "the god trick" (1998, p. 582), where knowledge is severed from both knowers and the contexts of its emergence. Anyone who has ever hunted in vain for an author of a webpage to cite to hold accountable for questionable information, or even to contact with a question, has likely experienced the uncanny feeling that there is more to the story than what appears. The omission of the human aspect of knowledge production from the web presents a dangerous veneer of a NPOV that is all too readily accepted in the name of efficiency.

At the other end of the continuum are zines and ezines with often brash communication that is decidedly linked to (g)local and particular people and histories. Licona (2012) argues that there are three overlapping primary functions of zines: (1) "zines are consciously pursuing coalitions to imagine and build communities based on shared affinities and a conscious and coalitional desire for social change"; (2) "zines are innovating new rhetorical strategies to address sex and gender"; and (3) "zines are enacting and provoking quotidian transformations in terms of production and consumption" (p. 23). In the digitization of zines and the production of ezines, new ways of inhabiting the web that respond to the limitations of NPOV writing are being explored.

It is important to note, however, that some zinesters and zine studies scholars are explicitly dismissive of the ezine form (Hays, 2017, p. 87), holding fast to a hand-to-hand paper process and transfer as integral to the definition and culture of zines. Many paper zines are aesthetically innovative and creatively constructed, meant "to be read and shared until they fall apart" (Woodbrook & Lazzaro, 2013, as cited in Brouwer & Licona, 2016, p. 71). The communities that such print copies draw together are dependent upon happenstance encounters in independent bookstores and cafés, personal relationships of hand-to-hand transfer at zine fairs, and networks of friends and acquaintances. However, as zine production rules have traditionally been that *there are no rules*, most zinesters are actively grappling with the tensions between zine and ezine overlap and divergence—rather than rejecting the latter outright. While potential losses might be experienced in the transmediation—the process of translating a work into a different medium—of paper to ezine production and distribution, there are also new connections that might be forged and spatially diffuse communities that might be networked.

ZINES FOR FEMINIST PRACTICE IN THE CLASSROOM AND BEYOND

My first experiences of zine making were with my gender, sexualities, and women's studies students over two semesters in 2020. My only prior experiences in publishing for a popular audience were as an undergraduate when I held a part-time job

(1999–2001) working as an office assistant at *Adbusters* magazine. Desirous of a broader audience for my students' work, I raised the idea with them of assembling a zine anthology of works from class. The DIY idea that our zine did not have to be overly polished or neutral appealed to me as a way to extend the critical feminist scholarship examined in the class to the world beyond.[6] Students responded positively to the idea. Three students, Kassia DeSouza, Madeleine Mei-Ling, and Akshayaa Ravindrababu, volunteered to edit submissions from their classmates and assemble the final copy of the first collaborative zine. A former student, Sarah McCarthy, came to the class to share what they had learned about self-publishing from their experience of editing a Creative Commons–hosted feminist student journal at Simon Fraser University and graciously volunteered as a student mentor for the project. Given the sensitive content of some of the personal stories shared, we agreed from the outset that pen names could be used to protect the identities of those who wished to publish anonymously. The primary audience for the zine would be the class itself and those friends, family, and community members we wished to share it with. We imagined the zine as an archive of the individual and collective explorations pursued in the class at a particular point in our lives and history. We also planned to circulate a few copies around our campuses and our broader community via "little libraries," those tiny shelters for free literature scattered around our neighbourhoods, which lent our zine its name: the *Little Feminist Zine.*[7]

When our class was rapidly shifted from face-to-face to online instruction with the government-mandated lockdown upon the outbreak of the COVID-19 pandemic, we pivoted to transform our physical cut-paste-and-copy plans to a digital platform. Our publication was now proceeding through remote meetings and web searching our way to rudimentary competency with Adobe InDesign. Some of the editors worked with "free" web-based publishing tools, but we assembled the final copies with the use of our college's software licence, which conferred greater privacy to our authors and control over the layout. The eventual zine produced is now hosted by Arca, an online digital repository of work from BC post-secondary institutions thanks to the support and guidance of Douglas College librarian, Gretchen Goertz (see Figure 14.1). The ezine experiment was then repeated in the fall 2020 semester under the leadership of volunteer student editors Lovepreet Smagh and Samiksha Chand.

It would be absurd to suggest that a collective zine, overseen by an instructor endowed with the responsibility to assign grades, could be a fully egalitarian endeavour. As there was no way around the fact of inequality within our editorial team, it was left to us to negotiate roles so that both the requirement of the institution, for me to assign grades, and the ideals of feminist praxis, to bring

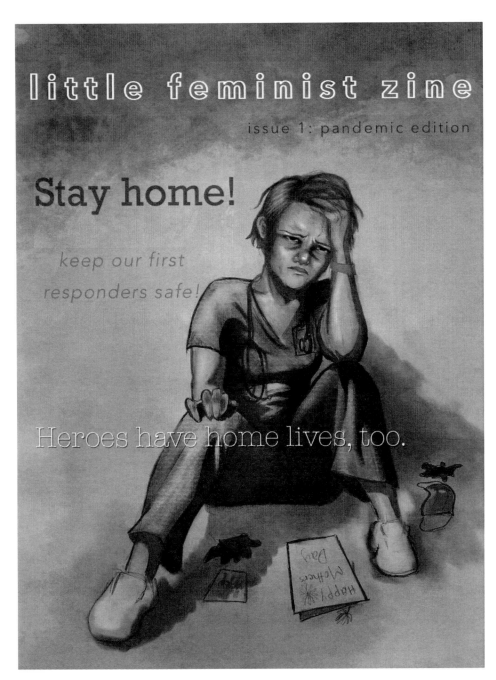

Figure 14.1: *Little Feminist Zine* Issue 1: Pandemic Edition. Original art by Jacqueline Atkinson.

our skills to the table and collaborate, might be reasonably respected. The project utterly depended upon the student editors believing that the intrinsic value of zine production compensated for some ambiguity around how their grades would be determined. The submissions from peers that the editors worked with were assessed for grades independently of the zine-making process. To me, it seemed that some of the most valuable learning for the students was in engaging with their peers about editorial decisions of layout and content. Of course, this kind of negotiation is a part of group work in many classes, but the personal nature of many of the contributions to the zines added additional layers of care and complexity to the conversations we had. With both editorial teams, anxieties about altering submissions from their peers were expressed. More than once, trepidation turned to deep mutual appreciation between authors and editors through the process of editing to clarify the prose and pair appropriate imagery. I think students benefited from the feedback of their peers in ways they would not have from instructor comments and a grade alone.

The contributions to our zines were drawn from class assignments, including but not limited to profiles of feminist icons, activists, and organizations; letters of apology and consolation to body parts terrorized by the "bikini industrial complex" (Nagoski & Nagoski, 2020, p. 151); critical reviews of gendered representations in popular media; "coming of age" autoethnographies; and found poems and infographics about reproductive justice. As already noted, we offered authors the opportunity to publish under a pen name, but our authors were not anonymous to the editorial team. This demanded a great deal of care and trust in author–editor and student–teacher relationships. At all stages of the writing and editing process, zine contributors were prompted to be mindful of their own comfort level with self-disclosure. As an editorial team, we worked to enhance the clarity of contributions without losing the particular voices and stories of our authors. This work demonstrated to us that zine production can help generate experience tackling the tensions between academic and activist feminisms and even be activism by facilitating all students to express their experiences and stories in an accessible format.

The ezines we made are web hosted with no comments section. We retain the ability to remove or suppress articles if at any time one of our contributors wants their work taken down. We do not invite the worst of the internet to come visit us or judge our success by the quantity of hits we get in the ways that corporate social media does. The ezines will only come up in a web search if you know what you are looking for or have been directed there (visit https://arcabc.ca/ and search "Little

Feminist Zine"). They are not meant to "go viral." The culture of zine circulation has never been maximalist. While corporate social media stresses feedback—likes and shares—zine circulation stresses reciprocity. Franklin (1999) elucidates this distinction: feedback is about "systems adjustment" and "improvement" but it "normally exists within a given design" (p. 43). Whereas reciprocity behaves according to only semi-predictable patterns, "reciprocal responses may indeed alter initial assumptions. They can lead to negotiations, to give and take, to adjustment, and they may result in new and unforeseen developments" (Franklin 1999, p. 43). As any cultural anthropologist will tell you, reciprocity is what all of the social and ecological relations that sustain us are made of. It's a part of both the foundation and aspiration of communication with others.

CONCLUSION

Can zines and ezines be technologies of resistance to the deepening structural and representative inequalities in our worlds? Can we create paper and e-nooks of reflection, recognition, and revitalization? In this chapter, I have traced some of the active debates in zine studies scholarship and relayed my own experiences with DIY feminist publication from the classroom. I wish now to end where I began, in dialogue with Ursula Franklin and her dichotomy of prescriptive versus holistic technologies. While I have by no means resolved any of the tensions inherent in bringing what I believe to have been holistic encounters with DIY publication into classrooms that still bear the prescriptive requirement of graded accreditation, I would like to think that this chapter has underscored Franklin's emphasis on engagement with the human and social impacts of technologies. I am not so naive as to suggest that we have no need for prescriptive technologies, in the classroom or elsewhere. The software tools we used to produce our zines wouldn't work if they didn't have a lot of prescriptive parameters. As Franklin (1999) suggests, we should always base our evaluation of the technologies we employ on our experiences in the "real world of technology," not on the utopian promises made or believed about it. I expect the perspectives of all of the contributors to our classroom zines to change over time, but this does not undo the value of marking a particular juncture in their "emergent political consciousness" (Honma, 2016, p. 42) and my own. After all, the particular ideas and experiences we have archived were formed in the contingencies of intersubjective and historically situated encounters. I plan to continue to examine and produce zines and ezines in my classes and invite correspondence from others doing likewise.

QUESTIONS FOR DISCUSSION

1. What examples of prescriptive and/or holistic technologies can you come up with from your own everyday life and experience? What are your positive and negative experiences of each?

2. What is your understanding of Adela Licona's (2012) conception of third space? Do you find it a useful concept to think with? Why or why not?

3. Would your classroom experiences be different if you were able to use all of the languages you speak for discussions and assignments? How? What do you think you might learn about yourself and your peers?

4. How have you been taught to assess information and sources for validity (the internal consistency and accuracy of information) and reliability (the consistency of a measure or outcome)? What skills would you like to build? Who could help you?

5. Do you have any experiences reading or making zines? If so, what are they? Do you know of any bookstores or zine fairs in your community?

INVITATIONS TO GO DEEPER

1. Want to try making a zine? Here are some good starting places:
   - How to Make This Very Zine (2004–present): "First created in 2004, *How To Make This Very Zine* is a single-page eight-fold set of instructions for making itself. It has since been translated into Arabic, Greek, German, Georgian, Khmer, Russian and Spanish." This is a good introduction to the tactility and accessibility of the paper zine form. https:// anneelizabethmoore.com/how-to-make-this-very-zine/
   - The Creative Independent, "How to Make a Zine": A useful introduction guide to the practicalities and ethics of zine making. https:// thecreativeindependent.com/guides/how-to-make-a-zine/

2. Interested in reading and exploring the tremendous diversity of digitized paper zines and ezines? Or ordering some by mail? Here are some great places to start:
   - People of Color Zine Project: "POC Zine Project's mission is to makes ALL zines by POC (People of Color) easy to find, distribute and share. We are an experiment in activism and community through materiality." https://poczineproject.tumblr.com/
   - Queer Zine Archive Project: "The Queer Zine Archive Project (QZAP) was first launched in November 2003 in an effort to preserve queer zines

and make them available to other queers, researchers, historians, punks, and anyone else who has an interest DIY publishing and underground queer communities." https://www.qzap.org/v9/index.php

- The Barnard Zine Library: the longest and most established post-secondary zine collection and zine research and teaching resource page. https://zines.barnard.edu/
- Broken Pencil: a quarterly "mega-zine dedicated exclusively to exploring independent creative action." https://brokenpencil.com/

READ MORE

Franklin, U. M. (1999). *The real world of technology* (rev. ed.). House of Anansi Press.

Haraway, D. (1988). Situated knowledges: The science question in feminism and the privilege of partial perspective. *Feminist Studies, 14*(3), 575–599. http://www.jstor.org/stable/3178066

Honma, T. (2016). From archives to action: Zines, participatory culture, and community engagement in Asian America. *Radical Teacher: A Socialist, Feminist, and Anti-Racist Journal on the Theory and Practice of Teaching, 105*, 34–43. https://doi.org/10.5195/rt.2016.277

Licona, A. C. (2012). *Zines in third space radical cooperation and borderland rhetoric.* State University of New York Press.

LISTEN MORE, WATCH MORE

There are no girls on the internet podcast, with Bridget Todd: https://www.tangoti.com/

Whose voices? podcast: https://podcast.whoseknowledge.org/

NOTES

1. My father made his living before retirement as a candlemaker and general manager of Circle Craft.

2. Hal Niedzviecki founded *Broken Pencil,* the Canadian equivalent to *Factsheet Five,* in 1995.

3. Both zine creation and autoethnography involve narrating personal and collective experiences and the broader social, historical, economic, and political context that have shaped these experiences. There are few formal, or even operational, definitions around of autoethnography. Just like zines, it is easier to point to examples of the genre than it is to define it.

4. The entire run of *Gidra* is hosted by the Densho Archives (http://www.densho.org).

5. I could not verify any additional information for Douglas J. Huffman online other than at the time of writing the article cited by Kemper, they were a resident of Newport Beach, California.

6. I know I am not the first instructor to feel responsible to the tremendous privilege of access— to life histories and experiences—that comes with being the recipient of term papers and final projects. Especially in classes that explicitly challenge students to confront not only particular histories and theories but also the unlearning of various internalized dominant cultural scripts, the need to keep assignments from becoming transactional—grading for word count and specific name and theory checking—is pressing. This is not to say that there is no content to be delivered, internalized, and properly referenced, but rather, the content might be more usefully encountered as a new set of tools to *play with* rather than received as a trophy for display on a shelf (or social media Slacktivism/virtue signaling).

7. For the second issue of the *Little Feminist Zine*, we opted to use LFZ as a masthead lest people take the word *little* as a descriptor of the ideas within that are anything but.

REFERENCES

Acey, C. E., Bouterse, S., Ghoshal, S., Menking, A., Sengupta, A., & Vrana, A. G. (2021). Decolonizing the internet by decolonizing ourselves: Challenging epistemic injustice through feminist practice. *Global Perspectives*, *2*(1), Article 21268. https://doi.org/10.1525/gp.2021.21268

Brouwer, D. C., & Licona, A. (2016). Trans(affective) mediation: Feeling our way from paper to digitized zines and back again. *Critical Studies in Media Communication*, *33*(1), 70–83. https://doi.org/10.1080/15295036.2015.1129062

Capistrano, D. (2021). *People of color zine project.* https://poczineproject.tumblr.com/

Clark-Parsons, R. (2017). Feminist ephemera in a digital world: Theorizing zines as networked feminist practice. *Communication, Culture and Critique*, *10*(4), 557–573. https://doi.org/10.1111/cccr.12172

Creasap, K. (2014). Zine making as feminist pedagogy. *Feminist Teacher*, *24*(3), 155–168. https://doi.org/10.5406/femteacher.24.3.0155

Duncombe, S. (1997). *Notes from underground: Zines and the politics of alternative culture.* Verso.

Franklin, U. M. (1999). *The real world of technology* (rev. ed.). House of Anansi Press.

Guzzetti, B. J., & Gamboa, M. (2004). Zines for social justice: Adolescent girls writing on their own. *Reading Research Quarterly*, *39*(4), 408–436. https://doi.org/10.1598/RRQ.39.4.4

Hays, A. (2017). Reading the margins: Embedded narratives in feminist personal zines. *The Journal of Popular Culture*, *50*(1), 86–108. https://doi.org/10.1111/jpcu.12504

Honma, T. (2016). From archives to action: Zines, participatory culture, and community engagement in Asian America. *Radical Teacher: A Socialist, Feminist, and Anti-Racist Journal on the Theory and Practice of Teaching, 105*, 34–43. https://doi.org/10.5195/rt.2016.277

Kempson, M. (2015). "My version of feminism": Subjectivity, DIY and the feminist zine. *Social Movement Studies Journal of Social, Cultural and Political Protest, 14*(4), 459–472. http://dx.doi.org/10.1080/14742837.2014.945157

Licona, A. C. (2012). *Zines in third space: Radical cooperation and borderland rhetoric*. State University of New York Press.

Miller, M., & Wilde, C. (2021). Queer zine archive project. https://www.qzap.org/v9/index.php

moor, b. w., & Zapf, W. (2021). Who we are. *Voices: Indigenous women on the front lines speak*. https://www.voicesfrontlines.com/whoweare/

Nagoski, E., & Nagoski, A. (2020). *Burnout: The secret to unlocking the stress cycle*. Penguin Random House.

Niedzviecki, H. (1997, August 23). Zines: Culture from the fringe. *Globe and Mail*, p. D11.

Piepmeier, A. (2009). *Girl zines: Making media, doing feminism*. New York University Press.

Poletti, A. (2005). Self-publishing in the global and local: Situating life writing in zines. *Biography, 28*(1), 183–192. https://www.jstor.org/stable/23541120

Potter, R., & Sellie, A. (2016). Zines in the classroom: Critical librarianship and participatory collections. In N. Pagowsky & K. McElroy (Eds.), *Critical library pedagogy handbook, volume 2: Lesson plans* (pp. 117–124). American Library Association.

Pratt, M. L. (1991). Arts of the contact zone. *Profession*, 33–40. https://www.jstor.org/stable/25595469

Rosa, J. (2019). *Looking like a language, sounding like a race: Raciolinguistic ideologies and the learning of Latinidad*. Oxford University Press.

Schilt, K. (2003). "I'll resist with every inch and every breath": Girls and zine making as a form of resistance. *Youth and Society, 35*(1), 71–97. https://doi.org/10.1177/0044118X03254566

Spiers, E. (2015). "Killing ourselves is not subversive": Riot Grrrl from zine to screen and the commodification of female transgression. *Women: A Cultural Review, 26*(1–2), 1–21. https://doi.org/10.1080/09574042.2015.1035021

Zobl, E. (2004). *Grrrl zine network*. http://www.grrrlzines.net/overview.htm

CONCLUSION

Coming Home to the Future: Start, Pause, Repeat …

Jennifer Jill Fellows and Lisa Smith

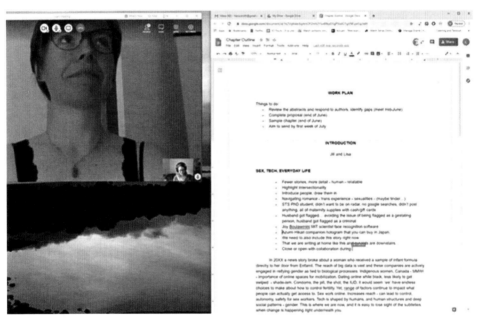

Figure 15.1: A Zoom Meeting with Jill Fellows and Lisa Smith Drafting the First Plan of This Book in Google Docs

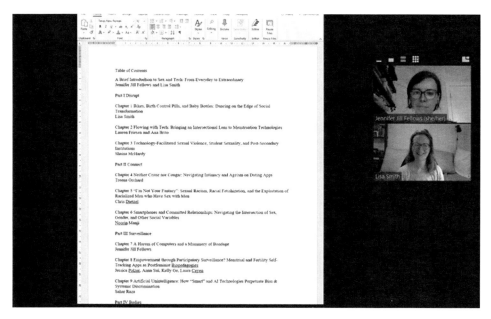

Figure 15.2: A Zoom Meeting with Jill Fellows and Lisa Smith Drafting the Final Table of Contents for This Book in Word

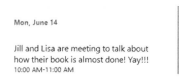

Mon, June 14

Jill and Lisa are meeting to talk about
how their book is almost done! Yay!!!
10:00 AM-11:00 AM

Figure 15.3: A Scheduled Zoom Meeting near the End of the Process of Pulling Together the Full Manuscript for This Book

START

It is amazing to us that this book is coming into being at all! Despite living in the same geographical region—we (Jill and Lisa)—have not been in the same physical space since February 2020. It is now, as we write this, June 2021, which means that much of the work of creating this book was done during the 2020 COVID-19 global pandemic (a fact that is reflected in many of the chapters). As we wrote this manuscript, existing inequalities were thrown into sharp relief around the world in a violent and brutal fashion as race, class, physical location, and gender became deciding factors in life and death. The impact of the COVID-19 pandemic is not only about health, and the casualties extend across our global community, impacting employment security, access to health and health care, mental health and social connection, and the basic necessities of life. Against this backdrop, technology was presented as a great lifeline as many people's work, education, social life, and family connections were pushed online. But this narrative of technology as a great saviour should be questioned and examined carefully—as authors have shown throughout this collection.

We wrote this text using a range of digital tools, from Google Docs to Zoom, to emails, to text messages, and even old-fashioned phone calls. We did it while both parenting children who were underfoot as daycares closed (affecting Jill's daughter) and schools shifted online (affecting Lisa's two sons and partner). In one respect, this rapid shift online may be celebrated by feminists as the invisible care work that has disproportionately fallen to women has now been made all too visible (as several of Jill's students were aware when her daughter made surprise cameos during her class). But though the care work has become visible in some aspects, little else has changed. Though we celebrate frontline care workers, many of whom are lower socio-economic status racialized women, we still expect them to work in increasingly dangerous jobs for very little pay and with little security. In addition, globally, women left the workforce in droves during the 2020 pandemic precisely because of the burden of care they now faced as schools and daycares closed. So, yes, care work has been highlighted for just how crucial it is, both paid and unpaid. But highlighting this importance has not, at the time of writing, led to any significant change and has placed a great number of people under a huge amount of stress—and in some cases risk.

The impacts of the pandemic have not been experienced or felt in the same way by everyone, and it has certainly affected the way this book came together in ways we could not have imagined as we sat in a coffee shop in Vancouver brainstorming one sunny December morning in 2019. But in some ways, releasing this book at this time seems just right. Now, more than ever, people are keenly aware of the effect that technology has on their lived experiences—for better and for worse. We hope that the theories, ideas, and concepts discussed in this volume can help serve as a guide to a critical analysis of tech and its use both in the age of the COVID-19 pandemic and beyond.

PAUSE

As we draw the text to a close, once again, we invite you, the reader, to take a moment to pause. Take time to digest what has been learned, consider the questions that have been raised, and identify areas for further exploration. There are many. The richness of this text comes from the many scholars who shared their wisdom, knowledge, lives, and experiences with us, for which we are so grateful. This text contains a lot of information from a multitude of authors in a variety of disciplines. It's a lot! It is important to take time to let these ideas settle. To this end, we invite the reader to return to the objective of this collection—to act as a guide for thinking about and synthesizing a range of pressing issues that relate to gender, sex, and tech. As we highlighted in the introduction, this collection is by no means an exhaustive reflection of all that could be said. During your pause, you should feel free to add or amend as needed by producing your own contributions to this field.

What Is Technology?

One thing we hope these chapters have encouraged you to do is see the world around you from a fresh perspective and recognize that technologies are everywhere, impacting us in multiple ways every day. We are, in the information age, fairly comfortable with addressing and identifying digital tech. But we may not be so quick to identify bicycles or menstrual pads as technological innovations that can have profound effects on our experiences. We hope these chapters have allowed some invisible technologies that you use in your day-to-day lives to become visible.

Indeed, the technologies that we use every day in many ways become invisible. They are taken for granted, as a given. In some cases, it can even seem like a given technological tool has always been there, as is the case when we automatically reach for our smartphones, ask Siri for help, or fill up a baby bottle for a midnight feeding. In these moments, we may not reflect on the technologies we use. It is all too easy to become complacent in relation to the technologies that surround us. We hope this text has provided space and opportunity to trouble the myth of technology as a given. One of our goals is to make space to really pay attention to the tech around us, to reflect on how it has changed over time and how those changes impact, and are impacted by, our lived experiences.

Who Does Tech Serve? Bringing Tech into Focus through an Intersectional Lens

In addition to thinking about what counts as technology, hopefully this book has pushed you to think about what sorts of stories are often told about technology. We often equate technology with progress, with hope, with power, and with knowledge. But in the chapters in this volume, we've seen that things are much more complicated than this simple narrative. Technology can bring progress but does not do so uniformly. It can give us hope but also leads to dangers. It can bring power, but that power is not evenly distributed across populations. And it can allow knowledge to be gained, but we should be critical of who is gaining that knowledge and what purposes they are putting the knowledge towards.

The most pervasive of these stories is probably the one of technology as progress. New tech is often assumed to be better simply because it is new. But this narrative of tech as progress obscures the countless ways in which technology is used to further white, patriarchal, capitalist, and hetero- and cisnormative ends. Many of the chapters in this text have illustrated that while advances in technology can be wondrous and helpful, things are much more complicated than a simplistic narrative of tech as progress would suggest. We encourage you to pause and reflect on the complicated nature of technology and consider the technology you use every day. Is it progressive? Whose interests are being served?

An Intersectional Feminist Guide

In short, our intention in writing this volume was to empower you, the reader, to think critically about the power and promise of technology by examining various technologies through the lens of intersectional feminist scholarship. Technology is not inherently one thing. It is complex and impacts different people in different ways because technologies are always already embedded withing existing relations of power.

When we examine technology through an intersectional lens, this both sharpens and broadens our focus. We can no longer think of technology as unproblematically progressive, for example, nor can we dismiss all technological innovation as harmful. We have seen that dating apps can promote and uphold racist attitudes at the same time that social media sites can be used for Indigenous activism. We have seen that smartphones can be used to effectively manage long-distance relationships and cultural norms of courtship while also being used to promote surveillance capitalism. Technology is not neutral, but nor is it automatically oppressive. Intersectionality means looking at things honestly, in context, and understanding the myriad of ways that people's social locations and lived experiences influence their use and perceptions of technology. As one of the editors, Lisa Smith, continuously said during the writing of this book: "It's complicated!"

It *is* complicated. But it is well worth doing the work. We hope you find this guide useful as you continue the work of troubling existing technologies that you use every day.

The Voices We Did Not Hear, the Voices That Are Not Here

This book was written and edited during the COVID-19 pandemic, a time that, as we stated above, exacerbated existing inequalities. Many of the authors in this collection face one or more axes of oppression and found their time was under increased strain, and their energies were stretched to capacity in meeting all the demands placed upon them. The editors recognized this, and we worked with authors and potential authors as much as we were able to support them. However, even so, there are voices that we were unable to include in this anthology. Despite our best efforts, we were not able to solicit a manuscript discussing the technology of pregnancy and parenthood (in vitro fertilization, breast pumps, etc.). Nor were we able to source a contributor exploring themes related to environmental justice movements and their various uses and critiques of technologies (planned obsolescence, reproductive justice, and online environmental justice activism). We were also unable to include a contributor examining sex robots and other sex technology, nor were we able to source a chapter looking at the increasing use of technology to manage old age. And there are still other voices that we were not able to include.

The editors speculate that these lost voices might have been due to the COVID-19 pandemic, but it is also possible that the pandemic was not the only reason, or even the most significant one, that these voices were not heard in this text. Sexism, classism, racism, and ableism are built into our social systems, including higher education. The pandemic has exacerbated these inequalities, but it did not create them. As such, the book itself cannot claim to be fully representative of the complicated ways people interact with technology, and we urge you, the reader, to consider voices you did not find in this text. Which perspectives were missing? What more would you like to know or explore?

When you identify these missing voices, please speak to your professor, a trusted mentor, or reach out to us and let us know! Ask for help in how to learn more about the missing voices you are interested in or begin the research yourself. We offer here a guide to get the discussion started, but a lot of work remains to be done.

REPEAT

At the start of this book, we asked you to pause and consider the technologies that lie around you within arm's reach. Now, at the end, we invite you to repeat this task again. Consider the technologies around you. Consider which of those technologies has been discussed by this volume. Consider what has been said. What hasn't been said. What would you say? How would you respond to the claims made here? Consider whether, if at all, your thoughts on technology have changed through reading this volume. Consider your own position. Consider what you have learned and what you have yet to learn.

And then, begin reading again! Read more. Think deeper.

And when you are ready, add your voice.

Contributor Biographies

This volume would not exist without the amazing scholarship of the following individuals.

Tamara Banbury is a PhD student in Communication and Media Studies at Carleton University, where her research focuses on the relationship of technology and the body, particularly embedded tech implants. Tamara's master's thesis in Legal Studies at Carleton focused on people she termed *voluntary cyborgs*—people who implant technology in their bodies for enhancement or augmentation, not for medical or rehabilitative purposes. Her MA thesis, *Where's My Jet Pack? Online Communication Practices and Media Frames of the Emergent Voluntary Cyborg Subculture*, was awarded a Carleton Senate medal for Outstanding Academic Achievement in 2017. In her PhD work, Tamara has broadened the scope of her research to include critical disability studies in her exploration of the implications of body autonomy, identity, and morphological freedom in relation to technological implants.

Ana Brito is an undergraduate student at Simon Fraser University, currently studying Sociology. She is interested in furthering discussions addressing sexuality, feminism, and inequality. Her work has appeared in *The Other Press* and *Canadian Dimension*.

Amber Brown is a mixed Métis woman with Scottish, British, and Hungarian roots hailing from British Columbia. Growing up on Kwikwetlem First Nation's ancestral territory, Amber is passionate about uplifting Indigenous futurism on the lands she calls home. Her bachelor's degree in psychology compliments her experiences as a youth coach, residential youth counsellor, and social work assistant. She continues to walk with purpose with the next seven generations in mind. Her vocational dream is to be a therapist specializing in Indigenous youths' wellness through culturally safe practice. As an artist, avid kayaker, and forager, Amber loves being on the land and celebrating the roundness of life. She is grateful for her connection to Creator and family for guiding her on her journey. Amber is thankful for being a part of this project and engaging in such valuable research. She prays this research inspires Canadians to protect the sacred through actions of solidarity.

Laura Cayen is an Assistant Professor in the Department of Gender, Sexuality, and Women's Studies at Western University in London, Ontario. Her areas of teaching and research include sexuality, media, popular culture, and methodological practice related to the analysis of digital and social media.

Christopher Dietzel is a postdoctoral fellow at Dalhousie University in Halifax, Canada. His research explores the intersections of gender, sexuality, safety, health, and technology. Chris is part of a collaborative project that investigates how dating app companies have responded to the COVID-19 pandemic, and he works on the IMPACTS Project, a seven-year Social Sciences and Humanities Research Council (SSHRC) partnership grant that aims to address sexual violence on university campuses across Canada and internationally.

Jennifer Jill Fellows is a faculty member in the philosophy department at Douglas College and a 2022 podcasting fellow for the Marc Sanders Foundation for public philosophy. She is passionate about academic podcasting and is currently involved in two podcasting projects: one called *Gender Sex and Tech: Continuing the Conversation*, which complements the material in this book, and another applying philosophical theories to video games. Her current research interests are in social epistemology and the metaphysics of personhood. She particularly focuses on trust, expertise, and marginalization in science and technology studies. In her spare time, she likes hiking, camping, playing video games, and playing three-chord songs on her guitar ... badly!

Lauren Friesen is an undergraduate student studying History and Gender Studies. Her work examines the intersections of race, gender, and class throughout history. She lives in New Westminster, BC, spending time writing, reading, and rollerblading.

Kelly Fritsch is an Assistant Professor in the Department of Sociology and Anthropology and Director of the Disability Justice and Crip Culture Collaboratory at Carleton University. She is the co-creator of *We Move Together* (2021), a children's book about ableism, accessibility, and disability culture. She is co-editor of *Disability (In)Justice: Examining Criminalization in Canada* (2022) and *Keywords for Radicals: The Contested Vocabulary of Late-Capitalist Struggle* (2016). She has also recently co-edited special journal issues of *Somatechnics*, *Feminist Formations*, *Catalyst: Feminism, Theory, Technoscience*, and *Studies in Social Justice*. Fritsch currently sits on the editorial board of *Disability Studies Quarterly*.

Kelly Ge is completing her Master of Public Health (Health Promotion) at the University of Toronto's Dalla Lana School of Public Health. Her interest in digital health studies and critical qualitative health research began during her undergraduate studies in health sciences at Western University in Ontario.

Jennifer Hites-Thomas has a PhD in Sociology from Simon Fraser University. Her scholarship examines gender, sex, and race with a particular focus on the medical production of cisitude, endosex bodies, and whiteness. She has co-authored publications in *Sexualities* and the *Journal of Gender Studies* analyzing how 'trans-friendly' mental health professionals determine which patients will gain access to medical transition. In her recent research, she investigates how medical discourses operate within gender confirming genital surgery for trans folks juxtaposed with how they function within 'male enhancement' for cis men. Her current project examines how medicine both defines the borders between intersex and endosex bodies and constructs the 'female' body as natural.

Angela Knowles is European, mostly Scottish and Icelandic, with some Algonquin First Nations heritage. She has grown up and worked on the Tsawwassen and Kwantlen First Nations lands. Angela enjoys creating art, reading, and being outdoors. She is passionate about Indigenous sovereignty and LGBTQ2S+ rights and hopes that this work reflects that. Angela's research for her Bachelor in Psychology focused on anti-Indigenous racism in academia, and she hopes to continue research in the area. Her future goals include continuing her education in Psychology and going on to become a therapist working in rural and underserved areas. She is grateful for the opportunity to contribute to this textbook and hopes that the work done in this chapter as well as the others will make an impact and be a thought-provoking read.

Noorin Manji is a Sessional Professor at the University of Waterloo where she teaches for multiple departments including the Arts First Program, Sociology and Legal Studies, and Global Business and Digital Arts. She specializes in work related to modern communication technology and human relationships. Dr. Manji's research focuses on smartphones and the ways in which they have had transformative effects on the very processes for which people use them. By building on her expertise in theory development, Dr. Manji has bolstered her exploration and understanding of the growing presence of smartphone technology by investigating new theoretical lenses through which their impacts can be framed and understood. Beyond this theoretical work, Dr. Manji also specializes in qualitative approaches to data collection, as she strives to authentically reflect people's lived realities through thick, descriptive representations of their perspectives.

Shaina McHardy is a PhD candidate at the University of Waterloo in the Department of Sociology and Legal Studies. With a background in criminology, her research focuses on interpersonal violence and victimization. From sexual assault and secondary victimization to the use of technology to violate others, her research aims to draw attention to Canada as a unique jurisdiction. Her current research explores how Canadian universities can and should respond to incidents of students using technology to sexually victimize one another in the hopes of informing future policy development and revision.

Treena Orchard is an Associate Professor in the School of Health Studies at Western University located in London, Ontario, Canada. She is a medical anthropologist who explores sexuality, gender, and the politics of health among marginalized populations to help create meaningful socio-political change with the people among whom she works. She uses qualitative and arts-based methods in her collaborative research initiatives, including her autoethnographic project on dating apps that will be published as a book with the AEVO imprint of the University of Toronto Press. Treena also loves creative writing, cats, interior design, and all things Joan Didion.

Jessica Polzer is an Associate Professor in the School of Health Studies and the Department of Gender, Sexuality, and Women's Studies at Western University in London, Ontario. Her research uses narrative and discourse methodologies to explore the gendered biopolitical implications and enactments of health-related technologies. Her previous work has focused on women's experiences of BRCA 1/2 genetic mutation testing, personal and media accounts of human papillomavirus (HPV) vaccination, and narratives of vaccine hesitancy.

Sahar Raza is the Project Manager of the National Right to Housing Network and a recent graduate from Ryerson and York Universities' joint Communication and Culture master's program. Her federally funded thesis research critically analyzed "smart city" projects and discourses in Canada to uncover the policy and social justice implications of corporate-made smart, artificially intelligent, and algorithmic decision-making technologies. She now works as a human rights advocate and public policy professional who continues to research intersectional Canadian issues rooted in colonialism, privatization, systemic discrimination, and an overreliance on AI technologies.

Lisa Smith is a Faculty Member in the Department of Anthropology and Sociology at Douglas College. Her research expertise lies in sexual and reproductive health, gender-based violence and the post-secondary context, and public and community-engaged sociology. She has several active research programs that examine the social and cultural dimensions of menstruation, as well as gender-based violence and the post-secondary context. In addition to publishing in academic journals and collections, Lisa broadcasts her work through community engagement, popular writing, and podcasting. When she is not professing, Lisa keeps busy with hiking, biking, music, and parenting her two fabulous kids.

Anna Sui is a PhD Candidate in the Health and Rehabilitation Sciences Graduate Program at Western University in Ontario. Her doctoral research explores the narratives of women seeking and receiving tubal ligation in Canada. Her other research interests include digital health, digital sociology, and digital research methods.

Kira Tomsons is a Faculty Instructor at Douglas College, teaching ethics, philosophy of law, and issues in Gender, Sexuality, and Women's Studies. She has written articles on rape and consent, companies and the ethics of care, and feminist considerations regarding euthanasia. Most recently, Kira's work has been looking at the ethics of lying to children as it pertains to the trivial (Santa and the Tooth Fairy) and the not so trivial (lies and omissions about parental heritage). When not struggling to clearly explain complex things, she hangs out with her wife, children, and two cats, playing video games, knitting, and dabbling with various art forms.

Jaime Yard has been full-time faculty in the Department of Anthropology and Sociology at Douglas College since 2013. She received her MA and PhD in Social Anthropology from York University in Toronto and her BA in Cultural Anthropology from Simon Fraser University. Her doctoral dissertation, *Working Natures: An Ethnography of Love, Labour and Accumulation on the British Columbian Coast*, received both the Canadian Studies Network dissertation prize and the York University Barbara Godard dissertation prize in 2013. In 2019, she was honoured with a Douglas College faculty-wide Humanities and Social Sciences teaching award. Jaime is a social and cultural anthropologist specializing in political ecology/environmental anthropology. She is also very interested in Anthropocene feminisms and the anthropology of work and performance studies. She has published in the journals *TOPIA: Canadian Journal of Cultural Studies* and *Emotion, Space and Society*.